DATE DUE

MR 18 '97			
MY 2 '97			
JY 30 '98			
JY 26 05			
MY 16 07			
JE 6 07			

DEMCO 38-296

INTERNATIONAL WOMEN'S WRITING

Recent Titles in
Contributions in Women's Studies

Mules and Dragons: Popular Culture Images in the Selected
Writings of African-American and Chinese-American Women Writers
Mary E. Young

Women, Community, and the Hormel Strike of 1985–86
Neala J. Schleuning

Edith Wharton's Prisoners of Consciousness: A Study of Theme and
Technique in the Tales
Evelyn E. Fracasso

Mothers and Work in Popular American Magazines
Kathryn Keller

Ideals in Feminine Beauty: Philosophical, Social, and Cultural
Dimensions
Karen A. Callaghan, editor

The Stone and the Scorpion: The Female Subject of Desire in the
Novels of Charlotte Bronte, George Eliot, and Thomas Hardy
Judith Mitchell

The Several Worlds of Pearl S. Buck: Essays Presented at a
Centennial Symposium, Randolph-Macon Woman's College,
March 26–28, 1992
Elizabeth J. Lipscomb, Frances E. Webb, and Peter Conn, editors

Hear Me Patiently: The Reform Speeches of Amelia Jenks Bloomer
Anne C. Coon, editor

Nineteenth-Century American Women Theatre Managers
Jane Kathleen Curry

Textual Escap(e)ades: Mobility, Maternity, and Textuality in
Contemporary Fiction by Women
Lindsey Tucker

The Repair of the World: The Novels of Marge Piercy
Kerstin W. Shands

Clara Barton: In the Service of Humanity
David H. Burton

INTERNATIONAL WOMEN'S WRITING

New Landscapes of Identity

Edited by
Anne E. Brown
and **Marjanne E. Goozé**

Contributions in Women's Studies, 147

GREENWOOD PRESS
Westport, Connecticut • London

n Data

International women's writing : new landscapes of identity / edited by
  Anne E. Brown and Marjanne E. Goozé.
        p.   cm.—(Contributions in women's studies, ISSN 0147–104X ;
  no. 147)
      Includes bibliographical references and index.
      ISBN 0–313–29045–8
      1. Literature—Women authors—History and criticism.   2. Identity
  (Psychology) in literature.   3. Feminist literary criticism.
  I. Brown, Anne E.   II. Goozé, Marjanne Elaine.   III. Series:
  Contributions in women's studies ; no. 147.
  PN481.I57   1995
  809'.89287—dc20   94–27950

British Library Cataloguing in Publication Data is available.

Library of Congress Catalog Card Number: 94–27950
ISBN: 0–313–29045–8
ISSN: 0147–104X

First published in 1995

Greenwood Press, 88 Post Road West, Westport, CT 06881
An imprint of Greenwood Publishing Group, Inc.

Printed in the United States of America

The paper used in this book complies with the
Permanent Paper Standard issued by the National
Information Standards Organization (Z39.48–1984).

10 9 8 7 6 5 4 3 2 1

Copyright Acknowledgments

The editors and publisher gratefully acknowledge permission to reprint the following copyrighted material:

Excerpts from Mariama Bâ, *Une si longue lettre* (Dakar: Les Nouvelles Éditions Africaines, 1980), and *So Long a Letter*, translated by Modupe Bode-Thomas (London: Heinemann Educational Books, 1981). Reprinted by permission of Les Nouvelles Éditions Africaines.

Excerpts from Christa Wolf, *Kein Ort. Nirgends* (Darmstadt: Luchterhand, 1979). Copyright © 1979 by Aufbau Verlag Berlin and Weimar. Reprinted by permission of Aufbau Verlag GmbH.

Excerpts from Christa Wolf, *No Place on Earth*, translated by Jan van Heurck. Translation copyright © 1982 by Farrar, Straus & Giroux, Inc., and Virago Press. Reprinted by permission of Farrar, Straus & Giroux, and Virago Press.

Arlette Smith, "Maryse Condé's *Hérémakhonon*: A Triangular Structure of Alienation." *CLA Journal* 32 (Sept. 1988): 45–54. Reprinted by permission of The College Language Association.

Contents

Acknowledgments

Support provided by the Vice President for Research and the Research Foundation at the University of Georgia and by the University Research Fund and the Dean of Arts Fund at the University of New Brunswick enabled our work together across the miles. We wish to thank Susan Canty Quinlan for her assistance and advice. Special thanks go to Sylvia Blain (UNB) for initial manuscript preparation. We are grateful for the technical assistance we received from Nancy Burnham (UNB), Michael Cabatu (UNB), Daniel Grant (UNB), Betty Stowe (UGA), and Cletus Stripling (UGA). Maureen Melino at Greenwood helped us negotiate the complex world of copyright permissions, and we are thankful for the aid of our production editor, Elisabetta Linton, as we prepared the final manuscript. We heartily appreciated Robert Gellert's fine culinary skills, childcare, and unwavering moral support throughout this project. Due, in part, to this book, we hope that Michèle Alexandra and all the little girls of her generation everywhere will have a strong sense of their identity.

Introduction: Placing Identity in Cross-Cultural Perspective

Anne E. Brown and Marjanne E. Goozé

International Women's Writing addresses vital issues in feminist criticism today: the interrelationships between female identity and place. In this book, "place" and "landscape" suggest both physical space (country, home, workplace) and metaphorical space (cultural and linguistic environment, sexual orientation, and sociopolitical practice). This collection by young and established scholars contains primarily new essays on women's writings in the second half of the twentieth century. It is the first to explore the diversity of identity in terms of "place."[1] Here we are using the terms "identity" and "self" as always gendered and socially influenced constructs. Because each of the following chapters locates identity within specific racial, cultural, sexual, national, and economic parameters, no single or fixed definition of identity can be universally applied. In fact, one of the goals of this book is, through the interpretation of literary works, to underscore the diversity of women's identities cross-culturally, while at the same time to foreground the common axis along which female identity is constructed. As Roberta Rubenstein notes: "To the extent that women—as both authors and characters—have internalized models of selfhood that overlap along the axis of gender and may diverge along the axes of national and ethnic origin, their narrative representations of the world express their diverse experience of boundary in both psychological and cultural senses" (8).

In an effort to emphasize the placing of identity inter- and cross-culturally, this collection brings together readings of twenty-nine writers from fifteen different countries. While some of these writers are well-known to English-speaking readers, many are not. Their works have influenced feminist discourses in their own cultures and abroad. By gathering together in one place analyses of such diverse works and writers, we aspire to create a space in which a dialogue can take place. This dialogue discloses both differences and commonalities, leading to an understanding of women's Otherness and Sameness. We do not wish to concentrate on differences so much that comparisons become impossible. Tzvetan Todorov elucidates the dangers inherent in an emphasis *only* on difference, in this instance in terms of race:

We are not only separated by cultural differences; we are also united by a common human identity, and it is this which renders possible communication, dialogue, and, in the final analysis, the comprehension of Otherness—it is possible precisely because Otherness is never radical. This implies not that the task is simple but that if we allow ourselves to believe in its feasibility, we can acquire an ever deeper understanding of Others. Affirming the existence of the incommunicability among cultures, on the other hand, presupposes adherence to a racialist, apartheid-like set of beliefs, postulating as it does insurmountable discontinuity within the human species. (374)

What Todorov calls "human identity" we translate as "gendered identity." This is not to say that women are not oppressed due to their politics, race, class, sexual orientation, nationality, or ethnicity but to stress the impact of the oppression they all share as women, even though this oppression manifests itself in different ways. For this reason, we refrain from adding up the number of ways in which each author or her characters discussed here are oppressed; we avoid quantifying another's experience.

Feminist criticism has begun to employ the term *gender* to stand for "the social, cultural, and psychological meaning imposed upon biological, sexual identity" (Showalter, 1-2). We use *identity* as always referring to the whole complex of factors contributing to the configuration of the gendered self as this self interacts with the world. As Showalter further points out: "Gender is not only a question of *difference*, which assumes that the sexes are separate but equal; but of *power*, since in looking at the history of gender relations, we find asymmetry, inequality, and male dominance in every known society" (3).

The virtual universality of male dominance would appear to leave no place for women or women's expression of their selves. Therefore, the woman writer is always in a sense "elsewhere," displaced from an ever shifting center. Jane Marcus reminds us: "For elsewhere is not nowhere. It is a political place where the displaced are always seen and see themselves in relation to the 'placed.' Dis/placement and difference as categories of political and gender exile from writing, speaking, and acting circulate around notions of fixed positions in a substantial Somewhere" (270). All women are exiled in patriarchal culture, while at the same time they must coexist with it.[2] Consequently, women perceive exclusion as imposed from the outside but also internalize their own expatriation. They are "expatriate in *patria*" (Benstock, 20). For the woman writer, exile can take other forms than physical exile. Women's writings both delimit and confront the patriarchal literary realm. The act of writing itself not only inscribes a site of resistance but equally is a means of empowerment. The writing provides a space within which the woman writer can locate and position her identity.

Many of the works discussed exhibit the writers' preference for first-person and autobiographical narratives. This preference illustrates their resistance to subjugation and their attempt to map new "modes of subjectivity" (Hekman, 189). Other genres, such as third-person narratives, film, and poetry, also serve as vehicles of resistance and empowerment. The authors in this collection all show how twentieth-century international women writers come together in their insistent concern with the configuration of gendered identity. This identity is never portrayed as fixed or solid. The interpretations presented here reveal two divergent but related aspects of this decentered identity. On one hand, the characters follow a path leading to a self-defined identity where the self can be fragmented and yet enriched. In these instances, fragmentation is synonymous with fluidity of identity, so that no preconceived barriers limit the possibilities for a self-defined subjectivity. When it lives under the sign of fluidity, fragmentation connotes self-empowerment and successful resistance to oppression. Fluid identity permits multiple facets of the self to emerge and multiple oppressions to be contested. It is then possible to live with and within contradictions.

On the other hand, fragmentation also results in failures to develop a self-defined subjectivity and, in the most severe instances, leads to madness and self-destruction. The obstacles placed in the way of self-empowerment are numerous and varied, but principally they can be identified as either an exclusive identification with a particular class or group or a total alienation from affiliation with others. Contradictory cultural messages and conflicts between personal desires and norms prove destructive.

All the chapters in this volume address the construction of identity in relation to racism, classism, heterosexism, or colonialism. Depending on the specific cultural environment, one or more of these may come into play. But in all instances, sexism is the primary signifier of oppression. It is refracted and multiplied by the experience of other forms of oppression. We do not wish either to minimize or overvalorize the impact of other forms of oppression on women. We speak from our positionality as Westerners who are ourselves not full participants in majority culture—as a French-speaking Canadian and a Jewish American—realizing that our ethnic and cultural positions do not completely mitigate our involvement with the modern Anglo-Saxon episteme. We share, however, Gayatri Spivak's view that it is not necessary to reject completely all Western constructs and ideas as long as they are not applied as concepts that are thought to be "transcendental or universal" (*Post-Colonial*, 76). Both chapter authors and we attempt to showcase how women artists of various backgrounds place themselves so as to name their own "worlding," rather than being seen as native informants whose sole purpose is to enlighten an Other (Spivak, "Three," 264).

For these reasons, the contributors employ a wide range of critical methodologies, ranging from sociocriticism to postmodernism. This diversity of theoretical approaches mirrors the diversity among the authors discussed and highlights a multiplicity of feminisms. They do not share a preordained agenda but instead map the complex interplay of placing identity in international women's writings. However, as feminist critics, they all enrich the ongoing dialogue by asking questions based on gender difference to give "a view of the woman writer less contentedly keeping to her separate sphere—and a particular kind of fiction—than powerfully straining against the boundaries that hem her in" (Anderson, vii). As opposed to offering a single feminist poetic, their chapters engender a dialogue among feminist critics.

Most contributors also engage in a dialogue with postmodern and postmodern-feminist theorists such as Foucault, Derrida, Kristeva, Irigaray, Lyotard, and

Hayden White. This engagement by feminists in the postmodern debate is a fruitful one, as Linda Nicholson explains:

Moreover, for some feminists, postmodernism is not only a natural ally but also provides a basis for avoiding the tendency to construct theory that generalizes from the experiences of Western, white, middle-class women. . . . postmodernism offers feminism some useful ideas about method, particularly a wariness toward generalizations which transcend the boundaries of culture and region. (Nicholson, 5)

Fraser and Nicholson go on to define a "postmodern-feminist" theory whose focus must necessarily be cross-cultural and comparativist (34). Although we heartily agree with this conclusion, we do not, as they do, see gender as only "one relevant strand among others" (34-35) but rather as the overriding criterion in the analysis of a complexly constructed female identity.

International Women's Writing joins in the larger project to map the intersections among national, cultural, racial, sexual, social, ethnic, and other spaces in the configuration of women's identity. The chapters in this book are presented in five sections. We did not categorize the chapters along geographical or linguistic lines, instead preferring to initiate a cross-cultural dialogue through the order of presentation. Some chapters would fit into more than one section. By placing them where we did, we chose to highlight certain concerns. This is by no means intended to limit the dialogue and interconnections to be made among all the chapters in the book. Indeed, readers will transcend our rather arbitrary boundaries and locate the numerous intersections among the various contributions.

I. MAPPING IDENTITY

This section addresses the remapping of women's identity in various cultures. The four chapters explore how the gendered self is constituted in relation to others and to community. Issues of sexuality, marriage, polygamy, and lesbianism inform the "placing" of women's identities within cultural environments.

The first work considered introduces many of these issues within the Muslim African context. Eva Rueschmann's contribution, "Female Self-Definition and the African Community in Mariama Bâ's Epistolary novel *So Long a Letter*," examines this most significant African novel, which marks a breakthrough in the literary expression of African feminist consciousness.[3] Rueschmann emphasizes the limitations imposed on Senegalese women's identity by sexism, classism, and racism. Colonialist, neocolonialist, and traditional African patriarchy shapes the unique realities of African culture influencing gendered identity. The definition of the self as embedded in a community distinguishes African women's identity. The epistolary form of Bâ's novel best captures this communally bred self, according to Rueschmann. In the letters of the narrator Ramatoulaye, the problems she encounters in a polygamous society concretize the dilemma of reconciling a communal self with "feminist aspirations for autonomy and self-realization as a woman." Rueschmann takes up the complex theoretical question of the dangers of applying Western feminist notions of identity to Bâ's characters.

Sheila Petty enters into a dialogue with Western feminist film theorists in her chapter, "(Re)Presenting the Self: Identity and Consciousness in the Feature Films of Safi Faye." Like Bâ, Faye is Senegalese, and she deals with similar issues of race, class, and gender in Africa. In the history of Sub-Saharan filmmaking, Faye is the first woman to have completed a feature film. Her films reflect the heterogeneity of African woman's experiences, portray the female self in relation to community, and define an African feminist film aesthetic that repudiates the embodiment of Africa in the female body. The mapping of the body as a metaphor for a continent exemplifies the problems women encounter in positioning their own identities within national, ethnic, and cultural boundaries.

These difficulties are exacerbated by the heterosexism that draws the boundaries for relationships among women. Anne Brown outlines three phases in the formation of the woman-identified self in "Sappho's Daughters: Lesbian Identities in Novels by Québécois Women (1960-1990)." The censorship imposed on the expression of lesbianism accounts for their only recent entry onto Québec's literary scene. She describes works by Louise Maheux-Forcier, Yvette Naubert, Jeanne D'Arc Jutras, and Marie-Claire Blais. This historical analysis maps the development and emergence of woman-centered identities from "unspeakable" to "self-naming." Inherent in "self-naming" are the breakdown of social isolation and fear of disclosure. Because lesbians continue to face discrimination by heterosexual cultures, they are confronted, as Blais has remarked, with their "exclusion from the planet" (qtd. in Brown). This exclusion is somewhat softened by the new women's community, which helps them forge a positive sense of self, while simultaneously broadening their expectations concerning the nature of their social role. Interestingly, their newfound expectations lead them to perceive their sexual orientation as simply one aspect of their identity. What eventually emerges from this shift in their perception of self is the realization that, until they have won the right to name themselves, their identity will continue to be threatened.

The fourth chapter in this section traces how the concrete employment of topographical imagery symbolizes both the characters' and the authors' attempts to place themselves within a patriarchal, post-Enlightenment, technocratic society that devalues and marginalizes them as artists. Marjanne Goozé's chapter, "Finding a Place for Christa Wolf: Gendered Identity in *No Place on Earth*," explicates the work of this well-known writer from the former German Democratic Republic in the light of unification. Rather than reading the novel as merely an allegory of Wolf's literary politics, Goozé relies on Wolf's own theory of "subjective authenticity" to explain the dialogue between the author and two figures of the Romantic era, Heinrich von Kleist and Karoline von Günderrode. Through them Wolf presents an imbricated complex of issues and relationships affecting the self-definition and self-expression of the artist and of the female writer in particular. Kleist represents the difficulties resulting from the artist's identification (or lack thereof) with the state, and Günderrode the exclusion of the female artist. There is literally "no place" for viable literary creation either within the limited space allotted to it by society or in a "u-topos," a utopia not bounded by time or geography.

II. DISRUPTING THE AUTONOMOUS SELF

The following five chapters all approach the concept of female identity in terms of decenteredness, fluidity, and multiplicity. Whereas in the first section, some of the female characters are seen to define their selfhood in connection to others, here the male-defined autonomous self is deconstructed and replaced by a female configuration of identity that transcends the boundaries of fixed identity.

Arlette Smith, in "Maryse Condé's *Hérémakhonon*: A Triangular Structure of Alienation," profiles the narrator Veronica's search for her African roots and identity. In opposition to most critics of the work, who view *Hérémakhonon* as a quest novel, Smith defines it as a *Bildungsroman*, where the evolution of Veronica's identity is of primary significance. Her travels to three continents—from the West Indies to France and Africa—transform her self-awareness. According to Smith, in the end, Veronica no longer idealizes or privileges any one of the three cultures out of which her identity is constituted but learns to accept the contradictions with which she must live.

Bharati Mukherjee's Jasmine character, like Condé's Veronica, experiences cultural fragmentation. The four names Jasmine has in the novel symbolize her fluid identity as she travels from India and across the United States. In "Colonial Discourse and Female Identity: Bharati Mukherjee's *Jasmine*," Suzanne Kehde argues that fluidity of identity is not only a strategy for survival but also "a site of flexibility." Especially for Third World women, "the operant discourses are always restrictive." Jasmine's personal liberation is a result of her willingness to negotiate the various discourses.

Peggy Sharpe, in "Fragmented Identities and the Process of Metamorphosis in Works by Lygia Fagundes Telles," elucidates how the Brazilian novelist Telles also locates the site for the construction of female identity in the woman herself. Referring to theories by de Lauretis and Alcoff, Sharpe observes that this site incorporates specific positional perspectives, in contradistinction to an imposed definition of the essentially feminine. Values are interpreted or constructed rather than passively predetermined. However, as Sharpe points out, Telles's characters all fail to accomplish this process of identity formation, because they remain trapped in the values representative of a decadent bourgeoisie. Telles, who is considered a successor to Clarice Lispector, makes language a central issue in her novel *The Bare Hours*, locating women's power in artistic endeavors and especially in the word.

Susan Porter's analysis of "The 'Imaginative Space' of Medbh McGuckian" also investigates the imagery of female artistry associated with women's bodies and lives. The "imaginative space" that the Irish poet McGuckian creates contributes to her displacement as a woman poet in a male-dominated literary canon, as an Irish writer in British literary tradition, and politically as an Irish Catholic in Northern Ireland. This space permits her to speak without distortion or overidentification with a specific cultural or political ideology. Porter places McGuckian in dialogue with Jacques Derrida in order to situate her poetry within postmodern critical practice, deconstructing gendered binary oppositions. This deconstruction enables McGuckian's ostensively feminine imagery to speak the voice of difference. Within the imaginative space, Porter shows how McGuckian's poems privilege the connections among women from different classes or ethnic groups.

The final chapter in this section, "Writing the Woman-Subject: Marguerite Duras, from Theory to Fiction" by Anne-Marie Gronhovd, brings together the deconstruction of colonial and male hegemonic discourses. Where Smith and Kehde focus on the fluidity of identity in writings by Third World women, and Sharpe and Porter point to the de- and reconstruction of female identity through language, Gronhovd demonstrates where, in Duras's spaces, the political intersects with the poetic, and theory with fiction. Gronhovd shows how the postmodern feminist theories of Luce Irigaray and Julia Kristeva challenge traditional notions of identity and thus open a space for the enunciation of the diverse identities among women in their specific historical and social locations.

All of these chapters indicate that the configuration of the gendered self cannot be enclosed in time or space. It is a continuous and ongoing process. The significant aspect of this refusal to be fixed and enclosed in patriarchal discourses manifests itself in the emergence of the woman as speaking subject, rather than as silent Other.

III. INNER AND OUTER SPACE

The chapters in the third section, "Inner and Outer Space," foreground the metaphorical aspects of place. These encompass mysticism, madness, and linguistic displacement engendered by colonialism, exile, sexism, and racism. The self acting in psychological or interior space is often juxtaposed with the woman as Other reacting to a male-dominant or exterior space.

Susan Canty Quinlan's chapter, "The Mysterious Space of Exile: *Punishable Songs* by Judith Grossmann," discusses the fictional autobiography of this contemporary Brazilian writer. Quinlan examines how in Grossmann's book, a critical subversion of language and form occurs as a part of the process of the search for an authentic self. Grossmann's acts of linguistic subversion not only disrupt patriarchal discourse but also point toward the creation of a new female linguistic order. Quinlan reinterprets the male-defined paradigm of exile/home as she forces a woman-centered rereading based upon her analysis of Grossmann's autobiographical presentation. The multiple interior and exterior spaces overlap and interact, breaking down traditional boundaries of nationality, gender, language, and experience.

The next contribution, "Inner and Outer Space in the Works of Esther Rochon" by Annick Chapdelaine, also exposes the breakdown of traditionally set barriers and highlights the development of new paradigms. But here the subversion of the paradigm occurs at the juncture of the spiritual and natural worlds, rather than in the linguistic order. In analyzing works by the Québec science fiction writer, Esther Rochon, Chapdelaine brings together Kristeva's deconstruction of the binary oppositions of male/female with the expression of Buddhist mystical thought in Rochon's texts. In this way, gender is no longer a barrier to enlightenment for either women or men. The "space" of outer space in Rochon's works allows for the creation of a new paradigm of equality based on the individual's quest for center and justice.

Nancy Topping Bazin, in her chapter, "Southern Africa and the Theme of Madness: Novels by Doris Lessing, Bessie Head, and Nadine Gordimer," focuses on the sociopolitical, and on madness as a response to the insanity and injustice of apartheid. The three authors offer examples of how shifting perspectives reveal the oppressive dynamic between an enforced social identity and the desire to develop an authentic self. Like Quinlan and Chapdelaine, Bazin analyzes the dismantling of binary pairs, but here the pairs are constituted primarily in terms of race, colonization (colonized/colonizer), and class, with gender as a component of each. Individual madness acts as a possible site of resistance against a collective societal madness that is never acknowledged. Bazin stresses that in the works of Gordimer, Lessing, and Head, the vision of the future as utopia or dystopia is dependent on discussions conducted in the present.

Madness is also a response to an oppressive situation in the two interpretations of Jean Rhys's *Wide Sargasso Sea* by Fiona Barnes and Deanna Madden. Taken together, the chapters, "Dismantling the Master's Houses: Jean Rhys and West Indian Identity" and "Wild Child, Tropical Flower, Mad Wife: Female Identity in Jean Rhys's *Wide Sargasso Sea*," provide a complex and thorough reading of this important postcolonial work. Barnes approaches the theme of place geographically, whereas Madden reveals how Antoinette Cosway (Bertha Mason) herself becomes a site of colonization. Barnes's analysis of what Adrienne Rich terms the "politics of location" (qtd. in Barnes) illuminates the homelessness suffered by the white Creole Jamaican heroine. She is caught between two cultures, and her situation is symbolized by the two Great Houses. Place, identity, and politics play interdependent roles in this retelling of Charlotte Brontë's *Jane Eyre* from the perspective of the "mad" wife. Madden's interpretation of the text works from the ternary structure of the novel to explain the different facets of female identity present in Rhys's protagonist, who grows up in a patriarchal and postcolonial culture. In Jamaica she can find no place in either the black or white communities; England rejects her as a tainted exotic. As madwoman in the attic, Rhys's character is denied a sense of belonging both to a place and to herself.

IV. RESISTING OPPRESSIONS

Discussed in this section are fictionalized sociohistorical critiques of women's struggles for emancipation and self-definition under totalitarian and fascist regimes, and machismo ideology. Women's involvement in resistance movements is seen to be an informing aspect of their identity formation. In her chapter "Isabel Allende and the Discourse of Exile," Marketta Laurila analyzes Allende's trilogy (*The House of the Spirits*, *Of Love and Shadows*, and *Eva Luna*). She explains how Allende's metaphorical and metanomic discourses reinforce the depiction of personal, familial, political, and national spaces in the three novels. The identities of the female protagonists are formed at the interstices of these spaces and played out in a specific historical context. These interstices mark the dialectical tensions between the repression and separation characteristic of androcentric space and a gynocentric space that allows for identification across gender and class lines. Even though the settings are precisely located, there is a deliberate blurring of national boundaries that symbolizes both the heroines' and Allende's resistance to imposed exile.

Also a political exile, Mercè Rodoreda writes from the position of an linguistic exile. Her Catalonian novel, *The Time of the Doves*, is discussed by Kayann Short in terms of the paradox of female identity. In "Too Disconnected/Too Bound Up," Short explores the positionality of the main character Natalia inside and outside the hegemonic discourses imposed on her as a working-class woman under a fascist dictatorship. Whereas Allende's female protagonists articulately resist the violence of male-dominated politics, Short elucidates how the oppositional strategy of Rodoreda's working-class heroine includes silence and inwardness. Both Laurila and Short highlight in their contributions how women's experiences of political oppression are different from, but no less significant than, men's. Short warns of limiting female identity to the male/female binary relation, "thereby foreclosing possibilities for oppositional strategies organized around intersecting locations of resistance."

The Western feminist ideal of the professional working mother is challenged by Margareta Thompson's reading of I. Grekova in her chapter, "Scientist and Mother: Portrait of the Heroine in I. Grekova's Fiction." This Soviet writer's composite heroine, outlined by Thompson, is usually a single mother alienated from any nurturing role. The configuration of female identity does not seem to be an issue and is therefore prominent by its very absence. On one hand, Thompson notes that Grekova's fiction cannot be categorized as feminist in Western terms, because her heroines are not cognizant of their own alienation from their children and their neglect of them. Grekova does not idealize the working mother but provides bleak yet realistic portraits of Soviet women. On the other hand, her realism does not comply with the dictates of socialist realism either. Grekova's own ambiguity toward her female protagonists, as well as her own political situation, makes it difficult to pin her down to any specific feminist or ideological position. She is a realist and not a dogmatist.

Vera Golini approaches the writings of Dacia Maraini in the light of the demands of Italian feminists for social change. "Italian Women in Search of

Identity in Dacia Maraini's Novels" specifically addresses issues of female conscience and consciousness within the topography of Italian culture. In contrast to Grekova's composite heroine, Golini delineates how Maraini's working- and middle-class female characters develop through increasing self-knowledge and maturity. Their self-actualization initiates their rebellion against traditional structures of oppression. Personal growth results in activist politics and a sense of identity linked to a larger community.

The four authors discussed in this section expand the boundaries of female identity by considering, in addition to gender, aspects of class, ethnic, and linguistic affiliation as they and their characters resist totalitarian, fascist, and machismo systems of oppression.

V. INTERCULTURAL SPACE

The authors presented in these chapters are all writing from a multicultural perspective, in that they all have adopted or inherited more than one set of cultural reference points. Each author belongs to an American minority and through her writing constructs an intercultural space in which the various facets of multiple identity are provided with a site of interaction and recognition. In this final section, the delineation of both physical and metaphorical "place" again comes into play. Marlene Goldman in her chapter, "Naming the Unspeakable: The Mapping of Female Identity in Maxine Hong Kingston's *The Woman Warrior*," discusses how Hong Kingston's reconceptualization of the novel form allows for the representation of women's fragmented identity. This transgeneric narrative incorporates the multiple contradictions generated by the clash of Chinese and American cultures, without dissolving the different exigencies of the two symbolic systems. Through the stories told by the Chinese-born characters, the narrator comes to understand the inherently precarious position she occupies, as she attempts "to map out . . . identity in the presence of the not-I." Goldman points out how Hong Kingston "must write in order to locate herself." Hong Kingston's writing brings forth an intercultural space that offers a model for portraying female identity that resists organizing life experiences into a coherent, solid, or linear construct. For these reasons, Goldman asserts that *The Woman Warrior* is a postmodern text.

In her analysis of Amy Tan's *The Joy Luck Club*, Gloria Shen also discusses how narrative technique—here, specifically, Tan's use of multiple narrators—subverts the narrative paradigm. Like Goldman, she draws parallels between postmodern theories and women's employment of narrative strategies that undermine the traditional authority of the third-person narrator. The montage effected by the eight narrators opens a space in which the unconnected fragments of life unfold. In this space, Tan illuminates the tensions and bonds between these Chinese-born mothers and their American-born daughters. The attempt by the daughters to establish their identity in contradistinction to their mothers is exacerbated here by ethnic and racial prejudices. The daughters' alienation from their Chinese identity is a barrier to understanding not only their mothers' experiences but also their own lives. Shen shows how through the act of storytelling—by means of the narrative itself—the intercultural gap between mothers and daughters is narrowed. In this way, the daughters come to understand and value their cultural history as Chinese Americans and as women.

In the next book examined, Paule Marshall's *Brown Girl, Brownstones*, the intercultural conflict surfaces once again in the relationship between mother and daughter. *Brown Girl, Brownstones* depicts an adolescent West Indian girl growing up in Brooklyn, New York, between two cultures. In this instance, the intercultural conflict moves beyond the familiar into an exploration of "same-gender bonding" across race and class lines (Abruña). Laura Niesen de Abruña argues in her chapter, "The Ambivalence of Mirroring and Female Bonding in Paule Marshall's *Brown Girl, Brownstones*," that racism, classism, and a history of slavery are very strong barriers to interracial same-gender bonding. These factors can also affect familial relationships, as we see in Marshall's novel. The protagonist, Selina Boyce, wants to identify at first with the dominant white culture. This process of identifying against oneself indicates that even in the nuclear family, cultural differences hinder female bonding. But as in Tan's *The Joy Luck Club*, limited reconciliation between generations and cultures occurs.

Niesen de Abruña traces the image of the mirror as metaphor for the emotional idea of bonding. Relying on theories of object relations by Winnicott and Chodorow (rather than on Lacan), Abruña attests to the positive nature of mirroring when the mirror reflects both ways. The self viewed in the one-way mirror is perceived by the subject as a "monster" in relation to a racial and cultural "norm." But the two-way mirror symbolizes the acceptance of differences.

In the fourth chapter, Tobe Levin examines a work by a writer who differs from the previous three in that the Jewish American-born writer, Jeannette Lander, lives in Germany and writes in German about a young Jewish girl growing up in segregated Atlanta, Georgia. *One Summer in the Week of Itke K*, like *The Joy Luck Club* and *Brown Girl, Brownstones*, is a female *Bildungsroman*. Levin notes in her chapter how "identity itself is a illusive and illusionary; the multilingual like the multicultural, displaces the self-identical." Jeannette Lander's work dramatizes an intercultural mix of codes: Yiddish and English, Yiddish and black English; and then all of these are put into a German that breaks native speaker rules. Itke can never truly be at "home" because she is a Jew in 1942 with Old World parents, living in a black neighborhood. Levin illustrates how Jews see themselves as similar to blacks because they are also a minority in the dominant southern white culture. However, Jews also benefit as whites in a segregated society. This partial access to three cultural spaces (white, Jewish, and black) precludes the possibility of Itke's achieving a unified identity. In this work, unlike the others in this section, issues of gender identity formation take a secondary rather than coequal place to the depiction of Jewish life in the diaspora: "There is no origin, no authentic self-identical culture to return to or create oneself out of, but only a dialectical interweaving of elements influenced by a concrete history, one of whose dominant traits is the displacement of entire peoples."

   Marilyn Elkins addresses the problematics of African American experience in the diaspora in three novels by Nella Larsen, Toni Morrison, and Andrea Lee. In pointing out how expatriate African American women, in contrast to their male counterparts, are viewed as exotics, Elkins foregrounds gender difference in identity formation. The protagonists go to Europe in the hopes of leaving aspects of themselves, as well as racism, behind. The women in the novels come to realize that, in spite of their attempts to enhance their "white characteristics," white Europeans define them exclusively in terms of their exotic "black characteristics." Their acknowledgment of their double marginalization—their objectification as both African Americans and women—creates a space in which living with contradictions is not self-destructive but self-enhancing.

   Living with contradictions and confronting the multiple oppressions that women face are recurring themes in all the following chapters. Some of the works examined offer successful models, while others depict the enormous difficulties women face. The remarkable and revolutionary changes in formerly communist countries, the dismantling of existing political structures, and the rise of nationalism and new nations point to the continued need to reassess the effects of these changes on women and women's own contributions to new social, national, and political structures.

NOTES

   1. Mary L. Broe and Angela Ingram's collection, *Women's Writing in Exile*, also touches on some of these issues, but limits itself to works in the English tradition.
   2. We rely here on the definition of women's exile offered by Angela Ingram in her "Introduction" to *Women's Writing in Exile*.
   3. In our introduction, titles of works not originally written in English will be given in translation. In the chapters, quotations for the literary works are provided in both the original language and in English translation.

REFERENCES

Anderson, Linda. Preface. *Plotting Change: Contemporary Women's Fiction*. London: Edward Arnold, 1990, vi-xi.

Benstock, Shari. "Expatriate Modernism: Writing on the Cultural Rim." *Women's Writing in Exile*. Ed. Mary Lynn Broe and Angela Ingram. Chapel Hill: University of North Carolina Press, 1989, 19-40.

Broe, Mary Lynn, and Angela Ingram, eds. *Women's Writing in Exile*. Chapel Hill: University of North Carolina Press, 1989.

Fraser, Nancy, and Linda J. Nicholson. "Social Criticism Without Philosophy: An Encounter Between Feminism and Postmodernism." *Feminism/ Postmodernism*. Ed. Linda J. Nicholson. New York: Routledge, 1990, 19-38.

Hekman, Susan J. *Gender and Knowledge: Elements of a Postmodern Feminism*. Oxford: Polity Press, 1990.

Ingram, Angela. "Introduction: On the Contrary, Outside of It." *Women's Writing in Exile*. Ed. Mary Lynn Broe and Angela Ingram. Chapel Hill: University of North Carolina Press, 1989, 1-15.

Marcus, Jane. "Alibis and Legends: The Ethics of Elsewhereness, Gender and Estrangement." *Women's Writing in Exile*. Ed. Mary Lynn Broe and Angela Ingram. Chapel Hill: University of North Carolina Press, 1989, 269-94.

Nicholson, Linda J. Introduction. *Feminism/Postmodernism*. New York: Routledge, 1990, 1-16.

Rubenstein, Roberta. *Boundaries of the Self: Gender, Culture, Fiction*. Urbana: University of Illinois Press, 1987.

Showalter, Elaine. "Introduction: The Rise of Gender." *Speaking of Gender*. New York: Routledge, 1989, 1-13.

Spivak, Gayatri Chakravorty. *The Post-Colonial Critic: Interviews, Strategies, Dialogues*. Ed. Sarah Harasym. New York: Routledge, 1990.

———. *"Race," Writing, and Difference*. Ed. Henry Louis Gates, Jr. Chicago: University of Chicago Press, 1986, 262-80.

Todorov, Tzvetan. "'Race,' Writing, and Culture." *"Race," Writing, and Difference*. Ed. Henry Louis Gates, Jr. Chicago: University of Chicago Press, 1986, 370-80.

PART I

MAPPING IDENTITY

Female Self-Definition and the African Community in Mariama Bâ's Epistolary Novel *So Long a Letter*

Eva Rueschmann

I am not indifferent to the irreversible currents of women's liberation that are lashing the world. This commotion that is shaking up every aspect of our lives reveals and illustrates our abilities.

My heart rejoices each time a woman emerges from the shadows. I know that the field of our gains is unstable, the retention of conquests difficult: social constraints are ever-present, and male egoism resists. (Bâ, *So Long a Letter*, 88)

[Les irréversibles courants de libération de la femme qui fouettent le monde, ne me laissent pas indifférente. Cet ébranlement qui viole tous les domaines, révèle et illustre nos capacités.

Mon coeur est en fête chaque fois qu'une femme émerge de l'ombre. Je sais mouvant le terrain des acquis, difficile la survie des conquêtes: les contraintes sociales bousculent toujours et l'égoïsme mâle résiste. (Bâ, *Une si longue lettre*, 129)]

In her feminist analysis of African women, *Speak Out, Black Sisters*, Awa Thiam points out that while women of the industrialized countries are engaged in the research and creation of a typically feminine discourse, their African sisters are struggling to recover their dignity, fighting for the recognition of their identity as human beings (153). Their identity as full individuals has been consistently denied to them by white colonialists or neocolonialists as well as by black males. African women have had to endure a triple oppression on account of their sex, class, and race. Unlike European and American women, African women are oppressed not only by the patriarchal and capitalist order, but they also suffer under colonialist or neocolonialist laws. The connection between sexism, racism, and class inequality has been suppressed in the African countries' struggle for independence after World War II in favor of the glaring racial problem. African men and women fought side by side to bring their countries out of colonialism, but after independence had been achieved, the old patriarchal order was resumed, and the African woman was once again kept in her traditional place.

The Négritude movement in Francophone Africa, led by prominent African writers like Léopold Sédar Senghor, has helped the black African male to recover his pride and self-worth but has done little for African women. In fact, many members of the Négritude movement assumed rather conventional attitudes toward the African woman by mythologizing her as the Great Mother, the root of the African people: "The African woman doesn't need to be liberated: She has been free for many thousands of years" (Senghor, qtd. in Topouzis, 70). Senghor here expresses a common view of the African woman as the powerful mistress of the house, but her power is a pseudopower, accorded to her by her male oppressors who equate the woman's role with African tradition.

For the longest time, the African woman was socially and spiritually defined by white male colonialists, by black African men, and by European and American feminists. By the 1960s and 1970s the time had come for African women to define themselves in their own words. Awa Thiam writes: "But what is the use of writing about Black women, if in so doing we do not learn what they are *in reality*? It is up to these women themselves to set the record straight" (14).

One of the most prominent women writers to emerge from the post-independence generation in Africa is the Senegalese writer Mariama Bâ, whose first novel, *So Long a Letter* [*Une si longue lettre*], received the Noma Prize for the best work published in Africa in 1980. *So Long a Letter* is a pioneering work among the genuinely feminist African novels, exploring women's social status and struggles in contemporary Senegal. In the words of African critic Abiola Irele, *So Long a Letter* is "a testimony of the female condition in Africa, while giving that testimony a true imaginative depth" (108). The novel articulates the fears and hopes, strengths and weaknesses, resolve, and ultimately, the sense of mission of the African woman.

Mariama Bâ was one of the first women in Senegal to receive a Western education and to experience the transition of a traditional African culture in the postcolonial period with all its social ramifications. Born in Dakar, Senegal, in 1929 to a father who later became the first minister of health in 1959, Mariama Bâ lost her mother at an early age and was brought up as a Muslim by her maternal grandparents. She attended the French School in Dakar and the École Normale in Rufisque to become a *femme cadre* (a professional woman) who taught primary school and was active for many years in the feminist movement in Senegal, Les Soeurs optimistes (The Optimistic Sisters), as well as in international women's organizations. She married the former minister of information (from whom she was later divorced) and had nine children. Many of Bâ's personal experiences as a Muslim woman in a society in transition are re-created in the personal voice of Ramatoulaye, the narrator of her novel whose experiences illuminate the broader social, moral, and emotional realities of middle-aged women in a polygamous society.

The letter referred to in the title is written by Ramatoulaye, a recently widowed mother of twelve children, to her childhood friend and confidant Aissatou, living in the United States. The compulsory seclusion imposed on her by Muslim law after her husband's death allows Ramatoulaye to review the thirty years of her marriage and the formative years of her "progressive" education as well as her friendship with Aissatou. Using the letter as a diary, she describes their experiences as young women who defied convention and family opposition by marrying across caste barriers for love. Ramatoulaye recalls their shattering sense of betrayal when both their husbands took second wives, and she reflects upon the differences in how each of them coped with their husbands' polygamy and its psychological destructiveness. Aissatou refuses to compromise, leaves her husband, and obtains a well-paid job as a translator at the Senegalese Embassy, which allows her to live independently and bring up her four sons. However, despite the deep injury Ramatoulaye's husband has inflicted upon her by choosing one of his daughter's schoolmates, Binetou, for a second wife, Ramatoulaye decides to accept his polygamy and professes her uncompromising love for him. Only after her husband's death does Ramatoulaye realize the extent of his repudiation and betrayal of his family and their exploitation by her husband's new in-laws and his adolescent bride. During the *mirasse* (the customary Islamic religious and juridical period during which the deceased's possessions and moral conduct are judged), Ramatoulaye reflects bitterly on the tradition of polygamy, which has had such a devastating effect not only on herself but also on the entire society. She realizes that her experience as a deceived and abandoned woman is not unique but a part of the repressive system of polygamy that afflicts many women in Africa. Despite Ramatoulaye's anger and depression, however, she never loses her inner dignity and emerges as a strengthened woman with a newly born consciousness of her own self. She confidently rejects two propositions for polygamous marriages and meets the challenges of being a mother to her "emancipated" daughters, one who smokes and another who has become pregnant out of wedlock. The letter ends with Ramatoulaye's joyously awaiting the arrival of her friend Aissatou:

Despite everything—disappointments and humiliations—hope still lives on within me. It is from the dirty and nauseating humus that the green plant sprouts into life, and I feel new buds springing up in me. (89)

[Malgré tout—déceptions et humiliations—l'espérance m'habite. C'est de l'humus sale et nauséabond que jaillit la plante verte et je sens pointer en moi, des bourgeons neufs. (131)]

To fully appreciate the cultural significance of the "new buds springing up" in the African woman and in her emergence in African literature, it is important to define the sociopolitical context from which a feminist writer like Mariama Bâ has herself sprung. *So Long a Letter* assumes its importance both as a breakthrough in feminist African consciousness *and* in its literary expressiveness against the unique historical realities of African culture and traditional gender relations.

African women have taken a long time to emerge as writers. Women were not admitted to institutions of higher education until a few decades ago, and they lacked the power to publish their own writing. Moreover, African women have been subject to an Islamic feminine ideal that devalues female self-expression as antithetical to beauty. In her book *Woman in the Muslim Unconscious*, Fatna Aït

Sabbah asks: "So why are silence and immobility—the signs and manifestations of inertia—the criteria of beauty in the Muslim woman? What does beauty have to do with the right to self-expression? Why, according to the canons of beauty in Islamic literature, does a woman who does not express herself excite desire in a man?" (3). The traditional role of women in African Muslim society as objects of desire does not allow for individual expression and a liberal education. In the name of traditional concepts of beauty, the African woman is silenced by her male counterparts, for the expression of her own desires represents a threat to patriarchal society. Thus, it seems to me all the more important to rescue and examine those women writers who break the silence and decorum in order to challenge the predominently male vision of the changing face of African society. This aspect has been neglected by male critics in an attempt to define African literature as a unified "other literature" and to attribute a single voice to the vast diversity of African literary expression.[1] However, in the wake of international feminism, an increasing number of articles and books have been published on African women writers and on women's social and political issues in Africa.[2] This recent development provides us with the missing *female* perspective of traditional Africa facing modern times, for the African woman will necessarily describe herself and her family and community differently than her male counterpart. She will speak in a different voice.

Western feminists' discovery of African women's texts and their interpretation of African women's experience, however, need critical examination. The question of the usefulness of Western feminism for African women remains to be considered. Is not the African woman once again being defined by an Other, this time by the white, educated, middle-class feminist? Although the problem of women's exploitation and oppression is global, Awa Thiam asserts that "the Black woman's struggle is of a different nature from that of her white sister" (55). Traditionally, the African woman is encouraged to define herself through her race rather than her gender. In African society, the individual self is much more rooted in the religious and familial tradition of community (rather than in the individualism of the West); hence, individual rebellion amounts to social suicide. The social structure and cultural tradition of Africa make it difficult for the African woman to readily adopt Western images of women's liberation without breaking completely with the indigenous community. Western models of feminism with their emphasis on individual freedom and fulfillment threaten to become yet another import of the colonizer. Eldred Jones, editor of *African Literature Today*, claims African literature still needs to be "decolonized" as Western modes and methodologies threaten to define African literature within the parameters of Western thought and tradition (vii-viii). Equally, Western feminist thought and criticism are not necessarily a cross-cultural mode of analysis because they typically defines the African female self within a Eurocentric cultural context. Rather than look at the attempts of African women to assert their selves as merely a first step in women's liberation, Western feminists need to rethink their own assumptions in their analysis of African women's writing and accept African women's voices on their own terms.

One way to avoid a "colonization" of African women's writing is to let these writers speak for and about themselves, that is, to examine the authorial voice of the female writer and how this voice constructs the self. It is highly significant, for instance, that Mariama Bâ chose the epistolary form for her first literary attempt to define an African woman's struggle for a "new way" of living. Along with the diary, or *journal intime*, and the autobiography, the letter serves as a powerful and direct literary form for the expression of the self. Rather than an object defined by a (male) Other, the female letter writer is her own subject; she defines her self, with her own words. Writing and reading are significant acts of self-definition for Mariama Bâ and for her letter writer Ramatoulaye in *So Long a Letter*. The letter captures the very act or process of writing. Its structure traces the evolving self of Ramatoulaye from a crisis situation (her abandonment and her husband's death) to a kind of spiritual renewal. The letter becomes an instrument of revelation and discovery, of self-discovery through communication with another woman, in this case, Ramatoulaye's bosom friend Aissatou. Mariama Bâ's sense of communal self, that is, of a self embedded in, and defined by, a community, is best captured in the epistolary form.

Like the autobiography and the diary, the letter as literary form allows the writing woman to be both subject and object. Women writers have preferred the narrative forms of first-person voice to conventional literary forms of representation because these forms allow them to assert their own subjectivity: the "I" is in the powerful position of defining itself and the world. The diary, letter, and autobiography are also nonlinear, fragmentary forms that are more suited to portray women's daily lives in their private sphere. What distinguishes the letter form from the diary and autobiographical novels is the desire for exchange, the call for response from a specific reader in the correspondent's world.[3] Unlike the interior monologue of the diary and the self-referential quality of the autobiography, the epistolary form implies both a specific reader *and* writer. The addressee of the letter (the "you") becomes a sounding board for the letter writer (the "I"): the first-person writing refracts events through not one but two prisms, reader and writer. Underlying the epistolary dialogue are common memories and experiences; the writer and reader often share experiences that are referred to in the letter and thus establish a communion of understanding.

In the beginning of *So Long a Letter*, Ramatoulaye addresses her friend and their common past:

Dear Aissatou, I have received your letter. By way of reply, I am beginning this diary, my prop in my distress. Our long association has taught me that confiding in others allays pain. . . . I conjure you up. The past is reborn, along with its procession of emotions. . . . We walked the same paths from adolescence to maturity, where the past begets the present. My friend, my friend, my friend. I call on you three times. Yesterday you were divorced. Today I am a widow. (1)

[Aïssatou, j'ai reçu ton mot. En guise de réponse, j'ouvre ce cahier, point d'appui dans mon désarroi: notre longue pratique m'a enseigné que la confidence noie la douleur.

. . . Je t'invoque. Le passé renaît avec son cortège d'émotions. . . . Le même parcours nous a conduites de l'adolescence à la maturité où le passé féconde le présent. Amie, amie, amie! Je t'appelle trois fois. Hier, tu as divorcé. Aujourd'hui, je suis veuve. (7-8)]

Virtually every section of the twenty-seven-part letter begins with Ramatoulaye's ritually recalling her friend's name, affirming her desire for exchange and contact in a common state of misery. Ramatoulaye emphasizes that this exchange is part of a long tradition of daily contact between the women of their respective families: "Our grandmothers in their compounds were separated by a fence and would exchange messages daily. Our mothers used to argue over who would look after our uncles and aunts" (1) [Nos grand'mères dont les concessions étaient séparées par une tapade, échangeaient journellement des messages. Nos mères se disputaient la garde de nos oncles et tantes (7)]. In a society dominated by men, the intimate dialogue between women is particularly meaningful for a definition of women's identity: common memories and experiences break the prison of isolation and create a link between individual women.

Communication between Ramatoulaye and Aissatou is all the more important as both women are faced with the dilemma of the "new woman" in a society caught between tradition and modernity; traditional values no longer provide an easy answer for the changing role of women in Africa. Both Ramatoulaye and Aissatou are among the first women in Senegal to receive a formal education in a white school, where they come into contact with Western views of women, love, and relationships. They defy the tradition of a prearranged marriage in order to marry the men they love. Their respective marriages to a lawyer and doctor promise to fulfill the dream of a new type of relationship based on respect and mutual consideration between enlightened individuals of the educated African elite. However, Senegalese society is still steeped in the Koranic concept of polygamy, and both women underestimate the pressure of social convention upon their husbands to take a second wife. Both women suddenly find themselves in the position of the "abandoned woman" and need to come to terms with the painful discrepancy between their ideal of love and the reality of a society unwilling to change the fundamental division between the sexes. Ramatoulaye's initial response to her husband's second marriage is disbelief, but after she realizes the finality of her situation, she becomes filled with self-doubts and depression: "I was not divorced . . . I was abandoned: a fluttering leaf that no hand dares to pick up, as my grandmother would have said" (53) [Je n'étais pas divorcée . . . j'étais abandonnée: une feuille qui voltige mais qu'aucune main n'ose ramasser, aurait dit ma grand'mère (79)]. Her depression reminds her of her friend Jacqueline from the Ivory Coast, who had a nervous breakdown when her husband continued his escapades with Senegalese women after their marriage. Through the skillful interweaving of the similar experiences of the three women, Ramatoulaye, Aissatou, and Jacqueline, Mariama Bâ provides a larger portrait of the female condition and the social "disease" of polygamy in Africa. Ramatoulaye recognizes that her predicament is not an isolated example but that many women struggle with degradation and humiliation by men in a polygamous marriage.

I have heard of too many misfortunes not to understand my own. There was your own case, Aissatou, the cases of many other women, despised, relegated or exchanged, who were abandoned like a worn-out or out-dated *boubou*. (41)

[J'avais entendu trop de détresses, pour ne pas comprendre la mienne. Ton cas, Aïssatou, le cas de bien d'autres femmes, méprisées, reléguées ou échangées, dont on s'est séparé comme d'un boubou usé ou démodé. (62)]

The letter is a means of communication for Ramatoulaye to reach out to all those African women who have experienced the humiliation of being a cowife. She empathizes with the women whose aging bodies have been rejected for younger, more supple ones. However, Ramatoulaye moves beyond mere commiseration and distinguishes herself from the vast number of abandoned women. She compares and contrasts the various reactions of African women to their predicament and defines her self in contrast and in relationship to her fellow victims. Thus the letter not only situates the female self within a community, but also allows the female subject to define herself in contrast to other women. However, Mariama Bâ always sees her letter writer's self-definition in relational terms.

The crucial dilemma that the African woman of today has to face is how to reconcile her communally bred self with her feminist aspirations for autonomy and self-realization as a woman. In her article on the "New Woman" in contemporary African novels, Beatrice Stegman writes:

African communalism implies a standard or value of submergence rather than self-realization. In traditional African societies, the role of each citizen is to perpetuate the status quo, to assure continuity of the clan, to work within tradition. . . . The "new woman," or feminist, rebels against such traditionalism because she evinces a theory of personhood where the individual exists as an independent entity rather than a group member, where she is defined by her experiences rather than her kinship relations, where she has responsibility to realize her potential for happiness rather than accept her role, where she has indefinable value rather than quantitative financial worth, and where she must reason about her own values rather than fit into stereotyped tradition. (90)

In her letter, Ramatoulaye presents the different forms of the price exacted by this conflict between tradition and modernity in contemporary African women: madness in the case of Jacqueline; exile, deracination, and isolation in the case of Aissatou and numerous other women who, unable to face a life on their own, remarried only to find themselves in a similar situation as before:

I counted the abandoned or divorced women of my generation whom I knew. I knew a few whose remaining beauty had been able to capture a worthy man, a man who added fine bearing to a good situation and who was considered "better, a hundred times better than his predecessor." The misery that was the lot of these women was rolled back with the invasion of the new happiness that changed their lives, filled out their cheeks, brightened their eyes. I knew others who had lost all hope of renewal and whom loneliness had quickly laid underground. (40)

[Je comptais les femmes connues, abandonnées ou divorcées de ma génération. J'en connaissais dont le reste de jeunesse florissante avait pu conquérir un homme valable qui alliait situation et prestance et que l'on jugeait "mieux, cent fois mieux que le partant." La misère qui était le lot de ces femmes régressait à l'envahissement de leur bonheur neuf qui changeait leur vie, arrondissait leurs joues, rendait brillants leurs yeux. J'en connaissais qui avaient perdu tout espoir de renouvellement et que la solitude avait mises très tôt sous terre. (61)]

Ramatoulaye understands that the specter of loneliness and despair leads many women to madness or self-denying compromise. She herself, however, declines two marriage proposals and imagines a future for herself beyond the dubious comforts of a second marriage. In a conversation with her brother-in-law, Ramatoulaye affirms that women can no longer be regarded as a piece of property and valuable asset to a man's socioeconomic status in society. She emphasizes that love is the only acceptable reason for marriage:

You forget that I have a heart, a mind, that I am not an object to be passed from hand to hand. You don't know what marriage means to me: it is an act of faith and of love, the total surrender of oneself to the person one has chosen and who has chosen you. (I emphasized the word "chosen.") (58)

[Tu oublies que j'ai un coeur, une raison, que je ne suis pas un objet que l'on se passe de main en main. Tu ignores ce que se marier signifie pour moi: c'est un acte de foi et d'amour, un don total de soi à l'être que l'on a choisi et qui vous a choisi. (J'insistais sur le mot choisi.) (85)]

The element of choice that Ramatoulaye emphasizes in this passage implies an *active* self that takes responsibility rather than a passive object. In the second half of the letter, Ramatoulaye writes of her difficult recovery, punctuating her narrative with the phrase, "I survived, I was surviving" (51) [Je survivais (76)]. She learns to drive a car, an act that is wonderfully symbolic of her new faith in her self, who is taking control. The affirmation of the self that is ritually enacted through the repetition of the "I" in the narrative continues and fulfills Ramatoulaye's trajectory from dejected, abandoned wife/victim to self-assertive woman. This trajectory began with Ramatoulaye's first picking up her pen in her state of distress to write "such a long letter" to her friend and ends with her determination to "go out in search of [happiness]" (89) [J'irai à la recherche [du bonheur] (131)]. By the end of her letter, the tone has shifted from hopelessness and despair to a feeling of quiet triumph and victory in having survived on her own.

Ramatoulaye's letter moves from her husband's funeral to the affirmation of life and the self, following the archetypal cycle of death and rebirth. Ramatoulaye uses the organic metaphor of the new plant growing out of the old soil not only to capture the regenerative qualities of the female self but also to illustrate her belief in social renewal from within the traditional African family and society. Just as the new plant needs its roots firmly planted in the ground, the "new" African woman should seek change and happiness within her indigenous culture. Ramatoulaye (as Mariama Bâ's mouthpiece) is a progressive, but certainly not a radical, woman; she does not want to annihilate completely the traditional African society but rather seeks reforms within the indigenous social structure which provides a sense of continuity and community for the individual African woman. Ramatoulaye's desire to achieve female independence within the traditional social structure is nowhere more apparent than in her attempt to meet the challenges of forging a new male-female relationship in African society. Her daughter, Daba, and her husband seem to represent a ray of hope, a potential new type of relationship that is based on equality, respect, and mutual consideration. For despite the many disappointments in her own marriage, Ramatoulaye affirms her ideal of the monogamous, eternal couple.

I remain persuaded of the inevitable and necessary complementarity of man and woman. Love, imperfect as it may be in its content and expression, remains the natural link between these two beings. . . . The success of the family is born of a couple's harmony, as the harmony of multiple instruments creates a pleasant symphony. The nation is made up of all the families, rich or poor, united or separated, aware or unaware. The success of a nation therefore depends inevitably on the family. (88-89)

[Je reste persuadée de l'inévitable et nécessaire complémentarité de l'homme et de la femme. L'amour, si imparfait soit-il dans son contenu et son expression, demeure le joint naturel entre ces deux êtres. . . . C'est de l'harmonie du couple que nait [sic] la réussite familiale, comme l'accord de multiples instruments crée la symphonie agréable. Ce sont toutes les familles, riches ou pauvres, unies ou déchirées, conscientes ou irréfléchies qui constituent la Nation. La réussite d'une nation passe donc irrémédiablement par la famille. (129-30)]

Mariama Bâ's idealistic outlook on the future of male-female relationships contrasts sharply with the view of Western feminists like Simone de Beauvoir, who has challenged the idea of the couple and who sees marriage as a "prisonhouse" for women.[4] Bâ's optimistic portrayal of marriage and the couple is grounded, on one hand, in her own strong belief in spiritual renewal and a destiny of perfection and, on the other, in her ideal of romantic love. Mariama Bâ admits the imperfect and problematic nature of the love relationship (which, for her, culminates in marriage); however, she believes that true love between two human beings is still the highest form of fulfillment of self and community. In her view, the unity of the sexes always will be the ideal that men and women must strive for, as it is the paradigm for the union of all opposites (past and present, nature and culture, death and life) *and* the foundation of a strong nation.

When Ramatoulaye came into contact with Western ideas of individual rights and personal fulfillment through her education, she was also introduced to the Western romantic ideal of the "couple," the exclusive love between man and woman that informs so much of Western literature. The monogamous relationship must have seemed a very attractive ideal to a woman who was forced to accept several cowives in her marriage. Nevertheless, there are obvious problems with this ideal concept of the "couple" in Western social reality. Simone de Beauvoir has argued that a form of polygamy exists in Western societies in the guise of prostitution and extramarital relationships.

A contrast and comparison between Mariama Bâ's and Simone de Beauvoir's views of monogamous love reveal a fundamental cultural difference in the ways African and European feminists envision the relationship between the genders and the social community. However, Beauvoir and Bâ agree that marriage in its traditional form is a threat to the individual identity of the woman, who becomes more or less an accessory to the man's life. Early in the letter, at her husband's funeral, Ramatoulaye laments:

This is the moment dreaded by every Senegalese woman, the moment when she sacrifices her possessions as gifts to her family-in-law; and, worse still, beyond her possessions she gives up her personality, her dignity, becoming a thing in the service of the man who has married her, his grandfather, his grandmother, his father, his mother, his brother, his sister, his uncle, his aunt, his male and female cousins, his friends. Her behavior is conditioned: no sister-in-law will touch the head of any wife who has been stingy, unfaithful, or inhospitable. (4)

[C'est le moment redouté de toute Sénégalaise, celui en vue duquel elle sacrifie ses biens en cadeaux à sa belle-famille, et où, pis encore, outre les biens, elle s'ampute de sa personnalité, de sa dignité, devenant une chose au service de l'homme qui l'épouse, du grand-père, de la grand-mère, du père, de la mère, du frère, de la soeur, de l'oncle, de la tante, des cousins, des cousines, des amis de cet homme. Sa conduite est conditionnée: une belle-soeur ne touche pas la tête d'une épouse qui a été avare, infidèle ou inhospitalière. (11)]

Beauvoir and Bâ describe in similar terms the compromises a woman has to make in marriage, but they arrive at quite different conclusions with regard to the value of marriage as a form of human relationships. Their different evaluations of marriage shed light on the self-definition of the African woman and illustrate why a Western definition of feminism may not be applicable to the vision of a "new" African female self.

Simone de Beauvoir postulates a discrepancy between love and sexual attraction and the socially required contract of marriage. She recognizes a more recent development that shows efforts to integrate sexuality, love, and marriage (primarily in the United States), but the married couple remains for her a hypocritical entity.[5] In contrast, Mariama Bâ feels love and marriage are not mutually exclusive and she attributes a great social value to marriage. Provided marriage involves the consent of two independent individuals who want to form a bond of love, the harmonious relationship between man and woman represents a source and reflection of the integrity of a whole nation, which is a major concern for African countries evolving from colonial dependence.

Whereas Beauvoir's orientation toward the male world of intellectual endeavor and career puts primary emphasis on the male/female dualism, Mariama Bâ includes an examination of the female power relations in *So Long a Letter* that provides a more complex picture of the dynamics of exploitation and abandonment of women in African society. In moving away from the stereotypes of male oppression of women, "Mariama Bâ is able to bring into sharp focus the part played by both male and female segments of society in this process" (Cham, 39). Ramatoulaye's letter, which is, on the most literal level, addressed to her friend Aissatou, represents an appeal to all African women to actively work toward a new identity and social change in their home country. The letter is directed, in particular, to all traditional mothers and mothers-in-law, who often play a major role in the disruption of their children's marriages out of greed and rivalry for social status. Ramatoulaye presents the disastrous effects of mothers like Aunty Nabou, Aissatou's mother-in-law, and Lady Mother-in-Law, the mother of Ramatoulaye's cowife Binetou, contrasting the traditional mother figure with a different model of motherhood that arises out of new female consciousness.

Aunty Nabou and Lady Mother-in-Law both exploit their power as mothers to undermine the efforts of women like Aissatou and Ramatoulaye who are committed to creating a new type of male-female relationship based on equality. Aunty Nabou, Aissatou's mother-in-law, is caught in the traditional caste hierarchy and cannot accept her son's marriage to Aissatou, the daughter of a lowly blacksmith. Aunty Nabou considers Aissatou a usurper who has soiled the royal family, and she embarks on what she calls an honorable mission to disrupt the "sinful" marriage. Using a strategy of calculated trickery, Aunty Nabou transforms her young niece Nabou into a second self, raising her in the tradition of the royal caste. She then forces her son Mawdo to take young Nabou as a second wife:

My brother Farba has given you young Nabou to be your wife, to thank me for the worthy way in which I have brought her up. I will never get over it if you don't take her as your wife. Shame kills faster than disease. (30)

[Mon frère Farba t'a donné la petite Nabou comme femme pour me remercier de la façon digne dont je l'ai élevée. Si tu ne la gardes pas comme épouse, je ne m'en relèverai jamais. La honte tue plus vite que la maladie. (48)]

Mawdo complies with his mother's wish, fulfilling his duty toward his mother, who took responsibility for little Nabou's education. In a polygamous society, where the relationship between husband and wife is not exclusive, the relationship between mother and son is all the more tenacious and powerful. Moreover, only through her children can a mother exercise any kind of control. For Aunty Nabou, Mawdo's marriage to young Nabou is not only a restoration of caste dignity but also a way to maintain control over her son (her "only man"), as young Nabou is basically an extension of her own self.

Lady Mother-in-Law, Binetou's mother, is the epitome of the mother who uses her power over her children to promote her own social position and material enrichment. Ramatoulaye sees her cowife, a school friend of her own daughter, as a "lamb slaughtered on the altar of affluence" (39) [un agneau immolé comme beaucoup d'autres sur l'autel du "matériel" (60)]. Binetou is not a partner committed to social, political, and moral ideals like Ramatoulaye; rather, she represents the "fountain of youth" for the vain man who wants to be part of the modern life-style of contemporary Africa. While Binetou uses her own female charms to manipulate a man's desire, it is ultimately her mother who uses her daughter as a pawn to ensnare Ramatoulaye's wealthy husband,

Modou Fall, and thereby rise out of poverty: "Having known poverty, she [Lady Mother-in-Law] rejoiced in her new-found happiness. . . . From then on, she joined the category of women 'with heavy bracelets' lauded by the *griots*"[6] (49) [Elle jouissait de son bonheur neuf, en connaissance de la misère. . . . Dès lors, elle accéda à la catégorie des femmes "au bracelet lourd," chantées par les griots (74)]. After Modou's death, Lady Mother-in-Law is forced to give up her newly acquired social position and returns to her humble origins. Binetou, who is already "dead inside" (as Ramatoulaye remarks), has no future without an education or professional skills. The child-widow is reduced to a position of total dependence on men. Lady Mother-in-Law ruined not only Ramatoulaye's marriage but also her daughter's life. Daba spells out her irresponsibility and harmful greed:

Remember, I was your daughter's best friend. You made her my mother's rival. Remember. For five years you deprived my mother and her twelve children of their breadwinner. Remember. My mother has suffered a great deal. How can a woman sap the happiness of another? You deserve no pity. Pack up. As for Binetou, she is a victim, your victim. (71)

[Souviens-toi, j'étais la meilleure amie de ta fille. Tu en as fait la rivale de ma mère. Souviens-toi. Pendant cinq ans, tu as privé une mère et ses douze enfants de leur soutien. Souviens-toi. Ma mère a tellement souffert. Comment une femme peut-elle saper le bonheur d'une autre femme? Tu ne mérites aucune pitié. Déménage. Quant à Binetou, c'est une victime, ta victime. (103)]

Mariama Bâ is clearly examining women's responsibility for perpetuating polygamy for their own self-interests. She is portraying mothers who become "victims victimizing victims" (Cham, 42). They are "women deliberately and maliciously sabotaging the happiness of other women in a male dominated society" (Cham, 47). The letter does not only represent a diatribe against male exploitation through polygamy but also a plea for female solidarity against domination and abandonment.

In contrast to Aunty Nabou and Lady Mother-in-Law, Ramatoulaye represents an alternative—more positive—role model of the African mother or mother-in-law. Ramatoulaye has enormous social power as a mother of twelve children, and there is great potential of abuse of that power. In the final part of the letter, her integrity and ability to relinquish power are put to the test as she has to face the pregnancy of her teenage daughter Aissatou. Ramatoulaye finds it difficult to accept the changing value system that affects her daughters' lives: "Does it mean," she asks, "that one can't have modernism without a lowering of moral standards?" (77) [Le modernisme ne peut donc être, sans s'accompagner de la dégradation des moeurs? (112)]. However, Ramatoulaye's maternal support and protection of her child in trouble prevail, which express Mariama Bâ's faith in the effort of women to correct the abuse of maternal power of the Aunties Nabou and Ladies Mother-in-Law. Ramatoulaye realizes and finally accepts the limits of parents' control over their children in contemporary society:

At that moment, I felt that my child was being detached from my being, as if I were again bringing her into the world. She was no longer under my protection. She belonged more to her boyfriend. A new family was being born before my very eyes. (86)

[À ce moment, je sentis ma fille se détacher de mon être, comme si je la mettais au monde à nouveau. Elle n'était plus sous ma protection. Elle appartenait davantage à son ami. Une nouvelle famille naissait à mes yeux. (125)]

Ramatoulaye's refusal to imprison her daughter in her own value system represents a step forward toward a more responsible and more healthy model of motherhood. Her compassionate treatment of her daughter is an outgrowth of her new awareness and definition of herself as an independent woman.

Indeed, Mariama Bâ considers the role of the mother as educator crucial for the process of social change. In an interview with Barbara Harrell-Bond she claimed: "So now we mothers, we mothers who have had the privilege to understand a little and to play a part in the creations of our sons, we have tried to raise them so that they do not grow up thinking of themselves as 'kings of the family.' This is the hope for the future" (211). The education of the younger African generation is a key to the social and personal transformation of the African woman. Education represents a field where women can exercise some control over the revision of gender roles in society.

In her letter, Ramatoulaye points out the various levels of insight and responsibility among the women whose lives have become interconnected through polygamy, and she defines her own sense of self in relation to these women's degree of self-awareness. Binetou is at the lower end of Ramatoulaye's scale of virtue because she lacks a sense of tradition and propriety. She did not love Ramatoulaye's husband when he married her, and she took her personal revenge by draining him financially. Young Nabou, however, grew up within a certain traditional religious framework and never had the education to look beyond her position. Ramatoulaye sees in her a certain innocence and admirable devotion that Binetou lacks. Ramatoulaye considers her friend Aissatou superior to both of them since she has taken individual responsibility for her actions and displays a sense of propriety and justice that comes from moral insight. Finally, Ramatoulaye is the only one of all these women who has reconciled traditionalism with feminism. Although she is looking forward to a reunion with her best friend, she senses Aissatou's cultural alienation and regrets that she has become Westernized to the degree that she does not feel comfortable with the indigenous African customs anymore:

So, then, will I see you tomorrow in a tailored suit or a long dress? I've taken a bet with Daba: tailored suit. Used to living far away, you will want—again I have taken a bet with Daba—table, plate, chair, fork. More convenient you will say. But I will not let you have your way, I will spread out a mat. On it there will be the big, steaming bowl into which you will have to accept that other hands dip.

Beneath the shell that has hardened you over the years, beneath your skeptical pout, your easy carriage, perhaps I will feel you vibrate. I would so much like to hear you check or encourage my eagerness, just as before, and, as before, to see you take part in the search for a new way. (89)

[Ainsi, demain, je te reverrai en tailleur ou en robe-maxi? Je parie avec Daba: le tailleur. Habituée à vivre loin d'ici, tu voudras—je parie encore avec Daba—table, assiette, chaise, fourchette. Plus commode, diras-tu. Mais, je ne te suivrai pas. Je t'étalerai une natte. Dessus, le grand bol fumant où tu supporteras que d'autres mains puisent.

Sous la carapace qui te raidit depuis bien des années, sous ta moue sceptique, sous tes allures désinvoltes, je te sentirai vibrer peut-être. Je voudrais tellement t'entendre freiner ou nourrir mes élans, comme autrefois et comme autrefois, te voir participer à la recherche d'une voie. (130-31)]

The letter expresses Ramatoulaye's need to reestablish the former closeness with Aissatou, to reaffirm their common struggle toward a new vision of the African female self. However, the letter also mourns the loss of Aissatou's indigenous identity. The final invocation of Aissatou indicates that Ramatoulaye no longer thinks her a "true African," and she finishes her letter on a note of personal pride in her loyalty to her own culture.

It is significant that Mariama Bâ chose Aissatou to be an interpreter and Ramatoulaye a schoolteacher in Senegal. Aissatou is living in exile in the United States, translating the ideas of other people who are, presumably, mostly male Senegalese and American representatives. In contrast, Ramatoulaye decided to stay in her native country to continue teaching in school. As a teacher, she is actively involved in shaping the minds of young Africans and in the creation of a new order in Africa. This power of creation not only defines her own self but affects the entire society. Ramatoulaye's female identity is shaped through her triple role as mother, teacher, and writer. As an educated *femme cadre* like Mariama Bâ herself, she has the creative power that the Aunties Nabou and the Ladies Mother-in-Law of the African society lack. She has learned to master the French language and can make use of the "power of the word" creatively to contribute to social change, that is, to share her experiences and thoughts with other women in Africa and the world. Thus this "long letter" moves from self-expression and self-reflection to communication with a community and the entire world of women engaged in a common struggle toward a new society: "I believe that books are an instrument of that development. We cannot go forward without culture, without saying what we believe, without communicating with others, without making people think about things. Books are a weapon, a peaceful weapon perhaps, but they *are a weapon*" (Bâ, qtd. in Harrell-Bond, 214).

NOTES

1. In his book *Women Writers in Black Africa* (1981), Lloyd Brown claims that "the women writers of Africa are the other voices, the unheard voices, rarely discussed and seldom accorded space in the repetitive anthologies and the predictably male-oriented studies in the field" (3).

2. Lloyd Brown's *Women Writers in Black Africa* is an early treatment of African women writers. A major work that discusses African women writers from a more feminist-critical perspective is Carole Boyce Davies and Anne Adams Graves, *Ngambika: Studies of Women in African Literature*. Katherine Frank discusses the usefulness of feminist criticism for the interpretation of African novels in her article, "Feminist

Criticism and the African Novel," which takes a look at African women in a socioeconomic context.

3. See discussion of the epistolary form in Janet Gurkin Altman, *Epistolarity: Approaches to a Form*, 89.

4. See Beauvoir's *The Second Sex* for her analysis of marriage in Western societies as a "bourgeois institution" that condemns women to a life of economic and emotional dependency:

> In marrying, woman gets some share in the world as her own; legal guarantees protect her against capricious action by man but she becomes his vassal. He is the economic head of the joint enterprise, and hence he represents it in the view of society. She takes his name; she belongs to his religion, his class, his circle; she joins his family, she becomes his "half." She follows wherever his work calls him and determines their place of residence; she breaks more or less decisively with her past, becoming attached to her husband's universe; she gives him her person, virginity, and a rigorous fidelity being required. (479)

5. Mariama Bâ is certainly aware of the love-money nexus in postcolonial society. If Ramatoulaye is at times completely engrossed in the ideal aspects of marriage, she also sees that, in a society incorporating Western capitalism, love cannot be detached from a socioeconomic context. Marriage, which is ostensibly based on love, provides material comfort, the "good life," especially for members of the lower castes who marry into the new African bourgeoisie. In the satire on the funeral rites of Ramatoulaye's husband, Mariama Bâ illustrates the eroding effect of the capitalistic system on traditional values.

6. Black African, of any nationality, who is part-poet, part-musician, part-sorcerer (see "Notes" in Bâ, *So Long a Letter*, 90).

REFERENCES

Aït Sabbah, Fatna. *Woman in the Muslim Unconscious*. Trans. Mary Jo Lakeland. New York: Pergamon Press, 1984.

Altman, Janet Gurkin. *Epistolarity: Approaches to a Form*. Columbus, OH: Ohio State University Press, 1982.

Bâ, Mariama. *So Long a Letter*. Trans. Modupe Bode-Thomas. London: Heinemann Educational Books, 1981.

————. *Une si longue lettre*. Dakar: Les Nouvelles Éditions Africaines, 1980.

de Beauvoir, Simone. *The Second Sex*. Trans. H. M. Parshley. New York: Vintage, 1974.

Brown, Lloyd. *Women Writers in Black Africa*. Westport, CT: Greenwood Press, 1981.

Cham, Mbye Baboucar. "The Female Condition in Africa: A Literary Exploration by Mariama Bâ." *A Current Bibliography in African Literature*. 17.1 (1984/85): 19-51.

Davies, Carole Boyce, and Anne Adams Graves, eds. *Ngambika: Studies of Women in African Literature*. Trenton, N. J.: Africa World Press, 1986.

Frank, Katherine. "Feminist Criticism and the African Novel." *African Literature Today* 14 (1984): 34-47.

Harrell-Bond, Barbara. "Interview with Mariama Bâ." *African Book Publishing Record* 6.3-4 (1980): 209-14.

Irele, Abiola. Review of *Une si longue lettre*. *African Book Publishing Record* 6.2 (1980): 108.

Jones, Eldred. "Editorial." *African Literature Today* 14 (1984): vii-viii.

Stegman, Beatrice. "The New Woman in Contemporary African Novels—The Divorce
    Dilemma." *Critique* 15.4 (1974): 81-90.
Thiam, Awa. *Speak Out, Black Sisters: Feminism and Oppression in Black Africa*. Trans.
    Dorothy S. Blair. London: Pluto Press, 1986.
Topouzis, Daphne. "Women of Substance." *Africa Report* 33 (May-June 1988): 70-71.

(Re)Presenting the Self: Identity and Consciousness in the Feature Films of Safi Faye

Sheila J. Petty

In *Ngambika: Studies of Women in African Literature*, Carol Boyce Davies argues that "African written literature has traditionally been the preserve of male writers and critics" (1). So, too, the situation repeats itself for filmmaking in Sub-Saharan Africa. It is commonly acknowledged that while the mid-1970s saw a significant number of women writers emerge and set out to ensure women's self-inscription into history and to reassess paradigms "canonized" by male writers, the same decade and, in fact, the whole history of Sub-Saharan filmmaking counts only one independent African-born woman director to have completed a feature-length film.

Safi Faye was born in Dakar, Senegal, in 1943. Her family belongs to the Serer ethnic group and comes from the village of Fad'jal, which is located south of Dakar. During the 1966 Dakar Festival of Negro Art, she met the French ethnologist and filmmaker Jean Rouch, who asked her to play a part in *Little by Little or the 1968 Persian Letters* [*Petit à petit ou les Lettres persanes 1968*], a film dealing with the "African" discovery and experience of French life. This brief acting experience led Faye to move to Paris to study ethnology and filmmaking. Since her first film, *The Passerby* [*La Passante*] 1972, she has completed several shorts and two feature-length films.

Françoise Pfaff has observed that *Little by Little or the 1968 Persian Letters* allowed Faye to

become acquainted with Rouch's technique of cinéma-vérité (an unobtrusive camera eye, spontaneous shooting, improvised nonprofessional acting, and mostly single takes), which was to influence her greatly in the course of her future career as a filmmaker. Yet, in retrospect, Safi Faye dislikes this film, questions its significance, and expresses severe criticism as to her own performance in it. (116)

Faye's reaction to Rouch's film clearly demonstrates her perception of how certain filmic practices have operated against the interests of Africans in an effort to "invent" and control their representation and identity in history.

In this chapter, I focus on Safi Faye's feature work in an attempt to show that the desire to control her own representation of identity has led the filmmaker to challenge the adequacy of "established" cinematic practices for the portrayal of African experiences. Simultaneously, I hope to demonstrate that while Faye's work explores issues of politics, memory and cultural identity, it also sets out to define an African feminist film aesthetic.

In reading Faye's work, it is necessary to recognize that she does not pretend to speak for all of Africa. She resists "typifying" the "African experience," and in so doing, she defies "the fixity of boundary relations between centre and margin, universal and particular, [which] returns the speaking subject to the ideologically appointed place of the stereotype—that 'all [Africans] are the same'" (Julien and Mercer, 5). Faye, however, also resists "typifying" the "female experience" and in this way respects the heterogeneity of African women.

In feminist film theory as in the women's movement as a whole, difference has been discussed primarily in terms of gender; race, class, and sexual orientation are rarely recognized as aspects of identity inseparable from gender. According to much of the work in feminist film theory, women's association with spectacle and icon (passive) and men's association with the advancement of the narrative (active), have contributed to women's objectification within the diegesis and in the eyes of the spectator in mainstream Hollywood cinema.

Laura Mulvey's pioneering article, "Visual Pleasure and Narrative Cinema," greatly informed by Freud and psychoanalysis, argued that:

the spectator's position, active and voyeuristic, is inscribed as "masculine" and, through various narrative and cinematic devices, the woman's body exists as the erotic, spectacular and exhibitionist "other," so that the male protagonist on screen can occupy the active role of advancing the story-line. (Mulvey, 162)

Her argument implies that identification with the advancement of the narrative is possible only through the appropriation of masculinity. In "Oedipus Interruptus," Teresa de Lauretis began to rethink the active/passive dichotomy and to explore the possibility of identifications with the narrative process "doubling up" with those associated with the image and the gaze (34-40).

De Lauretis's articulation of representation and spectatorship advanced somewhat beyond Mulvey's "transvestism," (in the sense of identification with a male), yet the either/or binary pattern has prevailed in feminist film theory. Laura Mulvey has since reflected that this type of argument lacks the capacity to "advance politically into a new terrain or suggest an alternative theory of spectatorship in the cinema" (162). She further contends that aesthetics that undercut dominant codes as well as aesthetics counterposed to those of orthodox cinema risk remaining within systems of dualistic opposition (162-64).

To understand Safi Faye's films by simply embedding them in European culture and white feminist film theory would have Faye reacting to the iconography and narrative structure of dominant classical cinema, a cinema already saturated with the taint of patriarchal assumptions and particular historical epochs. Faye would then be creating countercinema, cinema created in the context of, and produced by, Western oppression, rather than independent films associated with a particular culture and society. It must be understood that the breaking of hegemonic codes is not Safi Faye's grand project, for if it were, her films would constitute mere reactions to Eurocentric thought. Rather, her films chart an alternative to Western thought and its implied Other by striving to ensure that unique cinematic content and forms are being generated to probe African realities.

Safi Faye's feature work is invested with her own political and aesthetic project. Both *Peasant Letter* [*Kaddu Beykat*] (1975) and *Come and Work* [*Fad'jal*] (1979) effect critiques of sociocultural and political realities of the village of Fad'jal. *Peasant Letter* identifies the introduction of peanut mono-culture in the eighteenth century under French colonialism as the source of the villagers' present plight and proceeds to denounce "what Faye sees as the inadequate measures taken by her government to cure the ills of the Senegalese peasantry" (Pfaff, 119). While *Come and Work* continues the exploration of the peasants' present problems in terms of government policy and reform, Faye's concern is to show how oral tradition can preserve collective memory and forge cultural identity. Not surprisingly, this cultural identity becomes the subject of both films, and subsequently informs their narrative structure and use of cine-matic codes.

Critics have deplored the lack of "narrative thread" in Faye's work: the fact that not only is the heroine/hero impossible to distinguish from the other characters, but narrative functions do not always cause a progression in the story. In fact, the films are not bounded at both ends by the assertion of original synchronic order. Todorov has described narrative as a "movement between two equilibriums which are similar but not identical" (163). The move from one state (beginning) to the other (end) involves a phase of imbalance or disorder in which change occurs. Much of white feminist film theory's impasse derives from its understanding that to "refuse narrative is to refuse pleasure" (Kaplan, 32). But is narrative needed equally or in the same way in all societies and cultures? Is progression really vital to narrative structure, or is it vital only to Western narrative structure? I would argue that Safi Faye has created texts that defy the sadism of a narrative dependent "on making something happen, forcing a change in another person, a battle of will and strength, victory/defeat, all occurring in a linear time with a beginning and an end" (Mulvey, 22).

In both *Peasant Letter* and *Come and Work*, the "narrative" is not brought to resolution by the movements of self-present actants as Faye positions the heroine outside the visual image. Collective consciousness becomes the invisible heroine in *Peasant Letter* while *Come and Work*, as a historical evocation, seems at first to privilege cultural identity as the invisible heroine. The intrusion of the present, however, quickly imposes collective consciousness as the second invisible heroine. Faye's use of heroines rather than heroes is a celebration of Fad'jal's matriarchal roots.[1] Through these invisible heroines, Faye urges all African women to participate in the narrative quest, the object of which becomes collective survival in the face of drought and government reform. Each viewer/

subject controls her own representation of identity by constructing meanings from the quest appropriate to her experiences.

The positioning of the films' heroines outside the frame space and in the extradiegetic subverts the Western patriarchal practice of assigning woman an exhibitionist role and then proceeding to fragment her body for male pleasure. Kaja Silverman writes that "dis-embodying the female subject by allowing her to be heard without being seen, constitutes a challenge to the means by which we have previously known her, since it is precisely 'as body' that she is constructed" (135). Silverman is, of course, writing about Western cinematic practices where women filmmakers and critics have challenged the notion of the female body as a construct of the male gaze.

It would be totally absurd to claim that in Faye's films women's bodies function merely as ornamentation and as erotic objects of male desire within the diegesis and for the (male) spectator, since she ensures that shots of women are never invested with the sole function of an "aesthetic touch." The systematic use of long shots and a static camera ensures that women's bodies are never fragmented by close-ups and that the aesthetic value of the shots is not divorced from the moral code of community values as female characters function within a definable milieu.

By adopting invisible heroines and by employing a voice-over monologue in both her feature films, Safi Faye further rejects fragmentation by refusing a reading of the voice through the body. Rather than denying the heroine/subject an active role in the filmic discourse, Faye aligns her with a presence that transcends the diegetic. Together, these formal strategies forge what is perhaps Safi Faye's strongest feminist statement: recognition of African women's differences and repudiation of the embodiment of Africa in the figure of a woman. It has been argued that this "embodiment" is a "literary commonplace or topos, a recurring feature in a tradition that can be traced back at least as far as the Négritude movement of the 1930s" (Stratton, 112). It is by now a commonplace that this movement developed in reaction against the colonial attitude that Africans were savages in need of civilizing. Senghor's definition of Négritude as "the sum total of the values of the African world" (99) asserted an African essence free of western influence and encouraged a romantic nostalgia that glossed over contemporary problems.

This process of revaluation is not exclusive to African literature. While Stratton contends that the embodiment trope is a defining feature of the male written tradition (120), the same trope occurs in male-authored African film since its birth as a means of expressing (male) African essence and identity.[2] Women's function in these films is to embody the male vision of Africa as a "nation." The binary opposition of Mother Africa as the past or nation restored versus prostitute as the nation in present degraded state forcibly links woman to the male quest in the films and defines the boundaries within which she is allowed to function. In such male-authored films as *Woman, Car, Villa, Money* [*Femme, voiture, villa, argent*] (1972), *Black Star* [*L'Étoile noire*] (1975), *Karim* (1971), *Bronze Bracelet* [*Le Bracelet de bronze*] (1974), the hero must ultimately choose between the modern "prostitute" figure, the African woman dressed in a miniskirt, high heels and a wig, or the traditional "mother" figure, the African woman dressed in traditional clothes. Naturally, his choice determines his outcome in the film; the prostitute leads him to eventual ruin (*Woman, Car, Villa, Money*) or death (*Bronze Bracelet*), whereas "Mother Africa" leads him to reason and the reaffirmation of his cultural identity (*Black Star, Karim*).

The embodiment of Africa in the figure of the female enforces power relations characteristic of patriarchal cultures: subject/object, active/passive, self/Other (Stratton, 122), and denies women an equal role in the shaping of a national vision. Senghor's famous declaration that "the African woman does not need to be liberated. She has been free for many thousands of years" (45) contributes to the notion of power relations, for it idealizes and romanticizes the African mother in an attempt to camouflage the real situation of women in Africa.

Since many male-authored African films fail to achieve portrayals of women's real situations in both traditional and modern societies, *Peasant Letter* and *Come and Work* attempt to bring a feminist consciousness to African film by revealing, rather than glossing over, certain structures or uses of structures that continue to deny women equality. Both films acknowledge women's and men's oppression under imperialism but also recognize that, while modernism may have introduced new structures of oppression for women, certain inequalities that existed in traditional societies have been reinforced by colonialism.

The films carefully delineate how the introduction of peanut monoculture has increased women's oppression in modern rural Senegal. In *Peasant Letter*, for example, the women denounce the single-crop farming policy, which reduced women's rights to land and power. In many traditional African societies, land was controlled by the group; European laws, however, assumed that individual men in each family owned land. When the French introduced peanut cultivation during colonial expansion in order to reap profits from its export back to France, men were put solely in charge of cultivating the crop. The Senegalese male peasant, formerly self-sufficient, was suddenly forced to participate in this new monetary-based economy in order to pay the taxes levied by the French. Thus, the best land was seized for cash-crop production by men while women, who once participated equally in subsistence farming with men, were suddenly forced to cultivate all other crops for village consumption. In *Come and Work*, when the peanut crops do not need tending, the men gather for lengthy discussions in the village square, whereas the women must tend to the other crops as well as domestic chores. Not surprisingly, women complain about the men's laziness while images of women in the fields far outnumber those of men in a seeming affirmation by the filmmaker that women's labor output in subsistence farming in Fad'jal far surpasses that of men.

Yet, Faye's work moves beyond the limitations of boundaries created by such binary oppositions as past/present, tradition/modernism, and Mother Africa/prostitute, which are the central organizing principles of many African films. *Come and Work* as a deconstructive project offers a useful reading of the displacement of binary oppositions and the creation of new "space." Gardies has suggested that the two organizing principles of the film are thematic, on one hand (including life, death and work), and chronological, on the other (including seasons and times of day). According to Gardies, these two principles are simple in themselves but are organized in a complex manner lending a certain organizational density to the work (183). I would argue that the intermeshing of the real and the fictive, the recounted past and the lived present, adds a further dimension to the film's structure that necessitates a particular use of space and mise-en-scène.

Come and Work's mise-en-scène celebrates the social group's way and rhythm of life. Human relations, conversation and debates eclipse the obsession with time so characteristic of mainstream film's narrative logic. Through the constant use of static sequence-shots, characters are allowed the time it takes and the necessary space to complete gestures, actions, and dialogue. Closed form dominates the visual style of each scene involving a historical reconstitution. In these scenes, Grandfather recounts the past to the children, who form a complete circle within the frame. The portrayal of Grandfather as the living collective memory of the village involves a demarcation of his own space within this visual circuitry; the village "talking tree" serves as his backdrop just as the mat on which he sits and the spear he holds are his props. This ordering of space can be seen as a direct borrowing from the oral tradition, for it is together that the storyteller and his audience create the story. Audience interaction is portrayed through reverse-angle shots of the children asking questions and encouraging the teller to continue so they may experience the story.

As Grandfather's history of the village unfolds, we learn that Fad'jal was founded by a woman and that the village was once very prosperous. Grandfather's commentary moves back and forth between the diegetic and the extra-diegetic, the historical reconstitutions imposing elements of fiction from time to time. For instance, as the village's passage from a matriarchal society to a patriarchal society is explained, a villager dressed as a king appears on the screen. Interestingly enough, the real founder of Fad'jal is never contained by screen space just as Safi Faye's own voice-over commentary remains strictly extra diegetic. As the king of Sine rides across the screen, we are informed that he arrived in Fad'jal with the intention of conquering the village in a "peaceful" manner. The king and his court abused the traditional code of hospitality by moving from one neighborhood to another until there was nothing left to eat in the village. The villagers all understood the king's trick, but their sense of honor and dignity would not allow them to *not* well receive a guest. When a family could no longer fulfill its obligation toward such a distinguished guest, it would discreetly leave until, eventually, the whole village was forced to relocate.

Clearly, the king who symbolizes patriarchy turns women's values (matriarchal) against themselves in order to cause the ruin and exile of Fad'jal. His desire to dominate led to the eventual establishment of a patriarchal precolonial Fad'jal. Thus, one form of civilization has buried another as though the struggle between women's values and paternal law must end in unilateral defeat. Jessica Benjamin has asked:

Why must a patriarchal father supersede and depose the mother? If the struggle between paternal and maternal power ends in paternal victory, the outcome belies the victor's claim that the loser, the mother, is too dangerous and powerful to coexist with. Rather, it would seem that the evocation of women's danger is an age-old myth which legitimates her subordination. (156)

While Grandfather recounts the past in the present voice, the historical reconstitutions enacted by villagers conjoin with depictions of such present village activities as the gathering of salt and the harvesting of millet crops. Screen space accorded to villagers of the recounted past coalesces with that accorded to villagers of present-day Fad'jal, thus affording the spectator a sense of belonging simultaneously to the past and the present. Safi Faye has justified this structuring as reminiscent of the Serer tradition whereby an individual can be in the world of the living and that of the dead at the same time (Ruelle, 65). In *Come and Work*, visual and auditory images work to create a reference to the past in order to contextualize the present. If today's poverty is endured, it is because everyone continues to maintain a sense of solidarity by sharing everything. If exodus is tolerated today, it is because it has become a sign of courage to leave the village to look for work.

The historical reconstitutions are less an attempt to restore the mythical, mystical Africa so dear to members of the Négritude movement than a device to incite the viewer to read Fad'jal's present in the context of its past in order to safeguard the community's future. I do not believe the filmmaker is suggesting that the solution to Fad'jal's present ills is contained in the past. Rather, I would agree with Diawara, who, when discussing the films of Burkina Faso's Gaston Kaboré, observes that "a return to the inner-self or to African culture does not therefore mean a subordination to tradition for the director who uses oral literature. It is a questioning of tradition, a creative process which enables him to make contemporary choices while resting on the shoulders of tradition" (39). Interestingly, the film's final scenes provide a strong statement concerning the future of Fad'jal's identity. As the children are gathered at the foot of the "talking tree," Grandfather is noticeably absent from the shots. Each child recites bits of the "history lesson." Clearly, this generation will act as the "village library"[3] and will transmit the collective memory to future generations.

Safi Faye has declared that she makes her films "first of all for Africa, for African people" (qtd. in Martin, 17), and her use of cinematic codes certainly underscores this declaration. She describes her works as "collective . . . in which everyone takes an active part" (qtd. in Pfaff, 117). This philosophy converges with that of other filmmakers of the black diaspora whose cinematic practices place Africans at the center of text and discourse. Both *Peasant Letter* and *Come and Work* explore the possibilities of a mutually informing relationship between reader/viewer and text through their specific use of voice-over. Pascal Bonitzer observes that: "the voice-over represents a power, that of disposing of the image and of that which it reflects from a place which is absolutely other. Absolutely other and absolutely indeterminable. In this sense, transcendent. . . . In so far as it arises from the field of the Other, the voice-off is assumed to know: such is the essence of its power" (qtd. in Silverman, 134).

Safi Faye's voice-over commentary is not to be heard in territorial, conquering, all-knowing terms. Instead, it functions, to a certain extent, to organize discourse, provide indispensable information, and involve the viewer in what Gardies considers the semantic game of the audiovisual discourse (184). The filmmaker invites the viewer to associate her own voice with the "voice" of the village. *Peasant Letter* opens with the voice belonging to Faye/village announcing: "You're going to spend a moment with me." A series of long and extreme long shots captures the Senegalese countryside: a lagoon, fields surrounding Fad'jal, as the voice continues, "Here is my village. My parents are farmers." From this point onward, the "storyteller" assumes the viewer possesses the necessary cultural background to be called forth and inscribed in the identification process. Furthermore, as the audience is hailed, its presence is required to enter into dialogue with the voice/village, much like a traditional storytelling performance. As Faye continues with, "A peasant's annual income is twenty thousand francs C.F.A. [eighty dollars]. It has only rained three months," she is creating a dialogue with the Senegalese viewer, who would understand that in 1975 this income could not have lasted one person more than one month.

Come and Work also assumes a certain cultural knowledge on behalf of the viewer; as the men gather to discuss the government's projects for land reform and development, Faye's voice-over states that "on May 1, 1964, a law was passed declaring all land henceforth the property of the state." This intervention forces the viewer to ponder the changes that will occur within the Senegalese peasantry because of neo-colonial government reform and to consider the consequences of these very reforms on cultural identity. Further, it justifies and provides the context for Grandfather's history lesson.

Certainly Faye's "nonclassical" use of cinematic codes represents a commitment to reexamine "the image of Africa." Is she not responding to Fanon's call for new humane conditions and experiences in the postcolonial era? In *Peasant Letter* and *Come and Work*, cinematic codes form a cohesive unit to reorganize filmic enunciation around the discourse or ideology of "the community." The process of subject construction involves a necessary dialogue between viewer/subject and filmmaker/text/subject. *Peasant Letter* ends with a freeze-framed close-up of Faye's own grandfather looking at the audience as Faye's voice-over solemnly affirms, "This is the voice of the peasant—Kaddu beykat." In *Come and Work*, cinematic address constructs looks at the spectator, which are freed from the containment of frame space and the constraint of chronological film time. Thus, invisible heroism exists in a sort of timeless past/present/future. Both films meet Clyde Taylor's call for a postesthetic creative practice that "reconstructs knowledge" and "brings to black cinema a perception of its cultural practises as a crucial site of the contest out of which the human is being rewritten" (85). As subject, heroine, and spectator become one, a collective consciousness, an eternal collective village memory is called into concrete "being."

NOTES

1. I use the term *matriarchal* because Grandfather uses it in *Fad'jal* when he recounts the village's history to the children. Furthermore, when the *griot* arrives to name the village's ancestors for the children, he discusses how descent is reckoned through the female line right from Mbang Fadial, the village's founder.

2. The Guinean Mamadou Touré was the first African south of the Sahara to shoot a film. His twenty-three-minute short entitled, *Mouramani* (1953) examines the friendship between a man and his dog.

3. In *Come and Work*, Safi Faye quotes the Malian philosopher Hampaté Bâ, who observed that "in Africa, whenever an old man dies, it is as though a library has burnt down."

REFERENCES

Alassane, Mustapha, dir. *Femme, voiture, villa, argent [Woman, Car, Villa, Money]*. With Zingare Abdoulaye, Bintou Sawadogo, Sotigui Kouyaté, and Djingareye Maiga. Prod: (Niger), (Burkina Faso), and Ministère de la Coopération (France). 1972. 16mm., color, 75 min.

Aw, Cheikh Tidiane, dir. *Le Bracelet de bronze [Bronze Bracelet]*. With Nar Sene, Isseu Niang, Ngone Thioune,Christophe Colomb, Gorgui Diop, and Cheikh Tidiane Aw. Prod: Société Nationale de Cinéma and C. T. Aw (Senegal) and Ministère de la Coopération (France). 1974. 35 mm., color, 115 min.

Benjamin, Jessica. *The Bonds of Love: Psychoanalysis, Feminism, and the Problem of Domination*. New York: Pantheon, 1988.

Davies, Carol Boyce. "Introduction: Feminist Consciousness and African Literary Criticism." *Ngambika: Studies of Women in African Literature*. Ed. Carol Boyce Davies and Anne Adams Graves. Trenton, NJ: Africa World Press, 1986, 1-23.

de Lauretis, Teresa. "Oedipus Interruptus. " *Wide Angle* 7.1-2 (1985): 34-40.

Diawara, Manthia. "Oral Literature and African Film: Narratology in 'Wend Kuuni.'" *Présence Africaine* 142 (1987): 36-49.

Fanon, Frantz. *The Wretched of the Earth*. Trans. Constance Farrington. New York: Grove Press, 1968.

Faye, Safi, dir. *Fad'jal [Come and Work]*. With Ibu Ndong and his family. Prod: Ministère des Relations Extérieures, INA (France) and Safi Films (Senegal), 1979. 16 mm. and 35 mm., color, 108 min.

———. *Kaddu Beykat [Peasant Letter]*. With Assane Faye and Maguette Guèye. Prod: Safi Films (Senegal) and Ministère de la Coopération (France), 1975. 16 mm., black and white, 95 min.

———. *La Passante [The Passerby]*. With Safi Faye. Prod: Participation of Ministère de la Coopération (France), 1972. 16 mm., black and white, 10 min.

Gardies, André, and Pierre Haffner. *Regards sur le cinéma négro-africain*. Brussels: Éditions OCIC, 1987.

Julien, Issac, and Kobena Mercer. "Introduction: De Margin and De Centre." *Screen* 29.4 (1988): 2-10.

Kaplan, E. Anne. "Feminism/Oedipus/Postmodernism: The Case of MTV." *Post-modernism and its Discontents*. Ed. E. Anne Kaplan. London, New York: Verso, 1988, 30-44.

Maiga, Djingareye, dir. *L'Étoile noire [Black Star]*. With Djingareye Maiga, Aissa Indji, Mustapha Alassane, Damouré Zika, and Bernard Louno. Prod: Participation of Ministère de la Coopération (France), 1975. 16 mm., black and white, 95 min.

Martin, Angela. "Four Filmmakers from West Africa." *Framework* 11 (Fall 1969): 16-21.

Mulvey, Laura. *Visual and Other Pleasures*. Bloomington: Indiana University Press, 1989.

Pfaff, Françoise. *Twenty-Five Black African Filmmakers: A Critical Study with Filmography and Bio-Bibliography*. Westport, CT: Greenwood Press, 1988.

Rouch, Jean, dir. *Petit à petit ou les Lettres persanes 1968 [Little by Little or the 1968 Persian Letters]*. With Damouré Zika, Lam Ibrahima Dia, Illo Gaoudel, Safi Faye, and Mustapha Alassane. Prod: Films de la Pléiade, Musée de l'Homme (Paris) and C.N.R.S.H. (Niger), 1970. 35 mm., color, 96 min.

Ruelle, Catherine. "Faye, Safi." *L'Afrique littéraire et artistique* 49 (1978): 63-65.

Senghor, Léopold. *Léopold Sédar Senghor: Prose and Poetry*. Ed. and trans. John Reed and Clive Wake. London: Oxford University Press, 1965.

Silverman, Kaja. "Dis-embodying the Female Voice." *Re-Vision: Essays in Feminist Film Criticism*. Ed. Mary Ann Doane, Patricia Mellencamp, and Linda Williams. Frederick, MD: University Publications of America and the American Film Institute, 1984, 131-49.

Stratton, Florence. "'Periodic Embodiments': A Ubiquitous Trope in African Men's Writing." *Research in African Literatures* 21.1 (1990): 111-26.

Taylor, Clyde. "We Don't Need Another Hero: Anti-Theses on Aesthetics." *Critical Perspectives on Black Independent Cinema*. Ed. Mbye B. Cham and Claire Andrade-Watkins. Cambridge: MIT Press, 1988, 80-85.

Thiam, Momar, dir. *Karim*. With Sidy Casset, Fatim Diagne, Assane N'Diaye, and Fanta Traoré. Prod: Les Films Momar Thiam (Senegal) and Ministère de la Coopération (France), 1971. 16 mm., black and white, 65 min.

Todorov, Tzvetan. *The Fantastic: A Structural Approach to a Literary Genre*. Trans. Richard Howard. Ithaca, NY: Cornell University Press, 1975.

Sappho's Daughters: Lesbian Identities in Novels by Québécois Women (1960–1990)

Anne E. Brown

> What is a lesbian? . . . She is the woman who, often beginning at an early age, acts in accordance with her inner compulsion to be a more complete and freer human being than her society . . . cares to allow her. These needs and actions . . . bring her into painful conflict with people, situations, the accepted way of thinking, feeling, behaving, until she is in a state of continual war with everything around her, and usually with herself. (Radicalesbians, 172)

Prior to the 1960s, no mention of the woman-identified woman can be found in Québécois literature. In her thought-provoking book, *On Lies, Secrets, and Silence*, Adrienne Rich has written about the silence surrounding lesbians in literature: "Whatever is unnamed, undepicted in images, whatever is omitted from biography, censored in collections of letters, whatever is misnamed as something else, made difficult-to-come-by, whatever is buried in the memory by the collapse of meaning under an inadequate or lying language—this will become, not merely unspoken, but *unspeakable*" (199). Interestingly enough, it was during the Quiet Revolution[1] that lesbianism first dared to whisper its name on Québec's literary scene. The first literary portrayal of lesbianism can be found in Louise Maheux-Forcier's novel *Tinder [Amadou]*.[2] Published in 1963, this novel radically changed the literary landscape of Québec. Indeed, since then, a growing body of women novelists, following Maheux-Forcier's lead, have felt compelled to give voice to Sappho's daughters, to speak the hitherto unspeakable.

This chapter traces the emergence and evolution of the lesbian identity in women's novels between 1960 and 1990. I show that each decade corresponds to a particular phase in the representation of lesbian identity in Québécois literature and that by exploring a "different" or "other" perspective, the novelists in question begin to suggest "dimensions previously ignored and yet necessary to understand fully the female condition" (Zimmerman, 200).

The first phase (1960-1970) highlights the prohibition of the woman-identified woman's desire. This prohibition underpins the designation of the lesbian's identity as shameful, stigmatizes her "difference," and forces the lesbian into embracing the realm of silence. Conventions of male primacy and heterosexual dominance are shown to coerce lesbians into renouncing a female object of love in exchange for a male, while simultaneously encouraging them to repudiate their true sexual identity.

In the second phase (1970-1980), lesbian protagonists begin to demand the right to their "difference." The veil of secrecy that traditionally enshrouded them is rended, thus allowing the process of destigmatization to begin. The new gay/lesbian consciousness of the 1970s fosters a "public debate on 'homosexuality,'" and women writers begin to shy away from representing heterosexuality as "the only sexuality that existed or that *could* possibly exist" (Durocher, 14). Their woman-centered "discourse," based on the right to be different, unmasks the social foundations of heterosexuality and identifies the strategies of repression to which lesbians are subjected.

The third phase (1980-1990) focuses on lesbians' struggles to claim their true identity and to have their way of life legitimated. Prior to the generative moment in the novels discussed here, the lesbian protagonists have affirmed or accepted their women-identified identities, which they define as inborn, innate, and natural rather than chosen, adopted, or unnatural. The lesbians' perception of self no longer appears solely confined to the stifling and limited debate about sex and desire. In search of alternative values, women-identified women often give a disturbing account of the lesbian stigma that continues to set them apart from the dominant culture. In confronting their freely chosen women-identified life, lesbians resist, consciously or not, heteropatriarchal hegemony.[3] In resisting, it is clear that not only are lesbians returning to their "selves" by addressing their particular "difference," but they are also deconstructing the traditionally negative perception of their identity.

1960s: THE STIGMATIZED IDENTITY

During the 1960s, three writers—Marie-Claire Blais, Yvette Naubert, and Louise Maheux-Forcier—broke new ground in the history of the Québec novel by giving voice to lesbian experiences. It must be noted, however, that women-identified women have a relatively minor role to play in their narratives. More often than not, the lesbians are secondary characters. Thus relegated to the margins of the text, the lesbians are embryonic characters, protagonists who are just beginning to pierce the surface of the text. However small their voices, they nevertheless inflict a noticeable tear in the ominous shroud of secrecy that, up until then in Québec, cloaked all women-identified women and confined lesbianism to the realm of the hidden and the unmentionable.[4]

The lesbians depicted in the 1960s are cut off from a formal lesbian community. Understandably, they suffer from exclusion, alienation, and a loss of sense of self.[5] Their identity thus weakened, they are unwilling to make disclosures about their sexual orientation and often yearn to present, as does Marie, in Maheux-Forcier's *A Forest for Zoé* [*Une forêt pour Zoé*], a normative front that would help them "pass" in the "straight" world. During the Quiet Revolution, "passing" usually entails marriage. Because the dominant culture marginalizes their very existence while stigmatizing their identity, lesbians, as Maheux-Forcier implies, are reluctant to live outside the institution of heterosexuality. Fear "of having to explain herself" [d'avoir à s'expliquer (176)], causes Marie, for example, to become "cowardly" [lâche (176)] and break off her long-term lesbian relationship with Thérèse. This same fear forces her into heterosexual "coupledom."

Marie's abandonment of Thérèse is symbolic not only of her dread of public exposure but also of her irrevocable betrayal of her true self-identity. Having internalized the cultural message that lesbianism is abnormal and thus unacceptable, her fear of disclosure and her rejection of self are so strong that, a few years later, when she unexpectedly comes upon Thérèse at a beauty salon, she refuses to speak to her and will not acknowledge their past relationship. In brief, Marie's actions betray her deepest wish: to have all traces of her sexual orientation publicly and privately erased. Symbolically, her silence could be said to represent, as Stimpson suggests, "a passport into the territory of the dominant world" (246). Although Thérèse also marries in an attempt to mask her lesbian identity, she is less successful than Marie at integrating herself into the heterosexual order. Thérèse is unhappily married to a man for whom she has no sexual desire and who eventually rapes her. Prohibited from her lesbian subjectivity and confronted with an alienated/alienating identity, she retreats into an imaginary world where she suffers delusions and hallucinations.

Her story nevertheless ends on an encouraging note. Indeed, she is eventually rescued from her world of madness by Isis. The representation of the lesbian relationship between Isis and Thérèse is a positive one. Isis—named after the Egyptian goddess of birth and queen of the underworld—refuses to have her identity dictated to her or diminished by others. Her strong sense of self allows her to instill into Thérèse the desire to be "[herself] in the face of the world" [[elle-même] à la face du monde (185)].

This desire brings about Thérèse's rebirth. Rebirth is the process by which she reconfigures the boundaries of her identity. In the closing pages of *A Forest for Zoé*, Isis has left Montréal for professional reasons, and Thérèse—whose survival has been made possible by her lover's validation of lesbianism—is no longer willing to fulfill heteropatriarchal expectations of femininity or to posit herself as negative in the existing order of things: "Now, I walk the streets alone . . . if I happen to catch my reflection in shop windows, I like what I see" [Maintenant, je marche seule dans la rue . . . et s'il m'arrive de m'apercevoir dans les vitrines, je me trouve à mon goût (200)]. The final moment in the text demonstrates that lesbian relationships "are potentially of psychic and moral value" (Stimpson, 253). Thérèse has finally been able to reject the stigma attached to her lesbian identity, a stigma that Murphy describes as responsible for all lesbians' "experienc[ing] a time of internal struggle in order to accept [their] lesbian selves" (87).

In *Tinder*, an earlier novel, Maheux-Forcier had already exploited the theme of the lesbian who does not wish to live outside compulsory heterosexuality because of the negative social stigma attached to lesbianism.[6] Having internalized the lesbianism-as-sickness attitude of her society, Nathalie, one of Maheux-Forcier's lesbian protagonists, clearly expresses her inability to come to terms with her woman-centered self: "I am neither male nor female. I do not accept myself" [Je ne suis ni femme ni homme. Je ne m'accepte pas (66)]. Nathalie's identity is so splintered that she too chooses marriage as a means of "passing."

As a newlywed, Nathalie forms a lesbian relationship with Sylvia, a bisexual who urges her to come to terms with her sexual orientation: "Get up from under stifling prejudices and live your life as you wish" [Sors de l'étouffement des préjugés et vis ta vie comme tu la sens (150)]. Despite her lover's support, Nathalie is unable to imagine her lesbian subjectivity as powerful and positive. The tensions created by her experience of stigma and exclusion from the heterosexual mainstream, coupled with her clearly fractured psyche, are at the root of her inability to define her own identity, to signify herself to herself. This inability gives rise to an internal conflict symbolized by her alternating rejection and acceptance of self. Her self-hatred is further exacerbated by the fact that she is both physically and mentally abused by Julien, her authoritarian husband.

In an attempt to control every aspect of Nathalie's life, Julien does not hesitate to invade her privacy. While reading her mail one day, he discovers her "betrayal." Julien's subsequent violence does not stop Nathalie from answering her lover's letters. In these letters, Sylvia implores Nathalie to come live with her. Sensing that Nathalie is, mentally if not physically, escaping his grip, Julien attempts "to destroy Sylvia's image" [détruire l'image de Sylvia (156)] by discrediting her to his wife.

His strategy to bind Thérèse more closely to him fails miserably. Distraught by her husband's systematic destruction of the image that, symbolically and literally, "brings [her] back to life" [me rendait la vie (156)], Nathalie succumbs to an all-encompassing despair, shoots her husband, sets fire to their home, and immolates herself. Ironically, the motive for her violent deeds stems from a primal instinct: self-preservation. As she explains:

[I] will set fire to it [the house]! . . . Then Sylvia's three letters, they will burn too and they will burn in my mind at the same time as my hair and no one will touch all of that . . . no one anymore . . .

[j'y mettrai le feu! . . . Alors les trois lettres de Sylvia, elles brûleront aussi et elles brûleront dans ma tête en même temps que mes cheveux et personne ne touchera à tout cela . . . plus personne . . . (155)]

At a primary level, the murder-suicide signifies Thérèse's search for "an everlasting . . . peace" [une paix . . . jusqu'à la fin des temps (157)]. At a secondary level, it testifies to her fractured self, which renders her unable to openly challenge her husband's dominance and the heterosexist values of her culture.

During the 1960s, the lesbian as criminal is a recurring motif in novels representing women-centered characters. Mia, in *A Forest for Zoé*, and Mère Saint-Bernard de la Croix, in *Manuscripts of Pauline Archange* [*Manuscrits de Pauline Archange*], commit a reprehensible crime: child molestation. Both are teachers who are portrayed as unhappy and pathetic. Mère Saint-Bernard de la Croix teaches young convent girls. Mia, an alcoholic, gives private piano lessons in her home. Wishing to keep their lesbianism hidden from public view, they never speak openly about their sexual orientation. Living in the hermetically sealed worlds of convent and home, they correspond to Kallen's description of lesbians for whom there is an immense personal toll in covering their sexual orientation, such that they "privatize [their lives] to the point of utter social isolation" (54). Because their access to other lesbians is severely impeded by their fear of disclosure, they sexually abuse their young students. Their crime is neither justified nor justifiable. However, it can be argued that the stress involved in the "constant process of identity management or passing" (Kallen, 55) is so great that it is a contributing factor to their criminal behavior.

Manuscripts of Pauline Archange and, to a lesser extent, *A Forest for Zoé* and *Tinder* are novels that equate lesbianism with a "punishable deviancy" (Stimpson, 248). As they cry out for social justice and acceptance, the reader confronts the political reality of heterosexism. Because the novels present, in different ways, a significant number of lesbian characters as inauthentic and pathetic, one cannot claim that the writers are themselves free from heterosexual bias.

By equating love between women with self-destruction, sexual abuse, madness, alcoholism, and murder, the writers perpetuate the stigma that attaches itself to women who love women. Their texts can thus be categorized as belonging to a particular type of lesbian novel: narratives of damnation. As Stimpson argues, these narratives, at least at a certain level, reflect "larger social attitudes about homosexuality . . . [and] also extend an error of discourse about it" (245). Yet, if Blais's and Maheux-Forcier's portrayal of lesbianism seems sometimes oppressive, the fact remains that it overlaps with their deconstruction of certain myths about lesbians that circulated quite freely in 1960s Québec society. I contend, moreover, that Blais's and Maheux-Forcier's sympathies often lie with their lesbian protagonists, because the written expression of lesbian themes openly challenges the heterosexist foundation upon which Québéc society is built.

In Maheux-Forcier's, Blais's, and Naubert's narratives, the perceived enemy is located outside and inside the lesbian self. The outside is an oppressive heterosexist society that readily stigmatizes the lesbian's identity. Lesbians then internalize this stigmatized self. On one hand, the authors' portrayals of lesbianism suggest that the heteropatriarchal society is incomplete; this incompleteness pushes women into seeking solace in the arms of other women. On the other hand, lesbianism is a means by which some women attempt to fuse into a whole the various aspects of the female personality (mother, daughter, sister, friend, lover).

During the 1960s, lesbian protagonists often appropriate for themselves what Simone de Beauvoir calls "the treasures of femininity" (1: 498). With the exception of Mia and Mère Saint-Bernard de la Croix, they base their relationships with one another on the principles of reciprocity and exchange. In turn, they seduce or are seduced. Once their erotic passion is appeased, they readily transform themselves, like Nicole and Estelle in Naubert's *The Awakened Sleeper* [*La Dormeuse éveillée*], into maternal figures mutually "rocking each other" [se berçant (130)]. If, for example, Nicole calls her lover "little mother" [petite mère (129)], while Thérese, Maheux-Forcier's heroine, claims that her lover is both "[her] mother and [her] daughter" [[sa] mère et [sa] fille (153)], it is because, at a symbolic level, their lover's body has allowed them to be reborn as women who are now able to attach a positive value to their identity.

At a psychological level, they are searching for alter egos: "for moral and psychological equivalents. . . . Poignantly, painfully, they seek the mother as well. A mother waits at the heart of the labyrinth of some lesbian texts. There she unites past, present, and future. Finding her, in herself and through a surrogate, the lesbian reenacts a daughter's desire for the woman to whom she was once so linked, from whom she was then so severed" (Stimpson, 256). This search for a "psychological equivalent" and the attempt to re-create the mother-daughter bond are in a sense to fuse "with the archaic figure of our origin where the feminine sexual subject loses herself in the maternal" (Marini, 73). Yet many of the protagonists have been repudiated by their "real" mothers and sisters because of their sexual orientation. Among other things, lesbianism is thus for them "an aid in discovering how [they] may reconstitute lost families, becoming spiritual mothers and daughters for each other in time of need" (Ostriker, 74).

As the lesbian searches for a mirror image of herself (as sister, mother, lover, daughter) in her lover, she enters into a very complex process of trying to name herself. Past, present, and future not only are blurred, but become one in this relationship. Both women, simultaneously and alternately, play out all of the traditional female roles, while at the same time becoming each other's double. If lesbian love can be viewed as narcissistic by the very fact that it signals a desire of the Other who is also the same, it can also be described as an "anaclitic love" (Stimpson, 257). Partially stemming from a need to be supported and, conversely, from a need to support, this love has a very important role to play in the construction of lesbian identity. Indeed, it is due to the woman-centered relationship that lesbians, like Thérèse in *A Forest for Zoé*, must no longer derive their identity from a condemming Other, signified by the dominant culture, but rather from a same, one who lives under the same heteropatriarchal rules as they themselves do. This Other has no need of explanations for the simple reason that she understands all there is to understand about the lesbian condition. Ultimately, as the narratives suggest, the lesbian can come to know the full dimensions of her identity only if she follows Isis's example and forcefully rejects the negative label her homophobic society has attached to her identity.

1970s: REJECTING THE STIGMATIZED IDENTITY

During the 1970s, lesbian protagonists begin their long journeys out of the closet. The growing acceptance of homosexuality in Québec society propels them from the margins to the center of the narrative.[7] In *Georgie*,[8] for example, Jeanne D'Arc Jutras creates a space where the lesbian experience—from childhood to womanhood—can be minutely examined. Her novel is a kind of *Bildungsroman*, providing a fascinating account of a lesbian's coming to terms with her identity.

The first image that the reader has of the principal protagonist, Georgie, is of a young girl throwing her baseball glove and bat over a fence she subsequently climbs. As her name and her love of baseball suggest, Georgie does not conform to the stereotype of a young girl who plays only with dolls. Her "difference" is further intensified by the fact that Georgie is in love with her best friend, Irène Nelson. Convinced that Georgie's feelings for her daughter are unnatural, Madame Nelson forbids her to see Irène, while Georgie's own mother accuses her of being "perverted" [vicieuse (63)]. Hoping that her friends will be supportive, Georgie discloses her sexual orientation to them. Her honesty does not have the desired effect; all around her, "segregation established itself" [la ségrégation s'établit (63)].

This first lesson in the politics of rejection on the basis of sexual orientation forces Georgie back into the closet. From that point on, she embraces what sociologists call the "double life" syndrome. During her twenties and thirties, the greater part of her energies is spent in fabricating an existence built on layers of secrecy and deceit. She acknowledges her lesbian identity only in private and only in the company of other lesbians. By dichotomizing her private self and her public self, Georgie falls prey to what Krieger calls a "hiatus in identity" (98), a period in which a person is unable to formulate a clear definition of self.

This inability is further intensified by the fact that she suffers a double alienation—as a woman and as a lesbian: "Discriminated against as a woman, colonised, labelled with all sorts of names as a lesbian. . . . What is being a woman? Living one's life by surviving? And for a lesbian, what is living?" [Discriminée en tant que femme, colonisée, étiquetée de tous les noms en tant que lesbienne. . . . C'est quoi être une femme? Vivre sa vie en survivant? Et pour une lesbienne, c'est quoi vivre? (96)].

What, indeed, does living as a lesbian in the late 1960s and early 1970s in Québec entail? Georgie maps out the boundaries of the lesbian's world for us. First and foremost, women-identified women live in a society where their civil rights are denied: "no laws . . . protect us" [aucune loi . . . nous protège (142)].

This absence of legal protection leads to various abuses, such as when Georgie gets fired from her job because of her sexual orientation, or when her landlady refuses to renew her's and Diane's [her lover] lease under the pretext "that women like [them], depreciated her building" [des femmes comme [elles], ça dévalorisaient son building (142)]. Second, they are unable to claim for themselves the language of respectability. Perceived by the dominant culture as deviants, women-identified women are consistently labeled negatively. The term *lesbian* is itself:

a word so often used in a derogatory manner, linked to all the unimaginable perversions, a word launched like a missile to hurt, mutilate, degrade, a word pronounced with hatred, disgust, vengeance.

[mot si souvent employé de façon péjorative, rattaché à toutes les perversions inimaginables, mot lancé comme un projectile pour blesser, mutiler, dégrader, mot prononcé avec haine, dégoût, vengeance. (149)]

The verbal assaults to which these women are subjected and their loss of civil rights effectively sanction discrimination against them. These assaults illuminate the dynamics of power relations between lesbians and heterosexuals. This power relation pushes Georgie to declare: "No matter which way you [lesbians] turn, you are forced to ghettoize yourself even in your own ghetto" [De n'importe quel côté que tu t'tournes, on t'oblige à te ghettoriser même dans ton ghetto (142)]. In the heteropatriarchal society, the lesbian's status is that of an out-cast—a subclass of women too degraded and depraved to allow the heterosexual Other's recognition of them. Moreover, as bearers of the stigma of sexual difference, lesbians are cast as nothing more than convenient recipients of the negative pathological aspects of the self that the dominant culture projects upon them. In consequence, the subjugation of lesbians testifies, as Georgie implies, to the quasi-Nazi nature of the heterosexist society, in which all that is lacking to further oppress women-identified women is "the pink triangle of Nazism" [le triangle rose du nazisme (112)].

When Georgie makes this statement, she is in her late thirties, and she has just begun her desperate search for "the promised land" [la terre promise (175)], for a society in which the stigma surrounding lesbianism would be absent. This quest is signified in her wanderings from one province to another, one country to another, and even one continent to another. Her travels are in vain: "Else-where it's the same, everywhere it's the same thing" [Ailleurs c'est pareil, partout c'est la même chose (176)]. Given that there exists no place on earth where lesbianism is acceptable, Georgie finally realizes that she must search within herself for a positive sense of self. This retreat into the self enables her to disrupt the boundaries that have been imposed upon her identity.

In the novel's closing pages, Jutras's heroine is a spokesperson for lesbian pride and has positively redefined the edges of her identity. She now defines a lesbian as "a global woman, creative, with an emotional structure which is deliciously orientated towards women" [une femme globale, créative, avec une structure affective orientée délicieusement vers les femmes (152)]. If Georgie no longer registers a powerful ambivalence in her self-naming, it is essentially because she has come to understand that before others can celebrate her, she must first celebrate herself. In her mind, concealing one's lesbian identity is now tantamount to being ashamed of it, and disclosure is a consciousness-raising technique that serves to educate the dominant culture about the diverse women under the umbrella of lesbianism.

Georgie argues indirectly for the cultural acceptance of a desire traditionally categorized as evil, depraved, and sinful. Moreover, Jutras is engaged in what Boucher describes as the process of "deconstructing concepts of the 'natural' and the 'normal,' exposing them as oppressive constructs created by a phallocratic culture" (qtd. in Palmer, 48-49). Jutras's willingness to deconstruct the hetero-sexual norm is signified by Georgie's clear statement that homosexuality, like heterosexuality, is inborn: "it is innate, it is not acquired. One is a lesbian or one is not" [c'est inné, c'est pas acquis. On est lesbienne ou on ne l'est pas (151)].

During the 1970s, the perceived enemy is once again located outside, in heteropatriarchal society, and inside, through self-hatred of the lesbian self. Interestingly, with the exception of Irene, Georgie's first love, "passing" no longer entails marriage for women-identified women. However, they still suffer from the "double life" syndrome, the dichotomizing of their private world from their public world. This point is well illustrated by the following facts: Georgie is in her late thirties when she begins to disclose her identity to "straight" people, and all the other women-centered women in the novel opt, like their literary counterparts in the previous decade, to keep their identity secret. Because their identity is solely created "in the matrix of the lesbian subculture" (Ponse, 87), its boundaries are severely limited. Moreover, victims of various forms of discrimination, the lesbians depicted in *Georgie* are also economically disadvantaged. Like their sisters in real life, Jutras's women-centered women are "locked into a subordinate societal status, characterized by economic, political and/or social disadvantage (Kallen, 50). At the same time, a ray of light falls upon Jutras's bleak yet realistic portrait of the lesbian's identity. Georgie signifies this hope in her unequivocal statement of her lesbian identity on national television and in her newfound militancy; her activism intensifies her commitment to her lesbian identity. When women-identified women openly challenge the legitimacy of the heterosexual order by refusing to continue living under the conspiracy of silence, they strengthen their own identity while simulta-neously providing a strong ideological support for lesbian identities in general.

1980s: THE LESBIAN SEPARATIST STANCE

During the 1980s, there was an ongoing preoccupation with the assimilation of lesbian themes and protagonists in the works of Québec women writers. Contemporary women's narratives tend to disrupt fixed notions of identity, and writers usually avoid the trap of defining lesbian sexuality in heteropatriarchal terms. One of the leading authors of this new generation of women writers, Nicole Brossard, has openly adopted an authorial stance that ascribes special attributes to lesbians. Ponse terms this stance "the aristocratization of lesbian-ism" (98). Brossard writes: "Lesbians are the living proof of the 'genius' of women. All women would like to believe in this 'genius' of women, but only lesbians believe in it, are inspired by it, feel it" [La lesbienne est une preuve vivante du "génie" des femmes. Toutes les femmes aimeraient croire au "génie" des femmes, mais seule les lesbiennes y croient, s'en inspirent, l'éprouvent (109)]. If Brossard attributes superior, or at least special, qualities to the lesbian, others, such as Marie-Claire Blais, shy away from this dangerously élitist path.

In *The Angel of Solitude* [*L'Ange de la solitude*], Blais creates lesbians who are neither superior nor inferior to anyone else; they simply exist. Her refusal to "aristocratize" her lesbian protagonists makes her depiction of lesbian identities more realistic.

In terms of lesbian identities, the importance of *The Angel of Solitude* resides in the fact that its women-centered protagonists have already found their identity as lesbians when the novel opens. Since their identity is self-defined, they no longer feel the need to justify their lives to straight society. Hence, secretiveness and deception are not a way of life for them. As such, strategies for passing in the heterosexual world have been replaced by strategies for separation from the majority culture. One of these strategies consists in living collectively. The collective symbolizes women-centered space and reality. It also affords lesbians some measure of economic and emotional security in a society where heterosexual reality dominates everywhere else.

From a political perspective, the collective challenges the dominant culture's definition of a home and deconstructs the heterosexual notion of the family unit. From a psychological perspective, the collective breaks down the isolation that marked lesbian lives in the two preceding decades, thus giving women-identified women an on-going possibility to reinforce and validate their authentic selves. From a literary perspective, the collective constitutes a very practical device which allows Blais to portray a wide range of women-centered women in a realistic setting they control.

In *The Angel of Solitude*, lesbians find their centers inside themselves. Their source of identity moves beyond their sexuality; lesbianism becomes a whole of which sexuality is but one element. Here the sign *lesbian* is simultaneously erotic, personal, social, and political; it covers a wide variety of woman-bonding experiences. Because Blais's characters do not solely root their identities in their perception of themselves as lesbians, they tend to be multidimensional women whose identity options are varied.

L'Abeille (a painter), Doudouline (a musician), and Paula (a painter), for example, derive their primary identity from their careers. Johnie and Polydor define themselves as intellectuals with a strong commitment to feminist scholarship. Others, such as Gérard and Lynda, pride themselves in being marginal elements engaged in a cat-and-mouse game with the law. Gérard cultivates her marginality by adopting a male name and by selling drugs. As an ex-convict, Lynda's "love of danger" [amour du danger (35)] leads her to constantly court disaster. Less colorful than the other women in the collective, Thérèse sees herself, first and foremost, as a social worker with a mission.

These protagonists also clearly define themselves as women who love women. Yet, even at the level of their lesbian identities, Blais has chosen to highlight the singularity of each woman, her multiplicities. Blais thus sends a clear message to her readers: lesbians, like heterosexuals, do not all express their sexual identity in a similar manner. In *The Angel of Solitude*, one cannot speak of a "generic" lesbian identity, principally because the individuality of each lesbian serves to distinguish her from all other lesbians and, in the end, marks her identity in a very personal manner.

For example, some of Blais's protagonists correspond in many ways to Ponse's description of the "masculine lesbian" (179), as lesbians who repudiate "all characteristics, behaviors and attributes that are deemed feminine" (181). This is clearly the case for Gérard who, according to the other women in the collective, is guilty of sexual harassement, as when she "rips off the tweed cap of a young unknown woman whom she kisses" [arrachait la casquette de tweed d'une jeune inconnue qu'elle embrassait (27)]. Paula also adopts the "masculine" role. Like Gérard she is guilty of violence against women. In her case, the violence is both physical and sexual. She "beats women" [battait les femmes (73)], and her lovers insist that they "have been raped" [avai[ent] été violée[s] (89)].

One could argue that both Gérard and Paula's masculine traits—exemplified in their domineering attitude as well as in their physical or sexual brutality toward other women—are, at least partially, representative of the fact that they reject feminist values. Thus, in terms of identity formation, they have but two roles to choose from that would correspond to their inner self: the role of the passive, submissive female—the femme—and that of the aggressive male—the butch. As they are unwilling to adopt an egalitarian mode in their relationships with other women, one can only conclude that they choose to emulate the male role.

Some lesbians portrayed by Blais are militant, that is, lesbians who have "become politicized, usually through feminism, and/or gay liberation" (Ponse, 199). Polydor, for example, is a theology student who is struggling to become one of the first women ordained as a Catholic priest, simply because she wishes to "foster rebellion in women and gay priests" [semer la rébellion parmi les femmes et les prêtres gais (113)]. Johnie[9] is also motivated by a similar sentiment of rebellion, which helps to strengthen a positive sense of self. Throughout the novel, she is hard at work on her book: *From Sappho to Radclyffe Hall* [*De Sapho à Radclyffe Hall* (20)]. Her desire to add her voice to the voices of feminist scholars who seek to emphasize the relevance of lesbian writings never wavers.

As militant lesbians, Johnie and Polydor belong to a new generation of women-identified women. Their commitment to women is not only sexual and emotional but also political. Openly speaking the "unspeakable," they help to uncover biased attitudes towards women in general and lesbianism in particular. Their women-identified perspective offers them a privileged vantage point from which to challenge patriarchy and its corollary, heterosexism.

In *The Angel of Solitude*, not all of the protagonists' lesbian identities are as clearly defined as those of Johnie and Polydor. Lynda and L'Abeille, for example, sleep with both men and women. They do, however, live in a lesbian commune. Thus, Lynda and L'Abeille fit the profile of the "elective lesbian," a lesbian "who sees her heterosexuality as not as real nor as significant in defining the self as in lesbianism" (Ponse, 198). Marianne also conducts erotic affairs with both men and women. Yet she defines herself exclusively as a heterosexual. In a letter to Johnie in which she ends their relationship, she states: "You are a lesbian, and even though I am attached to you, I am not a lesbian" [Vous êtes une lesbienne, et malgré mon attachement pour vous, je ne le suis pas (109)]. Because of her refusal to acknowledge her lesbian tendencies, Marianne's identity is "idiosyncratic." She does "not draw the identity conclusion that [her] behavior would seem to impose according to the logic of social construction of sexual identity in both heterosexual and lesbian worlds" (Ponse, 163). Finally, Thérèse and Doudeline—because they are exclusively women-centered—are "primary lesbian[s]" (Ponse, 199).

As we have seen, the lesbian identity varies significantly from one woman to another in this novel. Blais's protagonists are masculine, militant, elective, and primary lesbians, or lesbians whose identities are idiosyncratic. Regardless of their differences, only partially situated at the level of their identities, they all share a common tendency. They challenge either directly or indirectly the hegemony of the heteropatriarchal institution, often through the mere act of openly loving another woman.

It should be emphasized, however, that even though Blais's protagonists do not perceive their selfhood primarily in terms of their sexual orientation, their society is still not prepared to accept them as productive and "normal" citizens who just happen to express their sexuality differently than the heterosexual majority. Consequently, they tend to succumb to a "contagious sadness" [contagieuse tristesse (44)]. This sadness underlines the fact that their minority status continues to have a negative effect on their mental health. Moreover, their outcast status is intensified by the fact that they are openly affectionate with one another in public. By blatantly trangressing the unwritten law of secrecy (a law that their literary sisters of the 1960s and 1970s usually respected), they expose themselves to a "censorship which mutilates them daily" [censure qui les mutilait chaque jour (29)].

This mutilation expresses itself in response to political and social oppression, symbolized by various forms of addictions or by an obsessive desire to travel. Johnie, l'Abeille, and Paula, for example, abuse both alcohol and nicotine. Doudouline suffers from an eating disorder, while both Gérard and Lynda are addicted to drugs. Most of them also suffer from an unrelenting wanderlust.

Their travels, like those of Jutras's heroine Georgie, are symbolic of their search for a place on earth where their lesbian status would not be repudiated in the larger society. Unfortunately, no matter where their travels take them, Blais's protagonists are confronted, as was Georgie a decade earlier, with their "exclusion from the planet" [exclusion de la planète (95)]. Contemporary women-identified women are still condemned to endure "the perpetuity of the Pink Rose" [la perpétuité de l'Étoile Rose (111)], which marked gays and lesbians for extinction under the Nazi regime. Like the lesbian protagonists of the 1960s and 1970s, Blais's characters are subject to insults and derogatory remarks because of the nature of their sexuality. Indeed, the word *lesbian* still retains "the same connotations of insult and of shameful scorn" [les mêmes connotations d'insulte, de mépris honteux (109)].

Thus, in the 1980s, a woman-identified woman's "conquest of a lifelong liberation" [conquête d'une libération à vie (111)] continues to be threatened. Even though lesbians of the 1980s, contrary to lesbians of the 1960s and 1970s, have a clearer sense of self (exemplified by their refusal to live a double life) and are less isolated because of their separatist stance (symbolized by their communal living), their lesbian selfhood remains threatened by an enemy located outside them and figured as the dominant culture.

In the 1960s and 1970s, fear of censorship and society's lack of understanding prevented the complete depiction of lesbian experiences in novels. In the 1980s, in response to gay liberation, writers began representing lesbians not monolithically, but as diverse from one another as heterosexuals. But the fact remains that antilesbianism has not been eradicated from Québécois society. The political and artistic force of Blais's work resides in her focus on lesbian subjectivity. She tracks the hatred of the lesbian as Other without idealizing her protagonists. In her descriptions, she foregrounds both their flaws and qualities. Blais brings to the forefront of the novel not only their contradictions but also the contradictions in a "free" society in which lesbians continue to be oppressed.

Taken together, the novels of Blais, Jutras, Naubert, and Maheux-Forcier perceptively retrace the path that Québec lesbians were forced to walk during the course of the last three decades. At the beginning of this process, they submitted to the unwritten law of silence that committed them to living double lives while simultaneously preventing them from exploring the nature of their personal and collective identities. Slowly but surely they rejected their stigmatized identity, thus opening up a new path leading to their separation from the majority culture. This separation coincided with women-identified women's complex definition of self, a definition that no longer stemmed solely from their sexual orientation.

During the last two stages of this journey, the word *lesbian* became a source of contention for many of them. The word has negative connotations for them because women-identified women had not chosen it for themselves. As the narrator of *The Angel of Solitude* so eloquently reflects: "Does not the [woman-identified woman's] dignity reside in her knowledge that she does not yet have a name which was named or namemable" [sa dignité n'était-elle pas de savoir qu'elle n'avait pas encore un nom qui fût nommé ou nommable (Blais, 111)]. If we are to believe Blais's narrator, lesbians have determined to reclaim completely their identities through the act of self-naming.

NOTES

An earlier version of this paper was presented at the American Council for Québec Studies Seventh Biennial Conference, Chicago, 1991.

1. The Quiet Revolution (1960-1970) is an expression commonly used to describe the political, social, and institutional reforms which were quickly set into motion soon after the death of Maurice Duplessis, leader of the right-wing National Union Party [L'Union nationale] and premier of Québec from 1945 to 1959. His death signaled the beginning of a new era for Québec, marked by the triumph of neoliberalism and neonationalism.

2. All translations in this chapter are my own.

3. Heteropatriarchal hegemony is particularly virulent in relation to women-identified women since it condemns them to a double oppression, as women and as lesbians.

4. In 1969, the Criminal Code of Canada was amended, and private sexual acts between two consenting adults were legalized. This document became known as the "homosexual bill," because it implicitly served to decriminalize homosexuality (Kallen, 60).

5. The creation of lesbian establishments such as bars and discos did not begin to proliferate in Québec until the 1970s.

6. Heterosexuality is defined as compulsory because it has always been "the principal organizing institution of personal life." Thus when homosexuality or lesbianism is acted upon, "it is punished by social ostracism and loss of civil rights" (Murphy, 87).

7. The late 1970s were watershed years in the gay and lesbian liberation movement and were "marked by extensive lobbying efforts . . . to have 'sexual orientation' listed among the specified non-discriminatory grounds in human rights legislation" (Kallen, 61). In 1977, Québec became the first Canadian province to do so in its Charter of Rights and Freedoms.

8. It is not possible for me in the space available to discuss all of the texts that portray lesbian characters in the 1970s. Indeed many authors (Marie Savard, France Théôret, Jovette Marchessault, Pol Pelletier, Louky Bersianik, Jocelyn Felx, Nicole Brossard, and Marie-Claire Blais) concern themselves in their writings with the question of lesbian identity and/or lesbian themes. Marie Claire Blais's *Nights in the Underground* [*Les Nuits de l'Underground* (1978)], for example, a novel in which the lesbian protagonists already have access to a lesbian community, is a literary first in Québec. I have chosen to limit my comments to Jutras's novel because her protagonists are still engaged in the struggle for self-love,and do not yet have access to a lesbian community.

9. Thus named by her friends because of her passion for Radclyffe Hall, who wrote about sexual love between women in *The Well of Loneliness* and whose lover called her John in private.

REFERENCES

de Beauvoir, Simone. *Le Deuxième sexe*. Vol. 1. Paris: Gallimard, 1949.

Blais, Marie-Claire. *L'Ange de la solitude*. Québec: VLB Éditeur, 1989.

————. *Manuscrits de Pauline Archange*. Montréal: Éditions du Jour, 1968.

Brossard, Nicole. *La Lettre aérienne*. Montréal: Éditions du remue-ménage, 1988.

Durocher, Constance. "Heterosexuality: Sexuality or Social System?" *Resources for Feminist Research* 19.3-4 (1991): 13-18.

Hall, Radclyffe. *The Well of Loneliness*. London: Virago, 1982.

Jutras, Jeanne D'Arc. *Georgie*. Montréal: Éditions de la pleine lune, 1978.

Kallen, Evelyn. "In and Out of the Homosexual Closet: Gay/Lesbian Liberation in Canada." *Culture* 6.2 (1986): 49-63.

Krieger, Susan. "Lesbian Identity and Community: Recent Social Science Literature." *Signs* 8.1 (1982): 91-108.

Maheux-Forcier, Louise. *Amadou*. Ottawa: Cercle du livre de France, 1963.

————. *Une forêt pour Zoé*. Ottawa: Cercle du livre de France, 1969.

Marini, Marcelle. *Territoires du féminin avec Marguerite Duras*. Paris: Les Éditions de Minuit, 1977.

Murphy, Marilyn. "Thinking About Bisexuality." *Resources for Feminist Research* 19.3-4 (1991): 87-88.

Naubert, Yvette. *La Dormeuse éveillée*. Ottawa: Cercle du livre de France, 1965.

Ostriker, Alicia. "The Thieves of Language: Women Poets and Revisionist Myth-making." *Signs* 8.1 (1982): 68-90.

Palmer, Paulina. "Contemporary Lesbian Feminist Fiction: Texts for Everywoman." *Plotting Change*. Ed. Linda Anderson. London: Edward Arnold, 1990, 43-62.

Ponse, Barbara. *Identities in the Lesbian World*. Westport, CT: Greenwood Press, 1978.

Radicalesbians. "The Woman-Identified Woman." *Out of the Closets: Voices of Gay Liberation*. Ed. Karla Jay and Allen Young. New York: Pyramid, 1974, 172-81.

Rich, Adrienne. *On Lies, Secrets, and Silence*. New York: Norton, 1979, 199-202.

Stimpson, Catherine. "Zero Degree Deviancy: The Lesbian Novel in English." *Writing and Sexual Difference*. Ed. Elizabeth Abel. Chicago: University of Chicago Press, 1982, 243-59.

Zimmerman, Bonnie. "What Has Never Been: An Overview of Lesbian Feminist Criticism." *The New Feminist Criticism*. Ed. Elaine Showalter. New York: Pantheon Books, 1985, 200-24.

Finding a Place for Christa Wolf: Gendered Identity in *No Place on Earth*

Marjanne E. Goozé

In the West, Christa Wolf has been the best-known writer from the German Democratic Republic. Her works have received widespread and serious critical reception by both the West German and international press, as well as by academics. Wolf's works have been translated into many languages, including English. Since the opening of the Berlin Wall and the unification of Germany, Wolf's place in German literary, cultural, and political life has been strongly challenged.[1] A controversy has arisen regarding her allegedly privileged position and her status as a critic of GDR society. Because she has not participated, as Christine Schoefer notes, in "the current political, economic and cultural annexation of the G.D.R.," the attack on her has intensified (Schoefer, 448).

Before unification, Wolf's significant place in German and world literature of the second half of the twentieth century seemed secure. Now, doubly marginalized as both a woman and a GDR writer, she has recently become an easy target of a West German press seeking scapegoats.[2] To deny Wolf her previously accorded place in world literature is to accede to the erasure of more than forty years of history. A renewed examination of her literary works and theories serves to counteract the attempted expulsion of GDR writers from the body of German and world literature. It is particularly fitting at this historical juncture to reread Wolf's 1979 novel, *No Place on Earth* [*Kein Ort. Nirgends*]. In this book, Wolf thematizes exactly these problematics arising out of the marginalization of the artist in a patriarchal, post-Enlightenment, capitalistic, and technocratic society. In addition, the novel deals with complex questions of gender identity and of the difficulties faced by women in particular.

Wolf assumes a unique place in speaking to an international audience while still addressing specific GDR concerns. Christa Wolf has herself drawn parallels between the experiences of those living in capitalistic and formerly socialist countries: "Perhaps our experiences are not so different. . . . I have lived here very intensively with a great treasure of experiences which I would not have wanted to miss. One can generalize these experiences, because in all industrial societies human potential is simply curtailed by the fact that efficiency and productivity are the primary values" (*Dialog,* 142-43).[3] These shared experiences result in common readers' reactions to her works. Wolf attributes this response across national boundaries to the patterns of work and life instilled in us ("Culture," 98-99). The only difference in reader response lies in male and female readers' reactions to her analysis of an immensely destructive patriarchy ("Culture," 99). However, these "differences" between East and West—the specific culture, history, and politics out of which Wolf is writing—cannot and should not be ignored. Her own relation to twentieth-century German history has been a significant component of her works.

Since Christa Wolf is a writer and literary theorist, and since her most of her works have an autobiographical component, this analysis of her ideas regarding the gendered identity of the artist in modern society first examines how her feminism and social critique evolved in her theories and early fiction. Her move away from the tenets of socialist realism and the development of her theory of "subjective authenticity" are crucial to an understanding of Wolf's work and her role in German literary politics and theory. The second part of this chapter more closely examines how Wolf employs the theme of "place" both structurally and metaphorically in the novel in confronting the issues of gender identity in modern culture and of the identity of the artist in particular.

Christa Wolf (née Ihlenfeld) was born in 1929 in Landsberg, a town east of the Oder River.[4] At the age of sixteen she and her family fled to Mecklenburg, which became part of the GDR in 1949. In 1948 she began studying German literature and joined the Socialist Unity Party (SED).[5] In 1951 she married the writer Gerhard Wolf; she is the mother of two daughters. Wolf worked for the writers' union and then was the editor of a major literary journal, writing many literary essays and book reviews. Her first literary work, *Moscow Novella* [*Moskauer Novelle*], published in 1961, endorsed the tenets of socialist realism advocated by the SED. Her second novel, *Divided Heaven* [*Der geteilte Himmel*] (1963), reflects her experience of briefly working in a railway factory and the reality of a divided Germany. By the mid-1960s she was criticizing socialist realism, and the publication in 1968 of her third novel, *The Quest for Christa T.* [*Nachdenken über Christa T.*], clearly marks her break with this aesthetic.[6] Loosened cultural restrictions in the early 1970s enabled the publication of a collection of her essays, *The Reader and the Writer* [*Lesen und Schreiben*], in 1971 and the release of a second edition of *Christa T.* in 1972. Wolf was able to travel widely in the 1970s, including a six-month visit to the United States in 1974. During this period, Wolf wrote her semiautobiographical novel about growing up under national socialism, *A Model Childhood* [*Kindheitsmuster*] (first published in 1976). In the wake of the expatriation of the poet and singer Wolf Biermann, Christa Wolf joined with other GDR writers in protesting this action. Many of these writers eventually moved to the West, Gerhard Wolf lost his membership in the writers' union and the SED, and Wolf was isolated.

In many ways *No Place on Earth*, which was first published in 1979, reflects Wolf's own situation. In the past, critics have read *No Place on Earth*, set in 1804, as an allegory of the GDR. However, the work must be seen as more than a veiled attempt to relocate in an earlier epoch her own situation and the literary politics of the GDR in the post-Biermann late 1970s. Wolf, who had once identified with the state, had distanced herself from it by the time she wrote the novel. Also, the novel clearly reflects Wolf's feminism. In the work, she enters into a dialogue with her main characters, two literary figures of the Romantic era, Heinrich von Kleist (1777-1811) and Karoline von Günderrode (1780-1806).[7] Through *No Place on Earth*, Wolf situates the disaffiliation of the writer from the state at the beginning of the nineteenth century.

Beginning with *The Quest for Christa T.*, Wolf's works exhibit a pronounced concern with the nature of female identity under national socialism, socialism, and early capitalism. While Christa T. has difficulty asserting her self-hood—"The difficulty of saying 'I'" (174) [Die Schwierigkeit, "Ich" zu sagen (170)], Günderrode confronts the enforced gender roles of the early nineteenth century. In an interview published in 1979, Christa Wolf explained her reasons for her interest in Günderrode: "I identify most easily with women. I have become increasingly interested in locating the roots of women's current conflict, their dissatisfaction with life" (*Fourth Dimension*, 87). Her interest in women's lives and experiences differs somewhat from that of First-World feminists in that Wolf does not feel she is writing "'emancipation literature'" in the sense of advocating economic and legal equality, because these were guaranteed in the GDR (*Fourth Dimension*, 75). Her interest lies in depicting women's "self-realization in a specific historical situation, since their self-consciousness, what they demand of life, goes beyond the opportunities society offers them" (*Fourth Dimension*, 75). Rather than emphasizing equality with men, Wolf focuses on differences in values and perceptions that she feels are positive: "I look at history to explain why it should be that women in our society relate to one another more naturally, more closely and intimately and with a greater readiness to live out certain values than men" (*Fourth Dimension*, 88).

This emphasis on the value of a subjectivity that is resistant to usurpation by a patriarchal, industrial, production-oriented society is also found in Christa Wolf's literary and aesthetic theories. These theories are most clearly expressed in Wolf's 1974 interview with Hans Kaufmann, "Subjective Authenticity," and in her four essays (written in diary and letter form) about the writing of her novel, *Cassandra* [*Kassandra*] Here she dismantles the barriers between subject and author. For Wolf, the process of writing is in itself an experience: "To my mind, it is much more useful to look at writing, not as an end product but as a process which continuously runs alongside life, helping to shape and interpret it; writing can be seen as a way of being more intensely involved in the world, as the concentration and focusing of thought, word and deed. . . . Suddenly everything is interconnected and fluid" ("Subjective," 59-60). Wolf's application of "subjective authenticity" to her own writing instigated her departure from the tenets of socialist realism in her thinking and writing. She could no longer accept "the authority of literary genres" (*Cassandra*, 278).

The main reasons for this rejection are the absence of female literary precursors and a belief that attempts by women writers to mold themselves to fit male-dominated aesthetics are essentially self-destructive (*Cassandra*, 295, 299). Instead, Wolf offers a model for writing and living based on relation to others to communicate:

the feeling that everything is fundamentally related: and that the strictly one-track-mind approach—the extraction of a single "skein" for purposes of narration and study—damages the entire fabric, including the "skein." Yet to put it in simplified terms, this one-track-minded route is the one that has been followed by Western thought: the route of segregation, of the renunciation of the manifoldness of phenomena, in favor of dualism and monism, in favor of closed systems and pictures of the world; of the renunciation of subjectivity in favor of a sealed "objectivity." (*Cassandra*, 287)[8]

The political, philosophical, and social crises in which the Romantics found themselves are analogous to Wolf's in the GDR after the Biermann affair. She perceived the trend toward enforced production and technocracy in her own society as just as threatening to the individual as nineteenth-century capitalism. Wolf notes: "I took these two figures in order to rehearse their problematics for myself" ("Culture," 89). Through these two historical figures and characters, Kleist and Günderrode, Wolf works through her exclusion from the GDR literary and political elite. She explores the larger issues of the relationship between the artist and society and of a gendered definition of the literary artist:

I wrote *No Place on Earth* in 1977. That was a time when I found myself obliged to examine the preconditions for failure, the connection between social desperation and failure in literature. At the time, I was living with the intense feeling of standing with my back to the wall, unable to take a proper step. I had to get beyond a certain time when there seemed to be absolutely no possibility left for effective action. . . . it was also a kind of self-preservation when the solid ground was pulled out from under my feet. ("Culture," 89-90)

This sense of being out of time and place, of no longer standing on the "solid ground" of her homeland in both a physical and cultural sense, opened Wolf's ears to the voices of her predecessors. In that "no place," she engages in a dialogue with them. The threat of expatriation was real. She was excluded and marginalized in the GDR. Wolf describes her life and experiences in the GDR as "the basis of my writing" (*Schreibgrund*) (*Dialog*, 148). This compound word, *Schreibgrund*, reveals how Wolf's writing replaced the ground that had been pulled out from underneath her: *Schreib* means "write," and *Grund* is also "ground."

This literal "writing ground" lies in her mind, and in *No Place on Earth* it prompts her as narrator to engage in a dialogue with Kleist and Günderrode that creates a poetical space that is at the same time "no place."[9] Kleist and Günderrode take on a presence for her (Bock, 148)—a presence that reaches beyond the normal boundaries of the historical novel or the writer's identification with her characters. *No Place* can be read as a fiction that rewrites "the dialogic relation between literature and history as historical fiction. The fiction appears as interpolated history—the rewriting of prior texts" (Herrmann, 118). Wolf's dialogue with Kleist and Günderrode is real because much of the text of the novel is composed of actual quotations from texts by Günderrode, Kleist, and the other figures.[10]

The German title of the book, *Kein Ort. Nirgends*, means "No Place. Nowhere." Critics have read the words "No Place" as a German translation of "utopia" or "u-topos." Accompanying this concept of "no place" is the idea of individuals removed from, and out of sync with, time. Wolf's atemporal non-place opens a place and moment of possibility for a reassessment of the past and the creation of the future (Fehervary, 141). Clearly, for the historical Günderrode and Kleist, their feelings of being out of place and time were alleviated only through their suicides—through self-removal from place and time. Within the novel, the title appears in a two-sentence paragraph: "Unlivable life. No place on earth" (108) [Unlebbares Leben. Kein Ort, nirgends (137)]. Wolf defines "no place" not as utopia but as "unlivable life" (Gidion, 168). This paragraph underscores the specific problems Kleist and Günderrode have with place and time: their selves—their identities—are irreconcilable with the demands of their spacial, social, and temporal environments. As Anna Kuhn suggests, there are three major themes to the work, "homelessness, alienation, and death" (153), and in my view, the first theme initiates the other two.

While the suspension of place and time, as well as the main theme of homelessness, forms the outer narrative structure of the work, the story of the meeting between Kleist and Günderrode is itself stringently marked by place and time. Situating them within this rigid framework highlights their social, intellectual, and gender misplacement. The meeting of the two is Wolf's fictional invention. She sets the story in June 1804. Friends have gathered at the home of the merchant Joseph Merten in Winkel on the Rhine. They have assembled one afternoon "For tea and conversation" (5) [Zu Tee und Unterhaltung (8)]. Present are Joseph Merten, his friend Nees von Esenbeck, a natural scientist, and his wife, Lisette, who is a close friend of Günderrode's. Bettine Brentano (later, von Arnim) and Günderrode are the only unmarried women present. Bettine's brother Clemens and his new wife, Sophie Mereau Brentano, have also been invited; both are authors, she, quite renown. Clemens's friend Friedrich Karl von Savigny, a jurist, is the last to arrive with his wife, Gunda, Clemens's and Bettine's sister. Heinrich von Kleist, who has been brought by his physician, Dr. Wedekind, is positioned as the outsider in this circle of family and friends; he is not acquainted with the guests. Günderrode is the emotional outsider; she is neither related nor married to anyone present. Indeed, her strong emotional attachments to Clemens Brentano and especially to Savigny haunt her.

The novel divides into two sections; the first is set indoors, and the second outdoors. The tea party at which they have gathered begins about two-thirty; at five the group decides to go for a walk outdoors. The indoor scene constitutes about two-thirds of the novel. Once outside, all are less constrained by social convention. They walk from the house down to the Rhine. After Clemens Brentano sings a song full of sexual imagery and dedicates it to Günderrode, she separates herself and Kleist from the group. Walking upstream, symbolically against the current of their social and political place and time, they begin to reveal their real fears and concerns.

The idyllic landscape is deceptive; it provides no long-term utopic space for Kleist and Günderrode. In fact, the site of meeting in *No Place on Earth* is later the site of the historical Günderrode's death. Here, Kleist, who shot himself on the shore of the Wannsee in Berlin, expresses, along with Günderrode, premonitions of death. In predicting their absence from both place and time through their deaths, Günderrode and Kleist have already removed themselves from the clear place and time indications that bind the other characters together.

For each, being out of place or unable to find a place has both actual and symbolic dimensions. Although they are both misfits, they manifest different aspects of social, cultural, political, and gender misplacement. Each may also be seen to represent different aspects of Wolf's own problems: generally speaking, Kleist reflects her political situation, and Günderrode reflects the problems Wolf encounters as a woman writer.

The indoor and outdoor settings allow us to see Kleist and Günderrode not only in two places but in various guises and relationships. The party indoors can be characterized as a masquerade, where some appear unaware that they are wearing masks, and others, such as Günderrode, are painfully conscious of everyone's concealed selves. At the end of their walk together, Kleist and Günderrode look at one another without masks: "Naked gazes. . . . Masks fall away, superincrustations, scabs, varnish. The bare skin" (108) [Nackte Blicke. . . . Maskierungen fallen ab, Schorf, Polituren. Die blanke Haut (137-38)].

The gaze does not free them but locks each into a fixed identity, an identity with which neither is comfortable: "We two, each imprisoned in his sex. That touching we desire so infinitely does not exist. It was killed along with us" (108) [Wir, jeder gefangen in seinem Geschlecht. Die Berührung, nach der es uns so unendlich verlangt, es gibt sie nicht. Sie wurde mit uns entleibt (138)]. Unmasked, they are disembodied ("entleibt," translated as "killed," literally means removal of the *Leib*, the "body"). They are ghosts incapable of any connection to others because they have none to their physical selves. By assuming multiple disguises, they are for a time able to evade the detection of their perceived sexual, professional, and other shortcomings by friends and family. But the price they must pay for their masks is very high; they are imprisoned behind them and are unknowable even to a desired other. Whether indoors or out, they cannot truly become a part of their surroundings, because they are always conscious of their own and others' masked identities.

Kleist and Günderrode confess to each other their confused gender identities. Being "imprisoned," they are alienated from their own bodies to the degree that they avoid physical contact. Even the thought of it frightens them. The uniforms they wear are also a part of the masquerade. Her convent habit and his military uniform seemingly define their "place" in the social order and they draw the physical boundaries of their lives. On one hand, Kleist and Günderrode desire to fit into their respective uniforms, their assigned roles. On the other, the uniforms conceal and mask their true identities and prohibit the development of their calling as artists. Günderrode and Kleist are, moreover, homeless even in their own clothes and bodies, because the socially enforced male and female gender roles bind them and limit their artistic aspirations. Since their roles are different, Günderrode and Kleist do not experience their homelessness in exactly the same way.

For Günderrode, enforced gender roles are the ultimate cause of most of her difficulties. Her conflict with social expectations displaces her physically, socially, and psychologically. Sent to live in a Protestant convent, she experiences "living conditions of the most restrictive kind" (15) [die beengtesten Verhältnisse (20)]. She envisions her place as even further confined, lying "on the hard narrow bed in the small room" (15) [in dem kleinen Zimmer, auf dem schmalen harten Bett (20)]. Her physical circumstances and her own nature form barriers to her development as a poet (103 [132]). Naturally shy, Günderrode is embarrassed by her own meager successes, such as when her book, published under the pseudonym Tian, is spoken of (21 [28-29]). She does not regret publication, only the revelation of the identity behind the pen name (21 [29]).

Yet Günderrode clearly has a strong commitment to her writing. Günderrode's poetry gives her identity a cohesiveness she can find nowhere else, while simultaneously allowing its expansion beyond set limitations. She expounds on this to Clemens:

Why do you refuse to admit that in poetry, as if in a mirror, I attempt to collect and to see myself, to pass through and beyond myself. . . . But everything we express must be truth because we feel it: there you have my confession of faith as a poet. (34-35)

[Warum wollen Sie mir nicht zugestehn, daß ich in der Poesie wie in einem Spiegel mich zu sammeln, mich selber zu sehen, durch mich hindurch und über mich hinaus zu gehn suche. . . . Aber alles, was wir aussprechen, muß wahr sein, weil wir es empfinden: Da haben Sie mein poetisches Bekenntnis. (45)]

Günderrode's aesthetic philosophy parallels Wolf's own theory of "subjective authenticity," in which writing is "a way of being in the world" and is in itself a type of experience ("Subjective," 58-60). Both may be a positive response to isolation, Günderrode's financial and social isolation, and Wolf's political isolation. But while, for Wolf, writing connects an already socially engaged writer with others and expands the boundaries of identity, for Günderrode, writing becomes in practice a replacement for life. The text offers her a home: "I am writing a drama, and my whole being is wrapped up in it. I project myself so vividly into the drama, I become so much at home within it, that my own life is becoming alien to me" (60) [Ich schreibe ein Drama, und meine ganze Seele ist damit beschäftigt. Ich denke mich so lebhaft hinein, werde so einheimisch darin, daß mir mein eignes Leben fremd wird (77)]. By writing poetry, she can transport herself into a world of her own creation, a world where there is love: "Poems are a balm laid upon everything in life that is unappeasable" (64) [Gedichte sind Balsam auf Unstillbares im Leben (82)].

As a woman poet and intellectual, Günderrode is socially an outsider. Her convent residence and meager finances distinguish her from the other tea party guests. She must always hold herself in check, perpetually in danger of being carried away by her own alternate vision of reality (8 [11]). She has built walls around herself that are nearly impossible to breach. Kleist observes from the outset "[a]n invisible circle is drawn around her on which one hesitates to trespass" (8) [Ein unsichtbarer Kreis ist um sie gezogen, den zu übertreten man sich scheut (12)]. As the people move about the room, Günderrode has isolated herself even among her friends. Rather than perceiving the parlor of the tea party as a safe space in which to interact and connect with others, she perceives the choreography (the artifice) of the social encounter; she recognizes the patterns they form as they move around the room as plotted on "a graph, a diagram" (36) [graphische Zeichnung (47)]. Günderrode is the disengaged observer, "quite detached from herself and all the others" (36) [abgelöst von sich und allen (47)]. Whereas in her works Günderrode seeks and may attain a kind of connection to others, she can find no place, no home, no special relationship for herself among her friends and acquaintances.

Her homelessness can be ameliorated and the love she desires can be attained only in death: "[I am strange to them, but they cannot say why. I know it:][11] I am not at home among them. There where my home is, love exists only at the price of death" (35) (Unheimlich bin ich ihnen, doch können sie nicht sagen, warum. Ich weiß es: Ich bin unter ihnen nicht heimisch. Wo ich zu Hause bin, gibt es die Liebe nur um den Preis des Todes (46)]. This sense of not being "at home" is "unheimlich," meaning both not at home and uncanny or unnatural. She feels so out of place that she imagines the ground giving way beneath her, so that the earth itself refuses to bear her (76 [97]). Death offers the ultimate hiding place (23 [30]). In the end, the only place for herself that she can conceive of is predicated upon her own non-existence. Death dominates her works, letters, conversations, and dreams. She connects her creativity with her death, as expressed in a line from her poetry she quotes to Kleist: "To give birth to what slays me" (97) [Was mich tötet, zu gebären [123].

This metaphor of birth further underscores Günderrode's highly conflicted gender identity. Her vocation as a poet and artist stands in opposition to society's expectations of her as a woman and to her own desire for heterosexual love. Even in her own mind, her identities as poet, lover, and "man of action" can be reconciled only by the man of her dreams:

She dismembers herself, making herself into three people, one of them a man. Love, provided that it is unconditional, can fuse the three separate people into one. The man beside her does not have this prospect before him. His work is the only point at which he can become one with himself. (117)

[Sie zerreißt sich in drei Personen, darunter einen Mann. Liebe, wenn sie unbedingt ist, kann die drei getrennten Personen zusammenschmelzen. Die Aussicht hat der Mann neben ihr nicht. Sein Werk ist der einzige Punkt, mit sich eins zu werden. (148-49)]

For Wolf, Günderrode represents all of the struggles, contradictions, and balancing acts faced by women (writers and otherwise). While the barriers encountered by Günderrode are primarily those of socially-constructed gender roles, Kleist's difficulties are also political and vocational—related to the newly regendered place of the artist in modern Western culture. His vocation as a writer ostracizes him from the masculine society he so wants to become a part of, while at the same time he criticizes it. Kleist is as conflicted by conventional definitions of masculinity as Günderrode is by those of femininity. His sense of homelessness, however, manifests itself somewhat differently than hers because of those definitions. As a late twentieth-century writer, Christa Wolf requires both figures, Kleist and Günderrode, to portray her concerns and illustrate her ideas. As a man in the early nineteenth century, Kleist's gender, artistic, and political identities play themselves out on a larger stage than is possible for Günderrode's.

Kleist's conflicts, however, are also developed in terms of a failed gender identity, resulting, as with Günderrode, in physical, social, and psychological homelessness. Wolf depicts most of Kleist's self-definition as a man in terms of gender opposition: he is a man because he is not a woman—the Other whom he fears: "He not wholly a man, she not wholly a woman . . ." (94) [Er nicht ganz Mann, sie nicht ganz Frau . . . (120)]. Kleist tells Günderrode that he cannot bear it "that nature has split the human being into man and woman" (104) [daß die Natur den Menschen in Mann und Frau aufgespalten hat (133)]. Günderrode, however, realizes that universal androgyny is not what he desires; he seeks, rather, a reconciliation between these elements of his own identity: "What you mean is that man and woman have a hostile relationship inside you. As they do in me" (104) [Sie meinen, daß in Ihnen selbst Mann und Frau einander feindlich gegenüberstehen. Wie auch in mir (133)].

The battle among the "masculine" and "feminine" elements within Kleist's psyche is tied to his acceptance of the capitalistic definition of career and work: "Who am I. A lieutenant without a sword knot. A student without learning. A civil servant without a post. An author without a book" (42) [Wer bin ich. Lieutenant ohne Portepée. Student ohne Wissenschaft. Staatsbeamter ohne Amt. Autor ohne Werk (55)]. He associates each of these vocations, in which he perceives himself a failure, with specific geographical locales. For many years, as a soldier, student, and writer, Kleist has been literally displaced and homeless. After all his travels he reflects: "Nowhere have I found what I was seeking" (66) [Nirgends hab ich gefunden, wonach ich suchte (85)].

Kleist defines his place in the world in negative terms. "Nowhere" has become a u-topos, where he can reconcile all aspects of his identity, including the conflicts between the masculine and feminine elements. Asked by Bettine to list three wishes, Kleist responds: "Freedom. A poem. A home" (86) [Freiheit. Ein Gedicht. Ein Haus (110)]. Yet he and Günderrode know these are irreconcilable (86 [110]). Each of these contradictory wishes has a geographic counterpart. The freedom and the poem can be attained only outside his Prussian homeland. In Prussia, however, circumstances prevent him from pursuing his vocation. He would have to take a civil service post, a job he finds degrading both to obtain and perform (63 [81]). France represents to him all that is not Prussian and remains an alternative even in the face of Napoleon's imminent invasion of Prussia: "It's a toss of the dice. France or Prussia. A civil service post or a literary career. Degradation with a modest income, or naked poverty with one's pride left intact" (70) [Würfeln. Frankreich oder Preußen. Ein Amt oder die Literatur. Erniedrigung und ein bescheidnes Auskommen, oder die blanke Armut und ein ungebrochnes Selbstgefühl (89)]. Kleist's thoughts vacillate during the party, but in the end he realizes he will return to Prussia and seek a position (113 [144]).

His contradictory wishes mirror Christa Wolf's. She shares his loyalty to "Prussia" (Dietrick, 217) and, to some extent, his dilemma. Both need to live there in order to fulfill their true vocations and find it difficult to meet its political and intellectual restrictions. As a Rhinelander, Günderrode's national loyalty is not a factor; she is accustomed to ever-changing borders and sovereigns (65 [83]).

Writing, however, proves to be an impossible vocation for both. While Günderrode cannot reconcile her vocation with her desire for love and socially imposed gender roles, Kleist's vocational choice undermines his desire to affect his time and surroundings. The barriers he encounters are put up by a new epoch that devalues the place of art and culture in modern society and, consequently, also its artists. The sciences have banished art to the margins. In a discussion primarily with the professional men at the party, Kleist questions the coldness of the new age:

The sciences? Which are in the process of forging iron bands around our hearts and heads? Which are paving the way to an iron century in which art will find itself standing outside with the doors closed in its face, and the artist will be an alien in the world? (78)

[Die Wissenschaften? Die sich daran machen, uns eiserne Reifen um Herz und Stirne zu schmieden? Die uns ein eisernes Jahrhundert vorbereiten, in dem die Kunst vor fest verschlossenen Türen stehen, der Künstler ein Fremdling sein wird? (100)]

The poet's role in this new order, as Savigny argues, is "to acknowledge the boundary between philosophy and life" (47) [hier an die Grenze zu führen, die zwischen Philosophie und Leben gesetzt wird (61)]. Kleist, however, refuses to draw the line between thought and action, idea and reality (46 [60]). Art's new place is to entertain, not to challenge us. The artistic realm will become the site for all our ideals, allowing us to maintain we still have them, without their interfering in our real lives or affecting power structures. Merten assigns Kleist his task: "The poet's charge is the administration of our illusions" (80) [Dem Dichter ist die Verwaltung unserer Illusionen unterstellt (103)].

As an amusing but insignificant figure, the (male) artist has been relegated the same place in the social order as accorded the "accomplished" wives of professional men. This feminization of the poet undermines Kleist's already questionable gender identity. Obviously, this feminization of the artist does little to assist women artists striving for wider recognition, since they must now compete with the feminized men for the space in the margins. In this space, Kleist and Günderrode are envious of the advantages each believes the other to possess. Kleist replies to her enunciated desire to be a man so as to act effectively in the world, expressing his own frustrations:

Don't you see how our masculine duty to act is by nature something that cannot be fulfilled, that we can only act wrongly or not at all! Whereas at least you are free to do as you like within the realm of ideas, which has been appointed to you.

Ideas that lead nowhere. So we, too, help to divide humanity into doers and thinkers. Don't we perceive how the acts of those who usurp the right to take action involve less and less reflection, fewer scruples? How the poetry of those who fail to act corresponds more and more to the aims of those who take action? (113)

[Sehn Sie nicht, wie unsre männliche Pflicht, zu handeln, uns unerfüllbar gemacht wird, daß wir nur falsch handeln können oder gar nicht! Während Sie wenigstens im Reich der Ideen schalten können, das man Ihnen zugeteilt hat.

Die Ideen, die folgenlos bleiben. So wirken auch wir mit an der Aufteilung der Menschheit in Tätige und Denkende. Merken wir nicht, wie die Taten derer, die das Handeln an sich reißen, immer unbedenklicher werden? Wie die Poesie der Tatenlosen den Zwecken der Handelnden immer mehr entspricht? (143)]

In spite of his earlier protests in his conversation with the professional men at the party, alone with Günderrode, Kleist reveals his own doubts and tacitly concedes the split between ideas and actions. He idealizes Günderrode's freedom from the demands of a paid job. The reaction to Kleist's statement in the second paragraph deflects his idealization by holding the "thinkers" just as responsible as the "doers." Also countered here is Kleist's envious feeling that women are allowed the luxury of ideas by stressing that they are free to think because they are barred from putting their ideas into action.

It is unclear who is speaking here, Kleist, Günderrode, or the narrator, who joins in their dialogue. This passage also applies to Christa Wolf's own situation and the literary politics of the GDR. Without the narrator's engagement with the two historical figures, they can teach us only about failure. The narrator gives all their struggles as writers—and as women and men—historical perspective.

The presence of the narrator lends the work its outer structure. Her presence in this narrative space opens a site of possibility for the writer both to think and to act in concord with an uncompromised self unrestricted by enforced gender or vocational roles. Clearly, Günderrode and Kleist never found this place in their lifetimes. Christa Wolf provides them and, most important, herself with it through the act of writing and the work itself. The role of the narrator raises the work beyond a merely negative example of how female and feminized writers are oppressed by their societies.

The internal monologues of Kleist and Günderrode and their dialogue with one another and the additional characters, as well as the narrator's engagement with them, are a concrete application of Christa Wolf's theory of subjective authenticity. The narrative self becomes involved with others. Yet, as she interacts with, and listens to, Kleist and Günderrode, the boundaries among author, narrator, and subjects become fluid. As was seen in the earlier discussion of Wolf's theories, there is an inseparable and logical connection between the fluidity of the female self as defined by Wolf and a female literary aesthetic. Within this aesthetic, female authorship presents a paradigmatic situation for writing *as* Other rather than *about* others (Fehervary, 146). The extensive use of citations allows the characters to speak in their own words. This helps maintain their separate identities apart from the author, narrator, and one another. Yet, at the same time, in the course of the novel, the narrator joins with the two protagonists in speaking as a "we" ["wir"]. Marilyn S. Fries describes these processes, as well as Wolf's other strategies in the work, as a "[d]isplacement of subject and object at every level" (48). The purpose of this "displacement" is, however, not an erasure of identity but is instead a redefinition of identity in terms of relations to others where all are permitted to be subjects, and objectification (even by the author) is avoided. Unfortunately, this redefinition appears possible only within the literary "no place" of the novel.

The "we" ["wir"] that emerges at the end of *No Place on Earth* has a utopian dimension. It incorporates Kleist, Günderrode, and the narrator. The "we" operates as a bridge in space and time. Most significantly, the utopian "we" responds to individual voices trapped in societally defined identities. The development in the book from the first-person interior monologues of Günderrode and Kleist to their dialogue and the infusion of the narrative voice into a "we" sublates the concept of gendered identity. There is a deliberate ambiguity of pronominal references in *No Place*, drawing the reader into the text as an active participant (Frieden, 276). The narrator introduces the first interior monologue with the simple question: "Who is speaking?" (4) [Wer spricht? (6)]. This question is repeated at the end of the work, before the narrator fully joins Kleist and Günderrode (113 [144]). Although there are a few early indications that Günderrode and Kleist set themselves apart from the others gathered at the tea party, their moment of recognition comes during their solitary walk along the banks of the Rhine. This moment is tied to their realization that each is trapped by an enforced gender identity: "Woman. Man. Untenable words. We, each imprisoned in his sex" (108) [Frau. Mann. Unbrauchbare Wörter. Wir, jeder gefangen in seinem Geschlecht" (138)]. In this passage, introduced by the narrator, it is virtually impossible to distinguish between Günderrode's and Kleist's words and thoughts.

Their dialogue has collapsed into a "we"; it is a plural of indefinite identity: "I am not I. You are not you. Who is 'we'?" (109) [Ich bin nicht ich. Du bist nicht du. Wer ist wir? (138)]. Seen in a positive light, their "we" does not signify loss of identity but is an extension and broadening of the self (Fehervary, 146). For some critics, this extended identity models an androgynous (Fehervary, 146) or "utopian ideal of ungendered subjectivity" (Herrmann, 120). The perception of androgyny and the negation of gender inherent in the word *ungendered* overlook, in my view, the far more complex self- and societal impositions of gender identity operating in the text. The reduction of these issues to androgyny posits what occurs between the two protagonists, and later the narrator, as a negation of predetermined and seemingly permanent gender roles, rather than as an extension of already indeterminate gender identities. Even though Kleist and Günderrode are unable to resolve their conflicts within a gender-based culture, alternatives may be conceived of that are more than a mere negation of a perceived universal binary gender structure. While, within the wider perspective of the book, the "we" may proffer a utopian vision, for Kleist and Günderrode (even as a "we"), there is no place for them to develop as individuals or as "we."

In the final pages of *No Place on Earth*, the narrator joins with the characters' "we." The narrator tosses in her lot with the outsiders whom she sees as possessing the freedom of the condemned: "[t]he freedom to love other people and not to hate ourselves" (118) [Die Freiheit, die Menschen zu lieben und uns selbst nicht zu hassen (150)]. If there is a truly utopian and idyllic element in this work, then it lies in the freedom to experience self-love and rid oneself of hatred. In terms of Wolf's own biography, this is clearly her goal. Regrettably, this utopia really is *u-topos*—no place. The final sentence of the book points toward the future: "We know what is coming" (119) [Wir wissen, was kommt (150)]. In speaking to the reader, this sentence reaches beyond tragic personal biography and is a prophecy of the modern technocratic society to come.

In the post-GDR world, Wolf continues to look ahead to a time when people will again recognize "a need for utopian thought" (*Dialog*, 162). The role of the author and the need for critical thinking should not be wiped out along the old borders. Wolf asserts that authors and writers should not give up their critical function or their history. In other words, writers should not accept the "feminization" of the author as portrayed by Kleist, but both women and men, through their subjective authenticity, should initiate a "femin*ist*ization" of the author. In this way, they will not cease to point out contradictions or challenge the powers that be "merely because the powers have changed whom we must confront" (*Dialog*, 168). Wolf insists on her own place and that of other GDR writers. Through her dialogue with the past and her vision of a place, she establishes a space for the writer as social and feminist critic within modern technocratic capitalism.

NOTES

1. The controversy surrounding Wolf and her writings has not abated since German unification in 1990.

2. Friederike Eigler points out how GDR literature has been seen as a negative and marginalized Other, and how feminist theory of identity construction offers a method of analyzing the reception of GDR literature in the West (2).

3. Most of Wolf's writings have been translated into English, only the most recent have not. Some of Wolf's essays have been published in both English and German in more than one location and are widely available. In the few cases, where only a German-language source is listed in the "References," the translation is mine.

4. This biographical sketch is indebted to Karen McPherson's overview of Wolf's life, published in her introduction to her collection of Wolf's interviews, *The Fourth Dimension*, vii-x.

5. The Socialist Unity Party was the name for the ruling party in the German Democratic Republic.

6. The book actually appeared in early 1969. Wolf faced enormous problems with the censors, and the GDR literary establish ment resisted publishing the book at all (Schreiber, 285-92).

7. Heinrich von Kleist's works have become a part of the modern German literary canon. Although considered unsuccessful during his lifetime, Kleist's dramas belong to the German classical theatrical repertoire, and his short prose works, especially his

novella, *Michael Kohlhaas*, are models of this genre. Kleist ended his own life by shooting himself in a double-suicide pact.

Karoline von Günderrode, on the other hand, has only in recent years received any critical attention. At the age of seventeen she came to live in a *Damenstift* in Frankfurt am Main—a Protestant convent for unmarried women from certain noble families. In spite of her situation, she wrote poetry and short drama. She studied modern and classical philosophy on her own, writing prose pieces reflecting this interest. During her lifetime, a volume of her writings was published under the pseudonym "Tian." Her life and work are defined by irreconcilable conflicts: she desired to be loved and accepted, and this conflicted with her passion for writing and intellectual pursuits. Her financial situation undermined her social standing (Goozé, 419). Günderrode's longing for action, was thwarted, as she saw it, by her femaleness: "I have no mind for feminine virtues, for feminine happiness. The wild, the great, the brilliant things are what I love. There is an ill-fated incongruity in my soul; and it will and must remain that way, for I am a woman and have desires like a man, without the strength of a man" (qtd. in Goozé, 419). Günderrode committed suicide by stabbing herself with a dagger she had carried with her for several years.

8. Parallels are evident here between Wolf's artistic theories and the relational models of female selfhood developed by American feminist theorists such as Nancy Chodorow and Carol Gilligan.

9. Ursula Püschel describes the whole book as a depiction of a poetic land of which we are to take possession (138).

10. Ute Brandes has discovered sources for more than ninety pages of Wolf's book. Wolf sets these texts and many fragments of texts in new contexts to shed light on characters, traits, and relationships (328-35).

11. The portion of the quote in brackets was omitted in the published translation. I have translated it.

REFERENCES

Primary

Works by Wolf

Cassandra: A Novel and Four Essays. Trans. Jan van Heurck. New York: Farrar, Straus, and Giroux, 1984.

Kassandra. Darmstadt: Luchterhand, 1983.

Voraussetzungen einer Erzählung: Kassandra. Frankfurter Poetik-Vorlesungen. Darmstadt: Luchterhand, 1983.

Die Dimension des Autors: Aufsätze, Essays, Gespräche, Reden 1959-1985. 2 vols. Berlin: Aufbau, 1989.

The Fourth Dimension: Interviews with Christa Wolf. Trans. Hilary Pilkington. Intro. Karin McPherson. London: Verso, 1988.

Divided Heaven. Trans. Joan Becker. Berlin, GDR: Seven Seas Books, 1965.

Der geteilte Himmel. Halle: Mitteldeutscher Verlag, 1963.

"Fortgesetzter Versuch." *Die Dimension des Autors. Essays und Aufsätze, Reden und Gespräche 1959-1985*. 2 vols. Berlin: Aufbau, 1989, 2: 339-45.

Im Dialog: Aktuelle Texte. Darmstadt: Luchterhand, 1990.

A Model Childhood. Trans. Ursule Molinaro and Hedwig Rappolt. New York: Farrar, Straus, and Giroux, 1982.
Kindheitsmuster. Darmstadt: Luchterhand, 1977.
Moskauer Novelle. Halle: Mitteldeutscher Verlag, 1961.
No Place on Earth. Trans. Jan van Heurck. New York: Farrar, Straus, and Giroux, 1982.
Kein Ort. Nirgends. Darmstadt: Luchterhand, 1979.
The Quest for Christa T. Trans. Christopher Middelton. New York: Farrar, Straus, and Giroux, 1970.
Nachdenken über Christa T. Darmstadt: Luchterhand, 1976.
The Reader and the Writer: Essays, Sketches, Memories. Trans. Joan Becker. Berlin, GDR: Seven Seas Books, 1977.
Lesen und Schreiben. Aufsätze und Betrachtungen. Darmstadt: Luchterhand, 1972. 2d, rev. ed., 1980.

Interviews

Kaufmann, Hans. "Subjective Authenticity." *Responses to Christa Wolf: Critical Essays.* Ed. Marilyn Sibley Fries. Detroit: Wayne State University Press, 1989, 55-75.
Meyer-Gosau, Frauke. "Culture Is What You Experience—An Interview with Christa Wolf." Trans. Jeanette Clausen. *New German Critique* 27 (1982): 89-100.
————. "Kultur ist, was gelebt wird." *Alternative* 144-45 (1982): 117-27.

Secondary

Bock, Sigrid. "Christa Wolf: Kein Ort. Nirgends." *Weimarer Beiträge* 26.5 (1980): 145-57.
Brandes, Ute. "Quotation as Authentication: *No Place on Earth.*" *Responses to Christa Wolf: Critical Essays.* Ed. Marilyn Sibley Fries. Detroit: Wayne State University Press, 1989, 326-48.
Chodorow, Nancy. *The Reproduction of Mothering: Psychoanalysis and the Sociology of Gender.* Berkeley: University of California Press, 1978.
Dietrick, Linda. "Appropriating Romantic Consciousness: Narrative Mode in Christa Wolf's *Kein Ort. Nirgends.*" *Echoes and Influences of German Romanticism: Essays in Honour of Hans Eichner.* Ed. Michael Batts, A. W. Riley, and Heinz Wetzel. New York: Lang, 1987, 211-23.
Eigler, Friederike. "November 1989: Collapsing and Cementing German Identities." Unpublished paper presented at the Women in German Conference, November 1991.
Fehervary, Helen. "Autorschaft, Geschlechtsbewußtsein und Öffentlichkeit. Versuch über Heiner Müllers 'Die Hamletmaschine' und Christa Wolfs 'Kein Ort. Nirgends.'" *Entwürfe von Frauen in der Literatur des 20. Jahrhunderts.* Ed. Irmela von der Lühe. *Literatur im historischen Prozeß,* Neue Folge 5 {Argument Sonderband 92}. Berlin: Argument, 1982, 132-53.
Frieden, Sandra. "A Guarded Iconoclasm: The Self as Deconstructing Counterpoint to Documentation." *Responses to Christa Wolf: Critical Essays.* Ed. Marilyn Sibley Fries. Detroit: Wayne State University Press, 1989, 266-74.
Fries, Marilyn Sibley, ed. *Responses to Christa Wolf: Critical Essays.* Detroit: Wayne State University Press, 1989.

Gidion, Heidi. "'Was mich tötet, zu gebären': Emanzipation as (tödlicher) Erkenntniss-prozeß—demonstriert an Kassandra, Günderrode, Kleist." *Anstösse* 32 (1985): 165-72.

Gilligan, Carol. *In a Different Voice: Psychological Theory and Women's Development.* Cambridge: Harvard University Press, 1983.

Goozé, Marjanne E. "Karoline von Günderrode (1780-1806)." Introduction, bibliography, and translation of letters. *Bitter Healing: German Women Writers from 1700 to 1830. An Anthology.* Ed. Jeannine Blackwell and Susanne Zantop. Lincoln: University of Nebraska Press, 1990, 417-26.

Herrmann, Anne. *The Dialogic of Difference: "An/Other Woman" in Virginia Woolf and Christa Wolf.* New York: Columbia University Press, 1989.

Kuhn, Anna. *Christa Wolf's Utopian Vision: From Marxism to Feminism.* Cambridge: Cambridge University Press, 1988.

Lennox, Sara. "Christa Wolf and the Women Romantics." *Studies in GDR Culture and Society* 2 (1982): 31-43.

McPherson, Karen. "Christa Wolf—An Introduction." *The Fourth Dimension: Interviews with Christa Wolf.* London: Verso, 1988, vii-xxvii.

Püschel, Ursula. "Zutrauen kein Unding, Liebe kein Phantom." *Neue deutsche Literatur* 27.7 (July 1979): 134-39.

Schoefer, Christine. "Germany Rewrites History: The Attack on Christa Wolf." *The Nation* (October 22, 1990): 446-49.

Schreiber, Mathias. "'Bonjour Christesse.'" *Der Spiegel* 44 (October 28, 1991): 285-92.

PART II

DISRUPTING THE AUTONOMOUS SELF

Maryse Condé's *Hérémakhonon*: A Triangular Structure of Alienation

Arlette M. Smith

Born in Guadeloupe, French West Indies, and having lived in Guinée, Sénégal and Côte d'Ivoire, Maryse Condé, with her novel *Hérémakhonon*, has taken us on a journey into an African past believed by many to be impenetrable. The novel was published in 1976, a date of special interest since, coincidentally, Alex Haley's *Roots* was also published the same year. The coincidence is not limited to the date of publication, however, since in its very general lines the subject deals with some of the same themes: a yearning for Africa as the depository of black culture and a trip to Africa in search of one's history. But the similarities of some of the themes accentuate all the more the very different orientations of the two works. While *Roots* is presented as an autobiographical narration, *Hérémakhonon* is a fictional work. In *Roots* the narrator, who is the main character, is a black American male whose search is successful, since he finds his African relatives. In *Hérémakhonon*, on the contrary, the main protagonist, a young black woman from Guadeloupe, undertakes a search which has generally been considered a failure, an interpretation to which this writer does not subscribe. A justification of my reading will follow in this essay. Maryse Condé, who is becoming more and more internationally known as a first-rate novelist and essayist, reported recently that she had returned to her native Guadeloupe in July 1986 to resume her permanent residence. She went on to say:

As it stands, the literary landscape of the French-speaking Lesser Antilles is far from being bleak. One by one the islands are recuperating their writers living abroad. . . . This will no doubt give rise to a healthy emulation, and according to the slogan of "Writings of the Islands," a literary competition organized by the Guadeloupe Center of Cultural Action, whose principal jury members include Daniel Maximin, Simone Schwartz-Bart and Maryse Condé, numerous are those who will say to themselves: "To your pens!"[1]

[Tel qu'il est, le paysage littéraire des petites Antilles de langue française est loin d'être sombre. Les îles une à une récupèrent leurs écrivains vivant à l'étranger. . . . Nul doute que cela créera une saine émulation et que selon le slogan d'"écriture d'Iles," concours

littéraire organisé par le Centre d'Action Culturelle de la Guadeloupe, avec comme
principaux membres du jury Daniel Maximin, Simone Schwartz-Bart et Maryse Condé,
nombreux sont ceux qui se diront: "A vos plumes!" ("Paysage," 2-3)]

The anticipated return to their native soil of those French West Indian writers,
who have been widely acclaimed and given exposure by the great publishing
houses of Paris, will certainly fulfill a major portion of Maryse Condé's dream.

In this essay,[2] after presenting a brief summary of the story in *Hérémakhonon*, while also giving a profile of the narrator/heroine Veronica, the writer
will analyze the novel's thematic structure, which will suggest the significance
of Veronica's quest. The novel opens as Veronica, then a philosophy teacher,
is arriving for the first time in an anonymous African nation recently independent. A considerable part of the novel is constituted by verbalization of her
stream of consciousness, a narrative device which allows the reader to be rather
well informed about her past, her present preoccupations, and her aspirations.
Veronica's life seems to conform to a pattern which could be divided into three
segments: first, her childhood and adolescence in Guadeloupe; secondly, her
nine-year stay in France, where she brilliantly completed her studies; and
thirdly, her present trip to Africa. Each of the three segments has the same
configuration to the extent that each of them is marked by similar events: a love
affair, a crisis, and a sudden departure which suggests a flight away from the
trying circumstances which had led to the crisis. In Guadeloupe her love affair
is with a young mulatto, Jean-Marie, and the crisis is precipitated by her
parents' outraged reaction when they discover the romance. Her welcomed
departure for France, which follows soon afterwards, is the result of her
parents' decision to exile her so that they may be spared any further humiliation
through her lack of discretion. Virtuous behavior is not the question here. The
parents' indignation is compounded by the complexities of the racial climate
peculiar to Maryse Condé's Guadeloupe, where self-respecting blacks strive to
avoid any appearance of subservience and lack of dignity in their rapport with
the mulattoes. At this stage, one dimension of Veronica's alienation is already
apparent: she is at odds with her parents—whose black bourgeois mentality she
rejects—and with her social milieu because she is critical of the color caste
system, which separates whites, mulattoes, and blacks and establishes a strict
tacit hierarchy between the three groups.[3]

In Paris, a few years later, she meets a French architect with whom she has
a happy romantic relationship which is marred by an accident having racial
overtones: while attending a social function with her white lover, she overhears
disparaging remarks directed at her by some male compatriots who resent the
sight of a black woman escorted by a white man. For the second time, Veronica's romantic relationship epitomizes the complexities, both racial and cultural,
which help to exacerbate her feeling of alienation: in Guadeloupe, she had not
been able to identify with the mentality and values of the Guadeloupeans, and
again in France, in spite of her immersion into French culture and her thorough
French intellectual training, she is made to experience a feeling of exclusion, of
"otherness." She sees herself as an oddity because she symbolizes cultural

inauthenticity resulting from her lack of a deeply rooted heritage which would have given her a stronger sense of self and of stabilizing wholeness. She perceives herself as the product of imperfectly woven disparate cultural strands: remote, blurred, distorted fragments of her African heritage, mixed with multiple elements of French culture which, despite the receptivity with which she assimilates them, she can never claim as indigenous to herself. Prompted to find a solution to this crisis, she decides to go to Africa, turning away from a hurtful situation, as had been the case in the Guadeloupean segment of her life. Her inability to relate fully to her milieu sends her on a search in an entirely new location.

As the original land of the black people, Africa represents for Veronica the source of their essential values. This continent offers blacks the most genuine image of themselves and provides them with the most adequate models. Africa, she hopes, will be a cure for her alienation. Her stay in this recently decolonized nation is shaped according to the familiar tripartite pattern: first, she becomes the mistress of one of the government leaders, Ibrahima Sory, who also happens to belong to one of the most ancient and noble families of the land; secondly, the crisis she experiences stems from several circumstances, both personal and political; and thirdly, Ibrahima appears to her, at first, as an emblem of the Africa she is seeking and as a descendant of a family who has been associated with the shaping and preservation of traditional Africa ever since the precolonial era. Thus, he is to her a symbol of the African past which, through the rupture caused by the slave trade, has been deported to the New World. Through her relationship with him she expects to recapture her vanished heritage in its integrity and to apprehend it free from the distortions it has undergone during the centuries. She hopes that, by learning about the African past from Ibrahima, she will be able to see that past restored in its continuity and her pride rebuilt. By this contact with the past, She hopes to recover her cultural authenticity and to have her fractured psyche unified:

I have come to rid myself of an ill: I know that Ibrahima will be the marabout's gris-gris. Through him, I will finally learn to be proud of who I am. . . . That man, he is the cure that I sought. I know he is the one who will reconcile me with them, with us, with myself.

[Je suis venue pour me guérir d'un mal: Ibrahima sera, je le sais, le gri-gri du marabout. Par lui, j'accéderai enfin à la fierté d'être moi-même. . . . Cet homme-là, c'est le remède que je suis venue chercher. Celui qui je sais me réconciliera avec eux, avec nous, avec moi-même. (*Hérémakhonon* 81, 111)]

However, no such thing happens. Veronica's hopes do not materialize because Ibrahima's concerns are focused much more on the present and the future of his people than on their past. He jokingly dismisses Veronica's expectations as romantic fantasies or ruminations of an overintellectualized mind.

The social scene is also a source of disappointment for Veronica, who has nurtured a vision of Africa embued with a mythical aura: the great African kingdoms, the land of serene and wise elders, and of happily lived communality.

What she finds instead is a young effervescent country in the process of defining its identity after colonial domination, searching for the political and economic options best suited to advance its development. Concrete African realities confront her: clash of ideologies, confrontations between factions, poverty, oppressive political power. At first she takes no interest in the prevailing agitation, cultivating an attitude of protective detachment, indifferent to everything except her wish to discover a cultural framework within which she can fit. Her disenchantment grows about Ibrahima's refusal to initiate her into Africanity, and under the pressure of the political unrest, she is made to perceive him gradually as a calculating and ruthless ruler. At the same time she also becomes more aware of the scope and gravity of the events which are taking place in the country. Finding herself in an Africa which she does not fully understand and with which she cannot identify, and now convinced of the impossibility of fulfilling her aspirations to discover her original cultural context, Veronica decides once more to leave, to turn away from a place where her own enigmas and contradictions cannot be solved or reconciled.

At this point the ternary structure, which could be discerned in the configuration of events making up Veronica's life, can be detected again, this time in the spatial organization of the novel. Indeed, her quest will have taken her in reverse to the three continents which played such a determining role in the destiny of the African slaves. She, in turn, travels the fatidic, inexorable triangular route which spells doom and inescapable sequestration for them. This spatial structure is symbolically meaningful. Both for Veronica and for her ancestors it is associated with the notions of discontinuity, uprooting, exile, a contingent sense of identity, and a feeling of "otherness." While the fate of the slaves is inscribed within the triangular journey, Veronica actually travels the totality of the space it delineates, and in both cases it has the same connotations. Psychologically and emotionally she experiences a sense of doom and imprisonment. She feels trapped by the three dimensions of her cultural heritage—Antillean, French, and African—which co-exist in her psyche without being able to blend harmoniously; she feels them to be irreconcilable. Her ethnic African heritage, her Guadeloupean sociocultural background, and her French intellectual training have transformed her into a person who is neither totally African, nor Guadeloupean, nor French.

Veronica's departure from Africa raises a few questions. Is it this time also an escape? Is she once more definitely locked within the three-sided prison of her alienation? At first, it may appear that each one of these questions could be answered affirmatively and that, indeed, her African heritage has destroyed her last hope of ever acquiring a meaningful identity. It is, however, possible to read *Hérémakhonon* as a novel which concludes on promising perspectives, although Veronica is not perceived as a triumphant heroine. This interpretation can be validated by a brief thematic analysis and a succinct study of the narrative structure.

The motifs which translate Veronica's alienation the most consistently are her preoccupation with the past, her search for cultural authenticity, and her narcissism. Her predilection for the past is evidenced in many ways: she ascribes the cultural disorientation of the Antilleans to their lack of deeply embedded roots; she first aggrandizes Ibrahima because he is the descendant of a long lineage and thus represents for her a vestige of the past; her own concerns, as reflected in her inner monologue, deal for a long while with her childhood recollections or her life in France; and she makes only fragmentary remarks about present circumstances—mainly, it seems, to bring back the past by association. But gradually a shift occurs in her temporal perspective, and she gains a more realistic, more objective view of reality as she loses her illusions about Ibrahima and as the turbulence of the local situation makes it more and more difficult for her to maintain her aloofness. Her obsession with the past also fades gradually. Her dreams of renewing contact with the vestiges of the African past are less obsessive, and she tries to understand the events which are taking place in the present. She becomes more and more a witness and emerges from the seclusion of her own subjectivity. She even admits that she would rather face the harshness of the present than slide back into the lulling comfort of the past:

Yes, one can forget everything. One can slide back into the past. I have noticed, however, that I want this less and less. It's almost as if the present had caught up with me. Not that I have gained anything in the deal. I even have to admit that I preferred my former phantoms.

[Oui, on peut tout oublier. On peut basculer en arrière. Or cela, je m'en aperçois, je le désire de moins en moins. Comme si le présent m'avait rattrapée à la course. Pas que j'aie gagné au change! Je dois même dire que je préférais mes anciens fantômes. (219)]

Through Veronica's own admission it is now obvious that she can analyze herself with greater objectivity than ever before. As narrator she is now better able to distance herself from her past character, which is a sign that she is freeing herself from her deeply entrenched narcissism. As a result, her outlook on the human environment also changes. While she had expected Africa to be a land culturally unspoiled by foreign influences, it now becomes clear to her that many Africans have adopted some of the cultural tics associated with the Europeans, and that African culture no longer exists in its pristine state.

The change which has occurred in Veronica's outlook and reactions constitutes one of the main arguments lending validity to a reading of *Hérémakhonon* as a positive novel in spite of a dénouement which suggests defeat. Also important is the determining of the type of narrative model after which a particular fictional work is patterned. Viewed as a quest novel, *Hérémakhonon* would indeed qualify as a story of failure, since in such narratives the objective outcome of the quest is the absolute criterion considered. Depending on his ability to reach the object which had motivated his search, the protagonist is characterized as a hero or an antihero. From this perspective, which is the traditional one, Veronica is definitely an antiheroine, and her search a total failure. But the narrative formula of *Hérémakhonon* may not be that of a quest; this novel can be read as a *roman d'apprentissage* [novel of apprenticeship], in which case Veronica's evolution would be of great significance. In such novels the emphasis is on the psychological and emotional development of the heroine through failures, misjudgments, and hurts, as in the case of Veronica, rather than on the happy or unhappy character of the outcome. It is true that her unhappiness is constant throughout the span of her life represented in the novel. She experiences rejection, humiliation, loneliness, anguish, self-doubt. At the same time, she also experiences a slow metamorphosis as her temporal consciousness focuses less on the past and more on the present, as her perception of cultural realities becomes less mythical and more historical, and as she becomes less self-oriented. Her transformation is fruitful because it amounts to an acquisition of knowledge. It is sign of her gradual liberation from the paralyzing effects of excessive introspection, from an immoderate fascination with the past, and from the idealization of any culture as a phenomenon of perennial sameness. In a *roman d'apprentissage* Veronica is viewed as the canonical heroine whose initial aspirations have not been fulfilled, but she has gained a clearer insight of herself and a more pragmatic outlook on her environment. With this in mind, it can be asserted that she has finally gained freedom from the entanglements and from the sequestration of her alienation. No longer trapped within the inescapable triangle, she leaves for France with a clear perception of her new self and with a lucid judgment concerning her misguided expectations:

This error, this tragic error I had to have committed, being who I am. I made a mistake, I chose the wrong ancestors, that's all. I sought my salvation where I shouldn't have. Among assassins.

[Cette erreur, cette tragique erreur que je ne pouvais pas ne pas commettre, étant ce que je suis. Je me suis trompée, trompée d'aîeux, voilà tout. J'ai cherché mon salut là où il ne fallait pas. Parmi les assassins. (312)]

Veronica acknowledges that she had set out on the wrong route and had misled herself. She now knows which ways to avoid. Awareness of one's errors is in itself a gain.

Veronica is the forerunner of those heroines/narrators who have subsequently appeared in Maryse Condé's novels: *A Season in Rihata* [*Une Saison à Rihata*] (1981), *Segu* [*Ségou*] (1984, 1985), and *I Tituba, Black Witch of Salem* [*Moi, Tituba Sorcière*] (1986).[4] In spite of a painful and harsh existence, woven with injustices and humiliations, Maryse Condé's heroines, like the author herself,[5] symbolize the dynamism of life, the ways of the world, and faith in oneself. Fiction and history join forces to form the substance of Condé's novels, and the determined quantity of these two elements gives evidence of an unfailing work of art based upon creative diversity and care for historical verity as well as for sensitive and responsive writing.

NOTES

This chapter was previously published in *CLA Journal* 32.1 (1988): 45-54.

1. The English translations are by Anne Brown; they do not appear in the original article.

2. This essay was read in part by the writer at the Forty-third Annual Convention of the College Language Association in Philadelphia, Pennsylvania, April 21, 1983.

3. On this problem, which lingers to a certain extent in the French Antilles, see Michel Leiris, 117-68. See also Robert P. Smith, JC., 783-90.

4. Maryse Condé wrote at least two plays before becoming famous as a novelist: *God Gave Him to Us* [*Dieu nous l'a donné*] (1972) and *The Death of Oluwemi of Ajumako* [*Mort d'Oluwemi d'Ajumako*] (1973).

5. Maryse Condé, who did her higher studies at the University of Paris, is well known in France, Africa, and her native Guadeloupe and one is beginning to speak of her more and more in the United States (Charlotte and David Bruner). In 1985, Condé taught Antillean literature and culture at the University of California at Los Angeles and has lectured at other U.S. institutions, including Howard University in Washington, D.C. In 1981, she was a professor of black African literature at the Sorbonne in Paris.

REFERENCES

Bruner, Charlotte, and David. "Buchi Emecheta and Maryse Condé: Contemporary Writing from Africa and the Caribbean." *World Literature Today* 59.1 (1985): 9-13.

Condé, Maryse. *Hérémakhonon*. Paris: Union Générale d'Éditions, 1976.

———. *Moi, Tituba sorcière*. Paris: Mercure de France, 1986.

———. "Paysage littéraire des Antilles." *Centre d'Études sur la littérature africaine et caribéenne d'expression française*. 1.1 (1987): 2-3.

———. *Une Saison à Rihata*. Paris: Éditions Robert Laffont, 1981.

———. *Ségou*. Paris: Éditions Robert Laffont, 1985.

Haley, Alex. *Roots*. New York: Doubleday, 1976.

Leiris, Michel. *Contacts de civilisations en Martinique et en Guadeloupe*. Paris: Unesco/Gallimard, 1955.

Smith, Robert P. "Michèle Lacrosil: Novelist with a Color Complex." *French Review* 47.4 (1974): 783-90.

Colonial Discourse and Female Identity: Bharati Mukherjee's *Jasmine*

Suzanne Kehde

> I was born in Calcutta. Yes, I am positive that Calcutta shaped me. Calcutta is a very special city—it's a world city, but at the same time it's a small town capable of exciting parochial passions and fiercely chauvinist loyalties. I am what I am because I was born into an upper-middle-class Bengali family in a city where to be Bengali was to be part of the mainstream. I didn't grow up in a multi-racial society in which to be Indian was to be a patronized or hated minority, as did V.S. Naipaul. North Americans don't always understand that an Indian growing up in India as part of the confident mainstream has a very different sense of self than an Indian growing up in a multi-racial country. . . . I feel lucky that I was born [1942] just before Independence—I know first-hand how precious liberty is. (Interview with Bharati Mukherjee, Hancock, 288-89)

For Jasmine, Mukherjee's eponymous protagonist, the kind of liberty she enjoys is a consequence of, rather than the reason for, her coming to the New World. An illegal immigrant from Punjab, who "phantom[s her] way through three continents" (101) on unscheduled flights landing on the disused airfields of the shadow world, she finally crosses the Atlantic in a sea voyage as horrifying as any suffered by the Mayflower pilgrims. Her first sight of America is no more attractive than Plymouth Rock was to them:

> The first thing I saw were the two cones of a nuclear plant, and smoke spreading from them in complicated but seemingly purposeful patterns, edges lit by the rising sun, like a gray, intricate map of an unexplored island continent, against the pale unscratched blue of the sky. I waded through Eden's waste: plastic bottles, floating oranges, boards, sodden boxes, white and green plastic sacks tied shut but picked open by birds and pulled apart by crabs. (107)

The "unexplored island continent" is not what Spivak calls "uninscribed earth" (133); it is aggressively inscribed with the signs of contemporary American culture. This passage, however, is not as simply ironic as it may appear in isolation. As throughout the novel, the relationship between the myth of Eden and the narrative trajectory is not that of parodic inversion. For example, nuclear plants may be dangerous, but they signal a country where hot water is taken for granted: "a miracle, that even here in a place that looked deserted . . . the tiles and porcelain should be clean, without smells, without bugs" (117).

Invoking the myth of America as Eden, Mukherjee brings colonial discourse into play. The image of Paradise has informed representations of America since the news of Columbus's discovery reached Europe at the beginning of the mercantile period. The Genesis account of Eden justifies a "natural" hierarchy based on gender and control of the natural world enforced by language. Man is the focus of power. All the resources of the earth exist for his welfare and pleasure. His right to rule legitimated by the Heavenly Father, Adam is the first patriarch; naming the animals while he is the sole human being, he establishes language as a function of domination. Eve is born into a preexistent hierarchy with only a father, thus entering an already constituted discourse with no one to speak for her as a woman; flesh of Adam's flesh, her identity is forever subordinated to his. This model provides the justification for the "natural" subordination of women to men and, by extension, the appropriation of the land, goods, and labor of the colonial subject, whose feminization is a condition of his subjugation.

As Doris Lessing's *Golden Notebook* and Angela Carter's *Passion of New Eve* suggest, the exploitative opportunities implicit in the myth are not available to women in the same configurations as to men because the myth constitutes women as already colonized subjects. This is not to imply that women cannot be colonizers, exploiters, or oppressors, only that their relationship to colonial discourse is more problematic. In Jasmine's case, her relationships to people she meets are defined by colonial discourse; that is, they attempt to construct her by the mechanisms of difference, resemblance, and desire. She may resist these constructions in some cases, acquiesce in others. Half-Face, the owner of the boat bringing her to Florida—whose injuries sustained in Vietnam might perhaps have suggested to him that colonizers do not necessarily escape unscathed—reads Jasmine as "one prime little piece" (115) who is so afraid of the Immigration and Naturalization Service that he can rape her with impunity, so docile he falls asleep while she is in the shower. When he sees her above him naked with her mouth open and blood pouring from her tongue, he is so startled he cannot prevent her from slitting one of his carotid arteries. Lillian Gordon, for whom "the world's misery was a challenge to her ingenuity" (131), scrutinizes Jasmine for marks of difference that must be erased lest they betray her to the Immigration and Naturalization Service: her jeweled sandals, her inability to manage escalators and revolving doors, her un-American gait. The Vadheras, earlier (legal) immigrants who give her shelter in New York, emphasize resemblance, trying to pressure her into the "modesty of appearance and attitude" proper to a Hindu widow (145). Educated people are interested in differences because "they are always out to improve themselves" (33)—in this case, by learning from her experience, which is perhaps democratic, as Jasmine sees it, but is also a kind of exploitation. The farmers she meets in Iowa, on the other hand, familiarize her because "alien knowledge means intelligence" (33). Rapists, sympathizers, intellectuals, and farmers read her according to their own desires.

In some cases, Jasmine uses her Otherness to construct herself according to the colonizer's desires. This behavior began with her marriage in Punjab (as a girl, she strenuously resisted the traditional Hindu engenderment of *woman*.) Taken in as an au pair, she wishes to become what Taylor and Wylie imagine her to be: "humorous, intelligent, refined, affectionate. Not illegal, not murderer, not widowed, destitute, fearful" (171). An Iowa farm banker falls in love with her "because I am alien. I am darkness, mystery, inscrutability" (200). Here is an example of what Homi Bhabha calls "the repeated hesitancy that afflicts the colonialist discourse when it contemplates its discriminated subjects—the *inscrutability* of the Chinese, the *unspeakable* rites of the Indians, the *indescribable* habits of the Hottentots" (97); however, it is colonial discourse used by the colonial subject to describe herself as she believes she appears to the colonizer. Once more, Mukherjee's use of colonial discourse is problematized. When a distraught farmer shoots and cripples Bud Ripplemeyer, Jasmine becomes what he needs—nurse, inventive sex partner, adoptive parent, expectant mother. Because she accepts them consciously, these identities provide sites of resistance for her. She never internalizes any one role—refusing to settle into being, she is always becoming. She draws attention to her multiplicity of identities: "I have had a husband for each of the women I have been. Prakash for Jasmine, Taylor for Jase, Bud for Jane, Half-Face for Kali" (197). Although she consciously adapts to these proffered roles, her exploitation is not cynical. She is not hypocritical in the sense that she pretends to be someone she is not while clinging to another image of her "real" self. Rather, she has never conceived of herself as a unified, single, transcendental subject, but as a contingent being—a position of considerable strength. Her fluidity of personality not only allows her to survive multiple trauma but also makes room for hope.

The myth of America as Eden disrupts an earlier mythology. Jyoti/Jasmine's earliest memory, with which the novel opens, is of a Hindu astrologer's prediction of her widowhood and exile. This the seven year old resists by asserting her own claim to wisdom, through which resistance she accidentally acquires her "third eye" (5). This star-shaped scar on her forehead (in the spot where Hindu women traditionally wear a *tika*) is thus an emblem of both her self-assertion and her power of foresight, forever throbbing with "pain and hope, hope and pain" (225). In the same way, as a twelve-year-old she resists her father's essentialist construction—"the thing is that bright ladies are bearing bright sons, that is nature's design" (51)—with a demand to be educated as a physician. Jasmine does not abandon Hindu mythology: she carries with her a small Ganpati (a version of Ganesha, the elephant god of knowledge); she makes frequent references to Lord Yama, the god of death, and others to Brahma, Vishnu, and Shiva. The myth of America as Eden begins to appear even before Jasmine/Jyoti thinks of coming to America. Her most desired characteristic in a prospective husband is his ability to speak English: "To want English was to want more than you had been given at birth, it was to want the world" (68). Prakash, who attempts to remake Jyoti into Jasmine, a new woman, yearns for America, where his fellow graduates live in houses with electricity twenty-four hours a day and hot running water, which becomes for Jasmine the enduring paradisal attribute. But the myth of America never displaces Hindu mythology. In America, Jasmine seems to embrace the idea of reincarnation: "[T]he Lord lends us a body, gives us an assignment, and sends us down. When we get the job done, the Lord calls us home again for the next assignment" (59). Though astonished by "the American need . . . to *possess* a vision so privately" (125), she responds to an anthropologist's claim to out-of-body experiences by saying, "[T]heoretically, I believe in reincarnation" (125)—a belief that underlies her ability to assume different identities. The colonial discourse of the American myth and the metaphysical discourse of Hinduism disrupt each other continually.

Juxtaposed to both these discourses is Jasmine's personal story of origin. Wishing to spare her fifth daughter both the pain of a dowryless bride and the exclusion from heaven of an unmarried woman, Jasmine's mother tried to strangle her at birth. Jasmine understands this attempted murder as an act of love. The act propels her into a new identity: "My grandmother may have named me Jyoti/Light, but in surviving I was already Jane, a fighter and adapter" (40). This personal myth of intertwined ends and beginnings helps Jyoti/Jasmine/Jane negotiate the American and Hindu myths without allowing either one to define her. Consequently, she can maintain the fluid personality necessary for survival in a contingent world.

For Jasmine, events that appear as ends may, in fact, be beginnings—her widowhood at eighteen, for example, which in India would have mandated a life of mourning as a companion to her mother in her native village. Instead, Jasmine takes Prakash's new suit to the campus of the Florida college where he had been accepted, there to burn it and with the intention to commit *sati* in the blaze. This sense of a divinely appointed mission supports her through all the difficulties of her journey—one example of the way elements from all her myth systems provide support at critical moments. America turns out to be a site of new beginnings for Jasmine in spite of her intention to make it the site of her end. Throughout, beginnings and ends are woven inextricably together, and both are steeped in violence. Jasmine sees new beginnings as the assumptions of new identities rather than as the simpler assumption of a new way of life: "There are no harmless, compassionate ways to remake oneself. We murder who we were so we can rebirth ourselves in the images of dreams" (29). These self-murders are the inner corollary of exterior violence, psychological suicides necessitated by the shift in power position attendant upon murder and rape. Jasmine does not see her rape by Half-Face as a satiric comment on America as Eden. The world is generally violent: her mother's murder attempt, and her husband's death at the hands of a Sikh fanatic both took place in India. Each of these acts of violence propels her into a new identity.

In spite of the realist surface of her fiction, Mukherjee sees identity as constituted by discourse rather than as a stable attribute of the transcendent, unified individual of the realist novel. The flexibility necessary for survival in a changing world comes from the understanding—either conscious or uncon- scious—of the discursive basis of identity and the willingness to negotiate the discourse(s). Jasmine's well-honed ability to survive depends on her resistance to definition by any one discourse. This is emphasized by the trajectory of Darrel Lutz's story. He is conflicted by two identities constructed from incompatible myths. The first is the myth of the midwest family farm he grew up with, the second of a more nebulous idea of getting off the land. Jasmine succinctly describes these two identities: "Crazy, Darrel wants an Indian princess and a Radio Shack franchise in Santa Fe. . . . Sane, he wants to baby-sit three hundred hogs and reinvent the fertilizer/pesticide wheel" (233). What provokes Jasmine to label these alternatives *crazy* and *sane* is unclear; they are, however, obviously incompatible. Needing to constitute himself as a single, unified personality, Darrel cannot live in this split condition. Suicide—a solution to difficult situations that Jasmine repeatedly entertains, then resists—is the only way he can imagine to resolve his conflict.

Jasmine/Jane's ruminations on Darrel's situation as the site of irreconcilable discourses provide a foil for her own colonized condition, which is augmented by her analysis of the subjectivity of Du, her adopted son. He is split in a much more complex way than Darrel Lutz, who is merely caught in a conflict generated by a single culture. Du, a Vietnamese orphan, is already split before coming to the United States. A "Saigon sophisticate" (220) whose family owned technological appliances like television, he was presumably displaced by the United States withdrawal from Saigon in 1975, which made him a refugee (once more, presumably, Mukherjee shows the consequences of his history rather than furnishing that history itself) in another country, most probably Thailand, where the Vietnamese are alien outcasts, herded into camps, surviving on "live worms and lizards and crabs so [they] wouldn't starve to death" (221). In Iowa, he tries to assimilate as quickly as possible. Seeing as Jasmine does that America is "a place where the language you speak is what you are" (11), he refuses to talk if he doesn't know the right English phrases. He rejects the role of colonial subject his teacher attempts to impose: "Yogi's [a nickname bestowed by his classmates] in a hurry to become all-American, isn't he? . . . They were like that, the kids who hung around us in Saigon. . . . I tried a little Vietnamese on him . . . and he just froze up" (28-29). In order to define the context of these comments, Mukherjee has Jasmine (silently) gloss them: "How *dare* you? What must [Du] have thought? His history teacher in Baden, Iowa, just happens to know a little street Vietnamese? Now where would he have picked it up?" (29). The benevolent teacher reminds the refugee of his own role as colonial aggressor—the representative of the most recent of a long line of colonizers, including the Chinese and the French—by equating Du with the beggar orphans Jasmine knows he would have despised. Barely veiled, American imperialism controls student-teacher relations in a high school in America, where in the cinemas and in the home innumerable movies show rivers full of corpses and tracts of leafless "jungle" while Vietnamese teenagers write of the beautiful forests and the white, sandy river beaches they do not expect to see ever again.

Mr. Skola's representative attempt to constitute Du as a colonial subject provides for Du a site of resistance and for Jasmine an opportunity to scrutinize an especially overt manifestation of the mechanisms by which the colonial subject is constituted. Through Jasmine, Mukherjee forwards an analysis of the constitution of the (male) colonial subject so complex and subtle that, in contrast to the way in which Jasmine's situation is generally presented, it needs to be articulated rather than implied. When Jasmine discovers that, although she has never before heard Du speak Vietnamese, he has "made a life for himself among the Vietnamese in Baden," she realizes that he is "a hybrid" (222). Here Mukherjee seems to use Bhabha's formulation of hybridization:

Produced through the strategy of disavowal, the *reference* of discrimination is always to a process of splitting as the condition of subjection; a discrimination between the Mother culture and its bastards, the self and its doubles, where the trace of what is disavowed is not repressed, but repeated as something *different*—a mutation, a hybrid. . . . [Hybridity] unsettles the mimetic or narcissistic demands of colonial power, but re-implicates its identifications in strategies of subversion that turn the gaze of the discriminated back upon the eye of power. For the colonial hybrid is the articulation of the ambivalent space where the rite of power is enacted on the site of desire. (96-97)

Bhabha's formulation explains Du's apparent attempt to become the all-American boy as mimicry rather than emulation, a site of resistance rather than acquiescence. Caught between two languages (and at least two discourses), Du establishes a position that not only enables him to deal with the conflict but empowers him to constitute that conflict as an opportunity for self definition. Jasmine sees him as hyphenated: "Du (Yogi) Ripplemeyer, a Vietnamese-American" (222). Although Du's hyphenation allows him to move between two cultures taking advantage of select features of each, his split condition precludes the desirable power position of the transcendent (male) individual—a position that male postcolonial theorists like Bhabha seem to want to reclaim for Third World men.

Jasmine, comparing her own state with Du's hyphenation, remarks that her "transformation has been genetic" (222). She apparently does not regard this transformation—so thorough as to require a biological metaphor—as a capitulation to the colonizer's demands; she does not constitute herself as hybrid or hyphenated Indian American. Her relationship to nationality cannot be the same as Du's not only because of their countries' different colonial histories, not only because the construction of *nationality* itself is specific to each nation, but also because of the difference of gender. Du has more to gain by maintaining his cultural and national identity. According to the Edenic myth that served as a blueprint for the depredations of the Old World, woman is the primary colonial subject; further, contemporary psychoanalytic theory holds that the sense of self depends upon differentiation from the Other, for signs of which the colonizer scrutinizes the colonized, just as gender categories are typically reinforced by policing the boundaries. Thus a male from a Third World country oppressed by a thousand years of successive colonial masters is inevitably constructed as a feminized Other by the imperial power. However, if he maintains ties with his native community, he may be able to retain at least a simulacrum of his position in his accustomed hierarchy. He will always outrank a woman or a Hmong peasant, for example. Jyoti/Jasmine/Jane has no comparable reason for remaining in touch with an Indian community, a vivid emblem of which is provided by the Vadheras in New York, for whom Jasmine was completely constituted by her marital history. She rejects the past they represent just as she rejects the nostalgia of the grade B Bombay movies they rent daily from the video store. She understands the attraction of clinging to the safety of a sanitized, burnished past but refuses it for herself: "To bunker herself inside nostalgia, to sheathe the heart in a bullet-proof vest, was to be a coward" (185).

America allows for a greater range of positive and negative freedoms (Sen, 49)—admittedly, the latter are constrained by the threat of (male) violence, but, as Jasmine remarks, in the Indian district where she was born "bad luck dogged dowryless wives, rebellious wives, barren wives. They fell into wells, they got run over by trains, they burned to death heating milk on kerosene stoves" (41). Even young, unmarried girls evacuating their bowels in a field before dawn may be attacked by mad dogs. As women have less to gain from ideologies of nationality, so they may be less invested in them. In both India and America, Jasmine's primary identification is as a woman, which she constitutes as a site of flexibility.

Thus, through her appropriation of the myth of America as Eden, Mukherjee brings colonial discourse into play; analyzing the construction of the colonial subject, she engages in a postcolonial critique of that discourse. Eschewing simple inversion, her critique of the myth, neither ironic nor parodic, takes the form of disruption: just as Jasmine's identity is disrupted, so are the various discourses that Mukherjee uses. The novel ends without closure. Jasmine sets off on a new life—or, rather, on a new version of a previous life when Taylor drives up and urges her to accompany him to California. Pregnant with Bud's child, and "caught between the promise of America and old-world dutifulness," she nonetheless chooses "adventure, risk, transformation" (240). She bounds out the door to the car "greedy with wants and reckless from hope" (241). There is no criticism of Jasmine (no longer thinking of herself as Jane) for her refusal to be pinned down to the past. Certainly, her acceptance of family configurations and caretaking roles (even of unorthodox ones) may be construed as a manifestation of the essentialist sense of self preached by her father, but it also suggests a willingness to recognize opportunity in unlikely situations. There is no reason to suppose that Jasmine, at twenty-four, still in the process of becoming, will be forever trapped in domestic preoccupations. Rather, Mukherjee endorses the fluid personality as a site of possibility, particularly for a woman, for whom in this novel the operant discourses are always restrictive, always forcing Jasmine back into the paternal essentialism, always (re)constructing her as the primary colonial subject. In this examination of the construction of national identity and gender identity, Mukherjee recommends not an ideology of female resistance but an ad hoc selection of useful features from whatever discourse is at hand—a resistance to ossification of identity, a resiliency articulated toward survival.

REFERENCES

Bhabha, Homi. "Signs Taken for Wonders: Questions of Ambivalence and Authority Under a Tree Outside Delhi, May 1817." *Europe and Its Others*. Ed. Francis Barker and Peter Hulme. Colchester: University of Essex, 1985.

Carter, Angela. *Passion of New Eve*. New York: Harcourt Brace Jovanovich, 1977.

Hancock, Geoff. "Bharati Mukherjee." *Canadian Writers at Work*. Toronto: Oxford University Press, 1987.

Lessing, Doris. *The Golden Notebook*. New York: Simon and Schuster, 1962.

Mukherjee, Bharati. *Darkness*. Ontario: Penguin Books, 1985.

———. *Jasmine*. New York: Grove Weidenfeld, 1989.

Sen, Amartya. "Individual Freedom as a Social Commitment." *New York Review of Books*, June 14, 1990.

Spivak, Gayatri Chakravorty. "Rani of Sirmur." *Europe and Its Others*. Ed. Francis Barker and Peter Hulme. Colchester: University of Essex, 1985.

Fragmented Identities and the Process of Metamorphosis in Works by Lygia Fagundes Telles

Peggy Sharpe

What is dark becomes clear only until the clarity returns to darken again; clarity is fleeting.

[O que é escuro fica claro até que o claro volta a escurecer de novo, a claridade é provisória. (Telles, *The Bare Hours* [*As Horas Nuas* (206)]¹

In 1980, Lygia Fagundes Telles made the following observation concerning women's writing:

It is natural for a woman author to lend a certain femininity to the work. But what ought to always prevail is the writer. That is, what she/he writes, independent of sex, social condition, etc. . . . I do not accept prejudices of any kind. . . . That is not to say that women should only speak about women, even though they might find it easier to describe women and feel their needs. I think that feminism is exactly the work that a woman must do. Her marked presence should be felt in all kinds of activities, hating each and every type of prejudice. (*O Globo,* July 4, 1974)

Although Telles admits that prejudice against women writers exists, she does not sanction the categorization of text or writer. As a result of her personal experience with marginalization in the fields of law and literature, she believes that each of us must undertake our own struggles with honesty and seriousness (*O Estado de São Paulo*, November 26, 1978).

Telles's struggle over the past forty-five years has produced a literary career of four novels and thirteen collections of short fiction. Although she was better known for her short stories during the beginning of her literary career, Telles's novelistic production has gained so much strength that she is now widely recognized as Clarice Lispector's successor. She was elected to the São Paulo Academy of Letters [Academia Paulista de Letras] in 1982 and to the Brazilian Academy of Letters [Academia Brasileira de Letras] in 1987. Her novelistic development began with the publication of *The Marble Dance* [*Ciranda de Pedra*] in 1954, followed by *Summer in the Fishbowl* [*Verão no Aquário*] in 1963. *The Girl in the Photograph* [*As Meninas*] appeared in 1973, and in 1981

Telles began work on her most recent novel, *The Bare Hours* [*As Horas Nuas*], which was completed and published only in 1989.

With each successive novel, Telles hones her stylistic technique while creating and re-creating her cast of fragmented female characters that populate her fiction. Despite their strength and sheer courage, these characters are usually unable to complete the process of metamorphosis that would free them from their solitude, decadence, and lack of identity.[2] This discussion examines the interplay between the recurrent themes and characters of Telles's previous novels that constitute the narrative space of *The Bare Hours*.

Telles was born in the city of São Paulo but spent her childhood in the interior of the state. She returned to the capital to pursue her secondary education, remaining there for her university studies as well. In 1939, she received her first university degree in physical education, and during the same year she began her law degree. Against the backdrop of São Paulo's elitist social milieu, the author attests to her position as observer of a significant historical period characterized by the decline of the bourgeoisie and the rise of the values of capitalism. In the face of these complex sociohistorical realities, which Telles has often described as fitting subject matter to record the decadence of the bourgeoisie, she sets out to intermingle the real and the imaginative, stressing that she uses reality as a point of departure to speak for those who cannot express themselves (Pinto, 112). Telles views fiction as something real: "[T]he imaginary or what already happened, or is happening or will happen. You cannot set this apart from reality" (*Folha de São Paulo*, July 6, 1983).

When Telles writes about women, she does not attempt to define the concept of woman, to establish fixed definitions about what is or is not essentially feminine. Rather, she describes the ways in which women interact with what Alcoff calls the "network of elements involving others, the objective economic conditions, cultural and political institutions and ideologies" (323). Alcoff reminds us that the external context within which a person is situated determines her or his relative position, "just as the position of a pawn on a chessboard is considered safe or dangerous, powerful or weak, according to its relation to the other chess pieces" (323).

Individual identity, on the other hand, is constituted, as Teresa de Lauretis postulates, by a historical process of consciousness, a process in which one's history "is interpreted or reconstructed by each of us within the horizon of meanings and knowledge available in the culture at a given historical moment, a horizon that also includes modes of political commitment and struggle" (8). If we accept de Lauretis's definition, then we must accept her conclusion, that "consciousness is never fixed or attained once and for all because discursive boundaries change with historical conditions" (8).

Consciousness, if it is not something posited in an unchanging symbolic order, is a "fluid interaction in constant motion and open to alteration by self-analyzing practice" (Alcoff, 315). The explosion of the boundaries that enclose Telles's female characters in a world devoid of human feeling represents a dynamic attempt to break open the sociohistorical conditions that delimit their barren existence. Through their attempts at self-reflectiveness, they are involved at every moment in the futile project of reconstructing their own history. This process allows them agency as subjects at the same time that it places them within particular discursive configurations that are linked to their sociohistorical conditions (Alcoff, 315).

The concept of positionality reconfirms what Telles reveals about her own feminist intentions—that there are no universal maxims about the feminine. One's identity is a political point of departure, a motivation for action and a delineation of one's politics (Alcoff, 323). Alcoff's postulations show how women use their positional perspective as a place where values are interpreted and constructed as opposed to the concept of a place where meaning can be discovered. In other words, the positional perspective is not the locus of an already determined set of values. Thus, woman is involved in an active fashion in the construction of her identity because it is the product of her own interpretation and reconstruction of her history as mediated through the cultural discursive context to which she has access (de Lauretis, 8-9). She is the dynamic element in any attempt to alter the context that offers her limited power and mobility.

With the explosion of language and narrative style that Telles achieves in *The Bare Hours*, she continues and even surpasses the legacy of Clarice Lispector. Whereas Lispector avoids plot and incorporates unusual and lyrical language patterns, Telles breaks with convention at every aesthetic level. In retrospect, the following comment about *The Girl in the Photograph* is a better description of *The Bare Hours*: "I think rupture is important, to break the established, to break off with all that which is the easiest, the most predictable. It is difficult to explain. To forget what I already know, to invent a new adventure in language" (*O Estado de São Paulo*, May 9, 1987).

Analogous with the linguistic revolution undergone at the level of the word, signifying Telles's final break with aesthetic convention, is the complete fragmentation of the female characters that leaves them with only the core of a human identity. The novel is held together by the disparate fragments of language of what used to be considered Telles's "well-behaved prose" (Wasserman, 50) and fragments of characters who all share common experiences with separation, disappearance, solitude, loneliness, and death.

Like Telles's previous novels, *The Bare Hours* has three female protagonists, all of whom live on the periphery, outside the structure of the traditional family where the individuals' interests are mediated through the Law of the Father. Telles's readers have already witnessed the destruction of the family as a social institution in her first novel, and the subsequent works have introduced us to a whole cast of female protagonists whose attempts at self-reflection are obstructed by the characters' incapacity to integrate the process of self-reflection with the external context of their lives. Since the protagonists are ultimately unable to fix anything more than their relative position in the process of identity making, they become like characters looking for an identity. Certain personalities are then reincarnated in subsequent novels, albeit with a different external context: "Until today, characters that I did not develop sufficiently, like Lorena from 'the Girl,' return to disturb me. They end up returning in another book, with another name.

I am writing and I realize that I was already with that character in another book. It is her return, only that its camouflaged" (*O Globo*, August 7, 1984).

In *The Bare Hours*, the central female figure is Rosa Ambrósio, the author as Other, an actress who anesthesizes her solitude and fear of aging with alcohol.[3] Rosa's cat, Rahul, is an innovative narrator whose disclosures aid the reader in putting together the missing pieces of the puzzle of Rosa's life story that do not make up part of her interior monologues. Rosa's daughter, Cordélia, is the reincarnation of Ana Clara from *The Girl in the Photograph*, who continually attempts to escape from the solitude of her identity crisis by living out her attraction for older men. Ananta is the young feminist psychiatrist whose strange metamorphosis and subsequent physical disappearance, reminiscent of Virginia's voyage in *The Marble Dance*, bring the narrative to an end but leave the novel with no closure.

In contrast to the female characters' torment, over their lack of ability to establish an individual identity, Telles's male characters are mere puppets. Indeed, the masculine universe of Telles's entire novelistic production seems to exist solely as a point of reference for the female characters' discursive attempts to journey into the realm of self-knowledge: "In my condition as woman, I speak about woman because I don't know men as well as I know us, even though I try to penetrate the masculine universe. But it is as woman that I relate to myself and that I open myself up to all fears and the symptoms of the unknown" (*O Globo*, December 6, 1980).

In *The Bare Hours*, the male trinity consists of Renato, Gregório, and Diogo. Telles has remained loyal to her objective to interpret the world from the female point of view, and even the male characters are seen through feminine eyes:

In my next book, the masculine characters are important because they are seen through the eyes of women. Of course, this does not take away their importance. We, women, cannot see ourselves. Somebody else is seeing us all the time: man, woman, elderly person, child. It doesn't matter. The whole time we are being analyzed by somebody, regardless of their condition. In this book, I consider the masculine characters as important as the feminine characters. Yes, there are masculine characters, but they do not act. It is the women who define these men. This is even a more truthful way of seeing. If the men were to define themselves, they would not be the same. (*O Estado de São Paulo*, May 9, 1987)

Renato is the stereotypical male aggressor who attempts to overpower everybody with his take-charge manner. However, his efficiency, organization, and self-confidence do not win him the affection of his cousin, Ananta. She is one female character who is an enigma to Renato. Alongside Renato Medrado are the three male figures of Rosa's past. Miguel was her first boyfriend, who died unexpectedly. Her husband, Gregório, was imprisoned and later also died. Diogo, the gigolo, is Rosa's third attempt at finding companionship. He was her lover even while Gregório was still alive, but Rosa dismisses him during one of his repeated instances of infidelity. His subsequent disappearance is a continual dilemma for Rosa, who uses the idea of his return as an escape to her encounter of self. In fact, beginning with Rosa's father, who disappeared mysteriously during her childhood, every intimate relationship Rosa has ever experienced with a man has ended in abandonment.

Rosa not only is abandoned by her father and her lovers but also experiences desertion by the women in her life. First, Cordélia announces that she is going to Australia with her elderly lover. With this, Rosa's imminent solitude is insufferable, and Telles focuses on her overpowering fear as Rosa seeks herself even more desperately in the Other. Finally, the asexual Ananta, Rosa's analyst, the ultimate knowing Other, also disappears in a strange metaphysical transformation with a third unknown Other who lives in the same apartment building as Rosa, Ananta, and Cordélia. In terms of companionship, only Rahul remains a constant, but he, just like everyone else in the novel, is unfaithful to Rosa. Rahul divulges Rosa's weaknesses and the inconsistencies of her character, stripping her of the rationalizations that prohibit her from discovering the hidden truths that would aid her in the process of self-acceptance. Instead, Rosa is left alone with her fear of the unknown.

Unable to withstand the loneliness, Rosa is incapable of anything productive, from the organization of events of her life to harnessing the creative and analytical powers of forging a true identity. This is reflected in the circular movement of her interior monologues, in the constant struggle to run from herself, in the fear of looking at herself in the mirror:

I could use up all the saliva in the world explaining it and I would not have explained it; what is interesting is hidden. I Know Everything, my mother's magazine used to say. Now I answer, I know nothing. I know that the body belongs to the Devil because it was after I broke off with my body that I got close to God.

[Eu poderia gastar todo o cuspe do mundo explicando e não explicava, o que interessa está escondido. Eu Sei Tudo, dizia a revista da mamãe. Respondo agora, eu não sei nada. Sei que o corpo é do Diabo porque foi depois que rompi com meu corpo que me aproximei de Deus. (50)]

There are both continuity and progression between the female characters of Telles's first two novels and Rosa and Ananta of *The Bare Hours*. However, unlike her spiritual sisters in *The Marble Dance* and *The Girl in the Photograph*, Rosa is older, more experienced, and aware that the enigma of life lies in the space beyond her body, beyond her lover, beyond her profession, even though she is unable to position herself effectually to reach and penetrate that space. Overwhelmed by fear, Rosa, as artist, would agree with Telles, as writer, that:

My only power is that of the word. I want to develop this up to the last drop that is not bitter. The truth is this: I am the fear, but I work with this fear. What's important is this, to work this fear with courage. I have moments of great courage; it is often necessary to treat the body like a horse that does not want to jump the fence, the whip. I whip myself, I beat myself, I try to overcome this fear and sometimes I win. (*O Estado de São Paulo*, January 9, 1983)

Throughout the novel, Rosa's story is juxtaposed with a simultaneous discourse on the status of women in the 1980s. Although each character has a particular point of view to advance on this subject, the composite depiction for Brazilian women is far from encouraging. As a point of departure, Rosa comments on the bonding between mother and daughter, positing that although her mother is her best friend, she does not believe that women like other women: "I agree but women hate women, still that climate of competition like the king reigning amongst the odalisques. Only that story about mother and daughter works. Sometimes" [Concordo mas mulher detesta mulher, ainda aquele clima de competição com o rei reinando entre as odaliscas. Só essa história de mãe com filha é que funciona. Às vezes (17)].

Rosa also admits to having cried at childbirth when she gave birth to a daughter, instead of a son, supposedly because girls suffer more than boys. On the subject of abortion and modern technology's ability to discover the sex of unborn children, Rosa mimicks the concerns of many feminists who are disturbed by the fact that, given a choice, many women still reflect their husbands' desires to have sons rather than daughters. Rosa observes that if this attitude were allowed to influence decisions on the desirability of unborn children, abortion could conceivably endanger the future of womankind.

Ananta responds to Rosa's concerns from a more rational stance: "The revolution is recent, Rosa. Think of a test tube that was shaken up, the water is murky but when the deposit settles, the water will clear up again. Even though the bottom is full of blood" [A revolução é recente, Rosa. Pense num tubo de ensaio que foi sacudido, a água fica turva mas quando o depósito se assentar essa água vai ficar límpida. Ainda que o fundo seja de sangue (122)].

Rosa counters Ananta's argument with a critique of the power structure that has corrupted woman's purity. Whereas women's choices are more open-ended today than they were in the past, self-knowledge is essential for resolving one's personal preferences. Rosa manifests the anguish of the process of self-acceptance when she admits that she was happier with herself back in the days when she was like:

those ancient women who used to embroider, [that] seemed so calm making pillows, rugs. Or was it all make-believe? Wouldn't the women be happier embroidering themselves? . . . I used to like myself, Ananta. Now I hate myself . . . to live with me, myself, horrible.

[aquelas antigas mulheres que bordavam [que] pareciam tão calmas fazendo almofadas, tapetes. Ou era tudo fingimento? As mulheres não seriam mais felizes se bordassem? . . . Eu gostava de mim, Ananta. Agora me detesto . . . conviver comigo mesma, horrível. (122)]

Ananta responds calmly, as has Telles in numerous interviews, that those who like to embroider would certainly be happier doing so, but each woman must make her own choices.

In response to Rosa's and Ananta's views on the issues of selfhood, Renato offers the reader the masculine critique of the feminist movement. He views Ananta's nonthreatening behavior as an acceptable form of feminism, and he even falls in love with this nonaggressive feminist who is involved with organizations that give social and legal aid to the large numbers of needy women who are victims of the social transformations women have experienced over the past several decades. Renato's behavior suggests that the feminist movement is worthy of male support, as long as it stays within the limits of charitable acts and does not challenge the power structure.

Ananta's puzzling disappearance from her apartment one afternoon spurs Renato into beginning an extensive search for her. Always preoccupied with the traffic and her watch, Ananta is reminiscent of the city and its impact on our contemporary lifestyle. Renato imagines that Ananta's association with various feminist groups might even be responsible for her disappearance. The narration of Renato's interaction with the police department, his frustration at not being able to locate Ananta, and the declaration of his feelings of love for her conclude the novel in the fashion of a detective story that has no resolution.

Closure is unobtainable for Rosa, Cordélia, Ananta, and even Renato who is left with only the faintest hope of finding Ananta. In the last analysis, solitude, even among the many inhabitants of the colossal São Paulo, is inescapable, and sanctuary from solitude is only momentary, as we learn from Telles in the novel: "What is dark becomes clear until the clarity returns to darken again; clarity is fleeting" [O que é escuro fica claro até que o claro volta a escurecer de novo, a claridade é provisória (206)].

If the agony of the process of writing is a metaphor for darkness, as Telles has sometimes described it, then we can equate clarity with the interplay between the explosion of language and recurrent themes that constitute *The Bare Hours*. Caio Fernando Abreu has appraised Telles's contribution in a slightly different fashion: "The first lady went crazy. God bless her: this craziness is sacred" (88). Whether Telles's most recent novel is seen as another fleeting moment of clarity in her brilliant literary career or as the result of the craziness of creativity, the result is indeed sacred.

NOTES

1. Except for quotes taken from *The Girl in the Photograph* [*As Meninas*], all translations are Susan Quinlan's and mine.

2. See Cristina Ferreira Pinto's discussion of the character Virginia in *The Marble Dance* [*Ciranda de Pedra*] in *O Bildungsroman feminino: quatro exemplos brasileiros*, 109-50. Pinto establishes Virginia as an exception to this rule in Telles's fiction.

3. In a personal interview with Lygia Fagundes Telles in São Paulo in July 1988, she described the protagonist of her next novel as an aging woman, alone and uncomfortable with the process of growing old, and insinuated that some of the protagonist's concerns were autobiographical in nature.

REFERENCES

Primary

Novels by Telles

The Girl in the Photograph. Trans. Margaret A. Neves. New York: Avon Bard, 1973.
As Meninas. Rio de Janeiro: Nova Fronteira, 1985.
As Horas Nuas. Rio de Janeiro: Nova Fronteira, 1989.
The Marble Dance. Trans. Margaret A. Neves. New York: Avon Bard, 1986.
Ciranda de Pedra. Rio de Janeiro: José Olympio Editora, 1954.
Verão no Aquário. Rio de Janeiro: Editora Nova Fronteira, 1984.

Interviews

"Histórias do desencontro: uma atmosfera de conflitos." Interview. *Última Hora*, July 17, 1958.
Medina, Cremilda. "Cinco escritoras questionam a literatura feminina." *O Estado de São Paulo*, November 26, 1978.
"Microentrevista com Lygia Fagundes Telles." Interview. *Folha de São Paulo*, July 6, 1983.
Paiva, Fernando, and Sílvio Cioffi. "Lygia: Meu único poder: a palavra." *O Estado de São Paulo*, January 9, 1983.
Priami, Elda. "Lygia Fagundes Telles." *O Globo*, December 6, 1980.
Ribeiro, Leo Gilson. "Lygia, imortal." *Jornal da Tarde*, May 9, 1987.
Schulke, Evelyn. "Lygia Fagundes Telles voltou a escrever um livro atual." *Jornal da Tarde*, December 7, 1973.

Secondary

Abreu, Caio Fernando. "As horas de Lygia." Review of *As horas nuas* by Lygia Fagundes Telles. *Isto É*, June 21, 1989.
Alcoff, Linda. "Cultural Feminism versus Post-Structuralism: The Identity Crisis in Feminist Theory." *Feminist Theory in Practice and Process*. Ed. Micheline Malson, Jean F. O'Barr, Sarah Westphal-Wihl, and Mary Wyer. Chicago: University of Chicago Press, 1989, 295-326.
de Lauretis, Teresa, ed. *Feminist Studies, Critical Studies*. Bloomington: Indiana University Press, 1986.
Pinto, Cristina Ferreira. *O Bildungsroman feminino: quatro exemplos brasileiros*. São Paulo: Perspectiva, 1990.
Wasserman, Renata R. Mautner. "The Guerrilla in the Bathtub: Telles's *As Meninas* and the Eruption of Politics." *Modern Language Studies* 19.1 (1989): 50-65.

The "Imaginative Space" of Medbh McGuckian

Susan Porter

> . . . Ireland—
> you have lived and lived on every kind of shortage.
>   You have been compelled by hags to spin
>   gold thread from straw and have heard men say:
> "There is a feminine temperament in direct contrast
>   to ours, which makes her do these things."
>   (Marianne Moore, "Sojourn in the Whale," 90)

Because she is an Irish Catholic from the North of Ireland, Medbh McGuckian is surrounded by insistent reminders of her national and religious identity. She belongs to a minority within political boundaries that in themselves cordon off a minority in Ireland as a whole, so that characterizing her by national and religious identity at the same time entails a certain marginalization. In addition, as a woman and an Irish poet, her sexual identity makes her a member of a group that has been doubly marginalized, by gender and by nationality, in the British literary tradition. In an early poem, "Champagne," the threat of marginalization, that is, of having one's identity characterized with an exclusionary aim, is alluded to indirectly: "[T]heir fictions hurt us" (*Flower Master*, 34). One possible response that such a "hurt" can elicit is hinted at in a more recent McGuckian poem, "Harem Trousers": "A poem dreams of being written / Without the pronoun 'I'" (*On Ballycastle Beach*, 43). The self that writes is hidden or even denied. The poem and the poet are identified as simply a space of writing, and McGuckian's poetry frequently seems to produce this effect of having no identifiable voice or no source in an individual consciousness. In the last stanza of "Harem Trousers" (43), for instance, the "room"

> . . . speaks of morning,
> A stem, a verb, a rhyme,
> From whose *involuntary* window one
> May be expelled at any time,
> As *trying to control a dream*

Puts the just-completed light to rest.
(43; emphasis added)

While McGuckian at times seems to "dream" of writing that approaches an "involuntary" expression of the dreamworld or the subconscious and in which consciousness, identity, and intention play little part, at the same time, her poetry clearly involves careful and conscious craftsmanship. Of course, she could not publish her work without the intention of developing an identifiable public voice.

With an awareness of the difficulties that place and identity pose for Northern Irish poets, Gerald Dawe writes about "the imaginative space necessary for their art to thrive"; this space, he continues, "may be the miniaturized world of Medbh McGuckian's domestic interiors" or "Frank Ormsby's increasingly mythic patch of unreasonable Belfast" (85). While Dawe is sensitive to the problems that Northern Irish poets encounter in speaking from their native "space," the very words *miniaturized, domestic,* and *interior* that he uses to characterize McGuckian's work demonstrate that he is less sensitive to the marginalization that customary gender distinctions produce. The terms that he uses here traditionally signal that the particular place from which she writes is feminine, further implying that it is to be regarded as less serious and significant than Ormsby's exterior, "mythic," and masculine "patch of . . . Belfast." A second critic, Michael Allen, alludes more directly to McGuckian's gender when, toward the end of a long and largely sympathetic review of *Venus and the Rain*, he alludes to McGuckian's "almost ideological insistence on the feminine" (60) but adds reassuringly, "In suggesting that Medbh McGuckian is 'almost ideological' in her feminine point-of-view I am not suggesting that she is a feminist" (63). The responses of these two critics to her poetry, for all their sympathy, illustrate some of the attitudes that have worked to inhibit, devalue, or even silence women poets. From Allen's review, one can extrapolate the particular double bind that a woman poet faces: to insist upon the difference of her gender identity serves to brand her voice as marginal, while to assert its centrality is seen as a threat from an "ideological" margin to the centrality of a largely male poetic tradition.

In his analysis of "Ode to a Poetess," a poem that explores the possibility of a male muse for the "Poetess," Allen shows his sympathetic awareness that the absence of women poets from a recognized tradition in itself makes it more difficult for contemporary woman poets to be heard. His analysis concludes: "[A]re we not, as readers, being asked to acknowledge (rationally) the provisional nature of the response we should make to an imaginative enterprise for which precedents are as yet in short supply?" (64) The search for a way into a poetic tradition, then, is one aspect of McGuckian's effort to develop a public poetic identity, that is, to find an audience and to make her voice heard. In "Ode to a Poetess," McGuckian makes direct reference to the search for a female poetic tradition in which to place her work. More indirect references to the dearth of precedents for the female poet's work and the marginal status of her progenitors pervade McGuckian's poetry, although, for the most part, they refer on the literal level to more traditionally feminine arts and only obliquely to women's poetry.

Such oblique reference in itself places McGuckian in the tradition of poets like Emily Dickinson and Marianne Moore, in whose writing a bolder claim for the poet's own work is often hidden behind a more traditionally feminine, self-effacing facade. Furthermore, it recalls Dickinson's dictum to "[t]ell all the Truth but tell it slant" ("1129," 506). Dickinson's poetry has clearly had an influence on some aspects of McGuckian's work, particularly her employment of vivid, dense images, whose logical connections are frequently obscure and whose semantics can be opaque. Placing oneself in such a tradition, however, entails at least two difficulties for McGuckian. First, the tradition itself is often seen as a marginal one because female. Second, "telling it slant" can mean telling it from such an oblique angle that meaning becomes nearly obscured, resulting in a quality in McGuckian's work that Allen refers to her "gnomic tendency" (Allen, "Foetal Tissue," 36).

The very qualities that enable a poet like McGuckian to challenge a central tradition also serve to exclude her from it by muting the impact of her potentially subversive message. In the face of such an impasse, one function of sympathetic criticism is to unearth or create a critical method that will make her work more accessible to the contemporary reader. In the case of McGuckian, there are similarities between her poetry and the writings of the contemporary philosopher Jacques Derrida (whose prose often seems as difficult to decipher as McGuckian's poetry) that suggest that some of his concepts could be fruitful tools for undertaking an analysis of her poetry. Derrida is concerned with questioning self-identity by insisting that difference inhabits even the most supposedly stable identity. His work endeavors to unsettle systems of thought in which the logic of binary opposition often functions to stabilize the identity of one of a pair of opposing terms by drawing an absolute line of distinction between the two and then by privileging one term over the other. In terms of gender difference, for instance, identifying a thing as masculine or feminine initiates a whole chain of associated opposition such as rational/emotional, active/passive, domestic/public, or central/marginal. At the same time, Derrida, along with such feminist writers as Hélène Cixous and Julia Kristeva, insists that differences like male/female or central/marginal must not, or cannot be, collapsed. Therefore, a critical approach based upon Derrida's notions about language and meaning can reveal ways in which McGuckian's poetry finally evades the particular obstacles to communication with a wider audience that she faces as a Northern Irish woman poet.

For instance, the first poem in *The Flower Master*, "That Year," presents challenges to the reader common to many of the poems in this volume. It opens: "That year it was *something to do with your hands*" (9; emphasis added), a phrase that has been used by generations of self-deprecating craftswomen. These "somethings" are then described in the poem's four stanzas. For example, stanzas two and three constitute a short catalog of seemingly unconnected childhood activities, chosen with no apparent plan, randomly, as a dreamy young girl might choose them herself:

I remembered as a child the red kite
Lost forever over our heads, the white ball
A pin-prick on the tide, and studied
The leaf-patterned linoleum, the *elaborate*

Stitches on my pleated bodice.
It was like a bee's sting or a bullet
Left in me, this mark, this sticking pins in dolls,
Listening for the red and white
(9; emphasis added)

The only obvious connection between the seemingly aimless play alluded to in
these stanzas and the other activities enumerated in the poem—such as playing
with rings or dying one's hair—is that they are all the typical occupations of a
little girl who is developing into an adolescent. However, at the center of the
poem is a short phrase, "elaborate / Stitches," that points toward a thematic
connection between these seemingly disparate activities. The patterns of stress
and alliteration that connect "studied and "Stitches," "patterned" and "pleated"
in the two lines linked by the phrase "elaborate / Stitches" alert one to a second
level of reference besides the obvious one of the typically feminine art of
stitchery: reference to the elaborate patterns of alliteration, stress, and interior
rhyme in each stitch of the poem itself.

The complex web of references in this poem, involving female craftsmanship
and poetry, immaturity and adulthood, the past and the present, is, in the termi-
nology of Derrida, "disseminated" throughout McGuckian's poetry. Barbara
Johnson's cogent definition of Derrida's use of the term in her introduction to
his book, *Dissemination*, makes the connection between McGuckian's poetic
technique and Derrida's concept of disseminated meaning even plainer: "*Multiple
coherences*. The unit of coherence here is not necessarily the sentence, the
word, the paragraph, or even the essay. Different threads of *Dissemination* are
woven together through the bindings of grammar . . . 'theme' . . . anagram-
matical plays . . . etc." (xvii). Johnson writes further of Derrida's methods:
"Because Derrida's text is constructed as a moving chain or network, it constantly frustrates the desire to 'get to the point'" (xvi). Similarly, this poem
frustrates the desire to "get to the point" by leading the reader in contradictory
directions, for to see an allusion to poetic patterns in "elaborate / Stitches" both
connects the poet with the feminine domestic arts, such as needlework, and
separates her as a poet (traditionally seen as a more masculine occupation) from
them. Furthermore, one can begin to see in the trace of a masculine/feminine
opposition that underlies the differences between poetry and stitchery the role
that dissemination plays in McGuckian's effort to escape the female poet's
particular disabling pitfalls. Derrida's disseminated meaning and refusal to come
"to the point" arise from his desire to escape two kinds of authoritative determination of meaning. The first involves his refusal to grant the supposed intentions
of the source of an utterance the status of the primary authority for determining
the meaning of that utterance. The second involves the conclusions of binary,

either/or logic in which a thing must be, for example, either central or marginal, male or female, domestic or political, private or public.

Both aspects of Derrida's notion of disseminated meaning are even more clearly illustrated in another poem in this volume, "The Seed-Picture." A close reading of the poem reveals that the oblique reference to disseminated meaning in the title is no coincidence but that dissemination is characteristic of this poem as it both reflects upon and illustrates McGuckian's poetic technique. For instance, McGuckian writes in lines that refer not only literally to the process of making a seed-picture but also figuratively to the process of writing her poems:

> The *seeds dictate their own vocabulary*,
> Their dusty colours *capture*
> *More than we can plan*,
> The mould on walls, or jumbled garages,
> Dead flower heads where insects shack . . .
> I only *guide them not by guesswork*
> *In their necessary numbers*,
> And *attach them by the spine* to a perfect bedding,
> (23; emphasis added)

The playfulness and the letting-go of authorial domination of meaning in these lines are in the spirit of Derrida's concept of dissemination. The authorial presence is humble, almost self-effacing; and one of the principal subjects of the poem, its reflection on poetry and language, is very nearly hidden, concealed within the description of the seed-picture. In Derrida's term, references to poetry are disseminated among the more obvious references to a simple craft. The creative process in either case, poem or craft, is characterized as guiding the placement of found objects. It entails participation in discovering meaning rather than striving for complete individual mastery of either form or meaning.

References to poetry and language and to "seeds" or "seed-work" in the sense of both the seed-picture and the potential for growth and transformation of seeds are "woven together through the bindings of grammar . . . 'theme' . . . and play" (*Dissemination*, xvii) in this poem: "vocabulary," "plan," "jumbled," "guide," "guess-work," "necessary numbers." Furthermore, all of these terms refer and are connected not only to poetry and the seed-picture but also to children—the quintessential work and production of women:

> The children come to me like a dumb-waiter,
> And I wonder where to put them, beautiful seeds
> With no immediate application. . . . the clairvoyance
> Of seed-work has opened up
> New spectrums of activity, beyond a second home," (23)

The phrase "the clairvoyance / Of seed-work" ties together the references to children and seeds, for "clairvoyance" evokes the anticipation of results with which "seed-work," in the usual sense of planting, is undertaken as well as the anticipation of adulthood that is always a part of child rearing. Then the references in lines 7-14, quoted before, to escaping from a plan and going beyond a plan, "jumbled," "only guide," "guesswork," indicate the limits of predictability and control involved in "clairvoyance" about the child's future form or "application." Children, indeed, "dictate their own vocabulary." In all senses of seed, then, and particularly as it connotes children, the work involved is partly guiding and partly knowing that what one guides is ultimately beyond any "author's" control and contains within it, from the beginning, elements that were not subject to her desires or intentions. The woman who is also a poet is prepared by her experience in the female world of "children," "home," "jumbled garages," and "seed-work" for the realization that words and arrangements of words also "capture / More than we can plan" (23) and carry within them the seeds of many and varied meanings.

The poem illustrates as well the second aspect of dissemination: the implications that questioning binary logic and interpretive authority has for the role of the woman poet. The two passages quoted from the first stanza have characterized traditional woman's work as, in some sense, liberating for the poet, but stanza two opens by alluding to aspects of "seed-work" that imply constraint rather than liberation. Bonding and continuity in these lines imply links with ancestral craftswomen but also with contemporary women who are not artists, such as Joanna, whose portrait the seed-picture is, and both sorts of bond with other women here are associations about which the contemporary artist can very well feel ambivalent:

Was it such self-indulgence to *enclose* her
In the border of a grandmother's sampler,
Bonding all the seeds in one continuous skin,
The sky resolved to a cloud the length of a man?
(23; emphasis added)

In the first stanza, "the clairvoyance / Of seed-work has *opened up* / *New* spectrums of activity, *beyond* a second home" (emphasis added). The final word of the poem is "liberation," but here at the beginning of the second stanza, at the very center of the poem, we find that the "bonding" within the seed-picture also implies "enclosure." "Bonding" is, at the same time, a reference to human bonds and to artistic form. The "continuous skin" can be read as self-reference to the poem and its form, which contain the portrait of Joanna and, inescapably, a portrait of the author herself—a poet with her roots in a feminine and domestic artistic tradition. Therefore, it can also be read as a reference to the poet's bonds with contemporary women and her artistic ancestors, whose aesthetic activity has traditionally been limited to domestic arts like the "grandmother's sampler." While the sky, with its suggestions of limitless aspiration, is reserved for men, women are enclosed in a traditional female space.

At the same time as these female bonds imply being enclosed within a domestic sphere, however, the various enclosures, both the poem and the picture as well as the female heritage, retain within them the seeds of liberation:

For the vicious beige circles underneath.
The single pearl barley
That sleeps around her dullness
Till it catches light, makes women
Feel their age, and sigh for liberation. (23)

As a work written about women by a woman, its subject, author, and even its audience can serve to relegate it to a female enclosure even while the poem's pattern of imagery is evoking the possibilities of opening up, splitting, and breaking out of externally imposed limits that fuel the desire for liberation expressed in these final lines of the poem. The seeming impasse between the poem's contradictory effects and implications is alluded to indirectly in the line that immediately precedes the lines about liberation: "the vicious beige circles underneath," which refers literally to Joanna's eyes in the portrait, but clearly in the context of the poem the reference to "vicious . . . circles" has wider implications. This impasse between "liberation" and "enclosure" can be seen as a refusal, like those in Derrida's philosophical writings, to "get to the point"; it is symptomatic of the artist's desire for a "liberation" that is also a "bonding" and thus of a desire similar to Derrida's to escape binary logic.

As we have seen, through the "seeds" of meaning that are disseminated throughout the quite conventional syntax and homely diction of this poem, the poet, like Derrida, questions certain kinds of poetic authority, those that are derived either from membership in an authorized poetic tradition or from poetic genius as a quasi-divine source of truth or meaning. Paradoxically, McGuckian could be seen to be claiming a different and characteristically female "authority," characterized by the letting go of claims about originality and finality. The humility in her refusal to claim mastery of meaning evokes and obliquely criticizes its opposite: the hubris characteristic of high modernist poets, such as Eliot and Pound, who think of themselves as members of a great tradition, or of Romantic poets, such as Shelley, who see themselves as fountains of poetic genius. The title poem of her first volume, "The Flower Master" (35), alludes to this paradoxical claiming and relinquishing of authority in the contrasting chains of association that "flower" and "master" carry with them: the traditionally feminine connotations of vulnerability and submissiveness with flowers and the traditionally masculine connotations of authority and power with mastery. In the body of the poem McGuckian again presents a reassuring front of traditional feminine artistic humility and social decorum by choosing flower arranging, origami, and needlework as her ostensible subjects, but this decorum is being undermined even as it is presented by the poem's erotic and sensual flower imagery. By combining feminine arts and eroticism and utilizing the cultural disorientation created through references to Japanese arts and custom, without having explicitly to defend her world, McGuckian subtly suggests that the reader view the female sphere from a different perspective. McGuckian takes a further risk in making this suggestion in the form of a seduction. The poet seduces the reader with her vivid and sensual imagery into metaphorically "stooping" to see the world from her viewpoint in the poem's play on the female artist as that stereotype of melodramatic fiction, the seductress.

Forcing the "special guest" to stoop to her "low doorway" in "The Flower Master" (35) is only one of the plays on mastery and sexuality disseminated through McGuckian's three published volumes of poetry. In stanza two of "Champagne" (34), for example:

> The mayflies' opera is their only moon, only
> Those that fall on water reproduce, content
> With scattering in fog or storm, such ivory
> As elephants hold lofty, like champagne. (34)

If the elephant's lofty ivory is seen as a phallic image, it can represent the illusion of a single source and arbiter of meaning and thus evoke the phallocentrism and phonocentrism whose claim to mastery of meaning is the target of Derrida's attack on binary logic. In actuality, of course, the tusks are not a source of anything; they have no reproductive function. The contrasting image of the mayflies' reproduction serves to deconstruct the illusion of a single, knowable origin of meaning or truth. Because it is, at the same time, a female (related to the "moon") image and a male image of insemination ("reproduce . . . scattering . . . ivory . . . like champagne"), sexual difference is contained within it; and because the mayflies' seminal potency exists only in their random "scattering," their reproduction is a paradigm of dissemination.

In *Venus and the Rain*, McGuckian's second volume of verse, authority, meaning, and difference are addressed more obliquely, but perhaps even more extensively, than in the *Flower Master* poems. In the two "Venus" poems, in particular, McGuckian further explores an earlier allusion in "The Theatre" (*Flower Master*, 42) to the sun as a source of illumination set in opposition to another source of illumination, the "bad light, on the stage of the summer theatre" (42). McGuckian's placing poetry and the light of the theatre in opposition to Socrates and the illumination of the sun in this poem is most obviously another reply to Plato's exclusion of poets from his Republic. When it is read in conjunction with the references to alternative sources of illumination (the sun, the moon, Venus, and the stars) in "Venus and the Sun" (9), the possibility also arises that McGuckian's reopening the quarrel between poets and philosophers has certain affinities with Derrida's critique of Plato in *Dissemination*. In this critique, which is part of his continuing attempt to "deconstruct" binary, either/or logic, Derrida moves from simply disrupting an old system of interpreting texts to advocating another system based upon what he calls "undecidables," a term defined most succinctly in *Positions*: "[I]t has been necessary to analyze, to set to work, *within* the text of the history of philosophy, as well as *within* the so-called literary text . . . certain marks . . . that *by analogy* . . . I have called undecidables . . . that can no longer be included within philosophical (binary) opposition, resisting and disorganizing it, *without ever* constituting a third term" (42-43).

In her earlier work, McGuckian was still working largely within the traditional binary sun/moon, male/female, Socrates/poet, philosophy/literature oppositions. The poet's remaining within the framework of these oppositions has the effect of virtually forcing her to be defensive in writing about her position as a woman poet in order to assert the value of both facts about her identity: poet and woman. In the "Venus" poems McGuckian is attempting to avoid this trap by finding a third term or pole of interpretive authority in an effort to undermine binary logic.

There is no doubt that one theme in "Venus and the Sun" is a reallocation of authority:

> The scented flames of the sun throw me,
> Telling me how to move—I tell them
> How to bend the light of shifting stars:
> I order their curved wash so the moon
> Will not escape. . . .
> . . . .
> I am the sun's toy—because I go against
> The grain I feel the brush of my authority, (9)

It seems obvious as well that the authority in question is the interpretive authority of a woman poet. Venus tells the sun's rays: "How to bend the light of shifting stars: / I order their curved wash so the moon / Will not escape" (9). Venus and the sun are poles of authority that, at the same time, oppose and influence each other. This indirect influence of Venus (whose dense atmosphere is highly refractive) on the sun's illuminating rays is a poetic substitute for the traditional passive reflection of the sun's rays by the moon, a reflection that becomes a feminine image in some contexts and a symbol of poetic imagination in others. The moon and its symbolic associations are not excluded from the poem, but female creative symbolism is relocated in the third heavenly body, Venus.

In the two "Venus" poems McGuckian makes use of both astronomical facts about the planet Venus and mythic associations with the Roman goddess of love. In "Venus and the Rain" (31), the goddess is more human, and her body and the "body" of the planet become a complex of birth symbolism and, by extension, of any human creative potential:

> On one occasion, I rang like a bell
> For a whole month, promising their torn edges
> The birth of a new ocean (as all of us
> Who have hollow bodies tend to do at times): (31)

The tangled imagery of planet and woman becomes almost indecipherably dense in the final stanza of the poem:

> I told them they were only giving up
> A sun for sun, that cruising moonships find
> Those icy domes relaxing, when they take her
> Rind to pieces, and a waterfall
> Unstitching itself down the front stairs. (31)

The final line of the poem is especially disorienting as it mingles references to the female body and the planet Venus with references to stitches and stairs, but to anyone at all familiar with McGuckian's poetry, neither sort of imagery is without precedent. The associations between stitchery and poetry (stiches) have already been explored. The reference to "front stairs" recalls "our low doorway" in "The Flower Master," both images referring to a threshold, a way in and a way out of buildings, of the female body, and ultimately of McGuckian's poetry.

Threshold imagery forms another cluster of references that is disseminated throughout her poetry. For instance, in "The Sofa" (*Flower Master*, 19): "I begin to scatter / To a tiny to-and-fro at odds / With the wear on my threshold." In "The Soil-Map" (*Flower Master*, 29-30) the metaphorical association among poetry, the house, and the female body is further elaborated. This poem abounds with threshold images, of loci that, like Derrida's "hymen" ("I drink to you as Hymenstown"), are "neither the inside nor the outside" (*Positions*, 43), such as "your two-leaf door," "the petalled steps to your porch," "your splendid fenestration / Your moulded sills" (29), "Hymenstown" (30).

In "Venus and the Rain," the threshold, the hymen, the place that is neither inside nor outside and thus serves as one of Derrida's "undecidables," is also the place of "unstitching," unraveling in the sense of interpreting or discovering meanings. "Unstitching" also suggests retracing the stiches, unpicking their orderly arrangement, and thus becomes a paradigm of the ending as a return to the beginning. The "to-and-fro" over the threshold then becomes a metaphor that includes the undecidability of beginnings and endings, a particular form of the undecidable that also manifests itself in "Venus and the Sun":

> But the stars are still at large, they fly apart
> From each other to a more soulful beginning;
> And the sun holds good till it makes a point
> Of telling itself to whiten to a traplight—
> This emptiness was left from the start; with any choice
> I'd double-back to the dullest blue of Mars. (9)

The undecidability of beginning and ending or of origin and end is consistent with Derrida's notion of "differance" (implying both *difference* as the producer of meaning and an endless *deferral* of identity between meaning and utterance). In contrast to the stars, points of illumination that "fly apart" and thus epitomize disseminated meaning, the sun, which is called a "traplight" in "Venus and the Sun" and causes a "burn" in "The Theatre," represents the dream of self-identity, meaning without difference or, in the terms of these poems, light without necessary shadow. "Venus," in both of her forms, with all of their implications becomes for McGuckian a complex symbol of "differance." In "Venus and the Rain," the planet itself cannot be viewed without difference.

> White on white, I can never be viewed
> Against a heavy sky—my gibbous voice
> Passes from leaf to leaf, retelling the story
> Of its own provocative fractures. . . . (31)

Unlike the moon, Venus appears brightest from earth not when it is completely illuminated but in the "gibbous" phase, when more than half, but not all, of the planet is illuminated. Observation of the deflection of the sun's light in this phase, however, led to both accurate and inaccurate scientific speculation. The deflection of light by heavy cloud on Venus aided Galileo in confirming the heliocentric theory while it also led observers to believe that Venus, which is, in reality, too hot for water to exist, was a planet where it rained continually. The gibbous phase of Venus, as an "undecidable" entity, epitomizes "differance," the mixture of truth and error, light and shadow in an endlessly changing form whose very changeable, unstable form made it possible for close observers to see a reflection of some part, but never all, of its real physical form.

The effect of introducing Venus as a symbol of "differance" or undecidability into the sun/moon opposition is that it enables McGuckian to avoid the inherent tendency in binary logic to privilege one term (in this case male or female) of an opposition over the other. By using the planet Venus as a symbol of "differance," McGuckian has also taken advantage of the certain association that her readers will make of the name "Venus" with the Roman goddess of love. When one becomes aware of both associations, an Apollo/Venus/Diana triad becomes another part of the web of dissemination in McGuckian's poetry. In the planetary, imagery Venus, the most brilliant planet seen from earth, because her heavy atmosphere deflects the majority of the light rays that reach it, takes its place along with the sun, the source of illumination, and the moon, a passive reflector of illumination. In the mythical allusions, Venus, a goddess associated with love and sexual union, joins Diana, the chaste huntress goddess associated with sexual abstinence, separation, and even hostility. When Venus becomes a "third term" in the sun/moon, Diana/Apollo dyad, the sexual union implied by the goddess of love aspect of Venus and the separation implied in the mythic associations between Diana and the moon transform the relationships among the three into an image that acknowledges and even insists upon both difference and unity and, most important, repudiates complete domination or submission by any of the three figures. All of the old associations with the sun/moon dichotomy—male and female, source and reflection, reason and imagination—are thus disrupted by the third term.

With such poems as "The Seed-Picture" and "The Flower Master," McGuckian has made a place for herself in a female artistic tradition by acknowledging her debt to the female heritage of domestic artistry. Her poetry pushes readers to look at this kind of work again and revalue it, free of prejudice against the domestic, the hidden, and the anonymous. Then in her "Venus" poems McGuckian combats the marginality that identification with a specifically female tradition threatens, by converting the sun/moon opposition into a triad in which each term serves to unsettle any easy identification of simple oppositions. The Venus imagery, with its allusions to illumination that comes as a result of light deflected, recalls again Emily Dickinson's "tell it slant," along with the attendant danger that such an indirect approach to communication can obscure meaning entirely. The speaker in some of McGuckian's more difficult poetry, such as the "Venus" poems, sometimes seems to come close to this sort of solipsism, but if the poems are read again with an awareness of words and images that recur throughout these two volumes, their obscurity recedes, and patterns of dissemination become apparent that enable the poet to assert difference in a way that need not form a new binary opposition between male and female, the center and the margin, or truth and imagination. Nor need her poems become a victim of the domestic interior/political exterior opposition into which assessments such as Gerald Dawe's would place her work. If her poetry unsettles bipolar opposition per se, it also unsettles this one and in doing so moves inevitably into the political sphere.

In Irish poetry with its always present consciousness of the potential conflict between English influence and Irish heritage, any disruption of the center/margin opposition must be salutary. Read with this literary and political tradition in mind, one can immediately see a new web of reference disseminated in McGuckian's poetry. In "The Seed-Picture," the "vicious beige circles underneath" that must be broken to achieve "liberation" from all of the vicious circles of her tradition take on a specifically political and historical meaning, as does forcing others to "stoop" to view events from a new angle in "The Flower Master." The enclosures in "The Seed-Picture" and "Mr. McGregor's Garden" (*Flower Master*, 14) imply political (the pale, Northern Ireland) and geographical (the island itself) enclosures as well as domestic ones; and, as my epigram from Marianne Moore's poem "Sojourn in the Whale" suggests, conceiving of the English/Irish difference in terms of a male/female opposition is not without its precedents. McGuckian's "miniaturized . . . domestic interiors" (Dawe, 85) escape into the public and political world and even far beyond to the cosmic expanse of the Venus poems. The imagery of planets and stars in these poems creates for McGuckian the sort of "imaginative space" necessary not only for Irish poets to thrive but for an Irish woman poet to speak to her political and cultural situation without, at the same time, having her poetic voice distorted or its implications limited by a too easy identification with contemporary factional or ideological debates.

After the cosmic expansion of McGuckian's imaginative space in the "Venus" poems, her most recently published volume, *On Ballycastle Beach*, seems at first a drastic contraction to the domestic sphere and, even more insistently, to the female body. However, this seeming contraction can also be seen as a form of expansion, for publication. Furthermore, the wider acceptance and acclaim that her work has received have opened up for her a more secure space from which to write about the experiences common to women. She has been able to escape the exclusion from the center that is so often the fate of writers who insist upon the importance of their identity as a member of any group regarded as marginal, and she has achieved this more central position by establishing a public identity that speaks through her poetry. One of the references in *Ballycastle Beach* that explicitly works to establish the centrality of the female experience is her identifying the "I" of "Sleep School" with "Pomona . . . Goddess of gardens" (15). Pomona here plays a role similar to Venus in McGuckian's earlier work in establishing a woman-centered body of mythological figures. As a goddess of fruitfulness, Pomona is a figure of female creative power. The goddess is referred to directly only in one poem, but references to female fruitfulness are disseminated in the poetry in this volume through chains of reference to apples and to the female body, particularly to breasts. For instance, in the poem, "Apple Flesh," she writes: "[M]y body tasted like apple flesh" (13). The allusion to breasts here is subtle but with an awareness of the many other such references in this volume, it is unmistakable. This passage alludes, in part, to the nurturing aspect of women's breasts, and at the same time it also evokes an identity between the female human body and the rest of the natural world, an identity McGuckian has referred to explicitly in a recent interview: "Men don't like to think of themselves as mammals; we have to" (McCracken, 20).

In the *Ballycastle Beach* poems, female creativity is associated more with a creative force in nature than with the craftsmanship tradition that was a central point of reference in the *Flower Master* poems. However, as in that volume, a certain humility is still a part of McGuckian's claims for poetic creation; for female creativity here does not imply romantic originality or quasi-divine creation *ex nihilo* so much as it does a remaking of what was already existing in another form. One example of the way that nature, creativity, and the female body are associated in McGuckian's recent poetry is the chain of reference in "Sea or Sky?" (17):

> The athletic anatomy of waves, in their
> Reflectiveness, rebirth, means my new, especially
> Dense breasts can be touched, can be
> Uplifted from the island of burned skin
> Where my heart used to be, now I'm
> Seeing eyes that, sea or sky, have seen you. (17)

Women's breasts are more traditionally associated with the nurturing function of motherhood and the womb with creativity, but the reference to breasts here is not so much to the nurturing aspect of milk as it is to the liquidity that identifies mother's milk with the fluidity of the sea. Thus, this passage pictures human creativity as participation in natural processes rather than as domination of the natural world. The woman and the sea merge into one another; the reference of "rebirth" could be to either body. Then, in the last line of the poem, the sea, in its turn, merges imperceptibly into the sky, that same limitless sky that was reluctantly ceded to males in "The Seed-Picture."

In addition to the allusion in this passage to female participation in the creativity connected with natural processes, the connectedness implied in the merging of one element or one body into another is for McGuckian a further way out of the opposition that defines feminine space as domestic and private, secluded from the world—in the words of Hélène Cixous: "inside a domesticated outside" (565). The way out of the domestic enclosure in "Sea or Sky" is somewhat different from that in the Venus poems, but water and the sky again refer us back to the natural world of those poems, as does the reference to a female mythological figure in the Pomona poem. In the first stanza of "Sea or Sky," the sun is an "echo of light . . . Improperly burning," whose recognizable outline is obscured by "the moisture-laden sky I should be working in" (17). Again, the blurring of any sharp distinction between sun and sea, light and water, emphasizes connection over distinction. The sun's light (with all of the associations it has had in McGuckian's poetry) is absorbed rather than deflected. The expanse of the sky (so often gendered masculine) is also absorbed into the expanse of the (traditionally, feminine) sea. McGuckian's imagery of the body is connected with the cosmic domain of the Venus poems through its association with disseminated references that begin inward with the female body and extend outward from clothing to houses, then to natural phenomena (especially the sea and water), and ultimately to the sky and the sun.

The political aspect of place is even more subtly alluded to than its natural aspect in the *Ballycastle Beach* poems. Ballycastle Beach itself is a threshold place between Ireland and the world beyond the "French-born sea" (59), and in one of the last poems in the book, "The Dream-Language of Fergus" (57), dissemination itself is given a specifically Irish political cast:

No text can return the honey
In its path of light from a jar,
Only a seed-fund, a pendulum,
Pressing out the diasporic snow. (57)

Ireland, too, has suffered from a diaspora because of the pressures, economic and political, to emigrate that have prompted so many to leave the Irish homeland. At the same time that emigration entails leaving a homeland, however, it also leads to the dissemination of elements of that place into new lands. Without being conquerors, emigrés have sown seeds of Irish culture over a wide part of the world—particularly through the power of Irish word craft, of poetry.

The poem just quoted also alludes even in its title, "The Dream-Language of Fergus," to a further sense in which her poetry in this last volume could be seen as a wider expansion of her imaginative space: further into the realm of dream and the subconscious. One of the central oppositions with which this volume plays is that between sleep and waking or between the subconscious and the conscious mind:

So Latin sleeps, they say, in Russian speech,
So one river inserted into another
Becomes a leaping, glistening, splashed
And scattered alphabet
Jutting out from the voice, (57)

Sleep and dream enter language and poetry as one river joining another. In McGuckian's poetic domain, "A poem dreams of being written" (43), and dreams and "dream-speech" both precede and inhabit poetry (29). In "The Dream Language of Fergus," the not "I" of both the subconscious inner world and the natural outer world inhabits the "I" of individual identity and consciousness. The dream poem, written without "the pronoun I" (43), works paradoxically both to question and to establish McGuckian's unique poetic identity.

McGuckian's approach to creating woman's language has much in common with that of feminist language theorists like Hélène Cixous and Julia Kristeva in that she has moved beyond unsettling conventional oppositions toward asserting the value of those elements so often placed on the feminine half of the gender divide, oppositions such as feminine dream/masculine consciousness or feminine irrationality/masculine logic. She has said of her poetic language: "I don't think my language is irrational; it has its own logic which may be the opposite of men's since we are of the opposite sex" (McCracken, 20). McGuckian's "dream-language," the "leaping, glistening, splashed / And scattered alphabet" (57) through which her woman's logic speaks, has much in common with Julia Kristeva's notion of the "non-speech, of a 'semiotics' that linguistic communication does not account for," a "semiotics" that commonly finds metaphoric expression as "milk and tears" (174) or, in terms of the disseminated references in McGuckian's poetry, the breast and water (rain, snow, rivers, the sea). In Kristeva's writing, the nonverbal has both mystical and natural maternal connotations; she finds this association between motherhood and the breast and mysticism exemplified in the phenomenon of the Christian mystic "who assumes himself as 'maternal'" (162). Similarly, McGuckian has made explicit associations between the sensual and erotic dimension of her poetry, and its religious or spiritual implications: "[I]f I'm erotic, maybe *agape* has a lot to do with it" (McCracken, 20). In this same interview, she further associated eroticism and Christian love with dreams of childhood and innocence: "People say the first seven years of life are the source of all poetry, and my state then was centrally Christian. I was baptized and sinless; dreams go back to perfection and that's what you aim for" (McCracken, 20).

McGuckian's spirituality is grounded in the female body, in the dreamlike, erotic, and yet innocent immediacy of the relationship between a child and its mother, which is suggested, above all, by the references to the breast disseminated through this most recent volume of her poetry. Without explicitly referring to any obvious traditional Christian symbolism, then, McGuckian's poetry places itself in a tradition of Christian mysticism and thus reveals its source in the remaining aspect of her poetic identity or her imaginative space: her Catholicism. Thus, once again, McGuckian has both retained her differences, her Irish nationality, her female sex, and her Catholic religion and also associated herself with a central tradition, the tradition of maternal imagery associated with mysticism. Whether the mystic be Protestant or Catholic, male or female, such imagery has traditionally been used to express the nearly inexpressible, and in McGuckian's poetry it becomes a foundation for poetic experimentation at the frontiers of linguistic communication where language shades into nonlanguage and private systems of symbolism shade into solipsism. Thus, her most recent poetry further explores the divides of traditional binary reasoning that would oppose speech to silence, consciousness to dream, public to private, male to female. In opening up this space of exploration, McGuckian's body of published poetry has provided her with both a distinctive voice and an attentive audience. She has acquired the two essential aspects of a poetic identity and of an authoritative poetic voice: the private imaginative space and the public poetic persona that make it possible for the poet both to engage in such experiments and to rely upon a sympathetic audience for her work.

REFERENCES

Allen, Michael. "Barbaric Yawp, Gibbous Voice." *The Honest Ulsterman* 77 (1984): 60-63.

————. "Foetal Tissue." *The Honest Ulsterman* 72 (1982): 36-43.

Cixous, Hélène. "Sorties: Out and Out: Attacks/Ways Out/Forays." Trans. Betsy Wing. *Contemporary Critical Theory*. Ed. Dan Latimer. Orlando, FL: Harcourt Brace Jovanovich, 1989, 558-78.

Dawe, Gerald. "Checkpoints: The Younger Irish Poets." *The Crane Bag* 6.1 (1982): 85-89.

Derrida, Jacques. *Dissemination*. Trans. Barbara Johnson. Chicago: University of Chicago Press, 1981.

————. *Positions*. Trans. Alan Bass. Chicago: University of Chicago Press, 1981.

Dickinson, Emily. "1129." *The Poems of Emily Dickinson*. Ed. Thomas H. Johnson. Cambridge: Belknap, 1955, 506.

Kristeva, Julia. "Stabat Mater." *The Kristeva Reader*. Ed. Toril Moi. New York: Columbia University Press, 1986, 160-86.

McCracken, Kathleen. "An Attitude of Compassions." *Irish Literary Supplement* 9.2 (1990): 20-21.

McGuckian, Medbh. *On Ballycastle Beach*. Oxford: Oxford University Press, 1988.

————. *The Flower Master*. Oxford: Oxford University Press, 1982.

————. *Venus and the Rain*. Oxford: Oxford University Press, 1984.

Moore, Marianne. "Sojourn in the Whale." *The Complete Poems of Marianne Moore*. New York: Macmillan, 1981, 90.

Writing the Woman-Subject: Marguerite Duras, from Theory to Fiction

Anne-Marie Gronhovd

In economics and politics, the female body has been a colony that has served the social corpus, the family space, and the organization of reproduction. Learning to comprehend and deconstruct these perfectly coherent systems in their relation to power, through their internal contradictions, brings forth an understanding of how women are perceived and perceive themselves in such a structure. This structure often enough is based on the relationship between gender and power and the multiple discourses, sex- and gender-related, that allow power to be exerted and created. Power has no stable and linear set of rules by which it abides. It functions from top to bottom and bottom to top. Power originates from scattered nerve cells that transmit energy at different degrees of inequality. The definition of power given by Michel Foucault articulates its inherent existence at all levels:

Relations of power are not in a position of exteriority with respect to other types of relationships (economic processes, knowledge relationships, sexual relations), but are immanent in the latter; they are the immediate effects of the divisions, inequalities, and disequilibriums which occur in the latter, and conversely they are the internal conditions of these differentiations; relations of power are not in superstructural positions, with merely a role of prohibition or accompaniment; they have a directly productive role, wherever they come into play. (94)

The deconstruction of the coherent systems of power that constrain women within traditional constructs creates a space where the woman-subject can be written. Literature written by women offers the intersection and articulation for the social, political, cultural, and literary necessities involved in the performance of the written text, be it critical literary theory or fiction. The performance that takes place in the writing and the reading of the woman's body traced by the mind of that same woman creates her identity as she invents herself. Women have had to move from the isolation of the solitary learner to the collective experience of knowledge shared. This has allowed them to requalify and reformulate the gender roles they play. Such an invitation better defines the localized and unstable character of power and transforms the roles played in the arena of gender representation in the interest of a greater social justice. By situating women and minorities at significant levels of representation (instead of non-representation, negativity, and absence), the relationship of victimization is upset so that the very rules of the game performed by the victimizers and the victims are exposed and consciously recognized by these performers. Power will never be abolished; thus, the question remains as to how one disrupts the logic of the unbalanced production of power and how one transforms the automatic mechanisms that trigger it. Once these movements are understood, one can participate actively within them and operate from (rather than passively comply with) them.

Feminism or one would prefer to think, feminisms, undertaken in a post-modern[1] light, allow us to reformulate the becoming-woman or becoming-man that is at the core of the postmodern vision. Feminisms (in the plural) seem preferable because they produce an articulation for different generations[2] of feminism, challenging the notion of identity and creating space for diversity among women in their historical and social times.

To explore such issues is to question ideologies versus genders. The contemporary literary endeavor has defined feminism and the feminine in new terms that construct a new subject: woman (and not Woman, avoiding thus the notion of category and escaping the confines of a unified concept of women that rejects diversity among women themselves). In texts of Marguerite Duras, Luce Irigaray, and Julia Kristeva, to cite only the authors analyzed in this chapter, woman is not only a new literary subject but a new active performer in culture and politics: a maker, not a consumer. The Other has become a speaking subject who is still searching for a language of her own. Her language has been a male language, and thus her representation has been a nonrepresentation in a *non-lieu* as it is produced in terms of negativity, nonpresence, and, above all, lack (void). How does one operate within this language that functions in the order of the symbolic? The mere fact of thinking or speaking is already recognizing unconsciously the intrinsic presence of the Law of the Father. This law is present in language as constructed by man and operating in Freudian and Lacanian discourses. The deconstruction and subversion of this universal language open a space of our own.

French feminists such as Julia Kristeva or Luce Irigaray, for instance, have worked within this deconstruction to produce new terms for this space. Julia Kristeva sees this space as potential. It is dynamic with its own pulsions, functioning much like the unconscious; even when it is static, it remains ephemeral. She defines it as the semiotic "chora" (from the Greek term). The "chora" exists always already superimposed on the symbolic. Kristeva explains it as a space where the preoedipal comprehension begins, a locus or the mother's body that releases the energy necessary to interact with the social:

The *chora* is a modality of signifiance[3] in which the linguistic sign is not yet articulated as the absence of an object and as the distinction between real and symbolic. We emphasize the regulated aspect of the *chora*: its vocal and gestural organization is subject to what we shall call an objective *ordering* [*ordonnancement*], which is dictated by natural or socio-historical constraints such as the biological difference between the sexes or family structure. We may therefore posit that social organization, always already symbolic, imprints its constraint in a mediated form which organizes the *chora* not according to a *law* (a term we reserve for the symbolic) but through an *ordering*. (*Revolution*, 26-27)

This concept of the "chora" is important as "she" prearticulates the notion of heterogeneity that is often repressed in language. Toril Moi explains in her introduction to the readings of Kristeva in *The Kristeva Reader* that without the understanding and the recognition of the "chora," we could not clear space for contradictions, disruption, and the unconventional: "It [*chora*] constitutes the heterogeneous, disruptive dimension of language, that which can never be caught up in the closure of traditional linguistic theory" (13).

Luce Irigaray offers another analysis of the deconstruction of the patriarchal discourse, the master discourse, very different in its questioning of the symbolic but similar in its objective of a woman-subject. In *Speculum of the Other Woman*, she shows how the concave perspective of the womb is perceived as an empty space (here, empty does not mean devoid of meaning but rather potentially ready to define the feminine in terms that would not be stifling to woman's psyche and social experience) reversed to a convex perspective, a sort of convex mirror. Irigaray uses, as she proceeds to explain it, the metaphor of the speculum as an instrument which penetrates to inspect and also reflects a concave image. Here the author deconstructs the patriarchal discourse which postulates a subject that has only the potential of reflecting what is speculating, thus making this speculation a narcissistic endeavor in masculine terms. Irigaray goes on, showing how this man-made language cannot represent femininity or women because it inspects and speculates itself and its own vision from the very first moment it penetrates the semiotic space that it violates:

Therefore, the feminine must be deciphered as inter-dict [*interdit*] within the signs or between them, between the realized meanings, between the lines . . . and as a function of the (re)productive necessities of an intentionally phallic currency, which, for lack of the collaboration of a (potentially female) other, can immediately be assumed to need *its* other, a sort of inverted or negative alter ego—"black" too, like a photographic negative. (*Speculum of the Other Woman*, 22)

In the light of feminist views that do not slip recurrently into the paradigms of masculine/feminine opposition as produced by male thinking, we can move from theory to fiction in a space where women invent themselves and emerge as new subjects independent from the persona the Other (in this occurrence, man) used to trace. The writings on Marguerite Duras are inscribed within a political and sexual pursuit that embraces the poetic. Marguerite Duras disrupts and reformulates the unified self by rejecting the "truth" and the "reality" of phallocentric discourse. On her path we are led to deconstruct the facets of the Western mind and hegemony, experience the process of mutation, and create new forms based on a progressive collective intelligence.

Marguerite Duras[4] explores an *écriture* of difference. Her style is not linear; her texts trace fragmented, interwoven patterns of lost moments and identities.

Through the pain of memory her heroines reach out for a becoming-woman:[5] becoming subject, a subject that emanates from her own feminine desires and not a powerless embrace of the masculine-built female paradigm. Duras is political in the sense that she takes the reader on an intellectual journey the nature of which is to upset the status quo in light of unity and disruption, allegiance and rebellion, stability and subversion.

Duras patiently reconstitutes throughout her novels a female subject whose body has taken on metonymically the shattered aspect of the textual body. In *Hiroshima mon amour* (1960), which is both text and film, the bodies inscribed in the text or the screen experience painful and violent mutations. The text opens with images of the mushroom of the explosion of the Bomb, the upper parts of the bodies of what seems to be a couple making love, and the shattered members of the victims of the Bomb. These fragments of the past (the Bomb in 1945) and the present (the love story of a French actress and a Japanese man in Hiroshima in 1957) are superimposed in the constant present of Hiroshima in the summer of 1957; they make the text and the film possible. This work is composed of suspended narratives of the past love story of the Frenchwoman and a German soldier in occupied France, in the city of Nevers, integrated into the making of the principal narrative, the making of *Hiroshima mon amour*. The "dis-membering" of the bodies and the scattered fragments of the story in Nevers in 1944 enable the Frenchwoman to "re-member" as she reassembles the pieces of the puzzle.

In Nevers, she experienced a state of madness as her German lover was shot:

Madness, it is like intelligence, you know. One cannot explain it. Like intelligence. It comes on you, it fills you and then you understand it. But, when it leaves you, one cannot understand it at all anymore.

[C'est comme l'intelligence la folie, tu sais. On ne peut pas l'expliquer. Tout comme l'intelligence. Elle vous arrive dessus, elle vous remplit et alors on la comprend. Mais, quand elle vous quitte, on ne peut plus la comprendre du tout. (58)]

By resurrecting Nevers, she resurrects her self. In Nevers her body was much like in a state of siege. The intelligence and madness of comprehension of the tragedy of life and death in her love affair with the German soldier and in the Hiroshima bomb are so violent that they can be resurrected only in fragments. These fragments come back after fourteen years with the fear of universal oblivion. "Re-membering" is like creating fiction. It cannot be the same once it is re-created, just like the documentary retracing Hiroshima after the Bomb, ironically revealing its false montage as the set is dismantled when the French actress goes back to shoot her last scene. However, the subversion of reality, the illusion that everything in *Hiroshima mon amour* is fiction, is qualified by the city of Hiroshima. In Hiroshima each word has an echo, a second gesture, a second meaning. Hiroshima is a multitude of universal givens: eroticism, love, and tragedy. The Frenchwoman reconstructs her self as she gives sense to her life in Hiroshima within the dimensions of her ordinary story. The Frenchwoman who was "[y]oung in Nevers. And then also, one time, crazy in Nevers"

[Oui. Jeune à Nevers. Et puis aussi, une fois, folle à Nevers (57)] reconstructs her past within the dimensions of history. In *Hiroshima mon amour*, Duras shows how the historical and ideological relationship between past and present creates a space in which mutations are comprehended as the dislocated bodies expel voices, haunting echoes of the past. Within the dislocation and the echoes, the heroine composes her self as she is starting to remember her German lover less. The awareness, as terrible as it is felt by the woman, brings forgetting and announces the emergence from madness:

Nevers that I had forgotten, I would like to see you again tonight. I set you on fire every night for months while my body set itself on fire at his memory . . .
    While my body sets itself on fire already at your memory. I would like to see Nevers again . . . the Loire [river that goes through Nevers].
    Charming poplars of the Nièvre [province]. I give you to forgetting.
    Four penny story, I give you to forgetting.

[Nevers que j'avais oublié, je voudrais te revoir ce soir. Je t'ai incendié chaque nuit pendant des mois tandis que mon corps s'incendiait à son souvenir . . .
    Tandis que mon corps s'incendie déjà à ton souvenir. Je voudrais revoir Nevers . . . la Loire.
    Peupliers charmants de la Nièvre je vous donne à l'oubli.
    Histoire de quatre sous, je te donne à l'oubli. (117-18)]

The state of madness experienced by the Frenchwoman in *Hiroshima mon amour* also pervades in *The Ravishing of Lol V. Stein* [*Le Ravissement de Lol V. Stein*] (1964). In *The Ravishing*, Duras exposes the colonizing of women through marriage. Lol must marry John Bedford (whom she barely knows) to show she recovered from her broken engagement with Michael Richardson, her husband-to-be: "Lol was thus married, without wanting to be, in the way that was convenient to her, without her having to go through the savagery of a choice" [Ainsi, Lol fut mariée sans l'avoir voulu, de la façon qui lui convenait, sans passer par la sauvagerie d'un choix (31)]. Whether Lol desires Bedford or not does not enter into account. He has laid eyes on her once, she seems like a good catch, and he decides to invade her space without any further question: "John Bedford asked for her hand in marriage without ever having laid eyes on her again" [Jean Bedford la demanda en mariage sans l'avoir revue (30)]. This body is being ravished and violated piece (eyes) by piece (hand) like a colony.
    Lol's family and friends had encouraged her to "make an effort." She "became a desert into which a nomadic faculty had thrown her in the endless pursuit of what? One did not know. She did not answer" [elle était devenue un désert dans lequel une faculté nomade l'avait lancée dans la poursuite interminable de quoi? On ne savait pas. Elle ne répondait pas (24)]. "To make an effort" means probably for her entourage that woman cannot let her body become sterile like the "desert." Much as the land and culture of a colony are exploited for their natural resources to the benefit essentially of the invader (the colonizer), Lol's body must serve the social corpus by marrying and reproducing within the family space. The role of women is often defined in terms of their potential to be mothers, this being for them a "human condition," as Adrienne Rich ex-

plains: "But the patriarchal institution of motherhood is not the human condition any more than rape, prostitution, and slavery are. (Those who speak largely of the human condition are usually those most exempt from its oppressions—whether of sex, race or servitude)" (33). Lol is this calm force, silent and subterranean, in the woman who still lives inside her. Her body, mind, and desires have been capitalized by others for her reproductive female potential. In the *Ravishing of Lol V. Stein*, Duras denounces the brutality of appropriating someone else's body, the violated innocence of a life and the injustice of imposing on victims the rules of the colonial system. Colonization is a political terrorist act that causes ravages for both the body and the mind; its victims become physically sick and mentally dysfunctional (Duras's mother was a victim of colonization in Indochina). Lol had to subvert the same repressive system by re-creating for herself the events of the ball where she witnessed the encounter of her lover, Michael Richardson, with Anne-Marie Stretter and their departure that same night. Lol never was given the time to feel the pain: "She was paying now, sooner or later, that had to happen, for the strange omission of her pain during the ball" [Elle payait maintenant, tôt ou tard cela devait arriver, l'étrange omission de sa douleur durant le bal (24)]. The absence, the hiatus that followed this important event in her life, can be filled only by her own understanding of it. Thus, she repeats the scenes of the lost moments, fragmented as they come, through memory. She composes a montage in which she decolonizes the self constructed by others, to replace it with her own self, emerging from the "ravishing" (in the Durassian sense, which intends to be double: rapture, ecstasy but also violent abduction and rape) of which she was a victim.

Knowing that the feminine is never represented in masculine discourse, Duras's writing participates in the semiotic realm, always superimposing it on the symbolic, making these realms coexist like the unconscious and the conscious. She writes between signs, between signifiers reconstructing the woman-subject from the perspective of difference. The reader is led to position herself or himself in a purely contextual rapport. As Trista Selous suggests: "In Duras's later work the figures are whittled down to a point where they almost lose their capacity to appear as 'being like us,' their desire being constructed entirely in the context of the structural relations around which the text is built, usually a sexual relation" (238).

Duras acknowledges desire through the female sexual difference so strongly present, although estranged by the male characters, that it is always able to appear as a subtext. This subtext has no control over itself; it pulsates in the other text, in the language of love and pain. Desire is in the Other, sacred in its original nature and violent in its difference. In *The Man Seated in the Hallway* [*L'Homme assis dans le couloir*] (1980), Duras's *écriture* draws the making of the woman-subject, even more than in *Hiroshima mon amour* and *The Ravishing of Lol V. Stein*. The author upsets traditional sexual identity in an introductory embracing of indistinct bodies. Although identified as "man"—Il [He]—and "woman"—Elle [She]—the couple is never assigned specific feminine or masculine roles. Furthermore, the woman's body and the body of the land surrounding them are reflected in specular images. The presence of this desiring body appears and disappears like the sliding forms of a palimpsest in the written bodies of the unidentified characters and the landscape:

In front of them [man and woman] the large unalterable foothills overlook the river. Clouds come, they move forward together, following each other at a slow regular pace. They go in the direction of the mouth of the river towards the indefinite immensity. Their dull shadows are light, on the fields, on the river.

[Devant eux, les larges vallonnements immuables qui donnent sur le fleuve. Des nuages arrivent, ils avancent ensemble, se suivent à une lenteur régulière. Ils vont dans la direction de l'embouchure du fleuve vers l'immensité indéfinie. Leurs ombres ternes sont légères, sur les champs, sur le fleuve. (10-11)]

As the river opens its mouth on the sea, it reconstructs the body of woman in a reflection that allows the same open dispersion of her sex and the rhythmic movements of life. The curves and the forms of this human body have metonymically shaped themselves on the landscape that lies beside her:

She would have started to move again. She would have been slow and long to do it in front of him who watches . . . I see that now she lifts her legs and spreads them apart from the rest of her body. She does it the same way she assembled them, in a conscientious and distressing movement, so strongly that her body, just the opposite of the preceding moment, mutilates itself in its entire length, deforms itself until it reaches a possible ugliness.

[Elle aurait recommencé à bouger. Elle aurait été lente et longue à le faire devant lui qui regarde. Le bleu des yeux dans le couloir sombre qui boivent la lumière, elle sait, vrillés à elle. Je vois que maintenant elle relève ses jambes et les écarte du reste de son corps. Elle le fait de même qu'elle les a rassemblées, dans un mouvement consciencieux et pénible, si fortement que son corps, tout au contraire du moment qui a précédé, s'en mutile de sa longueur, s'en déforme jusqu'à une possible laideur. (11-12)]

The female body becomes the body of the sea disseminating the feminine as multiple in its potential to produce the erotic. Luce Irigaray delightfully comes to mind: "So woman does not have a sex organ. She has at least two of them, but they are not identifiable as ones. Indeed, she has many more. Her sexuality, always at least double, goes even further: it is plural . . . But *woman has sex organs more or less everywhere*. She finds pleasure almost anywhere" (*This Sex*, 28). This powerful, strong, and intense use of the erotic in feminine terms is particularly felt in the Durassian *écriture*. In describing the heroine of *The Man Seated in the Hallway*, the narrator says:

I see the enclave of the sex between the spread lips and that the whole body freezes around it in a burn that augments. I do not see the face. I see the beauty floating, undecided, at the edges of the face but I cannot make it melt down to the point of becoming particular to it. I see nothing but its turned-away oval, the very pure plane, tensed. I believe that the closed eyes should be green. But, I stop at the eyes.

[Je vois l'enclave du sexe entre les lèvres écartées et que tout le corps se fige autour de lui dans une brûlure qui augmente. Je ne vois pas le visage. Je vois la beauté flotter, indécise, aux abords du visage mais je ne peux pas faire qu'elle s'y fonde jusqu'à lui devenir particulière. Je ne vois rien que son ovale détourné, le méplat très pur, tendu. Je crois que les yeux fermés devraient être verts. Mais je m'arrête aux yeux. (12-13)]

Duras gives the act of looking a whole new meaning that does not repress the touch to satisfy the look. The woman's sex does not represent "the horror of nothing to see" (*This Sex*, 25). In man's erotic economy, Irigaray argues that the female sex has been denied its existence, has been shut, denied its own pleasure. Duras thus does not hesitate to revitalize the desire and pleasure of these "spread lips" seen and accepted as the female erotic in action. The use of the word *plane* for the woman's face, in its laconic and precise nature, implies the thinness of the skin, the regularity and flatness of this surface, and evokes an undecided beauty, announcing the contradictions within it. This apparent calmness is disrupted and fragmented by Duras's outsider style. The body of the woman does not remain calm; it becomes violent against itself and the man's body. The violence reflects the actions of the man making love to her and violating the space he is penetrating. The writing pulsates as it mirrors the impure aspects of human nature, which are never able to offer a resolution.

Duras develops a corrosive narrative, a reflection of cruelty much too often part of the place reserved exclusively for women. In fact, the land of *The Man Seated in the Hallway* appears to be Indochina, already raped by multiple foreign hands and minds. The geographic allusion has a political tone that carries throughout the novel. The choice of Indochinese landscape recurring in Duras's work or the images of Hiroshima anguished by the apocalypse of the Bomb are not coincidental. Duras once said one cannot be intellectual if one is not political. The madness of Duras's mother after she bought an uncultivatable piece of land in Cambodia near Kampot, constantly invaded by the sea, to which she lost all her life savings, is superimposed as a subtext in several of Duras's texts. In *The Man Seated in the Hallway*, the sea comes back as an obsession. Eroticized in the confusion of violence, the geography of the scenery and the choreography of the lovemaking are not gratuitous; they trace a political itinerary. As the land brings back Indochina, colonization emerges. As the body of the woman is eroticized but also invaded, rape emerges. These acts both abuse somebody else's space. The body erotic (be it the land's or the woman's) intersects with the body politic. The words, the style subvert the natural order of things as the tension builds into rage, inter-shock but also *jouissance*, all ready to burst:

When he reaches the sex he has a renewal of strength, he crashes in its warmth, mixes himself with his sperm, foams and then he runs dry. The Woman's eyes half-open up without a look and close up again. Green.

[Lorsqu'il atteint le sexe il a un regain de force, il s'écrase dans sa chaleur, se mélange à son foutre, écume, et puis il se tarit. Les yeux de la femme s'entrouvrent sans regard et se referment. Verts. (16)]

In this chapter, theory and fiction are intersected to allow a better comprehension of the reconstruction of the woman-subject from the perspective of difference. Kristeva, Irigaray, and Duras write the woman-subject by exploring estrangement from and by dominant groups. These groups place women, ethnic and racial groups, gays and lesbians in situations of marginality. Marginality is very complex in its justification and representation of "abjection"[6] (the Other, fantasized as source of attraction and repulsion).

For Kristeva, marginality is emphasized as a question of "positionality." Moi shows how "what is perceived as marginal at any given time depends on the position one occupies" (166), thus giving the marginal the knowledge of the symbolic spectrum of law, order, and language. Certain groups are considered "abject" simply because they are placed in a discourse of marginality. Duras's fiction traces intellectually and politically the brutality and pain of marginality and difference. As she writes the woman-subject, she is outside, exploring revolution and liberation, and she is inside, equating writing and freedom. Duras delivers the articulation possible between a linear writing (pure representation of traditional values and ideological norms) and a jagged writing (disorienting representation of our fears, threats, and desires present in the most barbaric aspects of human nature). She opens new forms of expression where differences are suddenly rendered possible. When Duras's heroines create a space between norm and margin, the norm of society and the margin of madness, for instance, they extend boundaries where the political meets the poetic. Their language questions the "language of the Father" as a tool to unify meaning and to make it homogeneous.

The writing of the woman-subject is experienced in theories such as feminism (in the case of this chapter, French feminism) and postmodernism. These theories upset the status quo and have similar objectives in that they fragment and subvert the text, making it infinitely more self-reflexive, and dismantle the beliefs of unity that modernism tried to maintain within its preoccupation with myths and the crisis of temporal concepts. Thus, we can better apprehend how power, desire, and the unconscious function within the literary exchange. Duras fascinates the reader in that particular exchange, which is excessive, unsettling, and magical because it incites to "dis-member" traditional prose, "re-member" the omnipresence of desire, and celebrate the making of the woman-subject.

NOTES

1. One of the definitions of the term *postmodern* is suggested by Ihab Hassan as he describes what a postmodernist attempts to do:

> The postmodernist only disconnects; fragments are all he pretends to trust. His ultimate opprobrium is "totalization"—any synthesis whatever, social, epistemic, even poetic. Hence his preference for montage, collage, the found or cut-up literary object, for paratactic over hypotactic forms, metonymy over metaphor, schizophrenia over paranoia. (168)

2. The word *generation* has the sense that Kristeva gives it: a "signifying space, a both corporeal and desiring mental space" ("Women's Time," 33).

3. Kristeva defines "signifiance" in the following terms: "What we call signifiance, then, is precisely this unlimited and unbounded generating process, this unceasing operation of the drives toward, in, and through language; toward, in, and through the exchange system and its protagonists—the subject and his institutions" (*Revolution*, 17).

4. All translations from the novels of Marguerite Duras are mine.

5. This becoming-woman [*devenir-femme*] does not crystallize around a displacement of femininity as Deleuze, Derrida, and Lyotard capture the new woman, totally "de-centered" and "de-sexualized" (de Lauretis, 24). These male philosophers transgress their "new woman" to another man's Other, another metaphor of a subject. The term becoming-woman here identifies a subject in becoming, not differred in another metaphoric space but rather empowered with social, political, sexual differences recognized as her own.

6. I use the term *abjection* here as Kristeva uses it: "We may call it a border; abjection is above all ambiguity. Because, while releasing a hold, it does not radically cut off the subject from what threatens it—on the contrary, abjection acknowledges it to be in perpetual danger. But also because abjection itself is a composite of judgment and affect, of condemnation and yearning, of signs and drives" (*Powers*, 9-10).

REFERENCES

de Lauretis, Teresa. *Technologies of Gender*. Bloomington: Indiana University Press, 1987.

Duras, Marguerite. *Hiroshima mon amour*. Paris: Gallimard-Folio, 1960.

———. *L'Homme assis dans le couloir*. Paris: Minuit, 1980.

———. *Le Ravissement de Lol V. Stein*. Paris: Gallimard-Folio, 1964.

Foucault, Michel. *The History of Sexuality; Vol. 1: An Introduction*. Trans. Robert Hurley. New York: Vintage Books, 1978.

Hassan, Ihab. *The Postmodern Turn*. Columbus, OH: Ohio State University Press, 1987.

Irigaray, Luce. *This Sex Which Is Not One*. Trans. Catherine Porter with Carolyn Burke. New York: Cornell University Press, 1985.

———. *Speculum of the Other Woman*. Trans. Gillian G. Gill. New York: Cornell University Press, 1985.

Kristeva, Julia. *Powers of Horror: An Essay on Abjection*. Trans. Léon S. Roudiez. New York: Columbia University Press, 1982.

———. *Revolution in Poetic Language*. Trans. Margaret Waller. New York: Columbia University Press, 1984.

———. "Women's Time." Trans. Alice Jardine and Harry Blake. *Signs* 7.1 (1981): 13-35.

———, ed. and intro. by Toril Moi. *The Kristeva Reader*. New York: Columbia University Press, 1986.

Moi, Toril. *Sexual/Textual Politics: Feminist Literary Theory*. London: Routledge, 1985.

Rich, Adrienne. *Of Woman Born: Motherhood as Experience and Institution*. New York: Norton, 1986.

Selous, Trista. *The Other Woman*. New Haven, CT: Yale University Press, 1988.

PART III

INNER AND OUTER SPACE

The Mysterious Space of Exile: *Punishable Songs* by Judith Grossmann

Susan Canty Quinlan

> Exile is already in itself a form of *dissidence*, since it involves uprooting oneself from a family, a country or a language. . . . But through the efforts of thought in language, or precisely through the excesses of language whose very multitude is the only sign of life, one can attempt to bring about multiple sublations of the unnameable, the unrepresentable, the void. This is the real cutting edge of dissidence. (Julia Kristeva, "A New Type of Intellectual: The Dissident," 298, 300)

Judith Grossmann is a Brazilian writer of Jewish descent living in a traditionally Catholic and conservative city in the northeast of Brazil. Grossmann, unlike her more universally known contemporary, Clarice Lispector, is studied relatively little both within and without the Portuguese-speaking world. Grossmann's stream-of-consciousness, first-person narratives often mask larger philosophical issues in the disguise of dense, detailed, miniature portraits of the psychological considerations and issues concerning women.

I want to discuss several primary and interconnected issues in some detail in regard to Grossmann's work. The issues are interconnected in ways that lend themselves to specific studies about the status of contemporary Brazilian women's writing. These issues are also connected to theories and discussions of textual interpretation of linguistic exile or linguistic order. Such inquiries ask how it is possible to go about defining terms. When focusing on women-centered readings, does one begin from the author's own experiences, from the text, from the reader, from the country, from religion, or from any one of a dozen or more elusive categories?

I begin arbitrarily by examining the author's experience. I want to look at the work of a professionally relatively unknown and personally mysterious person, Judith Grossmann. Like other critics, I see Grossmann's work as autobiographical and mysterious. The author as the creator of, and a character in, her own text might then be introduced in the following manner:

Judith Grossmann, born in the 1930s and educated in Rio de Janeiro, Brazil, has spent most of her adult life as a Professor of Creative Writing and Literary Theory at the Federal University of Bahia in the city of Salvador da Bahia de

Todos os Santos in northeastern Brazil. In her formative years, Grossmann enjoyed a stay at the University of Iowa's Writers' Workshop and at the University of Chicago, where she obtained a master's degree in English. If I, as a reader, knew little else, I might assume a traditional Eastern European background for this woman, whose name could easily appear in any North American telephone directory.

I could rephrase her biography to read: Judith Grossmann, born to Jewish immigrant parents in pre-World War II Brazil, spent most of her adult life in the Afro-Brazilian culture of northeastern Brazil, where the predominant religious practices center around mystic, matriarchal ceremonies associated with the Yoruban-Bantu-inspired celebrations commonly referred to as *Candomblé*.[1] I would learn that many members of her immediate family are practicing followers of *Candomblé*, some of them even holding church offices.[2]

From either of these two introductions, any reader might assume that not only her specific cultural Jewish heritage but also the beliefs of her current community might influence Grossmann's work and inform the structured worlds present in her narrative fictions.

Concurrently, knowing that the writer follows in the footsteps of the more famous Brazilian-Jewish émigrée author, Clarice Lispector, any reader might assume that Grossmann exiled herself to a foreign country for a period of time before returning to her native Brazil in order to write more clearly about the problems facing women who differ from traditionally acceptable Latin American norms. In this respect, Grossmann also continues in the direction of such Spanish American writers as Luísa Valenzuela, Isabel Allende, Marta Traba, María Luísa Puga, and Elena Poniatowska, among others.

Each version of the preceding biographies is accurate to a point, provocative, and, most assuredly, speculative. All will have some bearing on the textual discussion of Grossmann's full-length narrative, *Punishable Songs* [*Cantos delituosos*], published in 1985. For a larger audience, my discussion will necessarily have to examine contemporary autobiographical literature written by women in a broad context. Here I want to focus on the context of linguistic meanings attributed to home/exile, law/order, or space/place.

In contemporary Brazilian literary studies, as in other literatures in general, much emphasis is given to the use of first-person autobiographical narrative and the relationship among space, place, and the specificity or subjectivity of meaning offered by this technique. By looking at Brazilian literature produced in the 1960s, 1970s, and 1980s, the reader can deduce that first-person narration results from a well thought-out critical position of subversion. Particularly in Brazil, this subversion has been precipitated by repressive governmental policies of extensive censorship. The only way to publish literature, political or not, was to cultivate the subtext to such a degree that the writer produced fictional autobiography, and the reader extrapolated the multiple meanings.

In an article on interpreting first-person narrative as fictional autobiography in the cases of contemporary Brazilian fiction, Nelson Vieira comments that: "an autobiographical narrative divulg[es] more than is intended through a voice which is that of an articulate, reliable, earnest narrator who is nevertheless a most vulnerable and unreliable character. . . . Self-conscious narrators inevitably become cosmically orientated, that is, they seem to make some order out of the chaos of their lives" (139-40). Vieira comes close to redefining traditional understandings of autobiography that explicate the model life where the subject is unified with itself and its environment through narration when he alludes to "self-conscious, cosmically orientated" narrators. He touches on a conceptualization of the unity or disunity of the self in relation to something else. Vieira calls this something else "cosmically oriented."

Vieira further asserts that this search is endemic to the contemporary Brazilian authors' quest for authentic expression and that the search in itself "is a form of literary and social commitment" (140). Can Vieira's description of the "socially committed stance" apply to this discussion of Grossmann's novel or, indeed, to any discussion of Brazilian women's literature of the 1980s? Probably not in the ways traditional critics envision social commitment. Grossmann uses her narration to divide or separate her character from any traditional community, as I later demonstrate. This separation calls into question Vieira's idea of social commitment. I also wonder if it is fair to supply this criterion, especially after the supposed *abertura* (opening) or lifting of the particularly oppressive censorship bans. Given the social strictures common to any theoretical discussion of what constitutes women's literary voices, I assume that Grossmann's texts offer more complex or, at least, less easily understood meanings as opposed to the texts considered by Vieira. What exactly does Judith Grossmann achieve with her first-person narrator in *Punishable Songs,* and how is it different from other political autobiography of the era? As important, how do I interpret a first-person narration that talks about itself in the third person? For these last two questions, I examine exile as a linguistic paradigm. I discuss this in terms of exile from content partly achieved by an exile from form. But where other critics have seen a lack of order from these techniques, I see important elements of ordered chaos.

Exile is a useful construct that enables an understanding of Grossmann's "traditionless" works. Exile also raises questions of specificity. Exile to or from what? Exile by whom? In referring to exile literature and its application to women's writing, I recall statements made by Ester Fuchs in an essay entitled, "Exile, Jews, Women, Yordim, I—An Interim Report," where she outlines the framework that Fuchs herself, as a reader and writer of women's texts, uses to understand meaning when confronted by what might be called "multi-marginalized" women's literature. Fuchs suggests that there is something more, something mysteriously akin to exile that the critic misses when she or he turns only to context: "When contexts become congenial to the examination of exile, it means among other things that one presupposes, or takes for granted, the concept of home. Beyond the exile/home dichotomy there must be another way of thinking about women in literature, feminism in the academy, I, Israelis, Yordim, the Holocaust, the universe, time, home, thinking, questions" (300). I pay particular attention to the concept of home and the space that this paradigm occupies throughout Grossmann's text in order to understand more fully the complex relationships of personal, collective, and fictive histories found in her works.

For Judith Grossmann, as for Esther Fuchs, exile is more than the displacement of a state of mind or a physical location or even a combination of these two ideas. Both Fuchs as critic and Grossmann as writer see themselves and their work as in a state of linguistic exile. The woman writer is exiled by the language she must use in order to name the "thinking" (Fuchs) that characterizes her ability to understand and interpret the world around her.

Linguistic exile, as an example of self-alienation, seems to be a central issue that counters Vieira's argument for Brazilian literature where "the narrator's personalized depiction of the values and beliefs" gives rise to "a clear picture of Brazil" (140) and the values and beliefs of Brazilians. I argue that Vieira's interpretive stance does not function for the woman writer. I also argue that exile links personal, female experiences that go beyond linguistic frontiers.

Linguistic exile negates many commonly held beliefs, such as the traditional concept of home, and forces one to reconsider or to rethink a text. I want to discuss the very rethinking of our spatial notions of a fixed, closed area called home from the vantage point of the linguistic exile of the protagonist, Amarílis, in *Punishable Songs*. In terms of deciphering fictive autobiography, I feel it is barely possible to skim the surface of the particular problems posed by a narrator's attempt to discuss self-identification and self-awareness experienced by a given protagonist. I can only offer extrapolations that may cross linguistic or cultural lines. Although linguistic exile can demonstrate a human (genderless condition), Majer O'Sickey points out the added bind women experience: "Women are exiled from symbolic language that structures law and social conventions, among which perhaps the most significant are parental and marital relationships. For women, exile from language means exile not so much from use of it as from the power to structure and restructure it" (372).

Linguistic exile and the ability to structure or restructure words in order to connote the real experience are the referent I use to examine the effects of abortion, a sustaining metaphor in the story *Punishable Songs*.

Grossmann's autobiographical story chronicles the absences of life, the inability of the lone female character to be seen or heard or understood and to be born or give life. *Punishable Songs* demonstrates the gap between the linguistic sign (woman) and its traditional referent (life). In the novel, Grossmann breaks down the idea that the autobiographical protagonist, the I who experiences, can consciously act without cost to herself and to the other subjects. The narrative, then, becomes an acting out or decoding or refutation of traditional Western symbolic logic.

To begin her literary process, Grossmann reverts to the familiar. Evoking the eighteenth-century classic of German *Sturm und Drang*, Goethe's *Sorrows of Young Werther*, *Punishable Songs* is a psychological diary of the state of mind of a woman who usually, but not always, refers to herself as Amarílis. The narration occurs in the alternating forms of diary entries and personal reminiscences that are juxtaposed without clear breaks. Not quite a coming-of-age novel or a traditional *Bildungsroman*, *Punishable Songs* details daily minutiae: feelings, love, meals, death, smells, children, physical activities, and childhood of this chameleon-like character who often resorts to disguising herself behind other names (Eu/I, Virgília, Glória, Anna).

Continuing with the parallels to German *Sturm und Drang*, the protagonist is an amalgam of both Goethe's Lotte and Werther. She has Lotte's dark, piercing eyes and wears Werther's clothes. Resembling Werther, Amarílis the protagonist's love interest centers around a mysterious married man. With a peculiar twist, this invisible male character, identified by the letter W throughout most of the text, is named only in the penultimate chapter. Of course, his name is Werther.[3]

Although never divulged in a linear fashion, the plot focuses on Amarílis's past and present love affairs, her abortion or abortion(s), pregnancy, the death of W, and the eventual possible death of her child, Roque. Nevertheless, every fact is ambiguous or vague. The events themselves are very often contradictory. The narrative space in which Grossmann recounts the life of Amarílis's child can be used to illustrate this separation from traditional storytelling. Sometimes Roque has died a natural death before birth, sometimes during his early childhood. Sometimes the child is never born. Sometimes Roque has been aborted. Amarílis, as the subject and experiencer of this autobiography, is exiled from the place and space of her own story by the lack of concrete facts in her own recasting of the events.

The novel's ending reinforces the idea of exile from place. *Punishable Songs* concludes with a chapter written in the third person that offers no closure and opens up yet another mystery. This chapter describes Amarílis's salvation as an ascension into heaven or a choice to continue life in a space associated with death. Amarílis's position in heaven, however, is also ambiguous. It is unclear whether or not she actually does die. The ascension into heaven of a living woman re-creates both a mystery of the Roman Catholic Church—the Ascension of the Virgin Mary—and a popular Brazilian northeastern folktale, *The Death of the Good Woman* [*A morte da mulher boa*], often a subject of *cordel* literature.[4] The folkloric renditions of difficult theological concepts are easily accessible to a generally uneducated Brazilian population in versions that stray far from the original theological beliefs. What Grossmann achieves here is the acting out of the distortions of truths: Virgin Mary > Mulher boa > Amarílis.

In this work, Judith Grossmann incorporates more than standard Brazilian folklore. She integrates scholarly literary references with the portrayal of real turn-of-the-century Brazilian literary figures (also noted for their excessive reliance on literary precursors) as characters, the brothers, Artur and Aluísio Azevedo, as well as the Portuguese poet, Antônio Nobre, for example. Curiously, these Brazilian and Portuguese authors all include the exile/émigré experience in their writings. It is not as surprising as it might seem for Grossmann to include references to Goethe's major work of German *Sturm und Drang*. Among the emigrant German-Jewish populations, Goethe was the embodiment of the Enlightenment and of humanistic ideals. He symbolizes all that is desirable in European culture. Many of Goethe's supporters and literary critics were Jewish.[5]

By referring to this German writer by name, incorporating his most famous characters in her work, and placing a new, inverted text on top of a well-known older one, Grossmann creates an external *Doppelgänger* effect. The author effectively achieves an illusion of form that serves as a counterpoint to her allusory spatial constructs.

This illusion/allusion reinforces the previously mentioned idea of woman's separation from symbolic language and text and of what I referred to as exile from the concept of home. Amarílis is not, nor can she be, an icon of assimilation as understood by traditional patriarchal readings. By consciously creating confusion between the I-protagonist and her multinamed others, between Amarílis as Lotte and/or Werther, for example, or by the use of Werther's name for the silent male figure, Grossmann deliberately distorts traditionally ordered assumptions and forces the use of an alternative logic to read the text:

Amarílis is made in Brazil, Amarílis is poor, Amarílis has the richness of poverty, Amarílis is extremely rich. The only thing that Amarílis has is her virgin body, her authentic name is Virgília, the name Amarílis only disguises or misleads her anatomy, her minor major mystery, her Madame and her King.[6]

[Amarílis é made in Brazil, Amarílis é pobre. Amarílis tem a riqueza da pobreza, Amarílis é riquíssima. O único que tem Amarílis é o seu corpo virgem, seu autêntico nome é Virgília, o nome de Amarílis é para disfarçar, despistar sua anatomia, seu menor maior mistério, Madame e o seu Rei. (61)]

Patterning her female character after Goethe's famous male one is only one more way for Grossmann to rethink the state of exile for this character.

Judith Grossmann uses another example of an almost perfect illusory form to capture her "formlessness," that of understatement. Remarking on the stylistics and use of Portuguese, the commentary on the book jacket explains:

She develops her narrative in a minor tone, very adequate for the subtlety of the analyses she makes, and that it would certainly be disturbing if the stylistic oddities would distract from the attention and the sensibility of the reader. The adaptation of form to content, the formal simplicity that is the result of a purifying process, evidence the dominion with which the fiction writer manipulates the instruments of her expression.

[Ela desenvolve a sua narrativa num tom menor, muito adequado à sutileza das análises que faz, e que certamente seria perturbada se estranhezas estilísticas desviassem a atenção e a sensibilidade do leitor. A adequação da forma ao conteúdo, a simplicidade formal que é resultado de um processo de depuração, evidenciam o domínio com que a ficcionista maneja os seus instrumentos de expressão. (*Cantos*, Orelha)]

Again, linguistic exile is reinforced through understatement within the naming process. Amarílis's own names evoke classical, pastoral poetry. These images indicate struggles with virtue, value and, structure. The pastoral images also suggest the contest between the artificial and the sociopolitical. The images suggest ways in which the protagonist discovers how to enter or how to act in a new world. Since the protagonists are at least doubly divided, into their character and that character's disguise, and since traditional considerations or formal organization in terms of the telling of the story about these characters is divided into possibilities of occurrences, it seems to me that the images and the occurrences underscore an alternative reading. I propose that there is a chaotic order or a form to the chaos that comes from the disparate sources of character and narration. If I can discern the form, then Amarílis and I can begin to solve some of these mysteries. As Amarílis herself remarks:

What is it that begins and ends, like a circle, with itself, that is like each one of us? How to handle this unbribable material? How to awaken sympathy for that which is only virgin, perfect, does not stray too far from itself? That which, when it is reached, ought to, by its very existence, eliminate the extrinsic obstacle.

Clothing comes out clean and fresh from washing machines, dryers, irons. The good smell of clean clothes. Heads are washed and combed and within them there is an order that never would be suspected by the outside world. Here is beyond, when each gesture was retaliated in its just measure and effected a justice never before dreamed of on the earth. Like when I made Arthur non-exist. A gesture is necessary in order to cancel that which, accidentally, exists on the face of the earth. Just like the Ninth Symphony ought not exist.

To live each day as if we were eternal, as if time did not exist, precisely because it can exist. Each minute, each second, petals. Just like time was never going to end, like it never brought danger to the skin. Within this long corridor, where time crystallizes itself.

About my name, there can be nothing. A sphere that begins and ends in itself. Not having anything specific in it, it can have everything.

I speak, I write from on high, without touching the paper underneath, touching only the page where this sweet, venomous foil drips, this pen. This was always my way of life, to skim over objects or never to touch them. The reason why I never learned to correctly sweep a floor, cook solid food, wash a piece of clothing.

My hands, that flutter, are crossed between my womb and my breast. Like those people who, even when they walk, keep their arms crossed. Position of the strangest, someone walking with their arms crossed.

To have a sister is something so improbable that I force a sisterhood with these women, in order to break the mystery and the secret. I do not see myself reflected in these mirrors, but I want to live together with these women, to feel the smell of them.

[Como é aquilo que começa e termina, como um círculo, em si mesmo, o que é cada um de nós? Como lidar com este material insubornável? Como despertar simpatia pelo que é virgem, só, perfeito, não vai além de si mesmo? O que, quando atingido, deve, por dever de existência, eliminar o extrínseco obstáculo.

A roupa sai limpa e fresca das máquinas de lavar, secar, passar. O cheiro bom da roupa limpa. As cabeças estão lavadas e penteadas e nelas há uma ordem que jamais se suspeitaria no mundo exterior. Aqui é após, quando cada gesto foi revidado em sua justa escala e vigora uma justiça jamais sonhada na terra. Como quando fiz inexistir Artur. Um gesto é necessário para cancelar o que, por acidente, existe na face da terra. Como a nona sinfonia que não deveria existir.

Viver cada dia como se fôssemos eternos, como se o tempo inexistisse, precisamente para que possa existir. Cada minuto, cada segundo, pétalas. Como se o tempo não fosse acabar, não trouxesse danos à epiderme. Neste longo corredor, onde o tempo se cristaliza.

Em torno do meu nome não pode haver nada. Esfera que começa e termina em si mesma. Nele não havendo nada de específico, pode haver tudo.

Falo, escrevo, sobrelevantemente, sem marcar o papel embaixo, marcando apenas a lauda onde escorre este doce florete envenenado, esta pena. Sempre foi o meu way of life tocar de leve os objetos, ou nem tocá-los. Motivo pelo qual nunca soube corretamente varrer um assoalho, cozinhar alimentos sólidos, lavar uma peça de roupa.

Minhas mãos, que esvoaçam, estão cruzadas entre o ventre e o peito. Como alguém que, mesmo quando caminha, está de braços cruzados. Posição das mais insólitas, alguem que caminha de braços cruzados.

Ter uma irmã é algo de tão improvável que forço uma irmandade com estas mulheres, para romper o mistério e o segredo. Não me vejo refletida nestes espelhos, mas quero conviver com elas, sentir-lhes o cheiro. (226-27)]

Using Jane Marcuse's definition, the voice of the protagonist, sometimes called Amarílis, sometimes Eu/I, sometimes Glória, Anna, or Virgília, represents a "triologic" discourse that challenges the law of the symbolic and does not set up clear-cut polar oppositions, such as black/white, male/female, good/bad (270). Here, for example, *Punishable Songs* presents a discourse that is exiled by virtue of its resistance to, and manipulation of, the gender-dominant tongue (male), the dominant cultures (Mediterranean-Afro-Brazilian), and, to an extent, the dominant religions (Afro-Catholicism). The mysteries occur in reading because the writer does not necessarily try to identify with the power discourse of her male counterparts. Rather, in Grossmann's case, as in the cases of other women writers in multimarginalized binds, she examines the power structure and then rejects the use of it. If this supposition proves valid, it will lead to the already strong argument that women writers do not examine a traditional male power structure in order to assimilate, subvert, or manipulate its use. Rather, women writers reject this power structure and replace it with a different one, a female one. As Julia Kristeva points out, female power structure is less associated with words and more associated with bodily feelings. As such, the structure ruptures the myth of the unified subject:

Art—this semiotization of the symbolic—thus represents the flow of *jouissance* into language. . . . Art specifies the means—the only means—that *jouissance* harbors for infiltrating that order. In cracking the socio-symbolic order, splitting it open, changing vocabulary, syntax, the word itself, and releasing them from the drives borne by vocalic or kinetic differences, *jouissance* works its way into the social and the symbolic. (qtd. in Majer O'Sickey, 369)

As a result of this explosion of the traditional paradigms, we can begin to reread this text, searching for the different structures. It is not that women writers such as Judith Grossmann do not subvert the symbolic; it is that they subvert it in untraditionally disparate ways. In *Punishable Songs*, we can begin to see how Grossmann subverts the home/exile dichotomy. She examines power, refuses to identify with it, and then rejects traditional uses of power through a series of apparent and not-so-apparent contradictions.

To initiate a dialogue about what is or what is not apparent in *Punishable Songs*, I illustrate my point about multiple exile with the following examples taken when Grossmann speaks about herself as a writer in the third person (I/Other). As a way of identifying the contradictions or forms of exile and the mysterious shapes they assume, I have taken Grossmann's own biographical sketch as a point of departure:

She was born in Campos, Rio de Janeiro State, on July 4, 1931, daughter of Joseph and Ethel Grossmann. She studied at the old Philosophy Department of the University of Brazil, currently the Department of Letters at the Federal University of Rio de Janeiro. . . . She began her career as a professor of creative writing and literary theory at the Federal University of Bahia. . . . Her sparse literary production can be found in literary supplements, newspapers, and national and international anthologies. In 1976, she received the Brazilian Prize for fiction.

[(N)asceu em Campos, Estado do Rio de Janeiro, em 4 de julho de 1931, filha de Joseph e de Etel Grossmann. Cursou a antiga Faculdade de Filosofia da Universidade do Brasil, atual Faculdade de Letras da Universidade Federal do Rio de Janeiro. . . . ingressou como professora de criação literária e de teoria da literatura no Instituto de Letras da Universidade Federal da Bahia. . . . Sua produção esparsa pode ser encontrada em suplimentos literários, periódicos e antologias nacionais e estrangeiras. Em 1976, recebeu o Prêmio Brasília de Ficção. (Nota bibliografica)]

Grossmann's biography continues to be marked by binary relationships. She is the daughter of two specific people, but they obviously do not have Luso-Brazilian names. She was born in the rural part of the state of Rio de Janeiro, educated in the city of the same name (country/city). From the more modern city of Rio de Janeiro, Grossmann moved to the more traditional city of Salvador de Todos os Santos, Bahia (liberal/conservative, cosmopolitan/rural). Salvador, because of its relatively unassimilated admixture of Africans, represents a culture foreign to the traditional Luso-Brazilian paradigm of European Catholics and to a more formal Judeo-Christian one. The author is educated at an institution that is no longer in existence, an institution that is renamed (past/present). It changes from the Philosophy Department to the Literature Department (praxis/theory). She teaches creative writing and literary theory (thesis/synthesis). It is as if Judith Grossmann assimilated her knowledge and her craft from all sides of all possible questions. From this vantage point I can begin to assess the writer's awareness of the multiplicity of the mystery she presents in *Punishable Songs*. Grossmann is as aware of the theory as she is of the theoreticians.

Further paradoxical parallels occur when she states that her work is difficult to find in print, the editions are sparse, yet most of her works are internationally published (local/universal). Some works receive prizes (known/unknown, good/bad). I could continue with the lists of oppositions and parallels, and yet I think there is sufficient evidence to refer back to Esther Fuchs's acknowledgment that it is necessary to redefine what is meant by exile from, and exile to, home. In rereading Grossmann's text, looking beyond the surface is very important.

The deductions possible from this small segment of her biography are as ephemeral as the substance of her narrative *Punishable Songs* and yet indicative of both the author's and the character's persona. Just as in Grossmann's own life, Amarílis experiences a separation of the I-narrator from the I-experiencer so that they do not mirror each other. In other words, there is no shared experience of the Other as either an opposite or a negation of self. This is most clearly evident in the use of the actual and fictional literary figures referred to earlier as a part of the structure. This lack of experience that denotes Nelson Vieira's "social commitment" is also seen by comparing the contradictions encountered in juxtaposing the working-class environment of an uneducated Amarílis with her linguistic ability to express pure emotion seen in several previous citations, especially those with interliterary disclosures.

Reading the autobiography in this fashion, one can begin to valorize "mystery" in a nontraditional construct. If there are multiple meanings in the autobiographical text, and these meanings refuse resolution, we have a definite continuum of the unknown or unknowable. If one understands a feminist strategy as permitting no return from exile because return is illusory, I think it is important to recognize that one permanent feature of women as speaking subjects can be illustrated by paradox. Ingeborg Majer O'Sickey defines this idea in the following manner: "Our exile from meaning, our condition of lack, is a permanent feature of our being as speaking subjects and can be alleviated or illuminated only through a double movement that recuperates meaning (understanding the buried life of the semiotic) by voluntary loss of it: that is, an embrace of our linguistic exile" (371).

It is my hope that as a result of this work, the use of intertextuality in women's writing that is not explained by ideological examinations will be examined. What the interior and exterior spaces show in Judith Grossmann's work are not so much the "plight" of being multimarginalized but rather what happens to women's writing when the Cartesian theory is inverted, or even discarded. If we can agree that processes of change are interconnected with the subject's discursive context, we can begin to understand the value of the explosive language and the problems of linguistic exile. This produces what has been previously likened to the nucleus of an atom, or a metaphysical space where there exists equilibrium. How one identifies this space is an ontological problem. It is a question with multiple answers that establishes a metadiscourse for the creative process and that transcends national boundaries.

NOTES

1. For a detailed discussion of *Candomblé* religious practices and their relationship to Brazilian women's literature, see Susan Canty Quinlan, *The Female Voice in Contemporary Brazilian Narrative*, Chapter 5.

2. In 1983, on the recommendation of Dr. Grossmann, I was escorted to a *Candomblé* religious center in the outskirts of Salvador to witness an observance of a celebration of women saints. My escort was a *pai-de-santo* or priest of the temple. This person was also Judith Grossmann's brother-in-law and a professor at the Federal University of Bahia.

3. Although there are clear references to the female characters in works by the Brazilian author, Joaquim Maria Machado de Assis, especially in relation to the name Virgília and to the story of Capitu, I am not going to explore this avenue here.

4. In the tradition of troubadour poetry, this popular Brazilian art form is often sung on market days and is for sale in cheap chapbook form all over the northeast. See Candace Slater, *Stories on a String*.

5. This was true up until the end of World War II—think of the many documented cases of Jews fleeing war-torn European countries with a volume of Goethe's poetry tucked among their belongings. This vision of Goethe would probably have been true for Grossmann and for her emigrant parents upon their arrival in Brazil (conversation with Marjanne Goozé).

6. All translations from the Portuguese texts are mine.

REFERENCES

Broe, Mary Lynn and Angela Ingram, eds. *Women's Writing in Exile*. Chapel Hill: North Carolina University Press, 1989.

Fuchs, Esther. "Exile, Jews, Women, Yordim, I—An Interim Report." *Women's Writing in Exile*. Ed. Mary Lynn Broe and Angela Ingram. Chapel Hill: North Carolina University Press, 1989, 295-300.

Grossmann, Judith. *Cantos delituosos*. Rio de Janeiro: Nova Fronteira, 1985.

Kristeva, Julia. "A New Type of Intellectual: The Dissident." *The Kristeva Reader*. Ed. Toril Moi. New York: Columbia University Press, 1986.

Marcuse, Jane. "Alibis and Legends: The Ethics of Elsewhereness, Gender and Estrangement." *Women's Writing in Exile*. Ed. Mary Lynn Broe and Angela Ingram. Chapel Hill: North Carolina University Press, 1989, 269-94.

Moi, Toril, ed. *The Kristeva Reader*. New York: Columbia University Press, 1986.

O'Sickey, Ingeborg Majer. "Mystery Stories: The Speaking Subject in Exile." *Women's Writing in Exile*. Ed. Mary Lynn Broe and Angela Ingram. Chapel Hill: North Carolina University Press, 1989, 369-94.

Quinlan, Susan Canty. *The Female Voice in Contemporary Brazilian Narrative*. Peter Lang: New York, 1991.

Slater, Candace. *Stories on a String: The Brazilian "Literatura de Cordel."* Berkeley: University of California Press, 1982.

Stern, Irwin, ed. "Judith Grossmann." *Dictionary of Brazilian Literature*. Westport, CT: Greenwood Press, 1988, 148-49.

Vieira, Nelson H. "Fictional Autobiography in the Novel, *Marcoré*: Confessions of a Brazilian Soul." *Luso-Brazilian Review* 20.1 (Summer 1983): 139-47.

Inner and Outer Space in the Works of Esther Rochon

Annick Chapdelaine

It is a known fact that fewer women than men read or write science fiction. The reason for this is quite simple: since science fiction is originally a technological form of literature, one simply has to refer to the doxa that women are not as attracted to science and technology as they are to arts and humanities.

As usual, however, exceptions confirm that women's struggle for recognition in the field of science fiction has proven just as difficult as in other genres of literature or in the sciences, for that matter. The first case in point is that of the founder of science fiction, Mary Wollstonecraft Shelley (1797-1851), author of *Frankenstein or the Modern Prometheus* (1818). That the critics of this famous work of science fiction sought to attribute Mary Shelley's creation to her husband, the poet Percy Bysshe Shelley, is strikingly symptomatic of a steadfast resistance to making room for women writers in a domain where mainly male writers prevail. For instance, her well-known successors, Jules Verne (1828-1905) and H. G. Wells (1866-1946), maintained a stronghold in the field that was never questioned.

As proof that women science fiction writers have difficulty achieving recognition, one simply has to turn back to the 1930s to when one of the greatest twentieth-century female science fiction writers, Catherine Moore, still felt that in order to make headway in the field, she had to resort to a purposely ambiguous signing of her first work, *Shambleau*, by the noncommittal use of her initials, C. L. Moore. One of her contemporaries, Leslie F. Stone, used the same subterfuge, and in the 1970s Alice Sheldon went as far as to change her name to James Tiptree Junior. Thus, just as in the nineteenth century, when women writers like Mary-Ann Evans and Aurore Dupin went under the male pseudonyms of George Eliot and George Sand, their twentieth-century counterparts in science fiction were driven to the same artifices to ensure publication.

In an article entitled "Women and Science Fiction" ["Les femmes et la science-fiction"],[1] Élisabeth Vonarburg, one of Québec's prominent science fiction writers, published a survey in which she examined 200 short stories and twenty novels in order to list the recurrent themes in science fiction works written by women. Her aim was to determine whether or not there exists a distinctly female form of science fiction. Although this question remained unanswered (Vonarburg, 11), the very process of compiling these themes revealed the authors' various concerns as demonstrated by their depictions of how things would be if the world were different. This, of course, is the premise on which science fiction is based.

According to Vonarburg, the subject dealt with most in science fiction written by women is the female body. The starting point for many stories is either a transformation that liberates women from their bodily shackles or, on the contrary, a staging of specific biological constraints. On one hand, stories portray "cyborgized" women—women whose violently mutilated bodies have been rescued by technology and thus made stronger or more beautiful. On the other hand, stories discuss the issue of women enslaved by their bodies. In these narratives, overweight, sick, or pregnant women are portrayed, the latter being given the option of reproducing by means of cloning. Also, many women are offered the possibility of making what seems to be the greatest dream of all come true: having the choice of being either a man or a woman. The relationship established between science and the female body is obviously portrayed as having both positive and negative consequences. The most interesting aspect of this is that the changes it makes in women's personal and social lives open up a wide range of reflections on male and female stereotypes.

Another popular theme in which women authors shed stereotypes is found in the portrayal of societies where there are more women than men or, in extreme cases, no men at all (Vonarburg, 10). Women's assertiveness is also expressed through heroines who have many parapsychological powers, such as telepathy or great intuitive abilities.

Thus, as Vonarburg aptly maintained, the main trend in science fiction written by women is the working out or destruction of female stereotypes. However, at the other end of the spectrum, male stereotypes are not spared either. In a violent indictment of patriarchal societies—Vonarburg counted more than twenty texts on this topic—women writers depict either adventurous heroes who meet unfortunate ends or men who remorselessly destroy the cosmic yin and yang balance and are duly punished for their actions.

Another interesting outcome of Vonarburg's survey is that she noted the various phases through which women science fiction writers pass in order to transcend sexual stereotypes in their work. Their struggle follows the same pattern as the feminist struggle that Julia Kristeva sees historically and politically as occurring in three phases (13-35). There is, however, an initial phase as well, coined by Vonarburg as female alienation (9) and which Elaine Showalter describes as a phase of "*imitation*" and "*internalization*" (13), where the heroes are male characters, and female characters are relegated to secondary roles. In what Kristeva sees as the first phase of the struggle, women demand equal access to the symbolic order (21). This is a period of liberal feminism referred to by Vonarburg as "virile assertion," whereby heroines are given strong male characteristics (9). It is followed by Kristeva's second phase, a period of radical feminism, where women reject the male symbolic order in the name of difference (24). Vonarburg refers to this as the "female assertion phase," where female characteristics are considered positive assets (9). Finally, in the third phase, which Kristeva supports, women reject the dichotomy between masculine and feminine as metaphysical (Vonarburg, 9; Kristeva, 33). According to Toril Moi, this position deconstructs the opposition between masculinity and femininity, therefore challenging the very notion of identity (Moi, 12). Kristeva writes: "In this third attitude, which I strongly advocate—which I imagine?—the very dichotomy man/woman as an opposition between two rival entities may be understood as belonging to *metaphysics*. What can 'identity,' even 'sexual identity,' mean in a new theoretical and scientific space where the very notion of identity is challenged?" (33-34). At this point, as Vonarburg explains, complete human beings begin to appear: men and women who are both rational and irrational as well as strong and sensitive (9). Women science fiction authors have by then achieved Kristeva's third stage (33-34), what Vonarburg calls "sexual integration" (9).

Esther Rochon, the most prominent female science fiction writer in Québec, belongs to this last category. In her works she has, indeed, broken down sexual boundaries. Her main characters are both men and women; sexuality alone does not define their identity. Rochon thus deconstructs the binary oppositions of masculinity and femininity. Having looked at the conclusions drawn by Vonarburg in her exploration of the main themes and phases in science fiction written by women, it is important to examine how they relate to Esther Rochon and science fiction written in Québec.

Women in Québec began writing science fiction during the Québec feminist movement of the 1970s, an offshoot of the Québec Quiet Revolution of the 1960s. During the 1970s, women science fiction writers plunged headfirst into a period when the genre at large was undergoing a complete change. Indeed, speculative fiction had started to replace space opera, hard science, and heroic fantasy, thus making way for both sociological issues and reflections on human nature (Nicot, 28-30). As we have already seen, these were the preferred themes of women science fiction writers. Also, the preceding generations of female science fiction authors at large had come to terms with the issue of establishing themselves in the genre, be it by signing their works or by focusing on the problematics of sexual integration. In 1974 Esther Rochon published her first novel, *In Praise of Spiders* [*En hommage aux araignées*].

To date, Esther Rochon has written six novels, approximately twenty short stories—most of which were published in two collections—and a number of essays on science fiction. She has two characteristics that distinguish her from other women writers in Québec. The first is that she abandoned her formal studies in mathematics in order to write science fiction. The second characteristic is a far more spiritual one. Her interest in Buddhism led her to become a member in 1980 of Montréal's Dharmadhatu, a Buddhist meditation center. On one hand, Esther Rochon challenges a prevalent prejudice against women: their apparent inability to deal with either science or science fiction. On the other, she provides an added dimension to this category of literature. Indeed, the general tendency of science fiction to abide by Western "outer space" standards is enriched in her writing by her exploration of Oriental "inner spaces." This particular blend of scientific precision and metaphysical issues makes for the originality of Esther Rochon's work. In fact, all her writings are constant illustrations of her belief in the complementarity of opposites, a balance between the yin and yang, the male and female forces of life.

This universal duality, a coexistence between what seem to be totally opposed paradigms, is an affirmative movement. It is portrayed as a dance in which Rochon's characters—men, women, mutants or extraterrestrial creatures—adapt to what in Buddhist terms is called "the spontaneity of reality" (Rochon, "Entrevue," 71). It is usually when her creatures are able to live this spontaneity that they discover what is one of Rochon's main themes: the "center," the first step of a quest enabling them to attain inner peace. This is followed by a striving for outer peace and justice.

In an article entitled "Daring to Actualize Utopia" ["Oser actualiser l'utopie"], Esther Rochon reflects on how women might create a new, more equitable society. She describes one of her models of female consciousness: Yeshe Tsogyel, a queen who lived in Tibet in the eighth century (Nam-mkha'i snying-po, 1983; Keith Dowman, 1984). First married to Trisong Detsen and later a companion of Padmasambhava, Yeshe Tsogyel greatly contributed to the spreading of Buddhism in Tibet. She was a writer who spoke many languages but whose own language was spiritual and directed far more at the heart and at visionary potential than at the intellect.

During Yeshe Tsogyel's life span, she managed, among other feats, to transform seven thieves who were about to rape her into "good" men. This was accomplished by helping them discover the awakening dimension of the sexual act—its communicative potential—as opposed to wielding their sexual power as a weapon against women. She also gave parts of her body to people who were in need of them; she understood the symbolic meaning of clouds, wind, fire, and trees and hid treasures of wisdom all over Tibet. Esther Rochon observes: "[s]he was a great lady"("Oser," 68). In Yeshe Tsogyel's songs and biography, utopia can be both pragmatic and poetic, and that is precisely what one finds in Rochon's work. How these two attributes come together in her characters' quest for the center or for justice is revealed by looking closely at the various forms she gives them in her collection of short stories, The Ferry [Le Traversier].

Before even trying to define the center, it is important to explain that there are many centers and that the center is, in fact, everywhere. It is there to be found, whether by chance ("The Labyrinth," Passage III ["Le Labyrinthe," Parcours III]), by falling in love ("The Ferry" ["Le Traversier"]), through a particular person one has loved ("The Labyrinth," Passages I and II ["Le Labyrinthe," Parcours I and II]), through the quest for beauty ("In the Stained-Glass Forest" ["Dans la forêt de vitrail"]), or by making an enlightening discovery about the union of pain and beauty ("The Double Junction of the Wings" ["La Double Jonction des ailes"]). There seem to be as many possibilities as there are people.

Various definitions of the center are given in the three Passages of the short story "The Labyrinth." In Passage I, it is defined in clear terms: "It is a place of fervor, of luminosity, of love. It exists eternally. It is in truth the point at which all worlds meet" [C'est un lieu de ferveur, de rayonnement, d'amour. Il existe de toute éternité. C'est vraiment le point d'accord de tous les mondes (19)]. Further on, when the story's heroine asks a civil servant what the center is, she is given a more vague answer: "Once you have seen the center, you are not completely the same person. . . . If more people know the center, it is good for us, for everybody" [Quand on a vu le centre, on n'est plus tout à fait la même personne. . . . Si vous trouvez le centre, c'est bon pour vous, pour nous, pour tout le monde (19)]. In Passage II of the same short story another heroine this time explains:

To experience the center for the first time is to be able to refer to that experience later by remembering, whether it is to orient oneself if one wants to return physically, or if one wants to radiate from oneself the calm and space which one has learned.

[Faire l'expérience une première fois du centre, c'est être capable plus tard de s'y référer, que ce soit pour s'orienter si on désire y revenir physiquement ou pour rayonner en soi-même et autour, le calme, l'espace que l'on y a connus. (28)]

A third heroine, in Passage III, attains the center easily; for her, it is a natural process. The way in which the center is perceived is clearly a personal experience as well.

Esther Rochon's portrayal of three women in these three quests for the center is not representative of her work as a whole, for both heroes and heroines alternate throughout her writings. Concerned by the issue of representing either men or women in literature, Hélène Colas asked Esther Rochon whether she established a difference between the parts played by men and women in her works. The author replied:

I know I'm prejudiced: my female characters are more down to earth, they tend to be more resourceful. My male characters, on the other hand, often seem arrogant or else they are at a loss in certain situations. I would like not to be prejudiced and to be able to say that all my characters are genuine. But then I know that my relationships with men and women are not the same and that that influences the relationships I have with my characters. For instance, I'm not afraid to have my female characters discuss cooking. Whilst with the male characters, I tend to be more subdued, or else I will be attracted to them as I am to the opposite sex. This comes through in my characters. . . . The men and women in my writings have different tendencies, but I guess it's simply that my own personal fantasies are then at work. For instance, by making most of my male characters experience pain, I am perhaps protecting myself as a woman, or perhaps, I am feeling a maternal protective instinct towards a man in pain. ("Entrevue," 72)

From this statement, it is clear that Esther Rochon portrays a socialized gender identity, not biological essences. She acknowledges different social and personal experiences for both sexes. Thus her textual productions are a highly complex, signifying process rather than a monolithic system.

In order to attain the center, men and women must experience departure or a separation. The motives for their quest are varied and not always idealistic.

Some characters are simply fleeing responsibilities at home ("The Labyrinth," Passage II). This is a crucial point in Esther Rochon's work: motives and actions are never judged. In due time the "spontaneity of reality," which can take any form—falling in love ("The Ferry"), unrequited love ("The Double Junction of the Wings"), a chance meeting with someone exceptional ("The Pink Velvet Tablecloth" ["La Nappe de velours rose"])—will help them to fully develop as human beings.

An impressive example of the ambiguous role played by the "spontaneity of reality" can be found in "The Pink Velvet Tablecloth," in which the two protagonists are women. One of them is a fourteen-year-old girl, the only surviving member of her family following a nuclear catastrophe in Montréal. This adolescent, caught up in the spontaneity of reality, is held hostage by two mutants who force her to lure lost survivors into their den as food. One day, the second female character appears, an old woman doomed to be yet another victim of these monsters. This woman senses what is happening, stares the girl in the eyes, and straightforwardly asks her why she is doing this. Taken aback, the girl immediately stops her murderous activities and follows the woman to New York, where, after a lapse of time, she becomes progressively remorseful. The wise woman then sends her back to the cave, where, for a period of four years, the girl metaphorically weaves her way back to sanity by weaving a pink tablecloth from the remnants of the corpses of the red and white mutants who had died of hunger after her departure. Finally, after she has come to terms with her violent deeds, she returns to New York, for she has become strong and wise enough to replace the old woman as the new leader of the survivors of the nuclear explosion. The experience of violence followed by peace has made her worthy of great responsibility. Evil that is assimilated and atoned for can make for "pink" serenity and wisdom.

In "The Staircase" ["L'Escalier"], Esther Rochon demonstrates once again that her choice of characters is not sexually stereotyped. Rochon herself explains that she had first created a male character and later chose a female character to play the protagonist. This character experiences the dilemma of having to find a balance between home life, professional life, social life and leisure activities (Chapdelaine and Paquet, 1987, personal communication; "Entrevue," 1987). According to Rochon, apart from the fact that she does find it easier to portray women because she can identify with them, she does not distinguish between the sexes when it comes to the problematics of being torn between various worlds.

The center or inner peace, which can be achieved only through a meaningful and inclusive acceptance of the various elements that coexist in the universe (no matter how terrible), is most impressively and poetically depicted in the story of "The Double Junction of the Wings." After the protagonist reveals to her son and daughter that she had wept her "gems," one by one, that they were the precious fruit of her sensitive perception of life, she is transformed into a dragonfly. Her wings consist of the important people in her life: her two children, the man who had taught her to weep gems, his fiancée, the man whom she had taught to weep gems, and his beloved. She is ready for the center, and here is what she finds as described by her young son, Trix. This time Esther

Rochon chose to portray a boy, thus proving that men and women alike, at one point in their lives, are ripe for enlightenment:

On the other side, I was dazzled. Gold gleamed everywhere. We were in a solid gold charnel ground. Gold water flowed into gold waterfalls on gold skeletons and gold carcasses. Laboratory rats with all their tumors and diseases—in gold; trephined cats, irradiated monkeys, pigs with bones shattered by machine tests—in gold; blinded rabbits, factory-grown chickens, battered children, disembowelled women—in gold. All of those who had tormented them—bureaucrats and officers who abused their power, torturers and sadists, butchers and ordinary laboratory workers—were also in solid gold, with rubies for eyes and mutilated as their victims were.

[De l'autre côté, je fus ébloui. L'or rutilait de partout. Nous étions dans un charnier en or massif. De l'eau d'or coulait en chutes d'or sur des squelettes d'or et des charognes d'or. Des rats de laboratoire avec toutes leurs tumeurs et leurs maladies—en or; des chats trépanés, des singes irradiés, des porcs aux os brisés par des tests de machine—en or; des lapins aveugles, des poulets d'élevage, des enfants battus, des femmes éventrées—en or. Tous ceux qui les avaient tourmentés—tortionnaires, sadiques, bureaucrates et militaires abusant de leur pouvoir, bouchers ou simplement personnel de laboratoire— étaient aussi en or massif, mais avec des yeux de rubis, et mutilés comme l'étaient leurs victimes. (58)]

As they fly over the charnel ground, suddenly:

When our wings renewed their humming to the orgasmic moaning of our rear wings, the charnel ground came alive, a perfumed breeze arose, songs and dances began, life made love to death, and suffering and joy echoed each other.

[Au vrombissement renouvelé de nos ailes, aux gémissements d'orgasme de nos ailes arrière, le charnier s'est animé, un vent parfumé s'est levé, chants et danses ont commencé, la vie faisait l'amour avec la mort, souffrance et joie se faisaient l'écho l'une de l'autre. (59)]

This transformation of the horrible into the beautiful, the worthless into the valuable, gives meaning to the most atrocious acts. It merges into an ultimate vision, the "gem of justice": "a globular iridescent gem that rested on a lapis-lazuli pedestal" [une gemme sphérique nacrée posée sur un piédestal de lapis lazuli (59)]. Later on, only Trix and his mother recall their voyage to the double junction of the wings. Here again, it must be noted that Esther Rochon does not favor one sex over the other, for the ability of human beings to see the center is not a male or female trait. The strong experience of perceiving pain and beauty, death and life, suffering and joy, as complementary will shape Trix and inspire him to lead a fairer life.

One day, many years later, when in his twenties, while visiting planet Vuln ravaged by war, Trix suddenly hears the beautiful sound of a piano playing. He approaches the pianist, and to his astonishment, sees that the man is wearing a gem. Trix then realizes that this is the stranger whom his mother had loved and taught how to weep precious stones. Now his mother's generous gesture will play a part in his own growth. Spurred by the emotion of her memory, he experiences a revelation:

When I raise my head again, a new dragonfly is in the process of being formed—on the top side of its four wings are Vuln, the room where we are, ruins, pain, sickness, and an inclination to laugh. On the under side of the two front wings are the gold creatures of the room my mother and I discovered. On the under side of its left rear wing are an immense piano and a pianist who plays with joy in spite of the war that took place, and on the under side of its right rear wing are my parents, my sister, my teachers and my companions from the labyrinth. And I am its head, its body, and its feet. I am the double junction of the wings.

[Quand je relève la tête, une nouvelle libellule est en train de se former: sur le dessus de ses quatre ailes se trouvent Vuln et la salle où nous sommes, ruines, douleur, maladie et envie de rire. Sur le dessous de ses deux ailes avant ont pris place les êtres dorés de la salle que ma mère et moi avions découverte. Sur le dessous de son aile arrière gauche se trouvent un immense piano et un pianiste qui joue avec joie malgré la guerre qui a eu lieu; sur le dessous de son aile arrière droite, il y a mes parents, ma soeur, mes professeurs et mes compagnons du labyrinthe. Et je suis la tête, le corps et les pattes, je suis la double jonction des ailes. (61-62)]

Full of love, he soars into the air while the anger and hatred of the destroyed planet vanish beneath him. Trix wants its people to live in harmony. At last he weeps his first gem, which he immediately recognizes as being the stone of justice he saw as a child. He has learned to live amid the contradictions of life, seeing beauty in horror, and is now prepared to act upon reality to transform it, to accept his mission to rebuild peace on the planet of Vuln. He thus confirms, in a true Buddhist way, that integrated acceptance and action can be complementary forces.

The principle of the spontaneity of reality, of its apparent arbitrariness, is so strong in Rochon's work that it is also possible to strive for justice without having experienced the center. In "Deep Down in Your Eyes" ["Au fond des yeux"], Corinne becomes a heroine simply because she is thrilled by the discovery of "voulques" (153), black- and white-winged extraterrestrial creatures imprisoned in her city. Her comfortable and dull life takes on new color, she falls in love with Francis, and together they decide to free the voulques. When Peter, who is on duty, sees them come into the prison, he is impressed by their courage and thinks: "[T]heir love was strong enough to open up cages!" [leur amour était assez fort pour ouvrir des cages! (184)]. Thus, strong love between men and women, another example of the complementarity of the yin and the yang, can also bring about justice. In this particular story, love makes Corinne and Francis transcend their material lives. They decide to set off with the strange voulques toward an unknown planet, leaving family and friends behind on earth. They soar to another world in an orgasmic surge of love and discovery. Perhaps this sudden impulse is yet another way of achieving the center. Each human being, whether man or woman, thus has a different fate to deal with. In how we perceive our fate and how we act upon it lies the true meaning of our identity and destiny.

In Rochon's stories, all lives are not as spectacular as those of Trix and Corinne. The helpless woman in "The Enclave" ["L'Enclave"] finds neither inner nor outer peace but still does what she can within her limitations: she writes a diary about her feelings of guilt over the discrepancy between her comfortable life on "Earth-Initz" [Terre-Initz] and the wars constantly waged on faraway "Earth-Ourillia" [Terre-Ourillia], a planet she can watch every night on the television news: "This is why I write here: a small enclave of truth in the enclave of our more or less murderous habits" [Voilà en somme pourquoi j'écris ici: une petite enclave de vérité dans l'enclave de nos habitudes plus ou moins meurtrières (90)]. Her awareness of injustice instead of indifference to it is already a step in the right direction, according to Rochon (Chapdelaine and Paquet, 1987, personal communication; "Entrevue," 1987). Rochon also states that the spontaneity of reality might give this helpless woman a chance to take action one day. She goes on to explain that this rather timid way of dealing with, or, rather, not solving, problems is still typical of several women in society today in the sense that the heroine does not take immediate action, that she chooses instead to write a diary without even being sure that it will ever be read. On the other hand, Rochon points out that consciousness of injustice is not a specifically feminine trait. Not only are men aware of injustice, but they also face it in different ways. Ultimately, how people react to situations counts—what they make of what they were born with and the conditions they were born in.

A most difficult aspect to understand in Rochon's worldview is that not react-ing to situations is just as acceptable as acting upon them: both change and nonchange have their raison d'être, just as both those who have found and those who have not found the center coexist in the world. In Passage I of "The Laby-rinth," the woman in search of the center realizes this:

It was there [in the day-care of the labyrinth] that I met for the first time people who had found the center. They looked totally ordinary, and rather boring. . . . In front of them I felt rough-hewn, barbarian. But that impression disappeared after a while. They existed, and so did I; nothing more.

[C'est là que j'ai rencontré pour la première fois des gens qui avaient trouvé le centre. Ils avaient l'air tout à fait ordinaires. Assez ennuyeux. . . . Devant eux je me sentais mal dégrossie, barbare. Mais cette impression-là s'est effacée avec le temps: ils existaient et moi aussi, rien de plus. (15)]

She is surprised to see that even those who discover the center can be ordinary. Rochon's sudden contrasting effects and strange juxtapositions are typical of Buddhist teachings in which, after seeing things as they are, it is for us to interpret events just as we would interpret texts and reach our own understand-ing of the world.

In an article published in 1973, Joanna Russ humorously states that science fiction is the "perfect literary mode in which to explore our assumptions about 'innate' values and 'natural' social arrangements, in short our ideas about Human Nature, Which Never Changes" (80). According to her, some of this exploration has already been carried out. On the other hand, she deplores the absence of "speculation about the innate personality differences between men and women, about family structure, about sex, in short about gender roles" (80). Russ's regrets apply to Esther Rochon in the sense that Russ would expect "human society, family life, personal relations, child-bearing, in fact anything one can name" to be "altered beyond recognition" in science fiction (80). However, in her work, Rochon mainly depicts societies that are reflections of present-day reality in social terms. Her spiritual concerns place her characters in an antiessentialist perspective, and in so doing she does question the "innate personality differences between men and women." In this sense, one could compare Rochon's vision to that of Kristeva's as explained by the feminist literary critic Toril Moi: "Applied to the field of sexual identity and difference, this becomes a feminist vision of a society in which the sexual signifier would be free to move; where the fact of being born male or female no longer would determine the subject's position in relation to power, and where, therefore, the very nature of power itself would be transformed" (172). Rochon transcends the restrictive closure imposed on men and women in present-day society, even though it is the society she depicts. She approaches the realization of Derrida's utopian view of a "relationship to the other where the code of sexual marks would no longer be discriminating" (76). Hers is a world in which, as Derrida describes it:

The relationship [to the other] would not be a-sexual, far from it, but would be sexual otherwise: beyond the binary difference that governs the decorum of all codes, beyond the opposition feminine/masculine, beyond homosexuality and heterosexuality which come to the same thing. As I dream of saving the chance that this question offers, I would like to believe in the multiplicity of sexually marked voices. I would like to believe in the masses, this indeterminable number of blended voices, this mobile of non-identified sexual marks whose choreography can carry, divide, multiply the body of each "individual," whether he be classified as "man" or "woman" according to the criteria of usage. (76)

Esther Rochon's writing is a mystical journey into science fiction, a journey that transcends the relationships between people by presenting them as sexually otherwise. This enables both men and women to place their identities, be they sexual, social, religious, or political, as they deem fit and according to the ethics of their own inner and outer spaces.

NOTE

1. With the exception of "The Labyrinth," Passages I, II, and III [Le Labyrinthe," Parcours I, II, III] and "The Double Junction of Wings" [La Double Jonction des ailes"], which were translated by Henry Polard, all translations of titles and excerpts are mine.

REFERENCES

Derrida, Jacques, with Christie V. McDonald. "Choreographies." *Diacritics* 12.2 (1982): 66-76.

Dowman, Keith. *Sky Dancer—The Secret Life and Songs of the Lady Yeshe Tsogyel.* London: Routledge and Kegan Paul, 1984.

Kristeva, Julia. "Women's Time." Trans. Alice Jardine and Harry Blake. *Signs* 7.1 (1981): 13-35.

Moi, Toril. *Sexual/Textual Politics: Feminist Literary Theory.* London: Routledge, 1985.

Nam-mkha'i snying-po. *Mother of Knowledge: The Enlightenment of Ye-Shes mTshorgyal.* Ed. Jane Wilhelms. Berkeley, CA: Dharma, 1983.

Nicot, Stéphane. "Un imaginaire en liberté." *Le français dans le monde* (May-June 1985): 28-30.

Rochon, Esther. *En Hommage aux araignées.* Montréal: Éditions de l'Actuelle, 1974.

―――. "Oser actualiser l'utopie." *Canadian Woman Studies/Les cahiers de la femme* 6.2 (1985): 66-68.

―――. *Le Traversier.* Montréal: Éditions de la pleine lune, 1987. The short stories cited are the following: "Le Labyrinthe," 7-32; "Le Traversier," 33-46; "La Double Jonction des ailes," 47-64; "Dans la forêt de vitrail," 65-82; "L'Enclave," 83-90; "L'Escalier," 91-100; "La Nappe de velours rose," 115-38; "Au fond des yeux," 139-88.

―――, with Hélène Colas. "Entrevue avec Esther Rochon, auteure de *L'Épuisement du soleil." imagine...* 28.6-5 (1985): 69-76.

―――, with Michel Lord. Interview. *Lettres québécoises* 40 (1985-1986): 36-39.

Russ, Joanna. "The Image of Women in Science Fiction." *Images of Women in Fiction.* Ed. Susan Koppelman Cornillon. Bowling Green, OH: Bowling Green University Popular Press, 1973, 79-94.

Showalter, Elaine. *A Literature of Their Own. British Women Novelists from Brontë to Lessing.* Princeton, NJ: Princeton University Press, 1977.

Vonarburg, Elisabeth. "Les femmes et la science-fiction." *Canadian Woman Studies/Les Cahiers de la femme* 6.2 (1985): 9-11.

―――. "Notes sur Esther Rochon." *Solaris* (Sept.-Oct. 1985): 19-23.

Wollstonecraft Shelley, Mary. *Frankenstein or the Modern Prometheus.* New York: Portland House Illustrated Classics, 1988.

Southern Africa and the Theme of Madness: Novels by Doris Lessing, Bessie Head, and Nadine Gordimer

Nancy Topping Bazin

However different their lives, Doris Lessing, Bessie Head, and Nadine Gordimer share the common heritage of having grown up in southern Africa. All three were profoundly affected by that experience. Their responses to the colonialist, racist, and sexist attitudes that permeated their lives have determined, to a major extent, the nature of their fiction. Their novels reflect the grotesque situations and bizarre human relationships created by prejudice, injustice, and the desire to dominate. These three authors focus on the mad nature of this social and political situation in southern Africa. In their works, dystopian and utopian visions of the future provide perspectives from which to view the nightmarish quality of the past and present. These writers seek to communicate the horror of what they have known and their longings for something else—other ways of being and acting than those that characterize not only most whites of southern Africa but also most people of all colors. Although other works by these women writers will be mentioned, this chapter focuses upon *Martha Quest*, *Briefing for a Descent into Hell*, and *Shikasta* by Doris Lessing, *Maru* and *A Question of Power* by Bessie Head, and *Burger's Daughter*, *July's People*, and *A Sport of Nature* by Nadine Gordimer.

There are degrees and forms of madness. Groups may judge an individual's behavior to be "mad" and commit that person to a mental institution. But individuals may also view various forms of group behavior as "mad." Group behavior imbibes a kind of madness when it is the product of racist, sexist, and class-conscious attitudes cultivated in a context of potential violence. In Doris Lessing's second novel, *Martha Quest* (1952), she demonstrates, through her descriptions of the daily sundowner parties at the Sports Club, the extent to which quite mad behavior can be socially acceptable. Martha, the protagonist, neglects her studies and her need for balanced meals and adequate sleep in order to participate in the frenzied lifestyle of her peers. These young whites spend every evening from 1935 through 1938 having a good time. Their leader is the wild, fun-loving, beer-drinking Binkie, whose rousing call to join in the fun is: "'Come on, let's-tear-it-to-pieces!'" (136). The young women are expected not

to "giggle when this wolf or that moaned and rolled his eyes and said, 'Beautiful, why haven't I seen you before, I can't take it, I'm dying,' as he clutched
his forehead and reeled back from the vision of her unbearable attractions"
(137). At these parties, a young woman typically has to endure being forcibly
kissed by a number of the so-called wolves, whose excuse is always their
inability to resist her charms. Martha feels that, in truth, for these young men,
"each kiss was a small ceremony of hatred" (157).

When Martha dances with Perry, he yells "like a tormented soul," or he
breaks "suddenly into writhing jive, his head crushed back on his neck, his eyes
closed, while he crooned . . . in imitation of a Negro singing" (155). Martha
begins to notice his eyes and the eyes of others; their eyes were "anxious, even
pleading" at the same time that their faces and bodies were "contorted into the
poses required of them." They appeared to be possessed, but "it was an exterior
possession that . . . left them free to judge and comment" (156). Frequently,
Martha notes this same kind of split personality in herself, as she finds her more
authentic self observing the mad behavior of her social self. Her observing self
seems to echo what she imagines Perry to say: "'Look how madly we are
behaving'" (159).

Perry serves to focus our attention not just upon madness in the way males
and females interact in this colonial society but also upon the rigid and strained
relations between whites and blacks. The Sports Club has an all-white
membership, but all the waiters are black. Suddenly Perry begins a "parody of
a native war dance. . . . But for this he could not be alone, he must be in a
group. . . . And soon a group of the wolves, headed by Perry . . . grunted and
sang." He sings the following words: "'Hold him *down*, the Zulu warrior, Hold
him *down*, the Zulu chief'" (206). Perry proceeds to tell one of the waiters to
dance and, when he will not, threatens him with violence. The terrified waiter
is forced to perform, and when he will not do it with any enthusiasm and runs
off, Perry is furious and offended. White males often charge blacks, women,
and other oppressed groups who are the butts of their jokes with lacking a sense
of humor. Perry's group truly feels "ill-used and misunderstood," and Martha
observes, "It was like a madness" (207). When she protests to her friend
Donovan, she is accused of becoming "'a proper little nigger-lover'" (208).
Sexism and racism are part of the colonialist lifestyle and philosophy of
domination that Martha Quest struggles to reject.

Thus, Martha breaks away from the Sports Club parties; but then she
discovers to her horror that her fiancé, Douglas Knowell, is normally one of the
Sports Club gang. The night she agrees to marry him, he goes "off the tack,"
heading for the Sports Club and his friends (224). Up all night, the "wolves"
"practically wrecked the town." They put "a chamberpot on the statue of Cecil
Rhodes" and red paint on every lamppost (225). As Shoshana Felman states in
her book *Writing and Madness*: "Madness usually occupies a position of *exclusion*; it is the *outside* of a culture. But madness that is a *common* place occupies
a position of *inclusion* and becomes the *inside* of a culture" (13). Madness is the
social norm within the white Southern Rhodesian culture portrayed in *Martha
Quest*.

Felman declares that "our entire era . . . has become subsumed within the space of madness" (14). Such is the world Doris Lessing portrays in *Shikasta*, written in 1979, twenty-seven years after *Martha Quest*. Toward the end of *Shikasta*, which Lessing labels space fiction, there is a lengthy trial during which representatives from a variety of countries and races testify against the mad behavior of the white race throughout the centuries; but the bulk of the trial consists of an indictment of the British who failed to protest what their settlers did in Southern Rhodesia:

From the very moment the white conquerors were given "self-government" they took away the black people's lands, rights, freedoms and made slaves and servants of them in every way, using every device of force and intimidation, contempt, trickery. But never did Britain protest. Never, not once. . . . *Britain had the legal and moral responsibility* to step in and forcibly stop the whites from doing as they liked. (328-29)

However, they did nothing "because of their inherent and inbred contempt for peoples other than themselves" (329). Lessing's story of madness does not stop there, for the representative of the white race who declares himself guilty goes on to ask why the other races have not learned from the whites' example: "'Why is it that so many of you . . . have chosen to copy the materialism, the greed, the rapacity of the white man's technological society?'" (335). Moreover, the whites have had no corner on this madness. Slavery was conducted "largely by Arabs and was made possible by the willing co-operation of black people" (338), and the Indians' treatment of the Untouchables is unmatched "for baseness" (337). In her fantasy, *Shikasta*, it is only after the holocaust of World War III that the rampant universal madness of the twentieth century seems to end. As Felman points out, often "the madness silenced by society has been given voice by literature" (15). Literary fantasy is the means by which Lessing gains the freedom to make us see ourselves and our time and place from a cosmic perspective. By calling into question predominant values and behavior, *Shikasta* makes evident the madness that the people of the twentieth century would like to deny.

Ironically, the madness of inclusion (in which madness is the norm) can coexist with the madness of exclusion (in which the social madness creates the mad outsider). Feminist theorists like Hélène Cixous and Catherine Clément point to the ways in which living in a patriarchal environment has repressed women and frequently led them to outbursts of hysteria or madness. In *The Newly Born Woman*, they observe that "societies do not succeed in offering everyone the same way of fitting into the symbolic order; those who are, if one may say so, between symbolic systems, in the interstices, offside, are the ones who are afflicted . . . with what we call madness" (7). Women, like the novelist, chronicler, and short story writer Bessie Head, are frequently among those who find themselves "offside," and it can be through literature that they find their psychological release from repression. In the words of Sandra Gilbert: "[T]he country of writing ought to be a no where into which we can fly in a tarantella of rage and desire, a place beyond 'vileness and compromise' where the part of ourselves that longs to be free . . . can write itself, can dream, can invent new worlds" (Introduction, Cixous and Clément, xviii).

Conceived in South Africa by the mating of an upper-class white woman and a black stable "boy," Bessie Head was born in the mental institution to which her ill-behaved mother had been committed. As a mulatto, Head was usually rejected by both blacks and whites. Living in a misogynous culture, she was mistreated by her sexist husband. As a South African in exile, she was treated as an outsider by the people of Botswana, the black nation to which she had fled to escape the oppression of apartheid.

In her novel *A Question of Power* (1974), Bessie Head articulates the experience of a black African woman driven "mad" by the madness surrounding her. She claims this book is "completely autobiographical" (Beard, 45). The protagonist, Elizabeth, having lived in South Africa under apartheid, knows that white people go "out of their way to hate you" (19). She is less prepared, however, to accept from the African male equally blatant hatred directed toward her as an African female. She finds the African's misogyny even more cruel than that of the white man, because it is less tempered by "love and tenderness and personal romantic treasuring of women" (137). The madness of misogyny added to the madness of racism becomes too much for her to bear, thus causing her breakdown.

Like racism, misogyny undermines the victim's self-esteem. In her hallucinations, two African males, Sello and Dan, use both heterosexuality and homosexuality to taunt her and make her feel inferior and degraded. To undermine Elizabeth's sense of herself as a woman, Sello uses Medusa, and Dan uses his "seventy-one nice-time girls" (173).

Sello displays before Elizabeth his attraction to Medusa's fantastic vagina: "It was . . . like seven thousand vaginas in one, turned on and operating at white heat" (64). The evil Medusa puts herself on display for Elizabeth: "Without any bother for decencies she sprawled her long black legs in the air, and the most exquisite sensation travelled out of her towards Elizabeth. It enveloped Elizabeth from head to toe like a slow, deep, sensuous bomb." Looking at Elizabeth with "a mocking superior smile," Medusa says, "'You haven't got anything *near* that, have you?'" (44).

Similarly, Dan taunts Elizabeth with the sexual superiority of his parade of women. He wants her to be jealous: "'I go with all these women because you are inferior'" (147). One of the key images in Elizabeth's madness is Dan "standing in front of her, his pants down, as usual, flaying his powerful penis in the air" (12-13). His women include Miss Wriggly-Bottom, Miss Pelican-Beak, Madame Make-Love-On-The-Floor, and Madame Loose-Bottom. Elizabeth takes heavy doses of sleeping pills to block out his all-night activities with these "'nice-time girls'" (128), for Dan sometimes tumbles these women into her bed: "They kept on bumping her awake" (127). Furthermore, he encourages them to use her personal possessions to clean up: "He was abnormally obsessed with dirt on his women. They washed and washed in her bathroom; they put on Elizabeth's dresses and underwear" (128). Dan also uses homosexuality to make Elizabeth feel excluded. He tells her that homosexuality is a "'universal phenomenon'" (138) and that Sello and his boyfriend "'do it all the time'" (139). Elizabeth's hallucinations are extensions of her experiences with her African husband: "Women were always complaining of being molested by her husband. Then there was also a white man who was his boy-friend" (19).

Recognizing the similarity between racists and sexists, Elizabeth calls them both "power-maniacs" who live "off other people's souls like vultures" (19). Elizabeth withstands the cruelty and torture of Medusa and the two men who inhabit her madness by not giving in to their view of her as nothing. At one point she tells Sello that he is making a mistake, for she is God, too (38).

Like Celie in Alice Walker's *The Color Purple*, Elizabeth finds herself forced by her experiences with racist and sexist attitudes to alter her concept of God. Like such feminist philosopher/theologians as Rosemary Ruether, Naomi Goldenberg, and Elizabeth Dodson Gray, Bessie Head's protagonist rejects the hierarchy in traditional religions and calls for a more egalitarian worldview. Elizabeth claims that people pray to a God they will never see, because God is, in fact, in ordinary people, not in the sky (197). Her ideal is to bring holiness down to earth. The Gods are, in fact, those "killed and killed and killed again in one cause after another for the liberation of mankind." She sees the Gods as "ordinary, practical, *sane* people, seemingly their only distinction being that they had consciously concentrated on spiritual earnings" (31; emphasis added).

As in Doris Lessing's space fiction works *The Marriages Between Zones Three, Four, and Five* and *The Making of the Representative from Planet Eight*, there is a movement toward mysticism in Bessie Head's *A Question of Power*. Elizabeth has been tested by the nightmare of madness. Once she has passed through this hell, her knowledge of evil helps her to rediscover and escape into its opposite—an impersonal, mystical love. She is transported into a state in which there are "no private hungers to be kissed, loved, adored. And yet there was a feeling of being kissed by everything; by the air, the soft flow of life, people's smiles and friendships." This "vast and universal love" equalizes all things and all people. Elizabeth emerges from her hell with a confirmed belief in such love and a "lofty serenity of soul nothing could shake" (202). At the end of the novel she recognizes that humankind's fundamental error is the "relegation of all things holy to some unseen Being in the sky" (205). Consequently, "since man was not holy to man, he could be tortured for his complexion, he could be misused, degraded and killed" (205). In short, people hurt other people, because they fail to perceive the sacredness—or God—in one another. The mystical experience of oneness is the ideal; assigning God a place in each of us is the means.

A mystical experience leads Lessing's protagonist to similar conclusions in *Martha Quest*. Martha Quest's perception is of the oneness of the universe. She experiences a slow, painful merging of her body with the animals, the grasses, the trees, and the stones. They "became one, shuddering together in a dissolution of dancing atoms" (52). Inherent in the moment is a message, that she must seize quickly, for "already the thing was sliding backwards" (53). What Martha intuits in that moment are the oneness and sacredness of all life. But she recognizes, too, the inadequacy of human beings, for we are unable to retain this knowledge long enough to live according to it.

Just as Martha tends to remember her mystical moment falsely as an ecstatic rather than painful experience, she quickly reduces the "difficult knowledge" (53) gained from the moment to the simplicity of a New Year's resolution or a religious platitude never to be taken seriously or put into practice. For example, because two small bucks were present and played integral parts in her painful process of becoming one with her physical environment, Martha resolves never again to kill a young buck. But she is immediately angry with herself, for she realizes that she will fail to keep this resolution. Her insight is prophetic, for the very next day she takes an early morning walk, carrying a gun as was her habit. She finds herself shooting a buck "almost half-heartedly, because it happened to present itself," and she is amazed when it falls dead (56). Here she is violating her resolve, not even out of a strong need or desire. She takes the dead buck home simply because she did not want to "waste the meat" (56). This is not atypical of Martha's experience; she is constantly finding herself doing what intellectually and even emotionally she does not want to do. Indeed, she knows better.

Doris Lessing resigns herself to the fact that this tendency to do what we know we should not because we "forget" is human nature. Human beings seem incapable of better behavior. Yet, persisting in behavior that ignores the interconnectedness of all individuals and all nature will bring on a major catastrophe—the cause and nature of which are left vague at the end of Lessing's novel *The Four-Gated City* but is specifically World War III at the end of *Shikasta*. Failure to acknowledge the oneness of the universe means that social, economic, political, and physical violence will continue until, Lessing suggests, human beings evolve into a higher consciousness or until something like a dose of radiation transforms their nature. Until human beings change, the current madness will continue.

As Doris Lessing shifts her perspective from the planet to the cosmos in her space fiction novels, she reiterates what Martha Quest learns in her special moment on the veld: "her smallness, the unimportance of humanity" (52). Martha learns she has been mistaken in "her own idea of herself and her place in the chaos of matter. . . . it was as if something new was demanding conception, with her flesh as host; as if there were a necessity, which she must bring herself to accept" (53).

Lessing again speaks of the Necessity in her 1971 fantasy novel, *Briefing for a Descent Into Hell*, and she speaks of the laws of Canopus in *Shikasta*. Both books suggest that human beings must submit to these higher laws if their species is to survive. Basically, they must acknowledge by their behavior the oneness of life. Both novels suggest that long ago this sense of oneness did prevail. Life on earth was once truly Edenic, but this harmonious way of life was lost in an ancient catastrophe. A future catastrophe will, it seems, restore it. Meanwhile, in both works, humans are condemned for thinking in terms of "I" instead of "we." From his own outer space, Charles Watkins, the mad protagonist in *Briefing for a Descent into Hell*, sees humankind as mad. According to his observation, saying "I, I, I, I, is their madness," for in fact "they form a unity, they have a single mind, a single being, and never can they say I, I, without making the celestial watchers roll with laughter or weep with pity." There has been a divorce between "the 'I' and the 'We,' some sort of a terrible falling-away" (109). Until the sense of We can be restored, envoys are sent to earth to "keep alive, in any way possible, the knowledge that humanity, with its fellow creatures, the animals and plants, make up a whole, are a unity, have a function in the whole system as an organ or organism" (128). This is an interim strategy until the human species evolves into higher consciousness: "'They have not yet evolved into an understanding of their individual selves as merely parts of a whole, first of all humanity, their own species, let alone achieving a conscious knowledge of humanity as part of Nature; plants, animals, birds, insects, reptiles, all these together making a small chord in the Cosmic Harmony'" (128-29).

Lessing thus puts into perspective the "'dividing-off, compartmenting, pigeon-holing'" (129) that causes racism, sexism, class consciousness, ecological problems, and world wars.

Through her fiction, Doris Lessing moves us from personal concerns (like Martha's with racism and sexism) to more general social, economic, and political concerns brought out, for example, as her protagonists in *The Four-Gated City* or *The Summer Before the Dark* change their clothes and roles and move through different classes of society to observe how differently they are treated. When Lessing turns to cosmic fiction, her focus shifts to philosophical and spiritual concerns. She carries us through the complexity of life back to the simple laws that govern it. In *Shikasta*, we read that our worst crime is arrogance—"a lack of humility and the curiosity that is based on humility" (320-21). There, too, she states her belief that "we are all creatures of the stars and their forces, they make us, we make them, we are part of a dance from which we by no means and not ever may consider ourselves separate" (40). This is the Necessity to which humans must submit, and that worldview has implications for what is proper in human behavior.

In her preface to *Shikasta*, Doris Lessing claims that there is an explosion of science fiction and space fiction in our time because "the human mind is being forced to expand" (x). In order to gain a better perspective on the present, the human mind must go both backward and forward through time. Like other writers about the future, Lessing goes back to the sacred literature of the past. Lessing states that science fiction and space fiction writers must explore "the sacred literatures of the world in the same bold way they take scientific and social possibilities to their logical conclusions." She says that we "make a mistake when we dismiss [sacred literature of all races and nations] as quaint fossils from a dead past" (x). In *Shikasta*, she shifts her readers' perspectives so that the present is illuminated by the ancient past and the far future. She retells the whole history of humanity from an ethical/religious perspective.

Like Bessie Head, Doris Lessing presents us with not only a vision of oneness but a necessity for oneness. The alternatives are too horrible to contemplate, and yet she makes us contemplate the inevitability of an ecological or nuclear catastrophe in *The Four-Gated City*, the inevitability of a breakdown in the effectiveness of government because of bureaucracies, elitism, and pollution in *Memoirs of a Survivor*, and the inevitability of World War III in *Shikasta*. All of these catastrophes occur because of our failure to think in terms of "we."

In Bessie Head's novels, as in Doris Lessing's, the blame is shared. There is no single race or nation that has a corner on the current madness and guilt. Bessie Head draws parallels between the egomania that causes the domination of women and the egomania inherent in each of the following: Nazi anti-Semitism, Ku Klux Klan behavior, black power fist-raising in the United States (*Question*, 47, 92, 132-33), the mistreatment of the African male as Kaffir (*When Rain Clouds Gather*, 171), and the black Africans' prejudice against "Coloureds" and especially against the Masarwa tribe (or Bushmen) in Botswana. One of the main characters in Head's second novel, *Maru*, is a Masarwa woman who was educated by a missionary so that she could teach school. But she is taunted even in the classroom by her students ("Since when did a Bushy go to school?"), and the principal thinks firing her will be unusually easy because she is a female as well as a Masarwa (17, 41). The character Maru reflects on the irony of black Africans, who treat others as the white man treated them:

How universal was the language of oppression! They had said of the Masarwa what every white man had said of every black man: "They can't think for themselves. They don't know anything." The matter never rested there. The stronger man caught hold of the weaker man and made a circus animal out of him, reducing him to the state of misery and subjection and non-humanity. The combinations were the same, first conquest, then abhorrence at the looks of the conquered and, from there onwards, all forms of horror and evil practices. (109)

In contrast to such horrors, Bessie Head and Doris Lessing give brief glimpses of what a utopian society might be like. In *A Question of Power*, Elizabeth is gradually healed by her relationship with the uneducated, hardworking woman, Kenosi, with whom she gardens. Her relationship with this woman keeps in sight the possibility of something quite different from the patriarchal relationships she has in her hallucinations: their "work-relationship had been established on the solid respect of one partner for another" (160). In *Martha Quest*, a symbolic picture of a utopia is provoked by the distressing sight of a native with a whip driving a team of oxen led by a small child (10). Martha feels an overwhelming sense of pity for the black child, son of "a harsh and violent man" rendered harsh and violent, one assumes, by the harshness and violence that characterize the racist society in which he lives. Then "her mind swam and shook" and "instead of one black child, she saw a multitude, and so lapsed easily into her favorite daydream"—that of the four-gated city where black, white, and brown adults watch with approval "the blue-eyed, fair-skinned children of the North playing hand in hand with the bronze-skinned, dark-eyed children of the South" (10-11). Out of the painful vision of the child, Martha fabricates the joyful vision of the city. Seeing the one provokes a quest for its opposite.

The sight of a violent black man in Nadine Gordimer's novel *Burger's Daughter* functions similarly as a recurring spur for the protagonist, Rosa Burger, to persist in her political activities. Such moments make her intensely aware of the necessity for an alternative. Born and raised by white activist parents in South Africa, Rosa Burger is driving along when she sees a donkey-drawn cart with a woman and child huddled in terror among the sacks. The black driver, frustrated by his own victimization, in turn, abuses his animal and his family. Rosa sees him standing on the moving cart:

Suddenly his body arched back with one upflung arm against the sky and lurched over as if he had been shot and at that instant the donkey was bowed by a paroxysm that seemed to draw its four legs and head down towards the centre of its body in a noose, then fling head and extremities wide again; and again the man violently salaamed, and again the beast curved together and flew apart. (208)

For Rosa, the donkey, cart, driver, and mother and child behind him "made a single object that contracted against itself in the desperation of a hideous final energy" (208). What that scene represents for her is:

the entire ingenuity from thumbscrew and rack to electric shock, the infinite variety and gradation of suffering, by lash, by fear, by hunger, by solitary confinement--the camps, concentration, labour, resettlement, the Siberias of snow or sun, the lives of Mandela, Sisulu, Mbeki, Kathrada, Kgosana, gull-picked on the Island, Lionel [her imprisoned father] propped wasting to his skull between two warders, the deaths by questioning, bodies fallen from the height of John Vorster Square, deaths by dehydration, babies degutted by enteritis in "places" of banishment, the lights beating all night on the faces of those in cells. (208)

Faced with so much suffering that she cannot determine when or how to intervene, Rosa's first reaction is to leave her native South Africa: "After the donkey I couldn't stop myself. I don't know how to live in Lionel's country" (210). But later in the novel, Rosa Burger realizes that she cannot stay away and ignore this suffering; her place is in South Africa. She must rejoin the struggle. This is symbolized by the epigraph for section two of the novel: "To know and not to act is not to know" (213).

Through writing her next novel, *July's People* (1981), Nadine Gordimer seeks an end to the psychological and social madness created by apartheid or any master-servant relationship. She reveals how even the white South African liberals are collaborators benefiting from racist policies. In this book Gordimer presents a dystopian vision of the future. Through it she can perhaps move white readers to take action to abolish apartheid and the many injustices suffered by blacks, thereby preventing the situation described in the novel from becoming a reality. In *July's People*, violence has erupted. With the help of Cuban and Soviet missiles, the black Africans are taking over the cities, and the white Smales family is saved, presumably from death, only by the ingenuity of their servant July, who allows them to escape with him to his village. However, in the village the power shifts from the whites to the blacks, just as it had in the city. Roles are reversed; July, the servant, becomes the master. Once again there is dominance rather than equality.

Through depicting in *July's People* what it would be like to be a white person abruptly thrown into a basically hostile black African village, Gordimer conveys a little of what the black person experiences when thrown into an alien white environment. To survive in the white world, July had to learn English; Bam and Maureen Smales need to know, but do not know, July's African language. Unable to speak and comprehend the dominant tongue, they are rendered powerless. Unable to understand local customs or methods of getting food and necessities, the Smales family becomes almost entirely dependent upon July for its survival. Because Bam cannot be seen driving his own small truck, called a *bakkie*, July keeps the keys. A little later, Daniel, one of the villagers, steals Bam's gun and goes off to fight against the whites for possession of the country. The Smales no longer have any police protection, and both the chief of the village and July have the power at any time to deny them the safety the village provides. On one hand, they are—like the urban blacks—invisible, nonpartici-pants in the social system; on the other hand, they are totally visible because they are watched closely by every villager.

Both Bam and Maureen Smales lose their status and traditional roles when they enter the African village. Their marital relationship is destroyed by this breakdown of their social order. Powerless, Bam can no longer support or protect his family. He does not know anymore how to speak to his wife, Maureen, because, without their roles, they seem to have no self or identity. He is unable to see this woman he lives with now either as Maureen or as someone functioning in any of her past roles—wife, mother, partner, dance teacher, daughter; therefore, he views this female as "her" (105). He views her as a presence whose "sense of self he could not follow because here there were no familiar areas in which it could be visualized moving, no familiar entities that could be shaping it" (105). Likewise, Maureen can no longer identify Bam as the man she had known back home in the "master bedroom." No longer able to function as her financial and physical protector, he seems useless; "she looked down on this man who had nothing, now" (145). When the village chief asks Bam to explain what is currently happening in South Africa between the blacks and whites, Maureen is quick to perceive that what he was really asking about was "an explosion of roles, that's what the blowing up of the Union Buildings and the burning of the master bedrooms is" (117). Similarly, July had lost his macho role and status when he had gone to the Smales to work, for Maureen had been his daily master and he her "boy." July tells her bitterly, "Fifteen years/your boy/you satisfy" (98). Just as Maureen lost her respect for her husband in the black African village where he had no power, the black African wife's respect for July had been permanently diminished by his lack of power in the white-dominated city. To become powerless and hence to lose control over one's own life mean a loss of social status but also a loss of self-esteem and a clear sense of one's own identity. This loss of identity and well-defined roles is central to the terror evoked by this South African dystopia.

In desperation, Maureen seeks to play a subservient and semi-intimate role with July. She discovers, however, that she, who had had control over his daily life, rather than Bam, the real white power, has earned all of July's hostility. Furthermore, she has absolutely no power over him anymore, for "his measure as a man was taken elsewhere and by others. She was not his mother, his wife, his sister, his friend, his people." His lack of response to her plea for a new kind of relationship makes her understand for the first time the true nature of their prior employer/employee interactions. She suddenly "understood everything: what he had had to be, how she had covered up to herself for him, in order for him to be her idea of him" (152).

More quickly than Bam, Maureen sees the total impossibility of their situation. July will obey black soldiers when they show up in the village just as he had obeyed whites, and for the same reason: he is powerless. By hiding his white family instead of staying in town to fight with his own people, July was already a traitor, a non-hero. So, too, in the village Bam is a nonhero. He will not fight with the village chief, who wants to defend himself against the revolutionary blacks. Politically, Bam is on the side of the revolutionaries; ironically, these same rebels may kill him.

It is not surprising then that, deserted by Bam and July, Maureen runs toward the helicopter that one day lands near the village. From the noise of the helicopter, "her body in its rib-cage is thudded with deafening vibration, invaded by a force pumping, jigging in its monstrous orgasm" (158). This masculine symbol comes down with "its landing gear like spread legs, battling the air with whirling scythes" (158). Concerned only for her own survival, Maureen is instinctively drawn toward this representation of male power. Her fantasy is of "a kitchen, a house just the other side of the next tree" (159). The book ends with the two words "She runs," and critics have speculated about what it is she is running toward. Will the helicopter contain saviors or murderers? If black men will be inhabiting the new master bedrooms of Africa, will Maureen be accepted inside?

In Gordimer's next novel, *A Sport of Nature* (1987), she develops further this desire of a white woman to share the future of black Africans as an insider. Being in the master bedroom with the new men in power makes that possible. The white South African protagonist, Hillela, crosses over the racial barrier effectively, marrying first a black revolutionary and then a black ruler. Under their aegis, she works continually and efficiently for the new black Africa. The latter part of *A Sport of Nature* is a fantasy in which we witness "the proclamation of the new African state that used to be South Africa" (337). Hillela can be part of the new world, but only because, as Nadine Gordimer says, "'Hillela is a kind of freak. She represents a break with all the ways that have been tried'" (Clemons, 78). Hillela is a "sport of nature" (defined in the epigraph as an "abnormal variation") in South African society, because she is free of racial prejudice. Distrustful of words, her decision making is determined by instinct and sexual passion. Meanwhile, her cousin Sasha, who makes decisions based upon political commitment, spends time in jail and then leaves the country. Despite his revolutionary commitment, he is unable to achieve the degree of integration into the black revolutionary societies of southern Africa that Hillela does through marriages.

Nevertheless, Hillela has to face the fact that the time was not yet right to realize her utopian dream of having an "African family of rainbow-coloured children" (223). Loving the skin and hair of the Other cuts at the root of racism; yet love between a few interracial couples cannot by itself alter an oppressive social structure. Moreover, this white female/black male attraction often hurts the black female—which a close reading of *A Sport of Nature* and Gordimer's next novel, *My Son's Story*, makes all too evident. Physical and spiritual love between whites and blacks is one way to undermine the madness of racism, but that love will be fragile in a struggle for dominance or in a racist or patriarchal context—white or black. Will the new African government itself be free of racism, and will black women be empowered? At the end of this futuristic novel, the answers to those questions are not clear. Still, the image of an interracial couple at the founding of the new African nation suggests that racial harmony may eventually prevail.

For Nadine Gordimer, as for Doris Lessing and Bessie Head, the future could be a dystopia or a utopia, depending upon the decisions we make in the present. Growing up in southern Africa made all three writers especially sensitive to the barriers between people. Barriers that separate, based on race or gender or class, breed madness in individuals as in social policies. Their novels suggest that experiencing mystical moments and/or witnessing moments of grotesque human violence convinced them that alternatives had to be found. Their dystopian fantasies and hallucinations help readers better understand the nature and the consequences of injustice and evil. Their utopian fantasies enable readers to imagine positive alternatives. In the words of Sasha, Hillela's cousin in *A Sport of Nature*, a utopia may be unattainable but "without aiming for it—taking a chance!—you can never hope even to fall far short of it" (187). He concludes that "without utopia—the idea of utopia—there's a failure of the imagination—and that's a failure to know how to go on living" (187). The novels of Doris Lessing, Bessie Head, and Nadine Gordimer make clear that to alter attitudes and behavior to support what is just, rationality and sanity are necessary. Until individuals not only know this but also act accordingly, the madness will continue.

NOTE

An earlier version of this chapter, entitled "Madness, Mysticism, and Fantasy: Shifting Perspectives in the Novels of Doris Lessing, Bessie Head, and Nadine Gordimer," appeared in *Extrapolation: A Journal of Science Fiction and Fantasy* 33.1 (Spring 1992): 73-87.

REFERENCES

Beard, Linda Susan. "Bessie Head in Gaborone, Botswana: An Interview." *Sage: A Scholarly Journal on Black Women* 3.2 (1986): 44-47.

Cixous, Hélène, and Catherine Clément. *The Newly Born Woman*. Trans. Betsy Wing. Introduction by Sandra M. Gilbert. Minneapolis: University of Minnesota Press, 1986.

Clemons, Walter. "South African Countdown: Gordimer's Angry Vision." *Newsweek* May 4, 1987, 78.

Felman, Shoshana. *Writing and Madness*. Trans. Martha Noel Evans and the author with the assistance of Brian Massumi. Ithaca: Cornell University Press, 1985.

Gordimer, Nadine. *Burger's Daughter*. New York: Penguin, 1980.

———. *July's People*. New York: Penguin, 1982.

———. *A Sport of Nature*. New York: Knopf, 1987.

Head, Bessie. *Maru*. London: Heinemann, 1972.

———. *A Question of Power*. London: Heinemann, 1974.

———. *When Rain Clouds Gather*. London: Heinemann Educational Books, 1972.

Lessing, Doris. *Briefing for a Descent into Hell*. New York: Bantam, 1972.

———. *Martha Quest*. New York: New American Library/Plume, 1970.

———. *Shikasta*. New York: Knopf, 1979.

Dismantling the Master's Houses:
Jean Rhys and West Indian Identity

Fiona R. Barnes

> As a woman I have no country. As a woman I want no country. As a woman my country is the whole world. (Virginia Woolf, *Three Guineas*, 109)

> As a woman I have a country; as a woman I cannot divest myself of that country merely by condemning its government or by saying three times "As a woman my country is the whole world." . . . I need to understand how a place on the map is also a place in history within which as a woman, a Jew, a lesbian, a feminist I am created and trying to create. (Adrienne Rich, *Blood, Bread and Poetry*, 212)

These two epigraphs chart the shift in emphasis from Woolf's modernist desire for a universal and utopian world without boundaries, to Rich's postmodern insistence on the importance of positionality and accountability in determining identity and perspective. This focus on the specificities and limitations of place (and the complementary issue of time) in the formation of identity and society is particularly germane to the writings of postcolonial writers. While modernist writers valorized the existential conditions of exile and alienation, self-consciously (and mostly voluntarily) pursuing "a strategy of permanent exile" (Steiner, 17) or what might be called deterritorialization, in contrast, postcolonial writers embark on a quest for a place to call "home." Postcolonial writers' inheritance is a state of exile; therefore, they attempt to counteract this enforced sense of homelessness with a dynamic process of reterritorialization.[1] To the modernist artist, dislocation and deracination were fashionable creative goals to be flaunted, whereas for the postcolonial writer these states are everyday realities of existence, and consequently are to be confronted on the most material of levels.

Central to postcolonial literatures and theories, then, is a concentration on the cultural and political ramifications of geography, the so-called sense of place.[2] In confirmation of Adrienne Rich's opening epigraph, postcolonial literatures affirm the idea that where you are in the world is an inextricable part of who you are and can become and that your geographic location determines your perspectives on self and society. It is this constant awareness of the mutual dependence of self and place that Rich terms the "politics of location" in an essay in which s ιe examines her own psychological development in the light of her geographic position. The complex network of place, identity, and politics that Rich exposes as central in her search for self-knowledge is, I contend, the central framework for Jean Rhys's examination of the identity of the West Indian white Creole in *Wide Sargasso Sea*.

Jean Rhys was born and brought up in Dominica, with a Welsh father and white Creole mother. At the age of sixteen she was sent to England, but she drifted on the fringes of society, an exile both "at home" in Dominica and in the "home country" of England, partially because of her anomalous position as a white Creole woman. Rhys examines this state of colonial alienation—termed "geographic schizophrenia" by Kevin Magarey (57)—in all of her novels, but most particularly in *Wide Sargasso Sea*. Rhys was doubly colonized, for, as a woman writer, she suffered under a form of literary colonialism; while she was treated as an outsider in English society, her novels were claimed by critics for the English modernist tradition.[3] In recent years, postcolonial critics have reclaimed her as a West Indian writer, but one who does not fit neatly into any preconceived place. Rhys's stance is a self-consciously marginal one, and this powerful liminality is recognized by the West Indian writer John Hearne as characteristic of both Rhys's and Wilson Harris's (a Guyanese writer) unique places in the West Indian literary tradition: "They belong; but on their own terms. Guerrillas, not outsiders" (323). It is significant, then, that Jean Rhys casts the protagonist of *Wide Sargasso Sea*, Antoinette Cosway, as a guerrilla within English society who ultimately manages to destroy the repressive societal structures that imprison her. In this way Antoinette becomes a more successful extension of Rhys herself, whose life was sadly limited and darkened by her experiences as a social outcast in England.

Indeed, all of Jean Rhys's other novels and most of her short stories are quite clearly autobiographical in content. Initially, however, *Wide Sargasso Sea* seems the most distanced from Rhys's actual life: it is set in the 1830s of post-emancipation Jamaica and it adopts a plot and characters created in the nineteenth century by Charlotte Brontë in *Jane Eyre*. Yet Rhys's novel is infused with her postcolonial perspective and dramatizes the lessons learned from her experiences as an exiled white Creole West Indian woman in England. By positioning *Jane Eyre* as the sequel to her own novel, Rhys demonstrates that the ugly facts of colonialism underpin the wealth and moral pretensions of English society, just as Antoinette Cosway's marriage to Rochester prepares the ground for Jane Eyre's future. It is clear from the following quotation that Rhys felt a personal challenge in Charlotte Brontë's unempathic depiction of Bertha Rochester, the quintessential madwoman in the attic, and that *Wide Sargasso Sea* is her archaeological excavation of Bertha's submerged history in order to open up the earlier text: "When I read *Jane Eyre* as a child, I thought, why should she think Creole women are lunatics and all that? What a shame to make Rochester's first wife, Bertha, the awful madwoman, and I immediately thought I'd write the story as it might really have been. She seemed such a poor ghost. I thought I'd try to write her a life" (Vreeland, 235). Yet Rhys does not merely construct the biography of the "poor ghost," Bertha Rochester. Instead, in *Wide Sargasso Sea* she tells at least two histories: the personal story of Antoinette Cosway (the "real" Bertha Rochester in Rhys's version) and a political narrative of English imperialism in Jamaica. Thus Rhys explores the inextricability of the stories of the individual colonial subject and the colonial history of Jamaica. At the same time, Rhys reclaims and reterritorializes the earlier oppressive text written by Brontë, enacting the narrative guerrilla warfare described earlier by Hearne.

The symbolic centers of colonialism and imperialism in *Wide Sargasso Sea* are the two Great Houses: Coulibri Estate, which houses the Cosway family in Part I, and Thornfield Hall, the Rochester domain portrayed in Part III. The parallel torching of these two edifices signifies the revolutionary destruction of two white families, whose heritages and cultures were founded on the exploitative economic, racial, and sexual relations of colonialism. These two doomed houses are built on the proceeds from colonial and imperial oppression, so that the families that inhabit these colonial structures cannot separate their identities or personal histories from the larger political histories.

While *Wide Sargasso Sea* proceeds chronologically, the burning of Thornfield Hall at the conclusion of the novel parallels the destruction of Coulibri in Part I, thereby circling back to the narrative beginning rather than emphasizing linear development or closure. Consequently, the concluding scene of the novel brings the personal and political histories of the text full circle, disrupting the teleological impetus of the narrative and reasserting the disruptions and inevitable resurgence of revolutionary history. Thornfield Hall, in all its grandeur and isolation, cannot escape the burning desire for vengeance kindled by the injustices of British imperialism, and it repeats the acts of vengeance that destroyed such Jamaican Great Houses as Coulibri.

COULIBRI ESTATE

Antoinette Cosway is the daughter of a deceased Jamaican plantation owner and his beautiful Martiniquan wife, Annette, who is left bankrupt by her husband's death and the emancipation of the slaves. *Wide Sargasso Sea* begins with Antoinette's early recognition that she and her family are different from everyone else and hence outsiders, living in lonely isolation at the end of a symbolically impassable road:

They say when trouble comes close ranks, and so the white people did. But we were not in their ranks. The Jamaican ladies had never approved of my mother, "because she pretty like pretty self," Christophine said. She was my father's second wife, far too young for him they thought, and worse still a Martinique girl. When I asked her why so few people came to see us, she told me that the road from Spanish Town to Coulibri Estate where we lived was very bad and that road repairing was now a thing of the past. (My father, visitors, horses, feeling safe in bed—all belonged to the past.) (465)

Antoinette's family suffers from the financial loss and social disintegration caused by the Emancipation Law of 1834, and this poverty, together with the loss of the male head of the family and the "foreign" status of Antoinette's mother, means that they live in a fallen Eden, estranged from other blacks and whites and held in contempt by both. This sense of estrangement and hostility affects even the natural landscape of Coulibri Estate for the young Antoinette:

Our garden was large and beautiful as that garden in the Bible—the tree of life grew there. But it had gone wild. The paths were overgrown and a smell of dead flowers mixed with the fresh living smell. Underneath the tall tree ferns, tall as forest tree ferns, the light was green. Orchids flourished out of reach or for some reason not to be touched. One was snaky looking, another like an octopus with long twisted brown tentacles bare of leaves hanging from a twisted root. Twice a year the octopus orchid flowered—then not an inch of tentacle showed. It was a bell-shaped mass of white, mauve, deep purples, wonderful to see. The scent was very sweet and strong. I never went near it. (466)

It is clear from Antoinette's fascinated dread that the wild natural profusion of the garden appears both enticing and threatening to her. While she recognizes its kinship to the Garden of Eden, Coulibri Estate is obviously a post-lapsarian world, where the tree of life has been supplanted by the sinisterly beautiful "octopus orchid." Antoinette's "home" is no place of refuge and security, and her powerful attraction to the beauties of her Jamaican environment is counterbalanced by the dangers that lurk for the unsuspecting white child. This estrangement from the place that should be home for the white Creole girl is later contrasted with the survival skills of the black Creole girl Tia.

Antoinette's alienation from her home is aggravated by the total neglect of her by her mother, whose love is focused on her retarded and invalid son, Pierre. Rhys constructs a polarity in the novel between two black and white mother figures: Antoinette's neglectful and febrile white mother, who is wholly male-identified and dependent, and the strongly independent and protective black housekeeper, Christophine, whose womanly powers are given magical status. Christophine accompanied Antoinette's mother from Martinique and consequently is regarded as a foreigner by the Jamaican blacks, yet she alone of all the characters manages to convert her outsiderhood into power. Nevertheless, her experience of alienation enables Christophine to sympathize with Antoinette's loneliness, and so she attempts to alleviate it by providing Antoinette with a black friend:

I never looked at any strange negro. They hated us. They called us white cockroaches. Let sleeping dogs lie. One day a little girl followed me singing, "Go away white cockroach, go away, go away." I walked fast, but she walked faster. "White cockroach, go away, go away, go away. Nobody want you. Go away." When I was safely home I sat close to the old wall at the end of the garden. It was covered with green moss soft as velvet and I never wanted to move again. Everything would be worse if I moved. Christophine found me there when it was nearly dark, and I was so stiff she had to help me to get up. She said nothing, but next morning Tia was in the kitchen with her mother Maillotte, Christophine's friend. Soon Tia was my friend and I met her nearly every morning at the turn of the road to the river. (469)

Tia provides a brief episode of friendship and companionship in Antoinette's childhood, but the painful end of this relationship confirms the earlier lessons learned from her father's death and her mother's withdrawal: happiness and trust are transient things.

Antoinette's relationship with Tia also teaches her that differences of race and color can prove insurmountable obstacles in her world. Antoinette admires Tia for her capacity for survival and her confident coexistence with her environment: "[F]ires always lit for her, sharp stones did not hurt her bare feet, I never saw her cry" (469). Antoinette never feels this harmony with Coulibri, her family home, or with Jamaica, her homeland. In fact, their meetings and games always take place literally on Tia's territory, and "[l]ate or early we parted at the turn of the road" (469), as if their relationship were "off-limits" in the white Creole world contained within Coulibri Estate.

The Cosways' poverty brings about Antoinette's friendship with Tia, and symbolically, money causes the destruction of Antoinette and Tia's friendship, although, ironically, the black Christophine had given the coins to the penniless white Antoinette. When Tia unfairly tricks Antoinette out of her few hoarded pennies, Antoinette reacts automatically by calling her a "cheating nigger." This racist slur prompts an answering stream of insults from Tia, obviously also learned from her elders, in which she declares that Antoinette's family are impoverished beggars: "Plenty white people in Jamaica. Real white people, they got gold money. They didn't look at us, nobody see them come near us. Old time white people nothing but white nigger now, and black nigger better than white nigger" (470). Here Tia makes a new distinction between the old planter class to which Antoinette's family belongs as a "white nigger" and the new English aristocracy, like Mason, in postemancipation Jamaica—the "real white people" who are the new elite because they are wealthy. The old plantation owners inhabit a liminal, tenuous position in the postemancipation Jamaican social hierarchy, because their poverty condemns them to a rank that the black Jamaicans obviously gleefully consider lower even than their own rank. This social "reclassification" is regarded by the black Creoles as partial reparation for the years of slavery and exploitation that the plantation owners caused.

Antoinette sees Tia only once again, and this meeting confirms our perception that while they share so many childhood experiences and desires, the colonial history of the island prevents full intimacy. The burning of Coulibri is the culmination of a brief period of prosperity after Antoinette's mother marries Mr. Mason, and he restores the estate. Mason is one of the new British representatives of colonialism who buy up bankrupt estates (or, in this case, marry widows and gain their property) and then introduce neocolonialism in the form of repressive laws that replace the old structures of slavery. Angered by these new oppressions and envious of Coulibri's restored wealth and reinstitution as the seat of white oppression, a black mob torches the house one night and forces the family to flee. As Antoinette watches her home burn, she clings in vain to Tia as her closest link to the land and to the few happy memories of the past:

Then, not so far off, I saw Tia and her mother and I ran to her, for she was all that was left of my life as it had been. We had eaten the same food, slept side by side, bathed in the same river. As I ran, I thought, I will live with Tia and I will be like her. Not to leave Coulibri. Not to go. Not. When I was close I saw the jagged stone in her hand but I did not see her throw it. I did not feel it either, only something wet, running down my face. I looked at her and I saw her face crumple up as she began to cry. We stared at each other, blood on my face, tears on hers. It was as if I saw myself. Like in a looking-glass. (483)

In this powerful passage of physical and emotional confrontation, Rhys drama-tizes the inextricable connectedness of Tia and Antoinette's lives through their personal and colonial pasts in Jamaica, but it is a link of mutual suffering and violence. In the confrontation between white and black in the West Indies, even the children are contaminated by the colonial history that endures; the whites still bear the marks of brutality ("blood on my face"), while the blacks still carry the memories of suffering ("tears on hers"). It will be some time before such a history can be accepted as past, and while in the interim Tia and Antoinette can recognize themselves in the other, they cannot cross the boundary of race and class. Rhys poignantly portrays this tragedy of alienation; both children are uncomprehending of the forces that control them and their reactions to each other, but both must suffer as victims of an inhumane colonial structure.

The torching of Coulibri Estate completes the destruction of the Cosway family and their plantation heritage. Antoinette's retarded brother dies in the fire, while her mother suffers a mental breakdown and is held prisoner (at Mason's orders) by two black attendants, one of whom rapes her in an ironic inversion of white colonial abuse of black slaves. After recovering from a serious illness, Antoinette is virtually incarcerated by Mason, albeit in a benevo-lent convent school, in preparation for her inevitable marriage with a British "gentleman" in need of a wealthy wife. Edward Rochester is just such a man, a second son with no immediate prospects of inheritance, who marries Antoi-nette Mason for the colonial fortune that will later help to finance Thornfield Hall. This marriage, like that of Antoinette's mother to Mason, mirrors the exploitative relationship between the marauding (masculine) colonial British power and the exploited riches (feminine) of the colonies.

Rochester assumes control of the narrative in Part II, as the male force seizes control of Antoinette's last link to Jamaica and her mother, the estate of Granbois, and tells the tragic story of the couple's exotic honeymoon, an interlude doomed to failure by Rochester's paranoia and racism. Convinced that he was the victim of an inferior marriage arranged by his own father and the Mason family, Rochester seeks to escape the imagined role of victim by adopt-ing the role of oppressor with vigor and victimizing the innocent Antoinette. He denies her his love, betrays her with one of the servants, then sends away her only protector and friend, Christophine, and takes Antoinette away from Granbois forever. Granbois was Antoinette's mother's estate, the last place where Antoinette felt known and loved, but because Rochester regards it as "alien" and "hostile," a place where women and their passions overwhelm him, he sells it, partly to punish Antoinette and partly to exert control over a female

space. Rochester's sale of Granbois and the banishment of Christophine serve
to exile Antoinette from her motherland and her last ties to Creole culture. As
Rochester also then denies Antoinette admittance to English society, he dooms
her to homelessness and alienation in both countries. However, Rochester's act
of revenge is more than matched by Antoinette's final act in Part III.

THORNFIELD HALL

The most obvious sign of Rochester's destruction of Antoinette Cosway's
Jamaican identity is his renaming of her as Bertha Mason, an act that prompts
her to tell him: "There are always two deaths, the real one and the one people
know about" (536). Once more Antoinette is trapped in a place and identity alien
to her, when Rochester transports her to England and Thornfield Hall against
her will. However, this time there are no sisters of mercy to instruct and
comfort her, as in the Jamaican convent, and no Christophine to defend and
protect her.

The final section of the novel begins, instead, with an unknown outsider's
voice, which coldly defuses the anguish and heartbreak of the second part of the
novel. An Englishwoman, Grace Poole, summarizes the time that has passed
since Antoinette's arrival in England. Ironically, Thornfield Hall is a refuge for
Poole and the other English women servants who have no other means of
support, while for Antoinette the place is a prison. The reader learns from Grace
that Antoinette's sense of freedom and defiance apparently lives on in Bertha
Mason, in contrast to the subservience and passivity of the English women
servants, whose only desire is to retire anonymously from a society that victim-
izes them. As Grace Poole acknowledges:

"After all the house is big and safe, a shelter from the world outside which, say what you
like, can be a black and cruel world to a woman. Maybe that's why I stayed on."
    The thick walls, she thought. Past the lodge gate a long avenue of trees and inside the
house the blazing fires and the crimson and white rooms. But above all the thick walls,
keeping away all the things that you have fought till you can fight no more. Yes, maybe
that's why we all stay—Mrs. Eff and Leah and me. All of us except that girl who lives
in her own darkness. I'll say one thing for her, she hasn't lost her spirit. She's still
fierce. I don't turn my back on her when her eyes have that look. I know it. (566-67)

This mansion provides a haven for Grace Poole and her fellow women servants,
but for Antoinette this English prison is a grotesque distortion of the security
and peace of her beloved convent, where the nuns have been transformed into
jailors. In Grace Poole's approbation of Thornfield Hall as a "shelter from the
world outside," Rhys exposes that gender is not a homogenizing or unifying
factor in society, for both racial and class differences cut across gender lines.
Antoinette is separated from Grace Poole by class and nationality, just as she
was split from Tia by the privileged status of her white skin. It appears that
male society's only "solution" to the existence of marginal, but powerful,
women figures like Antoinette and her mother is to incarcerate and isolate them

from others. As an outsider in the narratives of British patriarchal society, Antoinette has no "useful" role to play and no place to go: she must become the displaced madwoman in the attic that Charlotte Brontë portrayed. But in Rhys's narrative, Antoinette's presence permeates the house, a constant reminder of the English colonizers' repressive measures.

Despite Antoinette's restricted life at Thornfield Hall, she once again wrests control of the narrative, and her supposedly insane perspective provides a perceptive critique of the society that seeks to suppress and silence her. At night she steals the keys from her drunken keeper and explores the house, which convinces her that "[i]t is, as I always knew, made of cardboard" (568), a description that exposes the flimsy facade of English society and the hollowness that underlies it. Antoinette cannot believe that this empty, dark world can be the glorious England of legend, center of empire, particularly as it seems that "[g]old is the idol they worship" (573). These are telling descriptions of a society that Rhys has shown is built on greed and hypocrisy, revenge and exploitation.

Out of Antoinette's troubled dreams come the solution to her suffering and the means to expose the fragility of English society's structures.[4] For just as Tia learned to strike back at a colonial society that exploited and silenced her, so Antoinette finally learns how to avenge the wrongs perpetrated on her by a patriarchal colonial world. When Antoinette was working at cross-stitch in the convent, she would sign her name to the piece "in fire red" (489); now the burning of Thornfield Hall is revealed to her in a dream-vision as her final signature piece, in which she will destroy the cardboard world with her fiery red, "the colour of flamboyant flowers" (571). Clearly, this final act of defiance links Antoinette to both her own personal past and insurgent slave histories in the West Indies. Just as the black mob burned down Coulibri Estate, Antoinette's home, as the symbol of white exploitation and colonialism in Jamaica, so Antoinette will burn down Thornfield Hall, Rochester's home, as the symbol of white male domination and exploitation in England, with its economic basis in the oppressions of colonialism.

With this overthrowing of the main surface plot by the subterranean workings of the subconscious dream text, Rhys subverts the traditional nineteenth-century narrative closure for women's novels, with their customary dual choices of marriage or death. While Antoinette appears to be victimized by marriage and its accompanying imprisonment, her self-inflicted death will also bring about the triumphant destruction of her prison, the symbol of patriarchy and imperialism. Antoinette's dreams form a textual resistant narrative that counteracts the narrative supremacy of the dominant social text, a subversive narrative strategy that is revealed by the following excerpt as characteristic of women's writing in general:

The tensions that shape female development may lead to a disjunction between surface plot, which affirms social conventions, and a submerged plot, which encodes rebellion; between a plot governed by age-old female story patterns, such as myths and fairy tales, and a plot that reconceives these limiting possibilities; between a plot that charts development and a plot that unravels it. (Abel, Hirsch, and Langland, 12)

Antoinette's visions of Christophine, Aunt Cora, and Tia in the dream emphasize her link to strong Jamaican women figures and their defiant actions. While Christophine provides her usual protection to Antoinette as she proceeds with her revenge, Tia challenges her not to be frightened and to join her at the pool at Coulibri. These past companions appear more real to Antoinette than her present "real" life, and she hastens to join them in a rejection of the ghost life to which Rochester has condemned her.

As Antoinette assumes the role of a revolutionary guerrilla, the ugly figure of Bertha Mason, as portrayed in *Jane Eyre*, is transformed by Rhys into the personal and political triumph of a woman who overcomes persecution and exploitation in order to return to the maternal heritage of her island. Antoinette is nowhere so sure of her actions and so close to "home" as when she sets out to build her own funeral pyre from the edifice of British imperialism. This act of self-destruction achieves wider political dimensions, and an act of apparent madness is revealed as a valid response to such desperate circumstances.

Yet *Wide Sargasso Sea* does not end negatively with the act of self-destruction; rather it ends with Antoinette's decision to seize the initiative and boldly confront her own destiny: "Now at last I know why I was brought here and what I have to do. There must have been a draught for the flame flickered and I thought it was out. But I shielded it with my hand and it burned up again to light me along the dark passage" (574). Symbolically, Rhys leaves her protagonist with a ray of light to guide her hopes, as the darkness of ignorance, despair, and death is finally illuminated by the light of self-knowledge and revolt. Ironically, then, the novel ends with a common narrative device for romance novels: "*Wide Sargasso Sea* concludes with a dream come true" (Emery, 425), but the dream brings with it no stratagem for successful socialization, nor does it reconcile the hero and heroine, as conventional romances generally do. This is a dream of destruction, rebellion, and revenge, as the West Indian colonial woman literally destroys the edifices of colonialism that keep her captive and undermines the traditional narrative patterns that were designed to contain her story of resistance.

In her influential work, *Writing Beyond the Ending*, which discusses the resistant narrative strategies that twentieth-century women writers employ to break the constraints of the nineteenth-century romance plot, Rachel Blau DuPlessis analyzes some of the narrative "maneuvers" that Rhys employs in *Wide Sargasso Sea* to shatter the bourgeois individualism of *Jane Eyre*:

By a maneuver of encirclement (entering the story before) and leverage (prying the story open), Rhys ruptures *Jane Eyre*. She returns us to a framework far from the triumphant individualism of the character Jane Eyre by concentrating on the colonial situation. Through the realistic melodrama of black-white relations, Rhys allows us to see that the "personalities" of colonizer and colonized are transformed and fixed by their complementary functions. So it is with the relations between the sexes in a nineteenth-century arranged marriage; a woman from a colony is a trope for the woman as colony. *Wide Sargasso Sea* states that the closures and precisions of any tale are purchased at the expense of the muted, even unspoken narrative, which writing beyond the ending will release. (46)

By giving voice to the silenced Bertha Mason in the alter ego of Antoinette Cosway, Rhys reveals the story of the colonial subject that underlies and undermines the colonizing narrative of *Jane Eyre*. In this way Rhys exposes the gaps and silences that haunt the establishment of a nineteenth-century novel's "happy ending" or conventional "moral order." Yet Antoinette Cosway is no mere trope for "woman as colony"; she is also an individual caught in a tangled web of social, geographical, and historical factors that she struggles to unravel.

As a white Jamaican Creole woman, then, Antoinette inherits a nexus of colonial histories and oppressions that she cannot hope to overcome alone. Early in *Wide Sargasso Sea*, Antoinette's mother, in despair at the poisoning of her horse, declares, "Now we are marooned" (466), commenting on their physical isolation from both white and black Creole communities on the island. Mary Emery explains that the use of the word "marooned" is a conscious reference by Rhys to the original inhabitants of the island, the Caribs or Maroons. These natives struck a bargain with the British in which they won their freedom and some land in exchange for defense of the island against other foreign invaders and a promise to return fugitive slaves to their owners. In this way the brave Maroons became enforcers of other people's slavery, and consequently held an ambivalent position between the exploiters and the exploited in Jamaica. Emery persuasively argues that white women of the planter class in the West Indies inhabited a similar ambivalent position as the Maroons in the hierarchy of colonial power: "Perhaps as whites, they are especially privileged women; yet they cannot maintain that identity and privilege without the capacity to enslave others. The poisoning leaves them even more isolated, helpless to retaliate, and at the mercy of their own servants" (426). Consequently, as white Creole women, Antoinette Cosway and Jean Rhys have unique insights into this tragic interdependence of exploiter and exploited and the corrupting properties of power. Both Cosway and Rhys were marginal figures in a patriarchal colonial society, but the "double consciousness" that this liminality gave them enabled them to understand and sympathize with the oppression of the black Creoles in Jamaica.

When trying to explain her alienation from all social groups, Antoinette once translated a mocking song that Rochester heard a servant girl sing: "It was a song about a white cockroach. That's me. That's what they call all of us who were here before their own people in Africa sold them to the slave traders. And I've heard English women call us white niggers. So between you I often wonder who I am and where is my country and where do I belong and why was I ever born at all. (519) This desperate outburst from Antoinette is an emotional expression of the historical, political, and social forces that create the sense of alienation and marginality that white Creoles feel, caught between a hostile black community that resents their former power and English pretensions and a contemptuous but controlling English society that regards them as uncultured and alien. Only in the last dream-scene does Antoinette discover where she belongs—with the community of resistant women in Jamaica—and why she was born—to destroy what for her signifies the heart of darkness of British imperialism: Thornfield Hall.

Wide Sargasso Sea, published in 1966, is one of the first novels written by a woman to present a piercing analysis of the white woman as colonial subject, and to provide a "Third World" perspective on the destructive forces of imperial culture on women, black or white. Rhys analyzes a complex nexus of gender, geography, and history in her depiction of Antoinette Cosway's colonial identity and in her charting of Antoinette's search for a place to call "home." If at that particular time in history, and in those particular places in Jamaica and England, Antoinette (or Rhys) could find no place of her own, then her decision to destroy the prison constructed for her by English society can only be seen as heroic defiance against attempts to efface her. Unlike her mother, Antoinette learns the lessons taught her by the rebellious Jamaican black community, and her destruction of Rochester's house, Thornfield Hall, directly mirrors and re-enacts the Jamaicans' destruction of the master's house, Coulibri Estate. This final act brings Antoinette "home" to her Jamaican heritage, so that, to para-phrase the quotation from Adrienne Rich that began this chapter, Antoinette's story tells of the struggle "to understand how a place on the map is also a place in history within which as a woman, a white creole, a Jamaican, I am created and trying to create."

NOTES

The title for this chapter was inspired by Audre Lorde's essay entitled "The Master's Tools Will Never Dismantle the Master's House," in which she urges women to make difference into a strengthening and empowering factor rather than a divisive and destructive one.

1. For a discussion of the terms *deterritorialization* and *nomadism*, see the two influential essays by Gilles Deleuze and Felix Guattari. "What is a Minor Literature?" (*Kafka*) discusses how a minor literature works from within to deterritorialize the major language. In their essay, "Treatise on Nomadology—The War Machine" (*Thousand Plateaus*) Deleuze and Guattari advocate nomadism as the writer's subversive mode of deterritorialization in language and literature. However, while they fit Deleuze and Guattari's definition of a "minor literature" in most other aspects, I contend that many postcolonial writers particularly, women writers) seek to reterritorialize and position themselves more definitely in their works, rather than embracing nomadism.

2. The term *sense of place* has become a key phrase in colonial and postcolonial criticism. This is reflected in the fact that two anthologies of essays have been published with that title, one edited by Peggy Nightingale and the other by Britta Olinder.

3. See, for example, Alvarez's review of Rhys's work.

4. For a perceptive discussion of the role of dreams in both *Jane Eyre* and *Wide Sargasso Sea*, see Elizabeth Baer's "The Sisterhood of Jane Eyre and Antoinette Cosway."

REFERENCES

Abel, Elizabeth, Marianne Hirsch, and Elizabeth Langland, eds. *The Voyage In: Fictions of Female Development*. Hanover, NH: University Press of New England, 1983.

Alvarez, A. "The Best Living English Novelist." *New York Times Book Review*, March 17, 1975, 6-7.

Baer, Elizabeth R. "The Sisterhood of Jane Eyre and Antoinette Cosway." *The Voyage In*. Ed. Elizabeth Abel, Marianne Hirsch, and Elizabeth Langland. Hanover, NH: University Press of New England, 1983, 131-48.

Deleuze, Gilles, and Felix Guattari. *Kafka: Toward a Minor Literature*. Trans. Dana Polan. Minneapolis: University of Minnesota Press, 1986.

———. "Treatise on Nomadology—A War Machine." *A Thousand Plateaus*. Trans. Brian Massumi. Minneapolis: University of Minnesota Press, 1987, 351-423.

DuPlessis, Rachel Blau. *Writing Beyond the Ending*. Bloomington: Indiana University Press, 1985.

Emery, Mary. "The Politics of Form: Jean Rhys's Social Vision in *Voyage in the Dark* and *Wide Sargasso Sea*." *Twentieth Century Literature* 28.4 (1982): 418-30.

Hearne, John. "The Wide Sargasso Sea: A West Indian Reflection." *Cornhill Magazine* (Summer 1974): 323-33.

Lorde, Audre. "The Master's Tools Will Never Dismantle the Master's House." *Sister Outsider*. Freedom: The Crossing Press, 1984.

Magarey, Kevin. "The Sense of Place in Doris Lessing and Jean Rhys." *A Sense of Place*. Ed. Peggy Nightingale. St. Lucia: University of Queensland Press, 1986, 47-60.

Nightingale, Peggy, ed. *A Sense of Place*. St Lucia: University of Queensland Press, 1986.

Olinder, Britta. *A Sense of Place*. Göteborg: Gothenburg University Press, 1984.

Rhys, Jean. *Wide Sargasso Sea*. *Jean Rhys: The Complete Novels*. New York: Norton, 1985.

Rich, Adrienne. *Blood, Bread, and Poetry*. New York: Norton, 1986.

Steiner, George. *Extraterritorial*. New York: Atheneum, 1971.

Vreeland, Elizabeth. "Jean Rhys: The Art of Fiction [Interview] LXIV." *Paris Review* 21.76 (1979): 218-37.

Woolf, Virginia. *Three Guineas*. New York: Harcourt Brace, 1960.

Wild Child, Tropical Flower, Mad Wife: Female Identity in Jean Rhys's *Wide Sargasso Sea*

Deanna Madden

In *Wide Sargasso Sea* (1966), Jean Rhys has written a revision of Charlotte Brontë's *Jane Eyre*, placing Rochester's mad wife at the center of her text instead of the English orphan Jane. Drawing on the brief details of Bertha Rochester's life provided by Brontë, Rhys gives her protagonist, renamed Antoinette Cosway, a past in the West Indies, where she grows up as part of the white minority.

Like Brontë, Rhys is interested in exploring female identity, a concern reflected in *Wide Sargasso Sea*'s three-part structure, which corresponds to the three phases of Antoinette's life: childhood in Jamaica; initiation into sexuality and marriage, in Dominica; and subsequent life as Rochester's mad wife in England. Each phase adds a new dimension to her identity. Her destiny—the role she will play at Thornfield Hall—hovers over the text like a predestined event. The novel asks, Who is she and what made her like this? In Jean Rhys's version, the woman glimpsed by Jane Eyre at Thornfield Hall is a product of place, time, and culture, her identity shaped by race, class, gender, and the colonial experience.

Part I, an account of Antoinette's childhood, shows her growing up poor and wild in postcolonial Jamaica. From an early age she grapples with the problem of her identity as a member of a white minority in black Jamaica. The opening sentence introduces her sense of estrangement: "They say when trouble comes close ranks, and so the white people did. But we were not in their ranks" (465). Antoinette, as a child in Jamaica, feels caught between two worlds: white and black, colonizer and colonized.[1] She is isolated from both worlds, belonging to neither but existing in a strange limbo outside both. The whites reject her pretty young mother, Annette, for a number of reasons: they despise the poverty she has fallen into; they resent her attractiveness and think her vain ("The Jamaican ladies had never approved of my mother, 'because she pretty like pretty self' Christophine said" [465]); they disapprove of her sexuality ("She was my father's second wife, far too young for him, they thought" [465]); and they consider her an outsider because of her French heritage (as Daniel says, "French and English like cat and dog in these islands since long time" [515]).[2] Left impoverished by her husband's death and the abolition of slavery (the Emancipation Act of 1833), the young widow Annette Cosway finds herself and her two children shunned like untouchables. The blacks reject them as well, perceiving them as the enemy—white people, former slave owners, the colonizer and oppressor, the outsider who does not belong, interlopers. As a child, Antoinette finds herself cast out by both segments of her society and suffers from loneliness until she finds a playmate in her black friend Tia. The night when Antoinette's family is burned out by a mob of hostile blacks, Antoinette tries to turn to Tia, whom she sees in the crowd, and is violently rejected when Tia throws a stone at her. It is a painful lesson that she does not belong, that Tia, too, sees her as the outsider.

Throughout her childhood Antoinette feels torn between these two cultures, epitomized by two mother-figures—her white mother, Annette, and the black servant Christophine, both regarded by the community as outsiders from French Martinique. Annette ignores and rejects her, doting instead on her idiot son. Annette's main gesture to protect her daughter is to marry the Englishman Mr. Mason so Antoinette will not continue to grow up "wild" (471, 538). It is one of the few options—perhaps the only option—available to her as a white Creole woman in a patriarchal/colonial society where she is isolated from the black populace by her race and has no means of supporting herself and her children. Her only alternative to poverty and isolation is to trade on her looks and marry a man wealthy enough to take care of her and her children. Mr. Mason, an Englishman newly arrived in Jamaica, fits the bill.

Whereas Annette, for the most part, ignores her daughter, the second mother-figure, black servant Christophine, acts as nurturer and caretaker for Antoinette, both when she is a child and later when she suffers from the unhappiness of her marriage to Rochester. In the end Christophine is defeated by Rochester because she is an old black woman while he is a white man in a white, male-dominated society. She has her black magic, but he has recourse to the system of power installed by colonialism—the police.

The tropical world in which Antoinette's childhood is spent is lush, beautiful, but ominous, epitomized by the garden at Coulibri with its rank vegetation and blooming flowers. Colorful orchids hide roots that resemble snakes and octopi. Antoinette longs for safety, but the lesson of her childhood is that the world is a dangerous place. She is surrounded by people who consider her an interloper. It is a world poisoned by the colonial experience, the legacy of which is racism. She is perceived by the blacks in terms of her white skin: she is a "white cockroach" (469) and a "white nigger"(470).[3] In her conflict with Tia, the barely submerged racism erupts on both sides as they hurl racial slurs at each other. In a climate of such hostility it is no wonder that Antoinette feels confused about her identity: "Between you [blacks and whites] I often wonder who I am and where is my country and where do I belong and why was I ever born at all" (519).[4]

Mr. Mason, who, by his marriage to Annette, lifts the family from their low-class status to a position of respectability, is representative of the colonizer mentality. A newly arrived Englishman in the West Indies, he regards the blacks as harmless "children" and fails to perceive their hatred for the years of oppression and for the exploitative economic system created by colonialism, which leaves them poor but creates wealth for the colonizer. He does not see that the beautiful surface of Jamaica masks a dangerous undercurrent of violence that can erupt at any time. The culmination of this violence is the burning of Coulibri, when Mason is shown to be incapable of protecting his family. The destruction of Coulibri by the blacks is a symbolic rejection of the heirs of colonialism.

The fate of Annette, the Creole mother, prefigures that of Antoinette, whose French name echoes her mother's and suggests their affinity (Davidson, 22). Annette's life is also complicated by the issues of race, class, and gender. Her poverty makes it impossible for her to be accepted by the other whites. Her race and her marriage to Cosway make her hated by the blacks. After her husband dies, she is still young and attractive, and her estrangement is more than she can bear. Her feminine nature craves romance, love, beauty. Deprived of them, she sinks into lethargy and dotes on her idiot son. She comes back to life only when the promise of romance is renewed in the person of Mr. Mason. But she feels betrayed when he ignores her warnings and fails to avert the attack on Coulibri in which her beloved parrot burns and her son dies. She identifies herself with the parrot—with its beautiful plumage and clipped wings, killed by the fires of hatred. The trauma of Coulibri precipitates the madness that will cause her husband to have her locked away.

After Coulibri burns down, Antoinette, who was growing up "wild" (471) and neglected, is sent to a convent to be educated. She perceives the convent as a "refuge" (490) from the outside world, which she now knows to be so dangerous. But the convent may pose an even greater threat to her well-being. As a product of colonialism, it perpetuates colonial ways of thinking. Antoinette is regarded, like her islands, as terrain to be colonized, civilized, and, in general, made amenable to exploitation. The convent, in effect, educates her for a female destiny in a patriarchy. She is taught needlework, neatness of appearance, deportment, modesty, and chastity: lessons in how to be a well-bred woman according to white European standards. The nuns tell her stories of female saints who are "all very beautiful and wealthy" and "loved by rich and handsome young men" (489), stories as misleading and unrealistic as fairy tales. She does not see that she is being groomed to be a wife, to conform to a patriarchal concept of the female (and colonized subject) as docile, obedient, and subordinate. But on an unconscious level, she may recognize the potential for violence and violation behind the fantasy, the terrible knowledge that surfaces in a recurring nightmare of a man who menaces her in a walled-in garden.

The first time she has this dream is when her mother, Annette, is on the verge of involving herself with an Englishman as a refuge from poverty and isolation: "I dreamed that I was walking in the forest. Not alone. Someone who hated me was with me, out of sight. I could hear heavy footsteps coming closer and though I struggled and screamed I could not move" (471). The dream combines the ominous setting of a fairy tale (the forest where one can get lost or encounter the beasts of the imagination) with a female's fear of rape. It acknowledges the threat to her body and her self by a hostile male force. The second time she has the dream is after learning that her stepfather has arranged a marriage for her. This time the dream is more detailed:

Again I have left the house at Coulibri. It is still night and I am walking towards the forest. I am wearing a long dress and thin slippers, so I walk with difficulty, following the man who is with me and holding up the skirt of my dress. It is white and beautiful and I don't wish to get it soiled. I follow him, sick with fear but I make no effort to save myself; if anyone were to try to save me, I would refuse. This must happen. Now we have reached the forest. We are under the tall dark trees and there is no wind. "Here?" He turns and looks at me, his face black with hatred, and when I see this I begin to cry. He smiles slyly. "Not here, not yet," he says, and I follow him weeping. Now I do not try to hold up my dress, it trails in the dirt, my beautiful dress. We are no longer in the forest but in an enclosed garden surrounded by a stone wall and the trees are different trees. I do not know them. There are steps leading upwards. It is too dark to see the wall or the steps, but I know they are there and I think, "It will be when I go up these steps. At the top." I stumble over my dress and cannot get up. I touch a tree and my arms hold on to it. "Here, here." But I think I will not go any further. The tree sways and jerks as if it is trying to throw me off. Still I cling and the seconds pass and each one is a thousand years. "Here, in here," a strange voice said, and the tree stopped swaying and jerking. (493)

The feminine attire of long dress and thin slippers (is it an evening dress? Is it the gown the fairy tale princess wears to a ball?) represents the female role expected of her by a patriarchal society, or, in Fayad's words, "the ideal of femininity" (441). The dress and slippers hamper her steps, just as the female role hampers Antoinette's growth into an independent and resourceful woman. The dress is white, like a bridal gown, symbolizing virginity. She fears it will be "soiled," just as she fears she will be soiled/spoiled by the man in her dream. In the first dream she was pursued; now she follows the man, like a dutiful wife following her husband. She is oppressed by a sense that the awful violation about to befall her is something over which she has no control. The dark forest of fairy tales transforms into a "garden surrounded by a stone wall" (493). The image of enclosure suggests entrapment, confinement, imprisonment.[5] As Spivak explains, the "strange threatening voice that says merely 'in here,' invit[es] her into a prison which masquerades as the legalization of love" (269). The garden suggests the garden at Coulibri and by extension her tropical islands, besieged by European colonialism. The strange tree to which she "clings" is surely phallic, and as, O'Connor notes, the dream appears to end with "the sexual act itself" (186). O'Connor interprets the dream as being "about male power, the patriarchy, and women's masochistic relationship to men and to sex" (186). It also reveals Antoinette's fears of what marriage will be: she will be entrapped, violated, despoiled, and exploited like a colonized possession.

Antoinette's sense of helplessness in the dream reflects her powerlessness as a young woman in a patriarchal society. Dependent on her stepfather, she has little control over her destiny. She sees no choice but to obey like a dutiful daughter, to acquiesce to her stepfather's wishes. As the male authority figure in her life, he assumes the right to decide her future. He thinks he has only her best interests at heart, but he proves to be as blind in his choice of husband for her as he was to Annette's warnings about the hatred that surrounded them. Antoinette becomes a mere pawn in a game played by men, her value measured in terms of money—a dowry. It is the money her would-be husband covets, not herself.

The man whom Mason has arranged for Antoinette to marry is Edward Rochester,[6] an Englishman. As second son, Rochester will inherit neither property nor money from his father in England; thus, to secure his future, he must marry an heiress. Like Mason, Rochester represents the colonial mentality. As O'Connor notes, "[H]e embodies the character of the colonizing English: aggressive, controlling, urban, a warrior who captures wealth, property, and people" (170). He never doubts his superiority as a white Englishman. Staley describes him as "a dogged Englishman whose thought and values have crystalised; he is the egocentric male figure so convinced of his 'higher level of feeling' and intelligence that he can see no other point of view" (110). His attitude toward the black people of Jamaica and Dominica is condescending and racist. He refers to them as children; he thinks they are "lazy" (508), "stupid" (511), dirty (he is offended by Christophine's dress trailing on the floor), "half-savage" (564), and crude (he objects to their fractured English and their profanity). He distrusts them and feels uncomfortable around them. He neither understands nor respects their customs, as when he carelessly tramples the frangipani wreath that has been made to welcome him. The foreignness of the people repels him: the colored scarves worn by the women, their gold earrings, their patois, their black skin. He feels overwhelmed by what he perceives as an alien people in an alien place.

Antoinette, product of this environment, also strikes him as alien: "I watched her critically. She wore a tricorne hat which became her. At least it shadowed her eyes which are too large and can be disconcerting. She never blinks at all it seems to me. Long, sad, dark alien eyes. Creole of pure English descent she may be, but they are not English or European either" (496). Antoinette is so closely identified with her tropical islands that they seem to be extensions of each other. The landscape becomes engendered through this close identification, and Antoinette becomes a manifestation of place. Thus, when she embroiders at the convent, she expresses her sense of her identity in her choice of vivid tropical colors: "We are cross-stitching silk roses on a pale background. We can colour the roses as we choose and mine are green, blue and purple. Underneath, I will write my name in fire red, Antoinette Mason, née Cosway, Mount Calvary Convent, Spanish Town, Jamaica, 1839" (488-89). Her roses are green like the vegetation of her tropical islands, blue like the sky and ocean, purple like the mountains and the orchids. For her name, she selects "fire red"—symbolic of passion and destruction and reminiscent of the most searing memory of her childhood, the burning of Coulibri.

Part II, Antoinette's initiation into sexuality and marriage, reveals her sensuous nature, identifying her with exotic tropical flowers. On her honeymoon in Dominica, she is surrounded by lush flowers: roses, orange blossoms, frangipani, pink flowers, pink roses, pale flowers, orchids, moonflowers, oleander.

The air, heavy with their scent, disturbs Rochester, who objects to this heady profusion as he also objects to the perfume in Antoinette's hair. The island is a place of riotous color, scented flowers, flaming sunsets, breathtaking views—but for him it is too intense and overwhelming, like the heat: "Too much blue, too much purple, too much green. The flowers too red, the mountains too high, the hills too near" (498). Antoinette is identified in his mind with the place—beautiful, sensuous, lush, and strange. He dislikes her easy familiarity with the blacks; he expects her to treat them as inferior and Other, and when she does not, he sees her as Other: "She was a stranger to me, a stranger who did not think or feel as I did" (513). Just as her islands are not like England, she is not like Englishwomen. He distrusts her sensuality and beauty as much as he distrusts those aspects of the landscape. He has the urge to violate the mystery of the place and the mystery of the woman: "It was a beautiful place—wild, untouched, above all untouched, with an alien, disturbing, secret loveliness. And it kept its secret. I'd find myself thinking, 'What I see is nothing—I want what it hides—that is not nothing'" (509). He cares no more for Antoinette than for the orchid he tramples underfoot: "I remembered picking some for her one day. 'They are like you,' I told her. Now I stopped, broke a spray off and trampled it into the mud" (517). He recognizes that he does not love her. He categorizes what he feels for her as something shameful and inferior to love: lust ("I was thirsty for her, but that is not love" [513]). She does not fit his idea of a proper English woman: her chemise "hitched up far above her knees" is immodest and she throws a stone "like a boy" (510). Her fight with Amelie is unseemly. She should not be so passionate—it is not English. She should be more proper, more reserved; she should hide her feelings as he does: "How old was I when I learned to hide what I felt? A very small boy. Six, five, even earlier. It was necessary, I was told, and that view I have always accepted. If these mountains challenge me, or Baptiste's face, or Antoinette's eyes, they are mistaken, melodramatic, unreal" (519). From Rochester's perspective, he is the outsider, the exile, and Antoinette's tropical world is the alien place where he does not belong. He feels menaced in this Eden that harbors monster crabs, snakes, red ants, rats, and alien ways: the half-caste servant girl Amelie strikes him as "a lovely little creature but sly, spiteful, malignant perhaps, like much else in this place" (495). Because he distrusts the place so much, he distrusts Antoinette as well. He is only too ready to believe that she is alien and evil.

But the evil does not lurk in Antoinette; it lurks in the world around her, in the backlash of racial hatred against those with white skin and wealth—the ex-slave owners, the colonialists, the interlopers. James calls Daniel Cosway "the voice of Caribbean history" (57). His malice is the ugly underside of the tropical paradise, the same hatred that erupted at Coulibri. His hatred stems from his own mixed blood identity and his resentment at being rejected by the colonialist society that spawned him. He claims to be an illegitimate offspring of lecherous old Cosway, Antoinette's father, and thinks he is entitled to some share of her estate. That failing, he hopes to extort money from Rochester. At the same time, his spite is aimed at destroying Antoinette as a kind of revenge, because she symbolizes for him the colonialist system and the injustices it has created.

For both Daniel Cosway and Edward Rochester, Antoinette becomes a scapegoat, someone on whom they can displace their hatred and desire for revenge. Daniel Cosway has apparently selected Antoinette as a convenient target, when his anger should really be directed against her late father or some other white male colonialist.[7] Rochester's anger is really at his father and brother and the English tradition of primogeniture, which dictates that the elder son inherit the estate. Unable to strike back at father or brother, he displaces his anger onto Antoinette. As a female in a colonial/patriarchal society, she is a vulnerable target.

One reason she is vulnerable is that the society makes it difficult for her to defend herself. She attempts to avoid the arranged marriage to Rochester but is pressured into it by her stepbrother Richard and by Rochester himself. Once she is married, she becomes totally dependent on Rochester because all her money passes into his hands in accord with English law. Antoinette's stepfather, in arranging the marriage, has been concerned only with giving Antoinette what English custom prescribes as the desirable female destiny: marriage with a young man of good family (i.e., of the upper class). At seventeen, Antoinette is growing too old for the convent, and clearly something must be done about her. The best solution, from his point of view, is to marry her off while she is still at a marriageable age. Provision could have been made for her to retain some control of her money, but no one bothers to do this—not her stepfather or stepbrother, who cavalierly consider Rochester "an honourable gentleman" (527), or Rochester himself, whose primary concern is her money, not her welfare. Only the women—Aunt Cora and Christophine—are outraged at this arrangement. They see how the marriage will put Antoinette at the mercy of this man, and if he turns out to be a bad husband, she will be entrapped by her financial dependency, which is indeed what happens.

However, money is not the only factor that entraps Antoinette in her marriage. More entrapping is the love she feels for Rochester—a deep erotic love that leads her to desperately seek an aphrodisiac from Christophine in the hope of once more seducing the husband who has rejected her. She thinks that if she can seduce him again, she can win him back. This is why she will not listen to Christophine's advice to leave him. It is also why she is devastated when he betrays her with Amelie. Unlike Rochester, she does not separate lust from love. As Christophine tells Rochester, "She love you so much. She thirsty for you!" (555) Given her passionate nature, once she loves, she loves to excess. Not until she is completely broken by her experience does the feeling vanish, and then it is too late: she has lost hope and, with it, all sense of self-preservation.

Even more fatal than financial dependency and the vehemence of her love is her misfortune to fall in love with a man like Edward Rochester. On the surface he may appear to meet all the requisites for a husband, but beneath the surface is a twisted man.[8] Richard Mason and his father may consider Rochester an "honorable gentleman," but Aunt Cora thinks him "[s]tiff. Hard as a board and stupid as a foot . . . except where his own interests are concerned" (527), and Christophine declares he is "a damn hard man for a young man" and "wicked like Satan self!" (554, 567). If Antoinette is a product of the warm tropics,

Rochester is certainly a product of England, a place that is cold, sunless, and monochrome, where people speak perfect English and hide their feelings. He is not honest: he has no qualms about telling lies or pretending to feel what he does not, as when he urges Antoinette to marry him not out of love but to avoid the humiliation of being rejected by a "Creole girl" (503).

Rochester arrives in Jamaica steeped in bitterness over being forced to marry for money and his bitterness warps him.[9] His thoughts are paranoid as he imagines his father and brother have conspired to marry him off to a mad heiress: "As I walked I remembered my father's face and his thin lips, my brother's round conceited eyes. They knew. And Richard the fool, he knew too. And the girl with her blank smiling face. They all knew" (520). He imagines the women in Spanish Town look at him with pity after his wedding as if they know something he does not. He imagines Christophine and Antoinette are plotting against him: "Whatever they were singing or saying was dangerous. I must protect myself" (149). He is suspicious of everyone, imagining that Christophine is after money when she tries to persuade him to give some to Antoinette and set her free. He is greedy, marrying Antoinette for her money and having no qualms about leaving her dependent or destitute.

In his treatment of the blacks and of everything associated with their way of life, Rochester reveals himself to be racist and xenophobic. His warped mind makes him an easy prey for Daniel Cosway's malice. Repelled by half-caste Daniel's "yellow sweating face and his hateful little room" (534), he is still only too ready to credit Daniel's slanders against Antoinette—that she is promiscuous, that madness runs in the family, that Rochester has been tricked into marrying her, charges that exacerbate his paranoia and reinforce his conviction that she is not a proper wife, and hence he is justified in rejecting her. Perhaps what bothers him most is his revulsion at the idea that she is in any way linked to Daniel Cosway, what Erwin refers to as "contamination from contiguity, one racial term slipping or 'leaking' into another through sheer proximity, obsessively perceived as sexual. . . . Thus, for Rochester, Antoinette's sexuality itself is an index of racial contamination" (146-47).

Once he has an excuse for turning against Antoinette, Rochester has no qualms about hurting her. His sadistic tendencies have surfaced previously in his rough lovemaking that has left its marks on her body.[10] Now he comes up with a more fiendish idea: he will betray her with Amelie, knowing that Antoinette can hear their lovemaking through her bedroom wall. From this point on he is bent on destroying her. As Christophine charges, "All you want is to break her up" (552). He imagines himself as a hurricane that will destroy Antoinette like a tree in his path. He will crush her totally, destroy her very identity, demolish who she is. And so he strips her of her lovely Creole name that links her to her mother and her beloved West Indies and replaces it with an ugly English name, a name that is sexless, colorless, joyless—Bertha. He will rob her of her beauty and the innocent pleasure she takes in it: "She'll not dress up and smile at herself in the damnable looking-glass" (560). But most of all, he will take her away from her tropical islands: "She'll not laugh in the sun again. . . . She said she loved this place. This is the last she'll see of it" (560). As Kloepfer notes:

"[T]he most terrible punishment he [Rochester] can inflict on her is not abandonment or physical injury or death but rather exile from the land of the
mother" (152). In the end Rochester recognizes that he hates the place and the
woman: "I hated the mountains and the hills, the rivers and the rain. I hated the
sunsets of whatever colour, I hated its beauty and its magic and the secret I
would never know. I hated its indifference and the cruelty which was part of its
loveliness. Above all I hated her. For she belonged to the magic and the loveliness" (565).

In his determination to destroy Antoinette by stripping her of her identity,
Rochester imagines reducing her to generic woman and confining her within a
house, not in the kitchen or a bedroom, rooms symbolic of the traditional female
role in a marriage, but, oddly enough, in a remote top floor room:[11] "I drew a
house surrounded by trees. A large house. I divided the third floor into rooms
and in one room I drew a standing woman—a child's scribble, a dot for a head,
a larger one for the body, a triangle for a skirt, slanting lines for arms and feet.
But it was an English house" (559). She will be the mad wife in the attic—the
ultimate estrangement: cut off not only from other people and a traditional
female role but from her past, her place, and her self.

The question of madness specifically, female madness, is an important theme
in *Wide Sargasso Sea*. Are Antoinette and her mother mad because of an
inherited tendency to madness, as Daniel Cosway claims? Or are they mad
because the men in their lives choose to perceive them this way?[12] Daniel
Cosway claims madness runs in the family, that Antoinette is mad like her
mother. He cites her mother's withdrawal from society as evidence of her
madness, but it was society that ostracized her, not vice versa. If she retreated
from reality, it was because reality became too depressing to face; when Mr.
Mason arrives, she comes to life again. Her later madness, when Mason finds
it necessary to have her confined, has its inception in the burning of Coulibri.
The loss of Coulibri and especially of her beloved idiot son Pierre makes reality
again too intolerable. But is Annette initially shut away by her husband for this
reason or because she behaves in an unfeminine fashion by screaming at him?
(She blames him—with good reason—for the fire and Pierre's death.) Christophine explains Annette's madness like this:

They drive her to it. When she lose her son she lose herself for a while and they shut her
away. They tell her she is mad, they act like she is mad. Question, question. But no kind
word, no friends, and her husban' he go off, he leave her. They won't let me see her.
I try, but no. They won't let Antoinette see her. In the end—mad I don't know—she give
up, she care for nothing. That man who is in charge of her he take her whenever he want
and his woman talk. That man, and others. Then they have her. Ah there is no God.
(555)

Annette's madness begins as excessive emotion—grief for her dead son. It is not
a spontaneous eruption of madness: she is driven to it by others—the hatred of
the ex-slaves who have torched Coulibri, the husband who failed to see the
danger or heed her warning and remove his family to safety. Then she is shut
away, treated as if she is mad, abandoned by her husband, friendless, isolated.

The man in charge of her treats her as a sexual toy, and when the rumor spreads, the community brands her promiscuous—and sees this as more evidence of her madness. In the end, as Christophine says, she loses hope. Antoinette's last view of her mother shows a woman who has lost contact with reality—who is kept drunk to keep her mind blurred—who lives in the past with memories of a better time before Coulibri burned, before Pierre died.

Antoinette's madness follows a similar pattern. As a child she was isolated from other people, not because of any strangeness on her own part but because the community shunned her. She seems sane enough until Rochester torments her by withdrawing his love and then blatantly betraying her with Amelie.[13] Her overwhelming love for him leads to devastation at his rejection. By her reactions she seems to confirm his idea that she is mad, because his idea of sanity (like Mason's before him) is based on male definitions of female sanity and madness, definitions that reflect cultural assumptions about proper Victorian English female behavior.[14] Thus, the very excess of her emotion is seen by him as evidence of madness—the fact that she lacks restraint. He also categorizes her sensuality and eroticism as a sign of madness: "She'll moan and cry and give herself as no sane woman would—or could" (560). As Davidson explains, according to Victorian precepts, a man is permitted to experience passion, but a woman is not: "For her to take pleasure in the transaction would be depraved, unnatural, something that only a prostitute or a madwoman might do" (32). With his twisted mind, Rochester leaps to the conviction that she is promiscuous, a veritable nymphomaniac: "She thirsts for *anyone*—not for me" (560). Promiscuity, since it is not appropriate behavior in a Victorian English lady, serves as one more sign of madness. Antoinette's drinking, her attempt to bite him, the obscenities she screams at him—all these are for him further proofs of her madness since they represent unfeminine behavior.[15] At last, like her mother, she gives up, retreating into silence and a blank expression, so that Antoinette is transformed into "marionette"—a "doll" (553) something less than fully human, Rochester's possession and plaything: "My lunatic. My mad girl" (561).

Part III reveals Antoinette in her final incarnation as the mad wife in the attic at Thornfield Hall. Now she is totally estranged—exiled in a cold foreign land, friendless, confined and abandoned by her husband, robbed of her name as well as her money and her freedom, stripped of her former identity. As James notes, "Rochester kills Antoinette by destroying both her identity of place and her identity of soul" (60). She wanders in and out of the haze of madness, wondering, "What am I doing in this place and who am I?" (568). Her madness makes her doubly imprisoned: her body is literally imprisoned in the attic room, and she is imprisoned in a madwoman's body.[16] She has no looking glass to gain a sense of self from her own appearance, and when she does glimpse herself in a downstairs mirror during one of her nocturnal escapes, she does not recognize herself. She sees a "ghost," a "woman with streaming hair" (573). The only remnant remaining of her former life is the red dress redolent of tropic scents that hangs in her press. It is her signature color, the color of passion and destruction, "the colour of fire and sunset. The colour of flamboyant flowers" (571). But now she is Bertha, the madwoman with streaming hair, who wears a "grey wrapper" (572). It is little wonder that her stepbrother Richard fails to recognize her. She is no longer Antoinette. When she attacks him with a knife, it is no spontaneous outbreak of madness: her violence is precipitated by his maddening pronouncement that he is powerless to rescue her: "I cannot interfere legally between yourself and your husband," he tells her (570). Grace Poole, the lower-class woman hired as her warden, explains: "[I]t was when he said 'legally' that you flew at him and when he twisted the knife out of your hand you bit him" (570).[17] English patriarchal law contributes to Antoinette's victimization by Rochester by giving the husband not only control of his wife's money and property but also total control of her. As O'Connor notes, "Antoinette is, like her island, 'colonized,' her independence and autonomy subsumed to British culture and to British law" (193).

Yet she is not so totally in Rochester's control as he imagines. She learns that it is possible sometimes, while Grace Poole is sleeping, to steal her keys and explore the unreal world downstairs at Thornfield Hall. In a sequel to her earlier dream, she imagines that she has climbed the steps, and they are the stairs at Thornfield Hall—they lead to the room in which she is confined. But escaping that room, she imagines accidentally setting fire to Thornfield Hall, a fire from which she flees onto the battlements. Against the red sky, she sees images of her past in the West Indies, and she hears Rochester calling to her. When she looks over the edge, she imagines that she sees Tia inviting her to leap into the pool at Coulibri. It is a choice between the white Englishman who hates her and her black childhood friend Tia, a choice between her present at Thornfield Hall and her past at Coulibri, and a choice between two identities—Bertha and Antoinette. When she leaps, she chooses to return to a better time and place and identity—to her childhood before Coulibri burned, before she and Tia quarreled. When she wakes from this dream, she knows that the dream is an image of her destiny. She knows who she is and why she is there.

NOTES

1. Erwin comments that "*Wide Sargasso Sea* seems born of a historical moment when the older nationalism of the largely absentee English settlers of the early nineteenth century, who would have looked unquestioningly to England for their cultural identity, has given way, in the century between emancipation and the time of Rhys's beginning the novel, to the 'identity crisis' of the white former colonial at the end of empire" (156).

2. For an account of the historical background to this animosity, see James. He describes in detail how the French and English struggled for control of Dominica and other islands in the West Indies (46).

3. The term "white nigger" refers to her poverty, which puts her into a lower class than other whites. Nunez-Harrell explains that "white cockroach" alludes to the white West Indian woman's status as well as her skin color and that the term is gender-specific (281-82).

4. Nunez-Harrell notes that "Antoinette's challenge is to find her place, her identity, her life's meaning in her native land or to remain adrift in the mythical wide Sargasso Sea, languishing between England and the West Indies" (288).

5. Gilbert and Gubar have pointed out the prevalence of images of enclosure in women's writing (83-92).

6. Narrative point of view shifts in this section to Rochester's perspective. However, Rochester is not identified by name until Part III. Critics have offered several explanations for this. According to Spivak, the omission of his name denies him "the Name of the Father, or the patronymic," symbolizing his oedipal role in relation to his father and his victimization by "the patriarchal inheritance law of entailment" (270-71). Fayad contends he lacks a name "because he is his own 'subject' and thus free from objectification by naming and also because by not being named he becomes omnipotent, the god-like creator of Bertha's narrative text" (443). Another possibility is that, for the unsuspecting reader, delay of the name until Part III gives the ending more shock of recognition.

7. Christophine, the voice of wisdom in *Wide Sargasso Sea*, denies that he is Cosway's son, and so does Cosway himself. Nevertheless, some colonialist fathered him, even if Cosway did not.

8. Most critics seem to regard Rhys's Rochester as sane, even if he has his faults. Davidson takes this view but also grants that he is "psychologically disturbed" (28). Mezei questions his sanity, based on his fragmented narrative voice (205-06). One interesting perspective is that of O'Connor, who suggests that there are male and female ways of being mad and that whereas Antoinette manifests a female mode of madness by directing her aggression inward and wounding herself, Rochester manifests a male mode of madness by directing his aggression outward and wounding a female (167-68).

9. Wolfe calls this his "pawn complex" (142).

10. Rochester admits to himself that he experiences dark sadistic impulses during lovemaking: "I wonder if she ever guessed how near she came to dying. . . . It was not a safe game to play—in that place. Desire, Hatred, Life, Death came very close in the darkness. Better not know how close" (514).

11. See Gilbert and Gubar for their comments on the house as a common symbol of "female imprisonment" (85).

12. See Chesler's argument that madness is often a definition imposed by men on women who do not conform to their definition of correct female/feminine behavior. According to Rigney, "Most feminists see madness, first, as a political event. Female insanity, they argue, can in a majority of cases be explained by the oppression of women in a power-structured, male-supremacist society" (6).

13. Analyzing *Jane Eyre*, Rigney explains, "Bertha embodies the moral example which is the core of Brontë's novel—in a society which itself exhibits a form of psychosis in its oppression of women, the price paid for love and sexual commitment is insanity and death, the loss of self" (16).

14. As Fayad explains, "The 'sanity' that he [Rochester] advocates is the sanity of the 'norm,' or phallocentric order, and any infringement on that 'sanity' provokes an immediate attempt to destroy the source of that infringement" (443).

15. Chesler notes that traits in women like physical aggression, sexuality, and emotionálity "are feared and punished in patriarchal mental asylums" (31).

16. Gilbert and Gubar, discussing Charlotte Perkins Gilman's "The Yellow Wallpaper," point out how in that story "a supposedly 'mad' woman has been sentenced to imprisonment in the 'infected' house of her own body" (92).

17. Spivak observes, "[i]t is the dissimulation that Bertha discerns in the word 'legally'—not an innate bestiality—that prompts her violent *re*action" (269).

REFERENCES

Chesler, Phyllis. *Women & Madness*. New York: Avon, 1972.

Davidson, Arnold E. *Jean Rhys*. New York: Ungar, 1985.

Erwin, Lee. "'Like in a Looking-Glass': History and Narrative in *Wide Sargasso Sea*." *Novel* 22 (1989): 143-58.

Fayad, Mona. "'Unquiet Ghosts': The Struggle for Representation in Jean Rhys's *Wide Sargasso Sea*." *Modern Fiction Studies* 34 (1988): 437-52.

Gilbert, Sandra M., and Susan Gubar. *The Madwoman in the Attic: The Woman Writer and the Nineteenth-Century Literary Imagination*. New Haven, CT: Yale University Press, 1979.

James, Louis. *Jean Rhys*. London: Longman, 1978.

Kloepfer, Deborah Kelly. *The Unspeakable Mother: Forbidden Discourse in Jean Rhys and H.D.* Ithaca, NY: Cornell University Press, 1989.

Mezei, Kathy. "'And It Kept Its Secret': Narration, Memory, and Madness in Jean Rhys' *Wide Sargasso Sea*." *Critique* 28 (1987): 195-209.

Nunez-Harrell, Elizabeth. "The Paradoxes of Belonging: The White West Indian Woman in Fiction." *Modern Fiction Studies* 31 (1985): 281-93.

O'Connor, Teresa F. *Jean Rhys: The West Indian Novels*. New York: New York University Press, 1986.

Rhys, Jean. *Wide Sargasso Sea*. *Jean Rhys: The Complete Novels*. New York: Norton, 1985.

Rigney, Barbara Hill. *Madness and Sexual Politics in the Feminist Novel*. Madison: University of Wisconsin Press, 1978.

Smilowitz, Erika. "Childlike Women and Paternal Men: Colonialism in Jean Rhys's Fiction." *Ariel* 17 (1986): 93-103.

Spivak, Gayatri Chakravorty. "Three Women's Texts and a Critique of Imperialism." *"Race," Writing, and Difference*. Ed. Henry Louis Gates, Jr. Chicago: University of Chicago Press, 1985.

Staley, Thomas F. *Jean Rhys: A Critical Study*. Austin: University of Texas Press, 1979.

Wolfe, Peter. *Jean Rhys*. Boston: Twayne, 1980.

PART IV

RESISTING OPPRESSIONS

Isabel Allende and the Discourse of Exile

Marketta Laurila

> I wrote *The House of the Spirits* [*La casa de los espíritus*] as a means of drying the tears I carried inside and giving form to the pain to make it my prisoner. I attributed to literature the power to resuscitate the dead, to reunite the disperse, and to reconstruct a lost world. (Allende, "El canto," 276)[1]

Writing this work, as well as *Of Love and Shadows* [*De amor y de sombra*] and *Eva Luna*, in exile in Venezuela, Allende creates tension between a metaphorical and a metonymical prefiguration; while the former reflects her desire for unity, the latter relentlessly stresses the separation of exile. Prefigurative strategies, according to Hayden White, reflect structures of consciousness and give coherence to the diverse aspects of style in any narrative, historical or fictional (*Metahistory*, x-xi). The overiding image, or prefiguration, corresponds to a "secondary meaning below or behind the phenomenon 'described'" (*Tropics*, 110) and can be identified with one of four tropes: metaphor, metonymy, synecdoche, or irony. While a metonymical interpretation postulates separation, a metaphorical interpretation postulates identity among the members of society (*Metahistory*, 34-36). While the metonymical prefiguration reveals the inescapable reality of separation that marks Allende's texts, the metaphorical mode, which stresses identification and wholeness, provides her with the means of surviving her own exile by reconstructing her lost world. Allende's three narratives reflect an interplay and tension between the surface (content) and deep (prefiguration) levels as well as a back-and-forth movement between the tropes of metaphor and metonymy. The tension between wholeness and separation reflects the pain and ambivalence of exile, an experience that underlies all three narratives.

The three works trace a trajectory that begins in *The House of the Spirits* with the reconciliation of Alba, a character closely identified with Allende herself, to the violence of her reality within her country, a country easily identifiable as Chile. *Of Love and Shadows*, a more traditional, linear narrative, leads the female protagonist, Irene, to exile but leaves her on the border between her country, again clearly Chile, and another country through which she must pass to reach a democratic country in Latin America. Allende's third narrative, *Eva Luna*, defies the reader's expectation that the trajectory toward exile would be completed. In this work Allende prefigures her field as metaphor, postulating unity and identification, and, thereby, overcomes the separation of exile, prefigured as metonomy in *Of Love and Shadows*. The overriding image of metaphor, which stresses the identity between elements in the field, merges all Latin American countries into one generic country and negates the concept of contiguity and political borders. Eva Luna now does not have to continue Irene Beltrán's trajectory across the border into exile in a contiguous space. Allende's identification of *patria* or homeland with all of Latin America dissolves the spatial separation that informs political division between distinct nation-states, allowing her characters and herself (in exile in Venezuela at the time of the writing) to remain within her *patria* ("El canto," 275).

In their article on *The House of the Spirits*, Juan Manuel Marcos and Teresa Méndez-Faith clearly establish the correlation between the unnamed country and Chile through a series of references that describe historic persons and incidents, for example: Salvador Allende, "the new candidate of the Socialist Party, a charismatic, nearsighted doctor" (192) [el nuevo candidato del Partido Socialista, un doctor miope y carismático (172)]; Augusto Pinochet, "[w]rapped in an emperor's cape . . . his august mustache trembling with vanity" (377) [Envuelto en una capa de emperador . . . sus augustos bigotes temblando de vanidad (332)]; Pablo Neruda and his funeral; the popular manifestation in support of the new socialist government; the ideological debate within the United Popular party; agrarian reform and the expropriation of haciendas; the military coup of September 11, 1973; the bombing of the presidential palace, the Palacio de Moneda; the persecution of men with beards and long hair and women in slacks; the flooding of embassies by those seeking refuge; the creation of a military caste after the coup (296).

Within this concrete historical context, Isabel Allende creates dialectical tension between an androcentric space, representing the repression and separation characteristic of patriarchal hegemony, and a gynocentric space that offers the possibility of identification between sexes and all social classes. Once reconciliation is achieved among the primary representatives of the two spaces (Esteban, the patriarch, and his granddaughter), their parallel discourses are reconciled into one text. This double reconciliation, between characters and their discourses (Marcos and Méndez-Faith, 293), juxtaposes an alternative of love (a metaphorical prefiguration implying unity) to the violence of male-dominated politics (a metonymical prefiguration implying separation).

The gynocentric text of *The House of the Spirits* consists of a fragmented diary edited by Alba, who represents the last of four generations of women included in the narrative. Alba reconstructs the family saga from her mother's letters, her grandmother's diary, and entries from the administrative books of the family hacienda, Three Marias. Alba begins writing her text in her mind after her grandmother's spirit visits her in the concentration camp where the former, faint from torture, awaits death. Clara, the grandmother, informs Alba that to resist would be the best defiance and goes on to suggest that she write with her thoughts to keep her mind active and to distract herself from the pain of torture. The narrative ends as Alba painstakingly reconstructs the story because, as she states, her mission is not to prolong hatred but simply to fill the pages while she awaits the return of her lover and the birth of her baby, engendered either by her lover or the multiple rapes she suffered at the hands of the military. The act of writing and the appropriation of words empower Alba by making her an active subject contributing to the creation of meaning when she has the least amount of control over what happens to her physical body—imprisonment in the concentration camp, torture, and rape. Alba foils her jailers' attempts to subjugate and destroy her spirit just as her grandmother, Clara, who suggested that Alba write instead of giving in to her tormentors, had maintained the integrity of her inner self when faced with her husband's desire to control her spirit.

Alba's text is juxtaposed to that of her grandfather, Esteban Trueba, the patriarchal figure embodying all the characteristics of Latin American machismo. The two texts, the gynocentric and the androcentric, address the problems of personal and political violence, the objectification of women, and the suppression of women's vision of reality to preserve patriarchal hegemony. Doris Meyer examines these two discourses in light of Elaine Showalter's adaptation of Bakhtin's concept of the "double-voiced discourse" and points out the ironic twist of Allende's narrative; Alba's muted voice becomes the dominant one, while Esteban's voice moves from dominant to muted within the gynocentric space that Allende has created (361). Showalter explains, "We can think of 'wild zone' [the gynocentric space] of women's culture spatially, experientially, or metaphysically" (262). Allende includes all three conceptualizations: spatially in terms of Clara's increasing "zone" within the patriarchal home; experientially in terms of the lifestyle of the female protagonists; and metaphysically in terms of values that motivate the female protagonists. The metaphysical space, however, plays a dominant role, for within this space, or within female consciousness, Allende finds values that are to serve as models for an egalitarian and nonviolent reality.

The women in the narrative transform their muted voices into the dominant one through a process of "resocialization" (described by Dale Spender) that disrupts men's definition of reality and thereby challenges patriarchal hegemony (131). Spender explains that this definition of reality "accepts the existence of a single 'truth,' and an 'objective' way of proceeding towards it" (62). Chaos ensues for Esteban Trueba as the women surrounding him dismantle and transform this monodimensional reality, which he can no longer defend against the intrusion of other truths elaborated by the women around him. Clara changes the physical shape of the stately mansion that Esteban built as an androcentric space to rule over his wife and legitimate heirs. Through a series of additions, Clara transforms the house into a labyrinthine structure with protuberances, twisted staircases leading nowhere, doors suspended in empty space, winding corridors, and so forth. As the shape of the house changes, so does the role of the women in the Trueba family. The patriarch is displaced to a small corner of the massive house, while Clara lays claim to the large female space to which only women have access, where the irrational and supernatural mingle with everyday events.

In the discussion of her theory of intersubjectivity, Jessica Benjamin explains that, for women, spatial metaphors may represent the discovery of their "*own, inner* desire, without fear of impingement, intrusion, or violation" (128). Benjamin cites Winnicott's idea of active containment which represents "the ability to hold oneself, to bear one's feelings without losing or fragmenting oneself—an ability crucial to introspection and self-discovery" (128). The "irrational" expansion of the house in *The House of the Spirits* represents just such a process of introspection and creative self-discovery. Eventually all the Trueba women return to the house, where they develop their talents in a process of self-actualization. Clara dedicates herself to practicing her psychic powers, Blanca begins to earn a living making ceramic figures while she raises her daughter alone, and Alba undergoes a process of political consciousness-raising that leads her to embrace political ideas opposing those of her grandfather. As the physical shape of the house changes, the Trueba women subvert Esteban's expectations of his and his family's lives within the patriarchal home.

In addition to challenging Esteban's control of the patriarchal space, Clara challenges Esteban's notions of female emotions when, instead of jealousy or betrayal, she feels solidarity with the peasant women he rapes on the hacienda. Clara identifies not only with the women but with all who are oppressed and victimized by patriarchy. She develops a close friendship with the foreman, Esteban Segundo, for whom she has more respect than for her husband. Clara rejects the monodimensional reality of patriarchy with its hierarchy of privileges and emphasis on separation; she posits an egalitarian vision of society that negates both sexual and class divisions. The women of all social classes in the narrative gradually become aligned with the workers' and peasants' struggle, producing the dichotomy: women of all social classes, workers, and peasants versus the elite males of patriarchy.

Clara's daughter, Blanca, and her granddaughter, Alba, continue the process of identification by entering into relationships with the working and peasant classes. Both participate in a gradual process of social leveling. The reconciliation and identification that inform the ideology and the metaphorical linguistic protocol of the text lead to the final reconciliation between Alba and her grandfather, Esteban. Alba's love for him, in spite of his initial alliance with those who tortured her, as well as the love that she inspires in him, induces her grandfather to accept her belief in justice, independence, and dignity for all despite gender or class. Esteban, the prototype of the patriarch, can no longer defend his meanings. He learns that structures of patriarchy that oppress men and women, as well as his own violent acts, lead to hatred and more violence. As Esteban's power diminishes in the patriarchal mansion and in the political life of the country, he begins to shrink in size physically, bringing about the curse placed upon him by his sister, Férula. As Patricia Hart points out, however, by atoning for his previous attitudes and acts of violence, Esteban avoids dying alone like a dog, as Férula predicted (134).

Alba's final identification with all social classes, her reconciliation with her patriarchal grandfather, and her refusal to respond in kind to the hatred and violence of those who raped and tortured her induce her to remain in her country and to reject the option of exile. As reconciliation is achieved on this ideological level, the gynocentric and androcentric texts are reconciled into Alba's single text.

Of Love and Shadows, Allende's second narrative, is surprisingly traditional and romantic in its portrayal of the emerging love between Irene Beltrán and Francisco Leal and the brutality of the military junta in the wake of the 1973 coup d'état. The setting of this narrative is again clearly identifiable, through geographical and historical descriptions, with Chile and continues the historical narrative of *The House of the Spirits*. While the former focuses on Allende's rise to power and the ensuing coup, the latter addresses the problem of repression during the period immediately following the coup.

The text of *Of Love and Shadows* follows a linear structure interrupted by flashbacks that describe the background of the characters. The text follows Irene's awakening to the social and political injustices in her country, her active participation as she tries to help the Ranquileo family find their daughter, who was abducted by the military, her struggle between life and death after being machine-gunned on the street, and her escape with her lover to the border. Although the narrative traces Irene's movements between contiguous spaces—her home/the Leals' home, her country/a contiguous country—the reconciliatory spirit of both primary and secondary characters points to a metaphorical prefiguration that mitigates the overriding metonymical prefiguration of separation.

While the dialectical tension in *The House of the Spirits* leads to an ideological and discursive reconciliation, the chronological, linear discourse of an omniscient third-person narrator in *Of Love and Shadows* reinforces the image of contiguity. On the discursive level, the text leads irremediably to separation, to Irene's exile. The process of consciousness-raising moves Irene physically and psychologically from her familiar, safe bourgeois environment into that of the struggling intellectual, the Leal home presided over by the exiled anarchist, Professor Leal, and later into that of the impoverished peasant, the Ranquileo family. This movement within space, separating Irene gradually from her home, corresponds to a psychological separation from her previous values and from her former fiancé, Captain Morante. Yet the separation is coupled with a greater identification with different social classes as a result of Irene's consciousness-raising. The metonymical prefiguration on the discursive level—the physical and psychological separation of the characters from their former home, lifestyle and values—is brought into a dialectical relationship with the metaphorical prefiguration on the ideological level—identification with all social classes and personal integrity. The exaggerated stress on reconciliation and wholeness within society throughout the text, with its attendant metaphorical protocol, has induced María Inés Lagos-Pope to write:

Although the novel takes place in Chile, there are murderers and not only victims, these historical details are only suggested. The rest of the population is made up of friendly and mature people who, when they become aware of injustices, do not hesitate to join with the victims of oppression. Even though this conciliatory tone may be appealing and desirable, to eliminate any trace of malice in such a vast social spectrum and not to show the conflict either on the level of the narrative or of the characters, makes the novel lose interest. It presents a partial and idealized vision of a problematic and highly polarized situation. (213)

These reconciliations respond to Allende's need to overcome, on the ideological level, the painful separation that ultimately dominates the text on the discursive level. In *The House of the Spirits*, the tension in the narrative exists on both the ideological and discursive levels between the metaphorical and metonymical prefiguration, respectively, with a metaphorical resolution on both levels. In *Of Love and Shadows*, on the other hand, the tension exists between a metaphorical prefiguration on the ideological level and a metonymical prefiguration on the discursive level, with the latter dominating.

Lagos-Pope also notes and criticizes the absence of a strong male figure that represents the foundation of the repressive military apparatus as it exists historically. Three military officials who appear in the narrative (Irene's former boyfriend, Captain Gustavo Morante; Sergeant Ramírez, godfather to the Ranquileo children; and Pradelio Ranquileo) betray the fraternal order of the military when they become aware of its brutality and injustice. Gustavo Morante, who has dedicated his life to the military and has believed until this moment in the integrity of the institution, leaves the hospital where Irene lies between life and death, and he mounts a rebellion among the ranks. His decisive action is not well motivated, considering his long-term close association with the military and his recent breakup with Irene. His rapid conversion contrasts sharply with Esteban Trueba's (*The House*) gradual recognition of the abuses of the government that he has supported. Sargent Rivera, also a career soldier, frees Pradelio from his isolation cell while the other men watch, tacitly approving of the action, since the lieutenant had unjustly imprisoned him. Pradelio, admittedly with greater motivation, deserts and betrays his superior officer and friend when the latter abducts, rapes, and kills Evangelina, Pradelio's adopted sister whom he loves passionately. These military figures are clearly idealized, as Lagos-Pope argues, since they ultimately respond with compassion and value family, friendship, and honor over allegiance to the military.

Although Lieutenant Ramírez represents most closely the brutality and violence of the military, his actions respond less to the dictates of the military apparatus than to his damaged machismo, when he becomes visibly unnerved before his men the first time he executes a man and when Evangelina picks him up and throws him to the ground. His murder of Evangelina (and of the others found in the mine of Los Riscos) appears less frightening since it is the action of an individual rather than of a powerful institution.

Reconciliation also occurs between Beatriz Alcántara, Irene's mother, and Fernando Leal. Although the former never abandons her self-serving denial of the violence around her, she does eventually reconcile with Fernando, whom she blames for Irene's political involvement and the injuries she suffers because of this involvement. Fernando's great love for Irene, clear in his suffering at her bedside, induces Beatriz to forgive him.

As in *The House of the Spirits*, reconciliation is achieved through the power of love to overcome political and ideological barriers and to induce the protagonists to reject the violence of the military regime. In both narratives, although members of the military, Pedro García in *The House* and Lieutenant Ramírez in *Of Love*, rape, torture, or kill, their actions correspond to personal, rather than political, motives. Allende juxtaposes the hatred and vengefulness that inspire their actions, actions of males who dominate politics, to the love and reconciliatory spirit that motivate female protagonists.

Allende relieves the overriding image of contiguity and separation in the narrative through a circular movement in which Fernando and Irene reverse Professor Leal and Hilda's journey from Spain to exile in Chile. When Fernando and Irene leave Chile, Hilda asks them to go to Spain to the stone house that she abandoned, with its contents, in order to find her husband and go into exile with him. The text reads:

Fernando reflected on the capricious fate that had obliged his parents to abandon their home and go into exile—only for him, many years later and for the same reasons, to reclaim it. He imagined himself unlocking the door with the same turn of the wrist his mother used to lock it almost a half century before, and he felt as if during the same time his family had wandered in a great circle. (263)

[Fernando caviló en el destino caprichoso que obligó a sus padres a abandonar el lugar natal para ir al exilio y que tantos años más tarde tal vez se lo devolvía a él por igual motivo. Se imaginó abriendo la puerta, con el mismo gesto empleado por su madre casi medio siglo atrás para cerrarla, y sintió que en todo ese tiempo habían andado en círculos. (269)]

The metaphorical identification between Chile and the mother country Spain, the homeland of the Leal family where a house awaits the young couple, and the ideology of reconciliation, which weakens the novel, do not, however, assuage the pain of separation with which the novel ends.

In *Eva Luna*, Allende's Pan-Americanism provides an escape from the separation threatened in the previous work. The metaphorical prefiguration that underlies the work establishes identity among the elements in the field, abolishing contiguity and hence boundaries within space. All of Latin America is apprehended as one unified space, where countries are superimposed rather than contiguous. The negation of contiguity between Latin American countries negates exile, which refers to movement through contiguous space.

The action, therefore, occurs in a generic Latin America, rather than a specific country. The geographical descriptions and the political events, alternating episodes of dictatorship and democracy, are no longer identified with Chile as in the two earlier narratives. The political fluctuations affect the protagonists less than in the previous two works, and even the military appears less menacing. General Rodríguez, infatuated with Eva, behaves as a gentleman, withdrawing to wait for Eva to contact him. Even after the soap opera, written by Eva and laced with Rolf Carlé's clips of the assault on the prison, airs on national television, the general, contrary to our expectations of the military in Latin America, merely asks for Eva's cooperation and allows her to leave freely when she refuses.

Like Alba and Irene, Eva becomes involved in political activity through her love for a man, the street urchin, Humberto Naranjo, who later becomes Eva's protector and then joins the guerrillas. Unlike the other two protagonists, Eva never goes through a process of consciousness-raising and identification with class or other political struggles. She helps Humberto in his plan to free prisoners from Agua Santa strictly out of loyalty to her friend and former protector. Withdrawing to her private life after finishing her part in the mission, making false grenades, Eva learns of the outcome on the news. Her role changes from that of participant to that of spectator. Her identification with the less privileged (Elvira, La Señora and other prostitutes, the transvestite Mimi, street children) results directly from the nurturing and love she receives from these people in her picaresque journey through life.

While in *The House of the Spirits* the act of writing offered Alba a means to remember those who disappeared and to survive the experience of torture, which she could not control, in *Eva Luna* writing takes on the more important function of changing or creating reality. Long before she can write, Eva learned the art of storytelling from her mother, who *created* a world for her. Eva tells of her mothers' advice:

Words are free, she used to say, and she appropriated them; they were all hers. She sowed in my mind the idea that reality is not only what we see on the surface; it has a magical dimension as well, and, if we so desire, it is legitimate to enhance it and color it to make our journey through life less trying. (21)

[Las palabras son gratis, decía y se las apropiaba, todas eran suyas. Ella sembró en mi cabeza la idea de que la realidad no es sólo como se percibe en la superficie, también tiene una dimension mágica y, si a uno se le antoja, es legítimo exagerarla y ponerle color para que el tránsito por esta vida no resulte tan aburrido. (26)]

Eva, however, learns the value of storytelling when she imitates a peasant who chanted verses in exchange for coins or when she offers her stories in exchange for friendship, shelter, and affection. Storytelling and writing are like molding the "Porcelana" [porcelain],[2] a craft that Eva learns from one of her mistresses. Eva resists the temptation of this strange substance, which according to her, poses the danger that the artist might create a world of lies and become lost in it. However, not realizing the similarity, she falls into the same trap with words, with which she molds her own world.

When Rolf tells Eva that his beloved, retarded sister, Katharina, suffered a sad, lonely death in a hospital, Eva responds, "All right, she died, but not the way you say. Let's find a happy ending for her" (231) [Está bien, se murió, pero no como tú dices. Busquemos un buen final para ella (238)]. She proceeds to create a peaceful death for Katharina and a happy life for the rest of Rolf's family in Germany (232). In like manner, the "Porcelana" provides a successful, improbable, nonviolent ending to Humberto's plan to attack the prison. The guerrillas give the prisoners false grenades and rifles that Eva molds from this substance, which passes easily through the metal detection devices.

As Eva begins to write her own life in the script for the soap opera "Bolero," she tells the colonel that she likes to live her life the way it should be, as a novel. However, we suspect that she *writes* her life like she would like it to be. Eva herself says:

I suspected that I would reach the end [of the soap opera] only at my own death, and was fascinated by the idea that I was another character in the story, and that I had the power to determine my fate, or invent a life for myself. (225)

[Sospechaba que el fin llegaría sólo con mi propia muerte y me atrajo la idea de ser yo también uno más de la historia y tener el poder de determinar mi fin o inventarme una vida. (231)]

Eva leaves us to doubt her text by her contradictory final statements. She writes that she and Rolf loved each other for a prudent time until their love wore thin, only to contradict her statement with the following:

Or maybe that isn't how it happened. Perhaps we had the good fortune to stumble into an exceptional love, a love I did not have to invent, only clothe in all its glory so it could endure in memory—in keeping with the principle that we can construct reality in the image of our desires. (271)

[O tal vez las cosas no ocurrieron así. Tal vez tuvimos la suerte de tropezar con un amor excepcional y yo no tuve necesidad de inventarlos, sino sólo vestirlo de gala para que perdurara en la memoria, de acuerdo al principio de que es posible construir la realidad a la medida de las propias apetencias. (281)]

Eva, like Scheherazade, the protagonist of *One Thousand and One Arabian Nights* who postpones her death by telling the king stories (and who appears in the introductory epigram of Allende's narrative), invents her stories—her life—to survive the reality of her existence. The unconvincing and incongruent last ten pages of the text leave the reader wondering about Eva's fate and suspecting that her true story falls in the chasm between the world she fabricates with words, instead of the "Porcelana," and the unforgiving, violent reality of politics in Latin America. The text not only negates exile through its metaphorical apprehension of space, but also negates the need for exile through its reconciliatory representation of those in power. On the discursive level, the text also negates contiguity by proposing the possibility of multiple realities existing simultaneously rather than contiguously.

The House of the Spirits, *Of Love and Shadows*, and *Eva Luna* reflect Allende's search for a response to the violence of the military regime that forced many into exile. All three texts reveal a resistance to the exile forced upon the author herself. While the first narrative places faith on reconciliation and denies the need for exile, the second moves relentlessly toward separation. The third presents an unexpected reversal of the process begun in the second through its identification of all Latin American countries and the negation of boundaries within the continent. Although wholeness wins out over separation in the trajectory the three narratives trace, the pain of separation comes through clearly in Allende's discourse of exile.

NOTES

1. The translation is mine.
2. The English translation retains the Spanish "Porcelana" in italics since the word refers to an imaginary substance with somewhat fantastical properties rather than to real porcelain. I retain the Spanish "Porcelana."

REFERENCES

Allende, Isabel. "El canto de todos." *Evaluación de la literatura femenina de Latino-américa, Siglo 20: 2 Simposio Internacional de Literatura.* Ed. Juana Alcira Arancibia. Vol. 1. San José: Editorial Universitaria Centroamericana, 1985, 271-78.
———. *Eva Luna.* Trans. Margaret Sayers Peden. New York: Knopf, 1988.
———. *Eva Luna.* México: Edivisión, S.A., 1988.
———. *The House of the Spirits.* Trans. Magda Bogin. New York: Bantam Books, 1986.
———. *La casa de los espíritus.* México: Edivisión, S.A., 1988.
———. *Of Love and Shadows.* Trans. Margaret Sayers Peden. New York: Knopf, 1987.
———. *De amor y de sombra.* México: Edivisión, S.A., 1986.
Benjamin, Jessica. *The Bonds of Love: Psychoanalysis, Feminism, and the Problem of Domination.* New York: Pantheon Books, 1988.
Hart, Patricia. *Narrative Magic in the Fiction of Isabel Allende.* London: Associated University Presses, 1989.
Lagos-Pope, María Inés. "Isabel Allende, *De amor y de sombra.*" *Latin American Literary Review* 15 (1987): 207-13.
Marcos, Juan Manuel, and Teresa Méndez-Faith. "Multiplicidad, dialéctica y reconciliación del discurso en *La casa de los espíritus.*" *Evaluación de la literatura femenina de Latinoamérica, Siglo 20: 2 Simposio Internacional de Literatura.* Ed. Juana Alcira Arancibia. Vol. 1. San José: Editorial Universitaria Centroamericana, 1985, 287-98.
Meyer, Doris. "Parenting the Text: Female Creativity and Dialogic Relationships in Isabel Allende's *La casa de los espíritus.*" *Hispania* 73 (May 1990): 360-65.
Showalter, Elaine. "Feminist Criticism in the Wilderness." *The New Feminist Criticism: Essays on Women, Literature and Theory.* Ed. Elaine Showalter. New York: Pantheon Books, 1985, 243-70.
Spender, Dale. *Man Made Language.* London: Routledge and Kegan Paul, 1985.
White, Hayden. *Metahistory: The Historical Imagination in Nineteenth-Century Europe.* Baltimore: Johns Hopkins University Press, 1973.
———. *Tropics of Discourse.* Baltimore: Johns Hopkins University Press, 1978.

Too Disconnected/Too Bound Up: The Paradox of Identity in Mercè Rodoreda's *The Time of the Doves*

Kayann Short

The feminist critique of Western epistemology has exposed how women's perceptions of lived experience are different from those traditionally represented in political, historical, and social discourses. The idea that women speak "in a different voice," to borrow Carol Gilligan's influential title, has been particularly popular in the discussion of literature written by women because of its emphasis on "voice" as the written articulation of women's experiences. For example, at a panel on "Gender Poetics," African American poet June Jordan explained that she chose female personae for her poems because:

the political world is supposed to be a male world; it's supposed to do with the kind of power that women know nothing about. [But] whether or not we are actually in positions of political power, we are certainly affected by the exercise of political power. . . . It's very important . . . for us to understand that you cannot talk about what's happening in Central America or in the Middle East or in South Africa, without looking at that through the eyes, through the embodiment, in fact, of [the] response of a woman. . . . And I think that that gives to our understanding of these places and issues an entirely different perspective, which is at least as important as what you will encounter in the New York *Times*.

Similarly, in "Reading Contemporary Spanish Narrative by Women," Elizabeth Ordoñez suggests that since a woman's position is "often marginal to the making of history," yet "nevertheless suffers its effect," such "paradoxical experience, once considered natural law or female destiny by the dominant, male-defined culture, accordingly becomes restlessly problematical in the texts of women" (247). Difference, then, is not just a question of how women differ from men but of how women experience themselves in the paradoxical position of being marginal to, but affected by, hegemonic discourses of power.

The Time of the Doves, originally published in 1962 as *La Plaça del Diamant* by Catalan writer Mercè Rodoreda, lends itself to this feminist framework of paradox through the novel's portrayal of a woman's life in Barcelona during the turbulent period from the onset of the second republic to the aftermath of the

Spanish civil war.[1] Feminist critics such as Kathleen Glenn have pointed out how the novel presents "the other side of the story" from official accounts of the period, because of its consistent focalization and narration of events through the consciousness and voice of its protagonist, Natalia, a working-class woman struggling to survive against gender, class, and national oppression (60). Political names, dates, and statistics are strikingly absent from the narrative. For Natalia, the war is just a "piece of history" she has gotten "mixed up in," yet political events cause catastrophic changes in her life (125). She calls the establishment of the second republic "a day that made a notch" in her life, because with it her "little headaches turned into big headaches" when she takes a cleaning job to support her two small children since her husband is out of work (71). Rodoreda herself suggested a paradigm of paradox for *The Time of the Doves* by describing the period before she left Barcelona as "too disconnected from everything, or maybe too terribly bound up with everything, though that might sound like a paradox" (Rosenthal, 7-8). Writing the novel while exiled in Geneva, Rodoreda, like Natalia, was both shaped by, and alienated from, Catalan history and politics.

Yet the placement of women in a position of paradox can be, to borrow Ordóñez's term, "restlessly problematical" in that paradox itself is not a stable, static relationship between two terms but an uneasy, shifting place that seems to be no place. As Caren Kaplan explains: "This location is fraught with tensions; it has the potential to lock the subject away in isolation and despair as well as the potential for critical innovation and particular strengths" (187). Feminists warn of the risks of theorizing what Teresa de Lauretis calls "the nonbeing of *woman*": "at once captive and absent in discourse, [she is] simultaneously asserted and denied, negated and controlled" (115). De Lauretis links current discussions of female identity as "a process of continuing renegotiation of external pressures and internal resistances" with feminism's evolving conception of itself as a process that seeks to account for simultaneous and contradictory differences between women (137). As long as feminists view women's experiences singularly, along an axis of sexual difference, placing paradox as a trope for female identity risks reinscribing a closed system of oppression based only on male-female relations, thereby foreclosing possibilities for oppositional strategies organized around intersecting locations of resistance.

An alternative paradigm of paradox suggested by women of color includes the recognition that gender is only one aspect of a movement between margin and center. Race, ethnicity, nationality, class, and sexual preference—all culturally specific positions as well as particular relationships to language—must be included in any analysis of positionality.[2] María Lugones and Elizabeth Spelman, for example, call for a feminist criticism that will "engage in a mutual dialogue that does not reduce each one of us to instances of the abstraction called 'women'" (581), while Audre Lorde cautions, "The oppression of women knows no ethnic nor racial boundaries, true, but that does not mean it is identical within those boundaries" (97). Furthermore, cultural identities do not exist along parallel, coequal axes but interact and intersect within an imbricated system of practices.

In the field of American feminist literary criticism, feminist scholars are currently rethinking earlier assumptions about the universal nature of female experience as expressed in literature written by women and are actively engaged in an often painful critique of their own biases. This critique pertains not only to the reading of writers marginalized by the Anglo-European tradition in our own country but also to ethnocentric readings of works by writers of other countries.

With the end of the Franco regime in 1975, interest in Spain's growing feminist movement, as well as increased access to literary works by women, focused new academic attention on Spanish women's literature. Because this interest coincided with the growth of American feminist literary criticism as a discipline, works by Hispanic women writers were often read and discussed in terms of "women's roles" or "women's oppression." However, as Linda Chown warned in her 1983 review essay, early American feminist criticism of Spanish novels by women tended "either to consider the novels as aesthetic products independent of cultural tradition or evaluate[d] them in accordance with American feminist values," reading "the Spanish world either in reductive black and white terms or as a mirror reflection of American reality" (91, 96).

According to Chown, American critics often measured a character in terms of the "physical world"; they tended to "conceive of significant change as external or physical and to overestimate the importance of the social world" (96). These biases caused a misreading of Spanish women writers' "concern for the invisible, inner world and a belief in the possibility of internal harmony and authentic personal growth" (97). Chown cautioned that "this inner growth may be hard to 'read,' given the evident fragmentation and cruelty of physical, external circumstances" (98). By failing to place Hispanic women's writing in its own cultural context, American critics "render[ed] the world as a hopeless, alienating place for Spanish heroines" (96).[3]

Without consideration of the importance of inner reality to the texts of Hispanic women writers, it would be possible to label *The Time of the Doves* "a woman's story about a life turned in and imprisoned within itself" (Wyers, 301). However, placing the novel within a framework of paradox defined as a movement between multiple "centers and margins" allows a reading of Natalia's inwardness as an oppositional strategy of survival, a means of living within a dominant society hostile to the needs and desires of those it oppresses (Kaplan, 188).

As a young wife and mother, Natalia is exhausted from meeting the incessant demands of children, household, and her husband, Quimet's, doves: "I was worn out. I was killing myself working and everything seemed to go wrong. Quimet didn't see that I needed a little help myself instead of spending all of my time helping others and no one could see how I felt and everyone kept asking me to do more like I was superhuman" (107). Natalia is oppressed not only by traditional sex roles but also by class exploitation since her rich employers insist they can pay her less since she is selling them her work "wholesale" (82). Later, after fascist forces have almost destroyed Barcelona, Natalia considers suicide and murder rather than submit her children to slow death by starvation. Yet, despite, and perhaps because of, her struggles with gender, class, and national oppression, Natalia is not a victim. Rather, her life represents a woman's victory in a chaotic world turned upside-down by "a piece of history" (125). Rodoreda uses images of silence and inner reality to portray this working-class woman's identity as being "too disconnected from everything" and "too terribly bound up with everything" at the same time (Rosenthal, 7-8).

Rodoreda's narrative technique in *The Time of the Doves* blurs the distinction between external and internal awareness through her use of a first-person monologue that metonymically juxtaposes physical sensations and memories with details of setting and characterization in an often stream-of-consciousness style, as in the following passage from the beginning of the novel, just before the young Natalia meets her future husband, Quimet, for the first time at a neighborhood street festival in the Plaça del Diamant:

My petticoat had a rubber waistband I'd had a lot of trouble putting on with a crochet hook that could barely squeeze through. It was fastened with a little button and a loop of string and it dug into my skin. I probably already had a red mark around my waist, but as soon as I started breathing harder I began to feel like I was being martyred. There were asparagus plants around the bandstand to keep the crowd away, and the plants were decorated with flowers tied together with tiny wires. And the musicians with their jackets off, sweating. My mother had been dead for years and couldn't give me advice and my father had remarried. My father remarried and me without my mother whose only joy in life had been to fuss over me. (15-16)

Here Natalia's pain is displaced onto her surroundings—the plants are being "martyred" just as she is—and this martyrdom is equated with motherlessness. Because relationships between women are important in Spanish culture, both to provide supportive networks and to pass on traditions and knowledge, Natalia's motherlessness is linked to both her naiveté and her inarticulateness. At the beginning of the novel she says, "I really didn't have any idea what I was doing in the world" (38) and "We lived without words in my house and the things I felt scared me because I didn't know where they came from" (28).

In "A Woman's Voices: Mercè Rodoreda's *La Plaça del Diamant*," Frances Wyers perceptively parallels Natalia's silence under male domination with the suppression of the Catalan language during the Franco regime (a language from which Rodoreda, writing in Geneva, was doubly exiled): "This book, all words, is about speechlessness communicated in a language that is itself, at the time of its writing, being eradicated" (304). However, for Wyers the style of Natalia's narration is limiting:

Natalia's account is not an autobiography; there is no final taking stock, no deliberate tying of past and present, no psychological or moral distance between past feeling and present telling. Natalia never stands away from her world; she cannot categorize or judge; she does not tell us about her violence but she describes violent acts. Nor does she reflect on her position as a woman; she simply puts it before us. (307)

Because the novel's "only exterior projection is the narrative, the lament itself," the only location for hope or happiness is in the *author's* writing of the story as "literature comes to the rescue of characters who speak of passivity and impotence" (Wyers, 307, 308).

By negatively defining Natalia's silences, Wyers overlooks the significance of the paradox she herself implies: the novel is written by a character who "repeatedly protests her inability to speak" (301). This position is not accidental. As Clarasó points out, Rodoreda's previous novels (written, although not published, before *The Time of the Doves*) did not merge the roles of protagonist and narrator. In *The Time of the Doves*, however, this blending breaks down the boundaries between objective and subjective realities. *Natalia's* voice, not Rodoreda's, tells the story, a role reinforced in those rare moments when the narrator disrupts the diegesis. For example, when Natalia is describing the layout of her employer's home, she says, "I noticed all this later on, of course" and "I don't know if I'm explaining it clearly" (81). Such statements emphasize Natalia's concern with the process of recollection rather than reflection or judgment.

In fact, rather than limiting her role as narrator, Natalia's naiveté and silence are integral to it. Kathleen Glenn states that because Natalia "finds the world and her own place in it incomprehensible," the reader must "fill in the gaps, connect the blanks, and listen to Natalia's silences if he [*sic*] wishes to hear the other side of the story" (66-67). Mercè Clarasó relates this naiveté to Rodoreda's view of Catalonian political events:

Rodoreda's choice of a simple, unsophisticated woman like Colometa [the name her husband gives her] as the center of consciousness of a novel that describes the impact of the Civil War on the ordinary people allows her to make an unvoiced comment on the whole tragic business. Colometa's inability to see the point of any of it can be taken, on the surface, as springing from her own limitations; but it can also be taken as Rodoreda's way of saying the same thing, that the pointlessness is inherent in the situation itself. (150)

Thus Natalia's presence as both "articulate" narrator and "inarticulate" character embodies her paradoxical position as both outside and inside hegemonic discourse and problematizes the feminist ideal of speaking "in a different voice." Natalia's realization at the end of the novel that "I thought more than I said and I thought things you can't tell anyone and I didn't say anything" signifies neither silence nor speech but a moment of being in language, of lived experience as it is understood by the person experiencing it (200). Most important, for Natalia this statement represents the awareness of an internal voice that is able to exist in opposition to the society around it.

Rodoreda's refusal to locate her protagonist's identity in either silence or speech parallels the position of women writers like herself under the harsh censorship restrictions imposed by the Franco regime. As Janet Pérez and others have outlined, such writers found creative and subversive methods to circumvent the censors. One such method was to employ the guise of naiveté. The less intellectual the character, the less seriously the novel would be taken by the censors.[4] Although Rodoreda's characterization of Natalia as innocent and inarticulate should not be attributed solely to this motive, one reason *The Time of the Doves* was reprinted twelve times during the Franco regime may have been that, ironically, it was "only" about a woman's life and, therefore, not a political novel.

Just as the novel contextualizes and complicates definitions of silence and speech, images of inwardness represent not only confinement, enclosure, or isolation but also harmony and love. Images of termites burrowing in wood, waves crashing inside a shell, chicks forming inside eggs, and sap surging through trees all represent Natalia's heightened awareness of inner realities. Natalia often uses such concrete metaphors to express her innermost feelings. For example, when she suffers a guilty conscience at the beginning of the novel for breaking her engagement to one man in order to marry Quimet, she says, "I felt a pain that hurt deep inside me, as if in the middle of the peace I'd felt before a little door had opened that was hiding a nest of scorpions and the scorpions had come out and mixed with the pain and made it sting even more and had swarmed through my blood and made it black" (21).

Later, at the news of Quimet's death, the simile of a disorderly house reveals the shock and pain she has forbidden her "heart of stone" to feel:

I'd wake up at night and all my insides were like a house when the moving men come and shift everything around. That's what I felt like inside: with wardrobes in the front hall and chairs with their legs sticking up and cups on the floor waiting to be wrapped in paper and packed in straw in boxes and the mattress and the bed taken apart and leaning against the wall and everything all messed up. (139)

Throughout the novel, bodily images such as hearts, blood, guts, umbilical cords, and navels express connection—or the need for connection—with others. At the beginning of the war, when Natalia is worn out from the responsibilities of caring for two households, she wakes up in the middle of the night feeling like "someone had tied a rope around my guts and was tugging on them, like I still had that cord on my belly button from when I was born and they were tugging all of me out through my belly button. . . . Everything sucked out into nothingness again through that little tube that had dried out after they knotted it" (112-13). Here the image of an umbilical cord expresses Natalia's struggle to remain connected to her inner self, while at the end of the novel, the image of a navel links Natalia with her second husband, Antoni, during a moment of shared solitude: "and before I fell asleep as I was rubbing his belly my finger bumped into his belly button and I stuck it inside to stop it up so he wouldn't empty out" (200).

Bodily functions also symbolize life as it cannot be controlled or manipulated but only lived, as in this passage toward the end of the novel where Natalia remembers the belief of Senyora Enriqueta, an older woman who befriends the motherless Natalia, that "we had many interwoven lives and sometimes but not always a death or marriage separated them. . . . [and] those little interwoven lives fight and torture us and we don't know what's going on just like we don't know how hard our hearts work or how our guts suffer" (194). This passage also uses the imagery of weaving to express the interconnected nature of individual lives, representing both the interwoven moments of an individual life (as in the protagonist's progression from "Natalia" before her marriage, to "Colometa" when she is married to Quimet, to "Senyora Natalia" after his death) as well as the way one person's life is connected with another's.

Weaving also symbolizes Natalia's concept of her own existence as one individual thread joined with many others, not in an oppressive way but through love. As Spanish writer Carmen Martín Gaite remarks, "One is never free; the person who is not tied to something does not live" (Chown, 104). This sense of interwoven lives can be seen most dramatically after her daughter's marriage inspires Natalia's return to the neighborhood where she lived with Quimet, a place she has been afraid to visit since his death: "I felt like I'd already done what I was doing sometime before but I didn't know when or where, like everything was growing out of roots in some time without memory" (195). Here time is "without memory" because it is time without past, present, or future—time that is recursive in the sense of life always spiraling back on itself.

Earlier, Natalia experiences a similar sense of time as different from both the "unnatural" mechanical time of clocks and calendars and the "natural" time of biology when she realizes that her daughter is becoming a woman:

And I got a strong feeling of the passage of time. Not the time of clouds and sun and rain and the moving stars that adorn the night, not spring when its time comes or fall, not the time that makes leaves bud on branches and then tears them off or folds and unfolds the flowers, but the time inside me, the time you can't see but it molds us. The time that rolls on and on in people's hearts and makes them roll along with it and gradually changes us inside and out and makes us what we'll be on our dying day. (183-84)

Here time is both recursive and internal; it cannot be measured or marked in any way but only lived.

At the end of the novel, Natalia confronts the horrors of her past—war, death, poverty, starvation—when she returns to the plaza where, as a young girl dressed in white who "didn't have any idea what [she] was doing in the world," she stood at the edge of her future (38). Alone in the middle of the empty square with the buildings rising around her like the sides of a funnel, Natalia liberates herself from her past through a solitary scream that she calls "letting go":

and I covered my face with my arms to protect myself from I don't know what and I let out a hellish scream. A scream I must have been carrying around inside me for many years, so thick it was hard for it to get through my throat, and with that scream a little bit of nothing trickled out of my mouth, like a cockroach made of spit . . . and that bit of nothing that had lived so long trapped inside me was my youth and it flew off with a scream of I don't know what . . . letting go? (197)

Neither speech nor silence, Natalia's scream manifests inner emotion in a material image: a cockroach made of spit. That "little bit of nothing," itself a paradox, represents Natalia's life as both "too disconnected" from, and "too bound up" with, the experiences that have shaped her life as she has lived it. Told from the paradoxical position of expressing both the "other side of the story" and the story itself, the novel can offer no "happily-ever-after" ending, but the final image of flying birds and the word *happy* suggest that Natalia has found an inner harmony of peace and self-awareness.

In a 1973 interview with Mercè Rodoreda, Catalan critic and author Montserrat Roig wrote that Rodoreda's characters are "too wounded to die," that they have an instinct to live even while they contemplate suicide (39; my translation). In the same interview, Rodoreda herself stated that the only way to survive is "simply, to go on living," that "some hope always remains" (39). For Natalia, "living" during a time of political turmoil and devastation is an act of survival. To read *The Time of the Doves* as a novel of inwardness and silence without attention to its specific cultural context denies the power of these qualities as oppositional strategies. Instead, a focus on how women's identities are paradoxically both "externally constructed *and* internalized" (de Lauretis, 122; emphasis added) enables the recognition of Natalia's courageous struggle against the devastating effects of "a piece of history" (125). Having reached the end of the novel, we must go back and reread the epigraph to understand that this working-class woman's life presents not one stable position of female identity but a shifting, paradoxical one: "My dear, these things are life" (13).

NOTES

1. I am not including quotations from the original Catalan edition because it is not readily available in the United States and because I have used the English translation exclusively.

2. See Kaplan for a discussion of "positionality" in literature.

3. Like feminist criticism of American literature, recent feminist analyses of texts by Hispanic women are increasingly sensitive to cultural and historical contexts. See, for example, the special issue of *ALEC* edited by Mirella Servodidio, *Reading for Difference: Feminist Perspectives on Women Novelists of Contemporary Spain*.

4. From a lecture by Janet Pérez, "Post-War Women Writers of Spain." See also Linda Gould Levine, "The Censored Sex: Woman as Author and Character in Franco's Spain."

REFERENCES

Chown, Linda. "American Critics and Spanish Women Novelists, 1942-1980." *Signs* 9 (1983): 91-107.

Clarasó, Mercè. "The Angle of Vision in the Novels of Mercè Rodoreda." *Bulletin of Hispanic Studies* 57 (1980): 143-52.

de Lauretis, Teresa. "Eccentric Subjects: Feminist Theory and Historical Consciousness." *Feminist Studies* 16 (1990): 115-50.

Glenn, Kathleen M. "*La Plaza del Diamante*: The Other Side of the Story." *Letras Femeninas* 12 (1986): 60-68.

Jordan, June. "Gender and Poetics" conference, University of Colorado-Boulder, October 11-13, 1988.

Kaplan, Caren. "Deterritorializations: The Rewriting of Home and Exile in Western Feminist Discourse." *Cultural Critique* 6 (1987): 187-98.

Levine, Linda Gould. "The Censored Sex: Woman as Author and Character in Franco's Spain." *Women in Hispanic Literature: Icons and Fallen Idols.* Ed. Beth Miller. Berkeley: University of California Press, 1983, 289-315.

Lorde, Audre. "An Open Letter to Mary Daly." *This Bridge Called My Back: Writings by Radical Women of Color.* Ed. Cherríe Moraga and Gloria Anzaldúa. New York: Kitchen Table: Women of Color Press, 1981, 1983, 94-97.

Lugones, María C. and Elizabeth V. Spelman. "Have We Got a Theory for You! Feminist Theory, Cultural Imperialism, and the Demand for 'The Woman's Voice.'" *Women's Studies International Forum* 6 (1983): 573-81.

Ordoñez, Elizabeth. "Reading Contemporary Spanish Narrative by Women." *Anales de la Literatura Española Contemporánea* 7 (1982): 237-51.

Pérez, Janet. "Post-War Women Writers of Spain," University of Colorado-Boulder, September 24, 1987.

Rodoreda, Mercè. *The Time of the Doves.* Trans. David H. Rosenthal. Saint Paul, MN: Graywolf Press, 1986. Originally published as *La Plaça del Diamant*, Barcelona, 1962.

Roig, Montserrat. "El aliento poético de Mercè Rodoreda." *Triunfo* 573 (September 22, 1973): 35-39.

Rosenthal, David H. Introduction. *The Time of the Doves*, by Mercè Rodoreda. Trans. David H. Rosenthal. Saint Paul, MN: Graywolf Press, 1986, 7-11.

Servodidio, Mirella, ed. *Reading for Difference: Feminist Perspectives on Women Novelists of Contemporary Spain.* Special issue of *Anales de la Literatura Española Contemporánea* 12 (1987).

Wyers, Frances. "A Woman's Voices: Mercè Rodoreda's *La Plaça del Diamant.*" *Kentucky Romance Quarterly* 30 (1983): 301-9.

Scientist and Mother; Portrait of the Heroine in I. Grekova's Fiction

Margareta Thompson

For several years after 1956, the year of the Twentieth Party Congress and Khrushchev's speech denouncing Stalin, there was a temporary expansion of literary freedom in the Soviet Union, and a few works with cautious social criticism were permitted to appear in print. During and after the Brezhnev years, however, the traditional Soviet upbeat production novels and heroic war stories, faithful to the rules of socialist realism laid down in the charter of the Writers' Union in 1934, were once again officially supported, and little could be published that did not conform to these rules. The literary climate again started to improve after 1985, when *glasnost*, or openness, was officially proclaimed. Works that were suppressed for many years have since then been published in the Soviet Union, and new stories with hardly any traces of socialist realism are now written and can also be published there.

Throughout the last three decades, I. Grekova has written and published a number of novels and short stories. All of them have been quite popular with the readers, but in order to be published at all, they naturally had to conform to the basic literary standards of the time of publication. Even so, one of her stories, "Without Smiles" ["Bez ulybok"], could not be published until ten years after it was written. The guidelines of socialist realism were enforced more or less strictly over the years, depending on the prevailing political climate. For example, certain passages in Grekova's *At the Testing Grounds* [*Na ispytaniiakh*] were barely acceptable when it was published in 1967 but would have been unthinkable a decade earlier. They were too outspoken to be reprinted a decade later during the later Brezhnev years.

I. Grekova's dozen or so novels, novellas, and short stories can be viewed as a literary category of their own, because several common features occur in almost all of them: the main protagonist or an important secondary character is a working mother, the plot and the circumstances are realistically described, and much of the action takes place in a contemporary Soviet scientific setting. Furthermore, there are no completely positive heroes or despicable villains; this is a departure from the rules of socialist realism requiring clear-cut and recognizable positive role models and enemies. Among the important characters are many children, who are often either the narrators or the focus of the narrative, and they are usually somewhat neglected by their working parents or are even orphans, as in *Little Garusov* [*Malen'kii Garusov* (1970)].

Grekova's many works contain numerous heroines of different types, and it would take a long book to discuss all these characters in general.[1] Many of the women, however, both major and minor protagonists, have so many features in common that they appear related to each other or even seem to be the same woman. The very persistence of this heroine suggests that she is near and dear to the author herself, and, indeed, when her personal and professional circumstances are compared with Grekova's own, it is obvious that the similarities are more than coincidental. This recurring figure is a largely autobiographical reflection of the author. She has apparently invented and developed difficult situations that might have occurred in her own life.

Since this heroine is so significant in Grekova's works, it is worthwhile examining her more closely. I will examine some of the most noteworthy female figures in Grekova's fiction and then draw a composite picture of this character. In view of the facts that Soviet mothers of numerous children were given medals and that the common expression for "native land" is the feminine word *rodina* [birth land] or even *rodina mat* [mother land], one expects a positive image of the mother in Soviet literature. But, on the contrary, one of the striking characteristics of Grekova's heroine is a habitual neglect of her child, and this negative feature raises the question of how she fits into the didactic socialist tradition. What was, indeed, the official Soviet attitude toward motherhood? Does Grekova hold up her favorite heroine as an example for her readers to emulate, or does she on the contrary warn against the results of child neglect on a national scale? Are Grekova's works so popular with the readers because they depict life as it really is, with all its problems and disappointments, unlike the usual, artificially optimistic Soviet fiction? Can Grekova be regarded as a feminist who attempts to call attention to the unfair treatment of Soviet women and suggests ways to improve the conditions of women in the workplace? In an interview, Grekova explained that she lacks a vivid imagination; she can describe only what she knows and has observed ("Real Life," 10). Because we will examine her partly autobiographical heroines, it is necessary first to know a few facts about the author's own life. Grekova was born in 1907 and grew up in Leningrad, where her family survived the starvation during the years of the so-called "war communism," the social chaos of the first few years after the October revolution ("On the Use of Humour," 16). She became a mathematician who published over 300 mathematical works under her married name, Elena Ventsel. Her mathematical research had military applications, and she worked for a time at an air force academy. She currently resides in Moscow, where her three children are working as successful scientists (unpublished interview, with Helena Goscilo, 1988).

These and other autobiographical details are used in various combinations in most of her works. Her pseudonym I. Grekova is based on the French name for the letter "y," *i grec*. In mathematics the symbol "y" designates an unknown factor in higher equations. I. Grekova could equally well have formed her nom de plume from the letter "x," but the letter "y" lends itself more easily to the creating of a Russian name. It is noteworthy that she did not choose the masculine form for her pseudonym, namely I. Grekov. In fact, bibliographers usually supply a first name, Irina, probably finding the initial "I" unsatisfactory. The author herself has never given a hint as to whether there is any particular significance to her pseudonym. It is not uncommon for authors to divide their professional career from their literary one by using a pseudonym. One supposes that I. Grekova decided to use this rather witty name to distance herself from her fictional writing because of the polemics that might and did develop as a consequence of her controversial literary subjects.

Grekova's fiction contains hundreds of characters from different social and intellectual spheres, including single mothers. The status of single mother is very common in all levels of Soviet society, due partly to the shortage of men; not only did more men than women die in the war and the prison camps, but the life expectancy of men has long been low and is decreasing even now. There is also a high divorce rate. It would be a mistake, however, to regard Grekova's partly autobiographical heroine as invariably being the author's mouthpiece; as a matter of fact, male protagonists sometimes present Grekova's point of view on various issues.[2]

In the late 1950s Grekova finished her first story, "Beyond the Checkpoint" ["Za prokhodnoi"] (1962), which was brought to the attention of the prominent editor Aleksandr Tvardovskii. Although there is hardly any plot in this largely descriptive work, he immediately recognized her talent, published the story in his journal *New World* [*Novyi mir*], and encouraged her to continue writing.[3]

In both her next works, the story "Under the Streetlamp" ["Pod fonarem"] (1965) and the somewhat longer novella *The Hairdresser* [*Damskii master*] (1966), we meet Grekova's favorite heroine, the unmarried woman scientist with young children. Two years later, her autobiographical novel *At the Testing Grounds* [*Na ispytaniiakh*] (1967) was severely criticized in the press, and Grekova was dismissed from her position at the air force academy in retaliation for having published this work. The official criticism seems trivial now; it concerned veiled references to political events voiced by minor characters in the story. In spite of the strong opposition to this publication, however, other works she had written could again be published three years later. Her favorite character, the mature female scientist, figures also in the novella *Little Garusov* [*Malen'kii Garusov*] (1970), in the popular novel *The Department* [*Kafedra*] (1978), and in the later novels *The Rapids* [*Porogi*] (1984) and *The Break* [*Perelom*] (1987). The story "Without Smiles" ["Bez ulybok"], describing events in the late 1960s but published only in 1986, is almost completely autobiographical. Grekova has published several other stories, but the present discussion is limited to the works mentioned here.

The women scientists often featured in Grekova's fiction have never been wholly dependent on men and do not particularly want or need their company. Their first priority is their scientific work, and their children come in second place. On the whole, there is a development in Grekova's works from a rational to an emotional decision-making process and resolution of the conflict on the part of the heroine, but the early short story "Under the Streetlamp" does not reflect this development. This work contains almost all of the plot elements Grekova would use in her later fiction. Here we meet a war widow with grown-up children at a crucial point in her life—she has to decide whether she will marry a younger man. As she attempts to make up her mind, she is forced to reexamine her attitude toward her family. The reader has to guess what her decision will be; there is a noncommittal ending, which is unusual for Soviet fiction. This preoccupation with emotions suggests that the story may be as fully based on the author's own experiences as her more overtly autobiographical later works, mentioned here.

The narrator of the novella, *The Hairdresser*, the chief of a scientific institute, is Grekova's most prominent professional woman. A typical Grekova heroine, she is kept too busy by her administrative and teaching duties to devote much time to her sons or to take a serious interest in romance.

The physical setting of the maligned story *At the Testing Grounds* differs from most of Grekova's other stories, which usually have urban settings. The author claims that it is also the most directly autobiographical one (unpublished interview, with Helena Goscilo, 1988). The military testing ground of the title is located in a distant, dusty steppe, perhaps in Central Asia. One of the visiting ballistics technicians, a young woman, is patronized by the local authorities because of her gender. In one situation, a pilot refuses to fly the heroine to the testing site:

"I won't take family members, it's not allowed."
"You're crazy. This isn't a family member but a military designer, constructor Romnich. Don't you know? Everyone in the whole country knows this woman."
"I don't know. . . . It's a woman, just the same. I refuse to fly with a woman on board."[4]

[- Chlenov semeistva na bort ne bery. Ne imeiu prava.-Chto za bred! Eto ne chlen semeistva, a konstruktor boevykh chastei, Konstruktor Romnich. Neuzheli ne znaete? Etu zhenshchiny vo vsem Soiuze znaiut. - Ne znaiu. . . . Vse ravno - zhenshchina. S zhen-shchinoi na borty ne polechu. (16)]

She is also courted by a charming colleague, but instead of making an issue of the unprofessional treatment she is subjected to, she shrugs it off and concentrates on her work, as though considering it pointless to fight. Her situation was not uncommon at the time when the action takes place, in the 1960s, when women in the workplace everywhere, not just in the Soviet Union, encountered sexual harassment. Along with professional ambitions, she also has so-called feminine feelings; for example, she misses her child, whom she left behind in the city, but not enough to prevent her from extending her stay at this lonely testing area. Her husband does not occupy her thoughts at all, she does not feel guilty for neglecting her family, and she does not hesitate to admit this. In other words, she acts as a man presumably would act in her place. Later in the story her fellow scientist Skvortsov asks Lida:

"Do you love your work?"
"Very much," said Lida. "You know, when I think of my work, I get shivers along my spine."
"That's love. Aren't you homesick?"
"No. That is, yes, I'd like to hug my son. I have a boy, Vovka, he's two."

[- Liubite svoiu raboty? - Ochen',- skazala Lida. - Znaete, kogda ia dumaiu o svoei rabote, dazhe murashki po spine. - Vot eto liubov'. A po domu ne skuchaete? - Net. To est', da. Syna khochetsia na ruki vziat'. Syn u menia, Vovka. Dva emu. (83)]

The plot of this story departs from her autobiography, where Grekova's husband was one of the men at the research center. It is an interesting example of how Grekova, as it were, separated the married couple in her story and instead showed the women alone but self-sufficient in order to introduce the conflict between her treatment and her professional ambitions.

The sanctions taken against Grekova following the publication of *At the Testing Grounds* are described in the autobiographical story "Without Smiles," written in 1970 but published only in 1986. The nameless characters in this work have only descriptive nicknames, for example, the heroine's intimidating supervisor, Ominous. The narrator, clearly Grekova herself, is subjected to a so-called working-over at the institute where she is employed; that is, she is pressured to confess to some unspecified ideological error. During the period of her "working-over," nobody smiles at her. Artistically, this story is not a success, but it is important as both a social and a personal document.

As Grekova herself aged, most of her heroines also become older than, for example, the young technician in *At the Testing Grounds*. The middle-aged scientist in the novella *Little Garusov* is scatterbrained and looks ridiculous, but she is an excellent teacher, neglecting her own research to spend more time helping her students:

Marina Borisovna was generally liked at the institute, although she was considered eccentric and people sometimes joked about her. There were stories of how absent-minded, kind, and awkward she was.

[V institute Mariny Borisovnu voobshche liubili, khotia schitali chudachkoi i otchasti nad nei posmeivalis'. Tselye anekdoty khodili o ee rasseiannosti, dobrote i neleposti. (134)]

The scientist Marina Borisovna bears a marked resemblance to Professor Diatlova in *The Rapids*, who also looks absurd in her tasteless clothes and dyed hair:

He looked with sadness at her sparse orange curls, the unevenly painted mouth, the upturned pencilled eyebrows; one of them was cut through by a wrinkle. . . . She walked hurriedly along the hall like a blue elephant. She seemed to be wearing socks on her feet in spite of the season.

[On s zhalost'iu gliadel na redkie oranzhevye kudri, na nerovno nakrashennyi rot, na stoiachie podvedennye brovki, poperek odnoi iz kotorykh legla morshchina. . . . Ona toroplivo shla po koridoru, pokhozhaia na golubogo slona. Nogi pochemu-to byli v noskakh, nesmotria na sezon. (I, 45)]

The professor claims to have reached her high position only because a female scientist had to be promoted at the time, but in spite of her modest disclaimer she is respected by her colleagues. There are repeated detailed descriptions of how funny the lady scientists look; they act awkwardly, dress in flashy but tasteless clothes, and try to be womanly but lack feminine skill, since they are by choice scientists and presumably had to give up their femininity. Grekova's descriptions have a very personal sound; the reader concludes that these characters must be good-natured caricatures of the author herself, who was no longer young and slim when she wrote these books.

Grekova's popular novel, *The Department*, features a woman mathematician whose older son has assumed the responsibilities of the head of the family and treats his mother as an incompetent child. Her helpless private persona contrasts with her forceful professional one; she is a stubborn fighter for justice in her mathematics institute. It is not an exposé of prejudice against women, however; this particular conflict concerns a man, not a woman. Her home life is evidently of much less concern to her than her working life.

In Grekova's last novel, *The Break*, two new elements are evident. First, there is an increased attention devoted to exposing various incidents of social inequity and economic inefficiency. For example, the narrator is just bemoaning the dangerously neglected state of the Moscow streets when she slips on the ice, falls, and breaks her leg. The novel is so loaded with similar observations that it comes close to being a muckraking exposé. This social criticism has become commonplace in most of the post-*glasnost* works by Soviet writers, thanks to the lifting of most censorship control, but it has a detrimental effect on literary quality. Second and more significantly, this novel contains a loud and clear appeal for love between men and women, parents and children. The heroine, a physician, is completely devoted to her work and necessarily neglects her sons. During her convalescence after an accident, she reexamines her attitude toward people and realizes that she has not given enough love to her children. The stress on love in Grekova's latest work is duly noted with approval by at least one critic (Andrianov, 4). This emphasis on love and caring suggests that the author has, so to speak, mellowed in her old age and started to value the traditionally feminine value of love as highly as professional success, at least in principle. For herself personally, however, the high points in her life were associated with professional achievement. Grekova herself insists that the female protagonist of *The Hairdresser* speaks for the author when she says, "Neither love nor motherhood . . . yields so much happiness as those minutes [of professional achievement]" (unpublished interview, with Helena Goscilo, 1988).

Based on the character descriptions in the works mentioned, a composite portrait of Grekova's favorite heroine, appearing in almost all of her works as a major or minor protagonist, looks as follows: she is a no longer a young single mother with a responsible job, her career is more important to her than her private life, and she is successful and respected in her profession and suffers no significant discrimination because of her gender. Because of her dedication to her career, incidentally, always in a socially useful type of work, she is compelled to neglect her children. At first sight, one might wonder, how Soviet literary critics could permit such a negative portrait of a neglectful mother to appear in Grekova's works. Soviet literature is, after all, intended to be educational, and authors are expected to invent positive role models. There is, however, no consistent idealization of motherhood in the Soviet social structure, rather the opposite, and Grekova's image of a neglectful mother actually follows accepted socialist realist literary canons. The two undisputed Soviet classic novels *Cement* [*TSement*] (1925) by Fedor Gladkov and *How the Steel Was Tempered* [*Kak zakaialas' stal'*] (1934) by Nikolai Ostrovskii have female protagonists who are anything but caring. The emancipated wife of the hero of *Cement* sends her daughter to an orphanage to starve with barely a twinge of regret, and the hero's wife in Ostrovskii's novel refuses to look after her dying husband. This nonmaternal feminine ideal results directly from one of several failed good intentions of the Bolshevik revolution—to include men and women as equal partners in the economic life. Children and housework were to be taken care of on an institutional basis.

In reality, this goal was never reached. Even in normal times, cramped living conditions make it almost prohibitively difficult for a woman to have more than one child. Since two salaries are always needed by a family, this single child is, if possible, cared for by a grandmother. Thus, economic concerns force many Russian mothers to neglect their children and have multiple abortions. The Russian culture does not, of course, directly encourage child neglect, but many literary works, including those mentioned before, glorify women who do not regard motherhood as an important task. Grekova's unnurturing but professionally successful woman can be seen as merely a new incarnation or, more probably, as a reduction to the absurd of the old Soviet ideal working woman; she has acquired all the responsibilities but little of the help promised by the idealistic founding fathers of the Soviet Union.

In its main outlines, Grekova's attitude toward professional women, as reflected in her fiction, has not changed during most of her writing career. She was, after all, already fifty-five years old when her first story was published, and her opinions had already been formed. Her women struggle for professional achievement and regard this as their main concern, while treating the domestic problems as unavoidable impediments and their family life as definitely secondary to their careers (Mamonova, 139-40). Women who aspire to a professional career naturally have to invest more effort in their work and thus become more neglectful of their homes than women who have nondemanding jobs and save more energy for domestic chores. However, only the professional woman, like Grekova's heroines, get satisfaction from their achievements. They are lucky if they have help; Anna Kirillovna, the professor in *The Rapids*, asks herself:

Should I sacrifice myself, retire, become a professional grandmother? No, I can't. . . . All that I have achieved, I owe it all to my late mother-in-law Taisa Fedorovna, she was a real grandmother, modest, unnoticed, loving. A woman should know how to go unnoticed. . . . My whole life proves the contention that our [Soviet] women can achieve anything. I always sit on the stage on March 8; "See what she has accomplished, three children and a Ph.D.". . . . But I see the ghost of the modest gray Taisa Fedorovna beside me and think; she is the one you should honor.

[Pozhertvovat' soboi, uiti na pensiiu, stat' professional'noi babushkoi? Ne mogu. . . .
Spasibo za vse, chego dostigla, pokoinoi svekrovi Taisii Fedorovne. Ta byla nasto-
iashchei babushkoi. Skromnaia, nezametnaia, liubiashchaia. Zhenshchina dolzhna umet'
byt' nezametnoi. . . . Vsiu zhizn' byla na vidu, podtverzhdala soboi tezis o tom, chto
nashei zhenshchine vse dostupno. Vsiu zhizn' sizhu v prezidiume, kak v den' Vos'mogo
marta. Smotrite, chego dostigla; i troe detei, i doktor nauk. . . . A ia vizhu vozle sebia
skromnyi, seden'kii prizrak Taisii Fedorovny i dumaiu, vot kogo nado by proslavliat'.
(II 98)]

Grekova has mentioned in published interviews that she recognizes the fact
that not all women have the same talents and values, just as different men do not
have identical interests. This obvious fact has only recently been publicly
admitted in the Soviet Union where all women are expected to work, no matter
how useless and low-paying the job may be, and where it has been suggested
officially that housewives are parasites (Gladkov; Ostroviskii). The teacher in
Grekova's early story "The First Air Raid" ["Pervyi nalet"] (1965) illustrates
how a housewife feels as a result of this widely accepted attitude:

Liza Golubeva, thirty, mother of three, housewife. . . . Her husband earned well, they
had enough. There was no real need to work, and nowhere to leave the children. She had
to quit work. Liza was sad for a long time, even cried occasionally in the kitchen,
especially when the radio played. She felt that she was not a real person.

[Liza Golubeva, tridtsati let, mat' troikh detei, domokhoziaika. . . . Muzh Sergei
khorosho zarabatyval, im khvatalo. Priamoi nadobnosti rabotat' ne bylo, a detei ostavliat'
ne s kem. Prishlos' brosit' raboty. Liza dolgo ogorchalas', dazhe plakala po vremenam
v kukhne, osobenno kogda radio igralo. Ei vse kazalos', chto ona ne sovsem chelovek.
(103)]

The conflicts between the demands of motherhood and career have not been
solved satisfactorily in the Soviet Union or, indeed, in any society, and each
woman must find a workable compromise for herself. Personally, Grekova
herself has had more success in all her endeavors than any of her fictional
characters, but she confesses, surely tongue in cheek, that she had to neglect her
housekeeping ("Portrait of a Woman" ["Zhenskii portret," 13]).

Since Grekova writes almost exclusively about working women, one might
expect to find feminist tendencies in her fiction, but she propagates no such
ideas. She does not accuse men of suppressing women, nor does she seek out
and castigate incidents of professional discrimination against women in the
workplace, although such discrimination exists. In spite of the official effort
made in the Soviet Union to integrate the workplace as far as genders are
concerned, the resulting situation there is, nonetheless, not unlike the one in the
United States; women's salaries are around two-thirds of men's, and high-level
posts are disproportionately often held by men. Grekova makes no suggestions
of how to improve the status of women in Soviet society. Aside from a casual
remark in an interview about grown men who expect women to wait on them,
Grekova does not object in principle to the old-fashioned division of labor
between men-providers and women-caregivers ("Portrait of a Woman" ["Zhen-

skii portret," 13]). Rather than condemn all men for expecting female admiration, Grekova has in several of her works introduced positive male heroes, such as in *The Department* and *Little Garusov*. Grekova then cannot be regarded as a feminist in Western terms; she is a woman writer who writes about men, women, and children.

Considering the fact that Grekova's heroines, on the whole, fit within the social realist tradition and that the author offers no advice on improving the social position of Soviet women, what are the attractions of Grekova's fiction for her readers? Her works are always written in an unusually lively and conversational style, especially when compared with Soviet fiction in general (see Menke). More important, they faithfully and realistically depict the annoying trivia of a woman's everyday life and work. The heroines have to tackle the traditional demands of children, work, and careers, and they find different ways of dealing with their situations. In view of Grekova's preference for female protagonists, it is fair to say that Grekova's popularity is, above all, due to her serving as a sympathetic mouthpiece for Soviet professional women who may also be mothers and wives and who have to deal daily with all the same conflicts and frustrations that Grekova depicts so well. The absence in Grekova's works of direct feminist appeal is reassuring to Soviet readers who, according to Francine du Plessix Gray, are not comfortable with this movement.[5]

Without underestimating Grekova's contributions as a scientist, one could argue that her greatest impact on Soviet society is as a role model, albeit a rather intimidating one. She is a woman who succeeded both in having a satisfying career and in raising three children, just like many of her readers, but a little more successful, a heroine of everyday life. Representing and depicting such a positive image of Soviet womanhood, she might be expected to have escaped official reprimands, but, as we have seen, this was not so; she had to endure "workings-over" and see her works criticized, as did many other Soviet writers, male or female. Indeed, professional success cannot come easily to her or to any woman. In her own words, taken from her last novel, *The Break*: "[W]omen's tears bring people closer together" ["Ochen' oni sblizhaiut, bab'i slezy" ("Udary," 4)].

NOTES

1. In her dissertation, *Die Kultur der Weiblichkeit in der Prosa Irina Grekovas* [*The Culture of Femininity in the Prose of Irina Grekova*], E. Menke limited her discussion to a few female protagonists in a few works by Grekova but draws general conclusions based on her selected sample.

2. For example, the male protagonist Professor Zavalishin in *The Department* speaks for Grekova herself.

3. Aleksandr Tvardovskii wrote a favorable in-house review of Grekova's story; the review was published after his death in his *Sobranie sochinenii* [*Collected Works*].

4. All translations provided here are mine.

5. The recent book by Francine du Plessix Gray, *Soviet Women, Walking the Tightrope*, consists largely of a series of portraits of strong professional and activist Soviet

women; in several places, the author seems to suggest somewhat facetiously that a
"men's movement" is more needed than a "women's movement" in the Soviet Union.

REFERENCES

Primary

Works by I. Grekova

"Bezulybok." *Oktiabr'* (November 1986): 162-79.
Damskii master, rasskaz. Novyi mir (November 1963): 87-120.
Kafedra, povest'. Novyi mir (September 1978): 10-168.
Malen'kii Garusov. Zvezda (September 1970): 119-56.
Na ispytaniiakh. Novyi mir (June 1967): 14-109.
"On the Use of Humour Under War Communism." *Moscow News* 42 (1990): 16.
Perelom, povest'. Oktiabr' (August 1987): 72-149.
"Pervyi nalet." *Zvezda* (November 1965): 103-9.
"Pod fonarem." *Zvezda* (December 1965): 43-54.
Porogi, roman. Oktiabr' (October 1984): 3-51; *Oktiabr'* (November 1984): 81-180.
"Real Life in Real Terms." *Moscow News* 24 (1987): 10.
Russian Women, Two Stories. Trans. M. Petrov. New York: Harcourt Brace Jovanovich,
      1983.
"Za prokhodnoi." *Novyi mir* (July 1962): 110-31.
"Zhenskii portret v inter'ere." *Literaturnaia gazeta* (September 2, 1981): 13.

Secondary

Andrianov, A. "Udary schast'ia." *Literaturnaia gazeta* (October 7, 1987): 4.
Gladkov, Fedor. *Cement.* Trans. A. S. Arthur and C. Ashleigh. New York: F. Ungar,
      1960.
Gray, Francine du Plessix. *Soviet Women, Walking the Tightrope.* New York: Double-
      day, 1990.
Mamonova, Tatiana. *Russian Women's Studies, Essays on Sexism in Soviet Culture.* New
      York: Pergamon Press, 1989.
Menke, Elisabeth. *Die Kultur der Weiblichkeit in der Prosa Irina Grekovas.* München:
      O. Sagner, 1988.
Ostrovskii, Nikolai. *How the Steel was Tempered.* Trans. R. Prokofieva. Moscow:
      Progress, 1967.
Tvardovskii, Aleksandr. *Sobranie sochinenii.* 6 vols. Moskva: Khudozhestvennaia
      literatura, 1980.

Italian Women in Search of Identity in Dacia Maraini's Novels

Vera F. Golini

In 1985 the Presidential Committee of the Italian Council of Ministers published the proceedings of the Nairobi World Conference, celebrating the tenth anniversary of the United Nations for the Woman, promoting equality, development, and peace. This important document is prefaced by an announcement made in 1983 by the Italian president of the Council of Ministers, the honorable Bettino Craxi. In his Point 5.7 he states:

Great importance must be given to the problem of equality between the sexes which has found, in principle, some suitable solutions in the so-called law on equality issued in 1977. This law now exacts concrete and operative means of action to better fight against discrimination relating particularly to career development since discriminatory attitudes in the workplace tend to deny women positions that carry great responsibility.

Some suitable initiatives had already been put forth in the past legislature, and the Government must do all it can in order to pass and approve immediately a new law on the subject.[1]

Such a statement shows promise and initiative on the part of the Italian government, as it is gradually awakening to the reality of discrimination in the workplace and to demands Italian women have been voicing at a national level most vehemently in the past two decades; the inception of a real, united feminist movement coincided, not accidentally, with the centenary of the unification of Italy into a democratic republic completed in 1871. In May 1981, in a national referendum registering a 70 percent majority, Italians confirmed legislation providing for free abortion for women eighteen and over. The private, public, and national identity of Italian women is plagued by fluctuations between extremes of traditionalism (advocated by the Catholic Church) and liberalization catalyzed by leftist party politics; and between extremes of moral conservatism aiming at preserving the family as the focal social unit and materialistic consumerism resulting, in part, from Italy's emergence as an industrial superpower. The question of the Italian woman's identity is further complicated by regional, educational, and economic disparities that have persisted for centuries. The sense

of infinite variety in the national character of Italian women should be interpreted, in part, in the light of 400 years of continuous foreign domination
preceding Unification. More recently, as a result of legislative changes, people
from former fascist African colonies such as Somalia and Eritrea have taken up
residence in Italy, as have other people from disparate cultural and racial backgrounds. Some statistical information may help at this point to provide a more
concrete grasp of the private and public realities inherent in the lives of Italian
women in the past two decades.

The publication by the Committee for Equality entitled *Statistics on Italian
Women* [*Le donne italiane in cifre*] presents data on various facets of private and
public life. For example, the percentage of the female population receiving a
high school education in the decade 1972-83 has improved from 42.5 percent to
49.3 percent (*Instituto*, 25).[2] With respect to university, 2.1 percent of the
women hold a degree as compared with 3.6 percent of the men (*Instituto*, 24,
31). Here we see an obvious similarity in higher educational level between men
and women. If we then proceed to statistics related to employment, we notice
that while women in Italy made up 52 percent of the total national population in
1985, only 35 percent fourteen years old and over constituted the workforce
(Arangio-Ruiz and Guarna, 1). Of these, 34.5 percent had a high school and/or
university degree. Moreover, of the women in the labor force, 32.4 percent
were employed, while 58.1 percent were unemployed and looking for work
(Arangio-Ruiz and Guarna, 32). In the last decade, the level of education for
women has risen noticeably. Nevertheless, the rate of unemployment has
remained visibly high. Although 46 percent of university students are women,[3]
and there has been a noticeable improvement in the level of education for
women since the 1970s, as we have seen, nevertheless, the percentage of women
fourteen years old and over who choose to become housewives has remained
stable through time. Statistics taken in 1980 and 1985 show that in each instance, 41 percent were occupied with home and family, while those in the
workforce increased from 32 percent to only 34 percent (Arangio-Ruiz and
Guarna, 25-26).

Dacia Maraini is the most noted Italian woman writer who, since the early
1960s, has beeen persistently concerned with the private and public status of
Italian women. Through her literary compositions and very personal involvement, she has succeeded, for example, in effecting political change aimed at
correcting the retrograde and inhuman conditions in Italy's prisons for women.
The data provided earlier are of fundamental importance as the reader approaches the works of Dacia Maraini because they serve to confirm the fact that
Maraini's fictive protagonists represent the average Italian man and woman
harassed and frustrated by private and social problems that, to date, have not
found a solution through social or political action.

Maraini's dramas and prose concentrate on the development of the Italian
woman's identity through increasing self-knowledge and maturity either before
or after marriage. Her works focus on certain traditional themes permeating the
fiction of many women writers in Italy today: identity, family, memory, and
enclosure. Maraini's works represent the geographic, regional, economic, and

even linguistic diversity so characteristic of the contemporary Italian literary scene.

Dacia Maraini's contribution to Italian literature began with the publication of *The Holiday* [*La vacanza*] in 1962, when she was twenty-six. In the fifteen years that followed, she not only left her particular stamp on Italian literature but also acquired renown since her works were quickly translated into various languages, including Russian, Greek, and Polish. Aside from the books of interviews with important individuals in Italian society, *And Who Were You?* [*E tu chi eri?*], *The Child Alberto* [*Il bambino Alberto*], and her theoretical essays on Italian theater, *Making Theatre* [*Fare teatro*], and on literature, published in various journals, one can say that Maraini's entire literary production (consisting of eight novels, four collections of poetry, over twenty published plays, and one collection of short stories) studies the sociocultural and economic condition of women from adolescence to middle age in postwar Italy. Moreover, the women of the middle and lower classes of central and southern Italy are most often her protagonists. Among these we find housewives, students, teachers, artists, nuns, prostitutes, and even outlaws. On the other hand, the males who appear in these works can be lawyers, landowners and therefore independently wealthy individuals, self-employed businessmen, artists, students, student radicals, politicians. An overview of Maraini's prose works presents a panorama much like the occupational and economic status of the Italian population at large. This fact gives rise to at least two immediate considerations. First, far from being a literature of protest, Maraini's prose works reveal a carefully planned architecture in which the average reader can mirror himself or herself. Second, a close study of the existential predicaments of the female protagonists and the solutions proposed, such as separation, extending beyond the context of the novel, points to a more fruitful future life for these protagonists.

The thematic spectrum of Maraini's prose works does not present a great deal of variety. We find that problems of interpersonal relationships—preoccupation with emotional and sexual fulfillment, socioeconomic injustice, the struggle for survival on a day-to-day basis as well as on a more extended basis—constitute the thematic core of Maraini's prose production. In the midst of such central predicaments, female protagonists are generally impeded by social obstacles. Other characters actively or unknowingly affect change in the life of the protagonist.

This chapter considers the social implications in Dacia Maraini's *The Holiday* [*La vacanza*], *The Age of Malaise* [*L'età del malessere*], and *Woman at War* [*Donna in guerra*], while some references are made also to *Memoirs of a Female Thief* [*Memorie di una ladra*], and *The Train to Helsinki* [*Il treno per Helsinki*].[4] Each of the novels registers the female protagonist's arduous and painful journey toward a greater degree of maturity and self-knowledge in the light of human relations and values that have "nurtured" her and the society that has conditioned her to that point. To this end, each novel is written in the first person, making use of the internal monologue, direct narration to an imagined listener, or the medium of a diary, a form long associated with women writers. Each narrating style allows Maraini to present her female protagonists with great simplicity and realism, since the controlling and manipulating intelligence of the omniscient third-person narrator is absent. The subdued, serene mode of confessional narration, which at times verges on the monotonous, is a metaphor for the attitude of passivity that society has traditionally associated with the female sex. Maraini's narrative tone is both realistic and comic, at times aiming to deflate pretension and point out incongruities in the value system of the protagonist and the society that ensnares her. Each protagonist evolves toward an awakening to life. What she learns, whoever she becomes, directly or indirectly makes a statement about Italian society. Moreover, it is of signal importance to note that for each of the protagonists, maturation presupposes a "renunciation" of some sort, an act of will to sacrifice, in some instances, the expectant life that the protagonist conceives without wish or design.

In *The Holiday*, the fourteen-year-old Anna and her younger brother, Giovanni, are accompanied by their free-spirited father from Rome to a family holiday near Naples. The motivating force in the novel originates from Anna's desire for sexual initiation. The first person narration—a technique common to all of Maraini's novels and short stories—unveils Anna's most intimate thoughts and memories, at the same time making manifest an apparent listlessness, an indifferent state of near-somnambulism germane to each of Maraini's protagonists. Although some literary critics consider Anna passive and indifferent, she is, in reality, completely open to a sentimental and sexual education, to the idea of leaving the school run by nuns, venturing to a beach holiday: "We came running down the stairs and through the long corridor without meeting any nuns" (7) [Scendemmo le scale di corsa, e percorremmo il lungo corridoio senza incontrare una suora (1)]. Furthermore, she is far from naïve about sex since life in the private school is a microcosm of secret hates, jealousies, young lesbian affections, and mind games. Anna knows enough to ask questions, but no one cares about her enough to answer truthfully. Even the nuns chide her: "When we asked embarrassing questions they said not to think about that sort of thing. 'We don't talk about some things. Pray, my daughter.' Almost all topics were forbidden" (134) [Alle domande imbarazzanti ci rispondevano di non pensarci. "Non si parla di certe cose. Prega, figlia mia." Quasi tutti gli argomenti sono proibiti (115)]. Anna seeks to learn from the men around her those facts of existence that formal education in Italy so tenaciously denies. However, none of the male figures in the novel are capable of conceiving—let alone demonstrating—that equilibrium of affection and sexuality so fundamentally important to adolescents if they are to attain a serene vision of self and of reality outside the self. Anna's widowed father, who lives with the egocentric Nina, is too occupied with his work to tune in to Anna's particular search. The merchant's eighteen-year-old son, Armando, is attracted to Anna; however, handicapped by suicidal tendencies, he cannot develop a healthy emotional relationship. Moreover, the forty-year-old wealthy Sicilian, Scanno, can only be mystified by Anna's youth and freshness as he takes solitary pleasure in her nudity. She ponders: "I wondered if this was love. Like with Armando. On the one hand the contortion and the spasm; on the other, passive and arid nudity" (62) [Mi chiedevo se quello era l'amore. Come con Armando. La contorsione e lo spasimo da una parte, dall'altra la nudità passiva e arida (50)]. Even Giovanni, her younger brother, bets with his pals that he will be able to deliver Anna to the thirty-year-old homosexual, Gigio, who, in fact, has paid Giovanni for the pleasure of simply looking at his sister. Male critics have considered Anna inert and passive. Yet she is an average adolescent in search of guidance and enlightenment. Indeed, like Maraini's future heroines, she is not loquacious or vivacious. Not her character but rather her extreme youth and lack of experience which cause her to be subject to unforeseen actions. But it is equally true that the men involved with her, like the men in future novels, lend neither protection nor help to create an atmosphere conducive to fulfilling human activity and growth. Thus, it seems that in this first novel, as well as in her subsequent novels, Maraini creates a female protagonist victimized and passive, conforming to the traditional perception of women that males and society have maintained throughout the centuries. The task of Maraini's novels is to "educate" the initially naive protagonist to self-knowledge, which, in turn, toward the conclusion of the novel, brings about a spirit of rebellion and desire for amelioration. Personal maturation, then, becomes coupled with a keen awareness of the suffering and the complexities inherent in personal relations and human existence.

This first novel has as fictional setting the fascist society dominating Italy in 1943 and carries as subtitle "The Adolescence of a Woman as Object" ["L'adolescenza di una donna oggetto"].[5] The fact that Anna returns to the cloistered school not having experienced familial or erotic love, as she had hoped, registers, in part, a censure of the empty middle-class values of fascist society in Italy.

Between the fictional time of *The Holiday* and 1963, the fictional time of *The Age of Malaise*, no moral evolution has occurred in Maraini's fictional world or in Italian society. The modern city of Rome, where Enrica Battini lives and suffers, is enjoying an industrial boom, which, however brings no moral or spiritual enhancement to the lives of the many destitute, newly urbanized Italians who deserted their agrarian villages and patrimonies for a vilifying urban setting and its illusions of fortune. In this second novel, the seventeen-year-old Enrica is the only child of a poor, unhappy couple living in Rome. The puffy middle-aged mother is dying of cancer but continues to work at the post office to help support the family. The mother's search for a better life as a young woman was promptly stifled by marriage to a weak man: "My mother had come to Rome on her own to study. Then she had got married and her ambitions came to nothing" (69) [La mamma era venuta a vivere a Roma da sola e aveva studiato. Ma poi si era sposata e tutte le ambizioni erano finite nel nulla (63)]. Later in the novel, the drunken father, in a rare moment of lucidity, tells Enrica that they married out of obligation, not for love:

I've never been a real father to you. . . . You've been unlucky. Your mother and I conceived you without love. I've never given a hang about you. The only things I've ever cared for have been my little hobbies. I'm a fool. (137)

[Non sono mai stato un vero padre per te. . . . Sei stata sfortunata. Tua madre e io ti abbiamo fatta senza amore. Non me ne importava niente di te. Non mi è mai importato niente altro che delle mie manie. Sono un cretino. (121)]

The mother has come to terms with the failure of her marriage. However, she hopes for something better for her daughter. She encourages Enrica to continue her relationship with Cesare, the twenty-eight-year-old perennial law student from the upper-middle class. He, however, will marry a wealthy woman whom he does not love but who will be his meal ticket for life, as he has no intention of ever graduating or working. Enrica's sentimental and sexual attachments revolve totally around the opportunistic and callous Cesare, who first seduced her when she was fourteen. Because she truly loves him, she hopes against hope that they will be married. She becomes pregnant. Though still a poor student, the possibility of motherhood gives her sensations of genuine gladness: "It was wonderful to have a growing thing inside. Yes, being pregnant was out of this world" (102) [Era bello avere qualcosa dentro di sè che un giorno sarebbe diventato grande. Era bello essere incinta (91)]. But Cesare refuses all responsibility, as he automatically recommends and pays for an immediate but illegal abortion.[6] At this point Cesare stops seeing Enrica, accelerates preparations for his wedding, and suggests that he and Enrica resume their normal relationship after her abortion and his marriage.

Enrica's eventual decision to leave Cesare is prompted not only by his inhuman treatment of her but also by her disillusionment with other men who have touched her life: her father is basically unreliable; the young man from school, Carlo, who claims to love Enrica, is overly possessive of her and unable to lend her encouragement or a sense of self-worth. One day Enrica decides to accept a ride from a wealthy lawyer and earn some money as a prostitute. Having lived an unhappy family life, the protagonist begins to imagine that prostitution may be a lucrative occupation. However, during her initial experiences with the lawyer, she is completely repelled by the "titillating lathery rites"[7] he performs with her in his posh bathroom. As far as the role models in her life are concerned, Enrica implicitly rejects the possibility of growing up to become like her mother, victimized as she has been, by a weak man: "I didn't want to see her as she unfastened her brassiere. . . . The sight of her reminded me that one day I'd be the same way, fat and flabby and wrinkled" (12) [Cercai di non guardarla mentre si sfilava il busto. . . . Mi faceva pensare che un giorno sarei diventata come lei, grassa, con la carne flaccida e piena di rughe (13)]. Nor does Enrica find solace in the opulent villa of the middle-aged Contessa Bardengo, where she goes to work as a live-in companion and secretary. The widowed contessa, whose title is actually bought, befriends Enrica. But the young girl grows to dislike the contessa for her morbid attachment to the eighteen-year-old Remo, who deliberately makes the woman pine and suffer for him. Wherever Enrica turns, she is confronted by the empty lives of people devoid of moral fiber, whatever their intellectual or economic status may be. Even the contessa's old butler, who seems a tolerable individual, shows himself to be an opportunist with the contessa and the twenty-two-year-old maid. The butler gallantly announces his sexual prowess to Enrica:

I'm a special case, myself. I'm not like the others. I have a boy's physique. You ought to see me. I wear the women out. I can never get too much of it. . . . What disgusts me is to see the state this woman has got herself into. As for me I make a point of never falling in love. Nothing like that for me. (209)

[Io poi sono speciale. Non sono come tutti gli altri. Ho un fisico da ragazzo, lei dovrebbe vedere. Io le donne le stanco. Non sono mai sazio. . . . Quello che mi disgusta è vedere come si è ridotta quella donna per amore. Io non mi innamoro mai. Non ci casco. (185)]

He goes on to elaborate that he has enough stamina to make all three women in the house (the countess, the maid, and Enrica) happy if only they would allow it. Moments later Enrica decides that she must leave that house as soon as she is able to find other job.

Enrica's resourcefulness is necessarily limited by her very young age. Hers is a struggle for values and self-affirmation; but above all, she struggles to survive. Her reliance on Cesare is motivated by love but also by the hope for material security. She declines Carlo's overtures because she is not sure of his ability to stand firm in the face of a commitment. She leaves her own home and the contessa's residence, because although material survival is possible there, moral survival is not. In the end, Enrica leaves everyone behind because, having graduated from secretarial school, she can earn a living independently. Thus, through education, she has achieved a new freedom both from her impoverished condition and from the oppressive individuals who have burdened her existence. Accordingly, the novel closes on a positive note as Enrica bids a final good-bye to both her lovers and looks forward to the summer:

Summer is just around the corner, I said to myself, and I'll start a new life. Meanwhile I must go back to the villa. The next day, I promised myself, I would get up early and look for another job. (220)

[L'estate è vicina pensai e presto incomincerà per me una nuova vita. Ma intanto devo rassegnarmi a tornare alla villa. Il giorno dopo mi sarei alzata all'alba per andare a cercare un impiego. (195)]

The two novels that followed, *Memoirs of a Female Thief* and *Woman at War*, also conclude with a firm resolution by the protagonists to seek a more personally fulfilling existence. The former work was, in part, inspired while the author was conducting a study of the Italian prison system for women for a newspaper, *Paesesera*. The protagonist is modeled after a real woman, a thief in her early fifties. Within the fiction of the novel, the protagonist, Teresa, overcomes countless risks and commits an endless array of petty crimes. She is tossed from women's prison to women's prison, where both inmates and nuns who are security guards often subject her to barbaric treatment as well as pressures for sexual favors, which she relentlessly rejects, at times risking her life for doing so. She falls in love with a temporarily repentant male thief, marries him, and has a son, who is taken from her by her husband's two spinster sisters. Throughout her life Teresa maintains an undaunted sense of loyalty to her child, her men, and her female friends, thieves like herself. This very loyalty often brings her ruin. The two elements most precious to her, personal freedom and unconditional sincerity, are the very conditions she finds most difficult to attain in the midst of the society into which she was born and from which she is unable to extricate herself. From the moment of birth, when she was thought to be stillborn: "[M]y father was about to throw me in the garbage bin" [mio padre stava per buttarmi nell'immondizia (1)], until her early fifties, when she finally decides to trust no one and struggle on her own, Teresa's life is a brutal battle for survival. Near the conclusion, while still in jail, Teresa resolves to change her life by living in a more "regular" manner, inspired by the middle-class values of her son and his leisure-loving wife. Teresa promises herself:

Enough is enough; when I get out I want to stop being a thief; I want to get a job as a seamstress, even if I can't sew, what does it matter . . . I'll borrow to buy some cloth, and after paying for the first instalment I'll change my address. I want to make a peaceful home for myself with Ercoletto and Orlandino in a nice and quiet place. I never want to go to jail again.

[Quando esco, basta, voglio smetterla di fare la ladra, mi voglio trovare un lavoro di sarta, anche se non so cucire, che ci fa . . . comprerò della stoffa a rate e dopo la prima rata cambierò indirizzo. Voglio mettere su casa, con Ercoletto e Orlandino, tranquilla, quieta, in un posto bello, pacifico. In carcere non ci voglio piú tornare. (297)]

However, since remaining free from attachments to people or possessions is Teresa's highest ambition, and even her honest intentions are based on ruse and evasion from responsibility, it will be impossible for Teresa to settle for a life of middle-class values, as she proposes to do. About her protagonist, Maraini has remarked that "Teresa will always remain a petty thief of chickens and wallets, just like when she was eighteen" (qtd. in Chiesa, 3)]. Nevertheless, throughout her struggle for survival, Teresa has learned self-reliance, which, toward the conclusion, works to her advantage. The reader is thus led to expect that outside the fiction of the novel, the quality of life of this picaresque character will improve.

Among the many subjects broached by *Memoirs of a Female Thief*, the social criticism that naturally arises from the fertile, dynamic fabric of the novel, there is also the subject of an impossible marriage. However, the fundamental problem of survival faced by the protagonist is the moving element of the work, overshadowing the subject of conjugal love. In *Woman at War*, through an exploration of problems inherent in a typical middle-class marriage, that Maraini breaks down the patriarchal marriage plot that sanctions private violence against women. Here the problems of poverty, survival, or lack of education are absent, leaving the author free to deal with the intrinsic psychology of her characters pitted against a middle-class society that tolerates political repression, mutual exploitation, and economic opportunism.

Giovanna and Giacinto are a financially secure young couple: she is an elementary school teacher; he, a mechanic. Raised in Sicily, she lives in Rome with her husband. In August, like most Italians, they go on holidays. The novel that unfolds on a small island, Addis, near Naples, is written in the form of a diary and spans five months, during which Giovanna awakens to the realization of her vacuous marriage, her spiritless teaching, her immature husband, her dangerous ignorance of social issues, and her own lack of aspirations. For the first two weeks she lives out her holidays as a perfect wife and companion whose unquestioned points of reference are the kitchen, the market, and the conjugal bed. She makes love with the same listlessness with which she does the dishes and the shopping. Nor does she find serious objection with her husband's manner of pleasing himself without regard for her needs:

We make love. Quickly, as usual, without giving me time to come properly. I tell him to wait for me, but he says that if he doesn't hurry he loses momentum and then he can't make it. He's in a rush to grow big . . . to explode as if he'd lose something if he hesitated. . . . So I lie there panting and tense only half aroused. I can't stop him or restrain him, and when I grab him he's already come. (11)

[Abbiamo fatto l'amore. In fretta, come al solito, senza darmi il tempo di arrivare in fondo. Gli dico di aspettarmi. Ma dice che se non fa presto gli passa la voglia. Ha fretta di gonfiarsi . . . di esplodere, come se indugiando potesse perdere qualcosa. . . . Così io rimango a metà, ansante, contratta. Non so fermarlo, né acquietarlo, né trattenerlo. Quando lo afferro è già scappato. (11)]

Through her friendship with Suna, a wealthy young woman semicrippled by polio, Giovanna comes to realize that she merely puts up with her marriage, that socially, intellectually, and physically, she and Giacinto do not share the same inclinations or vision of life. She becomes certain that she is Giacinto's source of emotional security, that his need of her is founded on habit, rather than on reciprocal caring and affection. In the course of the novel, the island of Addis emerges as a metaphor for the Italian peninsula, teeming with corruption and vice. Gradually Giovanna opens her eyes to this corruption and is repelled by it. Suna initiates Giovanna to painful realities. Through Suna she comes in contact with a group of radical youths who, by questionable means, intend to effect political changes but fail. The two women decide to conduct surveys in and around Naples, recording how husbands and fathers compel their wives and children to undertake illegal, ill-remunerated piece work at home, where the women lack both space and proper lighting. While Giovanna visits a young friend in a local hospital, she witnesses the abominable sanitary conditions. As a guest at the home of her husband's young fishing companion, she is brought face-to-face with an egocentric father involved in contraband activities. He bullies his sons and takes pride in their oppressive sexual prowess exercised on foreign women tourists. On this same island, Giovanna observes the gallant young males whose lucrative nightly pastime consists of giving the wives of wealthy foreign industrialists the entertainment that their overly busy husbands send them to Italy to buy. Anthony J. Tamburri rightly observes: "The majority of men in the novel consider sexual gratification a male's prerogative. In their eyes, enjoyment by the woman is either inconceivable, or at least shameful" (144). The protagonist has thus developed a critical distance from life while on the island. On her return to Rome, Giovanna realizes that her colleagues, like her former self, are not sincerely committed to educating the young about social and existential realities. She finds this intolerable and effects a drastic change in her teaching methodology. Throughout the novel, Giacinto is a suffering spectator of his wife's gradual but certain metamorphosis. She encourages and seeks to inspire him to assist her or at least to be receptive to her growth in self-awareness. Not only does Giacinto find her development false and unnecessary, but he feels threatened by it:

"You see, you have changed. . . . That bitch has put you against me. You've lost your sweet nature, you've become hard, moody, just like that shit Suna. You've become spoiled, and what's happened to that sweetness of yours which I loved so much, where the hell has it gone?" I gave in to him against my will. Out of meekness, out of habit, out of love, I don't know. . . . My satisfaction however soon turned to anger, indeed into hatred against the inertia of my body, against the perverse sense of duty which held me from rebelling against the submissiveness which I always allowed to dominate me. Something was burning my throat and I couldn't spit it out. (246)

["Vedi che sei cambiata . . . quella stronza ti ha messo contro di me; hai perso la tua natura, sei diventata dura, musona, come quella troia di Suna, ti sei guastata, e la dolcezza tua, e la dolcezza che mi piaceva tanto dove cazzo è finita?" L'ho accontentato contro voglia. Per mitezza, per abitudine, per amore, non so. . . . La soddisfazione però si è trasformata presto in rancore. Anzi odio. Per la passività del mio corpo, per l'inerzia buia e fangosa di quell'abbraccio, per il dovere che mi tratteneva dalla rivolta, per la remissività perversa da cui ero invasa. Qualcosa mi bruciava in gola, ma non riuscivo a sputarla. (234-35)]

The only means of changing Giovanna into her original self, Giacinto suspects, is through the traditional method of limiting her freedom by giving her a child. Near the end of the novel, Giacinto makes the error of forcing a pregnancy onto Giovanna by coaxing her to make love against her will and amid her protests that she is without contraceptive protection. She judges his aggressive act as a conjugal rape and a blatant revelation of their irreconcilable differences. Giacinto's emotional and physical tyranny has given the protagonist the strength to face up to the severe limitations of her marriage, which she chooses to renounce; at the same time, she terminates her pregnancy. Both the separation and her illegal abortion take place just before the conclusion of the novel, when Giovanna is left alone. Her inner self, however, has been enriched by the presence of the courageous Suna. Giovanna faces her future alone, in the wake of the death of her young friend. Suna's instructive influence and encouraging examples have carved for Giovanna a path leading her to deeper self-knowledge and increased awareness of flawed traditional values:

I said goodbye to him at the front door. . . . I felt like kissing him, hugging him, feeling his strong arms around my waist. But then he would have dragged me home. I told him

I wanted to be left alone and I closed the door in his face. . . . Now I'm alone and I must start everything all over again from the beginning. (282)

[Sul portone l'ho salutato. . . . Avevo voglia di baciarlo, di stringerlo, di sentire le sue braccia forti attorno alla vita. Ma dopo mi avrebbe trascinata a casa. Gli ho detto che voglio stare sola. Gli ho chiuso il portone in faccia. . . . Ora sono sola e ho tutto da ricominciare. (268-69)]

Maraini's style is defined as "lyrical realism" (Freedman, 6). Lyrical realism is defined as simplicity of language, firmness of tone, coupled with concrete images and references that demonstrate that significant social changes can be achieved through understanding, intuition, compassion, self-analysis, and, above all, constructive self-criticism. In each of the novels mentioned, the protagonists, having been unquestioning products of a specific cultural milieu, looked to others for survival, acceptance, and gratification. Each one learns, however, that to continue to conform to certain values inculcated by family and an antiquated educational system implies considerable suffering as well as loss of personal consciousness and freedom. Except for the very first protagonist, Anna, who is only fourteen, each of Maraini's women, with resolution and a degree of optimism, decides to take responsibility for her individual existence.

Almost a decade after *Woman at War*, having produced a number of success-ful feminist plays, Maraini published *The Train to Helsinki*, whose protagonist not only is politically aware but also lives her life with a comfortable degree of detachment. The continuous flashback style of narration affords the reader an intimate view of the genesis of Armida's maturation. In fact, the novel ends with the protagonist in the kitchen still peeling the potato she had taken up at the beginning of her narration: "I'm peeling a potato. I stop, holding the dripping knife in one hand and the half-peeled potato in the other" [Pelo una patata. Mi fermo col coltello gocciolante in una mano la patata mezza pelata nell'altra (3)]; and, in like manner, in the conclusion, Armida reflects in a tone of amused irony, "I'm still here holding this potato which in its white, shiny and soft con-sistency seems to lock within itself forever the sad and at the same time grand mystery that Miele is" [Io sono qui con in mano questa patata che nella sua bianca lucida e tenera compattezza pare racchiudere per sempre il misero e nello stesso tempo grandioso mistero di Miele (267)].[8] The painful discovery about life and love made by the protagonist eighteen years earlier is that, in the name of love, individuals fetter and exploit each other; that true love means not possession and enslavement but freedom for the individuals involved; that, in the final analysis, love, like life, is like a work of art, a work of precision that each one of us, as an artisan, must refine individually and, at times, in solitude.

The novels prior to *The Train to Helsinki* provide examples of men and women groping for substance and meaning. At the conclusion, the author brings her protagonists to a renouncement of past values and to an attitude of openness toward change. Indeed, in the conclusions of Maraini's earlier novels, the protagonists cast away the shackles of outdated values as they envision an open-minded existence capable of encompassing experiences and human growth transcending traditional parameters. This frame or vision that Maraini attributes to her protagonists seems to parallel Umberto Eco's critical concept enunciated in the title of his work *Open Work [Opera aperta]*. Published in the same year as Maraini's first novel, Eco's work elaborates the idea that while the valid work of art should, in form, be suited to its times and, in content, mirror the spirit of the times, it should nevertheless remain open to new modes of thought that may be even antithetical to traditional ones. Maraini brings her protagonists to the point of maturity in which, for the first time, they are able to engage in a sincere quest for identity and meaning. However, in each case the active search is realized outside the fiction of the novel.

This individual solution by the woman that is based on severance from one's historical past and present social milieu while standing resolutely on the threshold looking to the future has been proposed before, by Henrik Ibsen in *A Doll's House*, Sibilla Aleramo in *A Woman*, and other less prominent artists whose protagonists begin their enlightened existence as the work of art concludes. However, in *The Train to Helsinki*, her last work of fiction of the 1980s, Maraini created an atypical heroine who has grown to wisdom and independence before the novel begins. Armida has not found complete happiness, nor does she seek it since she does not believe in its existence. Instead, she employs her energies in constructive social action for the purpose of bettering the collective community that she inhabits and loves. The novel portrays exemplary characters, both male and female, in the late 1960s who are occupied in a united effort toward international brotherhood and peace. The vital element that we do not find between men and women in the earlier novels by Maraini and yet radiates throughout *The Train to Helsinki* is the Aristotelian concept of *amicitia* or friendship. In the novel, through the person of Armida, friendship between men and women is given a higher value than love since love can thrive on the mutual refinement and respect that friendship generates. Friendship, then, can serve as the catalyst to worthwhile relationships and a greater degree of justice between the sexes. In this novel, Maraini seems to be demonstrating an idea that the renowned British feminist Mary Wollstonecraft put forth in 1792 in her treatise *A Vindication of the Rights of Woman*:

Love, from its very nature, must be transitory. To seek for a secret that would render it constant, would be as wild a search as for the philosopher's stone, or the grand panacea and the discovery would be equally useless, or rather pernicious to mankind. The most holy hand of society is friendship. It has been well said, by a shrewd satirist, "that rare as true love is, true friendship is still rarer." (qtd. in Gilbert and Gubar, 151)[9]

Adriana Zarra in her article "Being a Woman: A Blessing or a Curse?" ["Essere donna: condanna o promozione?"] maintains that by giving renewed impetus to fundamental but somewhat neglected human values,

the woman can propose a type of culture centered on the other hand on the quality of being able to receive and on unselfish behaviour. . . . Thus we will come to understand that the most important realities of life—art, love, culture itself—help to shape mankind. . . . It is clear that this culture of tomorrow should not be brought about by women exclusively, but perhaps it will have to originate from those "female" values which nurtured particularly by women, are however common to everyone, including men. It will be therefore, a culture created by everyone, but promoted by women. (120)

Thus, people can make revolutions, and governments can pass laws in order to bring about change.[10] Yet, the first courageous steps toward real change for understanding and improved interpersonal relations on both the private and public spheres must take place within the self. Through her female protagonists, Maraini ridicules the retrograde practices of the political establishment and exhorts Italian women to take concrete, courageous steps toward a clearer understanding of self.

NOTES

1. The committee responsible for the translation of the Proceedings of the Nairobi World Conference is the Commissione Nazionale per la Realizzazione della Parità tra Uomo e Donna. The long title of the document, *Strategie future d'azione* etc., in translation would read: *Future Strategies of Action for the Progress of Women and Measures for the Realization, Within the Year 2000, of the Goals and Objectives of the Decade of United Nations for the Woman: Equality, Development, and Peace*. The translation from this document is mine.

2. When no page number is given for the English translation, the translation is mine.

3. Arangio-Ruiz and Guarna further indicate that of these women, one-third go into traditional study areas leading to degrees in "languages and literature" (23-24).

4. Maraini's novels have been widely translated into English, French, and other major European languages. Maraini's *The Age of Malaise* (1963) won the Formentor International Prize for an unpublished work by a young writer. As a result of the prize, awarded by publishers from thirteen countries, the novel was immediately translated and published in the thirteen languages of these countries.

5. Critics, such as Luigi Baldacci in "Una figlia della noia moraviana," have alluded to the possibility of Maraini having been inspired by Moravia's *La noia* [*The Empty Canvas*] (1960). However, Maraini wonders whether Moravia may have derived some inspiration from her since they had met, and he had asked Maraini to live with him, which they began to do one year later. On this matter see the introduction to *La vacanza*, ix.

6. This novel was not published in Spain immediately, as it was in the twelve other countries that donated the money for the Formentor Prize. Nor was the function held in Cape Formentor on the island of Mallorca that year, as was customary. It was held, instead, in Corfù. Some speculated that the Spanish government would not admit the Italian publisher Einaudi, who brought out a volume of anti-Franco songs. Alfred Chester of the *Herald Tribune* (May 5, 1963, 5) seemed to think that the subject matter (the pregnant adolescent who gets an illegal abortion) sparked the controversy and censure.

7. "Life Is a Steamroller," *Time*, May 17, 1963. The name of the critic is not given.

8. Maraini's optimism on relations between men and women is expressed more in recent fiction than in terms of real life. The national magazine *L'Espresso* published a letter of reply by Maraini ("Giocando e sparando che male ti fo?" ["My Playing and Shooting Can't Hurt You"]) to the Italian philosopher Gianni Vattimo, who in the preceding number of *L'Espresso* (October, 13 1991, 46-48) reviewed Ridley Scott's recently released film in Italy, *Thelma & Louise*. Maraini objects with cynicism to the

male director's portraying the female protagonists committing acts of violence with casual and remorseless ease similar to the Bonnie and Clyde stereotypes. Maraini's cynical observations convey the notion that even if, in time, women come to be regarded as equals, they will not yet have won men's right understanding of women's intimate inner life (*L'Espresso*, October 20, 1991, 46-47).

9. The satirist to whom Wollstonecraft alludes is the French epigrammist de la Rochefoucauld.

10. After decades of national debates and demonstrations, Italian working women seem to be reaping some benefits. A 1990 issue of the national magazine *L'Espresso* carried a cover story by Chiara Valentini, "Donne o schiave," June 17, 1990, 6-11, questioning whether working women aren't also "slaves." The article presents women's views on the commitment work-family, the long hours involved in each of these fundamental areas, how, consequently, the family (and by extension, the national) lifestyle is impoverished.

REFERENCES

Primary

Works by Maraini

The Age of Malaise. Trans. Frances Frenaye. New York: Grove Press, 1963.
L'età del malessere. Turin: Einaudi, 1982.
Il bambino Alberto. Milan: Bompiani, 1986.
E tu chi eri? Milan: Bompiani, 1973.
Fare teatro. Milan: Bompiani, 1974.
"Giacondo e sparando che male ti fo?" *L'Espresso*, October 20, 1991, 46-47.
The Holiday. Trans. Stuart Hood. London: Weidenfeld and Nicolson, 1966.
La vacanza. Milan: Bompiani, 1980.
Memorie di una ladra. Milan: Bompiani, 1984.
Il treno per Helsinki. Turin: Einaudi, 1984.
Woman at War. Trans. Mara Benetti and Elspeth Spottiswood. London: Lighthouse, 1984.
Donna in guerra. Turin: Einaudi, 1984.

Secondary

Arangio-Ruiz, G., and Fernanda Guarna. *Le donne italiane e il lavoro* [*Italian Women and Work*]. Istituto Centrale di Statistica. Milan: Mondadori, 1985.
Baldacci, Luigi. "Una figlia della noia moraviana." *Il Popolo*, May 9, 1962.
Chiesa, Adolfo. "Dacia e la ladra." *Paesesera*, April 29, 1972, 3.
Eco, Umberto. *Open Work*. Trans. A. Cancogni. Cambridge: Harvard University Press, 1989.
———. *Opera aperta*. Milan: Bompiani, 1989.
Freedman, Adele. "Writing Enables Maraini to Burst Out of Her Shell." *The Globe and Mail*, March 3, 1987, 6.

Gilbert, Sandra M., and Susan Gubar, eds. *The Norton Anthology of Literature by Women*. New York: Norton, 1985.

Istituto Poligrafico e Zecca dello Stato. *Decennio delle Nazioni Unite per la donna: uguaglianza, sviluppo, e pace*. Rome: 1985.

————. Committee for Equality. *Le donne italiane in cifre* [*Statistics on Italian Women*]. Rome: 1986.

————. *Strategie future d'azione per il progresso delle donne e misure alla realizzazione, entro l'anno 2000, degli scopi e degli obiettivi del Decennio delle Nazioni Unite per la donna: uguaglianza, sviluppo e pace*. Rome: 1985.

"Life Is a Steamroller." *Time*, May 17, 1963.

Moravia, Alberto. *La noia*. Milan: Bompiani, 1964.

Tamburri, A. J. "Dacia Maraini's *Donna in Guerra*: Victory or Defeat?" *Contemporary Women Writers in Italy: A Modern Renaissance*. Ed. S. L. Aricò. Amherst: Massachusetts University Press, 1990, 139-51.

Testaferri, Ada, ed. *Donna: Women in Italian Culture*. Toronto: Dovehouse, 1989.

Valentini, Chiara. "Donne o schiave." *L'Espresso*, June 17, 1990: 6-11.

Zarra, Adriana. "Essere donna: condanna o promozione?" *Donna, cultura e tradizione*. Ed. P. Bruzzichelli and Maria Algini. Milan: Mazzotta, 1976.

PART V

INTERCULTURAL SPACE

Naming the Unspeakable: The Mapping of Female Identity in Maxine Hong Kingston's *The Woman Warrior*

Marlene Goldman

In *A Room of One's Own*, Virginia Woolf raises questions concerning women's identity and the problem of inscribing this identity in literature. Such questions must be addressed if women writers are to convey a sense of their own experience, rather than simply reiterate a male perspective. In particular, Woolf argues that, due to the differences between men and women's experience, women cannot expect to utilize traditional literary forms: there is "no reason to think that the form of the epic or of the poetic play suit a woman any more than the [traditional, male] sentence suits her" (74). Although Woolf claims that the novel form is still young enough to be "soft" in a woman's hands, contemporary women writers have shown that even this form must be reconceptualized if it is to represent their unique understanding of identity and its relationship to gender, race, and class.

Maxine Hong Kingston's work *The Woman Warrior* provides a powerful example of one author's experimental treatment of the novel form. For reasons that I will outline, *The Woman Warrior* can be classified as a "postmodern" text. Blending "fact" with fiction, autobiography with folktale elements, the work maps out the contradictions that arise from a collision between two distinct cultures. As a Chinese American, Kingston refuses to portray her identity as unified. She refuses to dismiss the complexities generated by the clash between cultures. Instead, she weaves these contradictions into her text to arrive at a more expansive, although precarious, inscription of identity.

In describing the work as "postmodern," I am suggesting that it shares certain features common to postmodern literature. For one, the text demonstrates an awareness of the "constructed" nature of meaning—an awareness that meaning is developed and produced within particular systems of representation. For instance, the narrator's mother tells her children stories to test their "strength to establish realities" (Kingston, 5). Thus, realities do not exist preformed out there in the world. Instead, they must be "established" by each individual. As Patricia Lin Blinde puts it in her essay on Kingston, life as portrayed by the novel is "a complex network of fictions" (65).

A second feature of a postmodern text concerns its paradoxical relationship to literary convention. These works challenge the conventions even as they exploit them, and they also depend on the reader's familiarity with these conventions (Hutcheon, 32). Third, as a "memoir," *The Woman Warrior* shares yet another feature common to postmodern texts in that it foregrounds a concern regarding the ability to understand the past or, more specifically, "to know the past in the present" (Hutcheon, 35). In blending "factual" subject matter with folktales, for example, the text presents a radical challenge to traditional assumptions regarding the process of constructing both personal and public history.

Finally, in its exploration of history, the text, like so many postmodern works, does not represent typical historical figures: the warriors and victors. Instead, it gives voice to the "story and the story-telling of the non-combatants or even the losers" (Hutcheon, 38). In fact, all five chapters in Kingston's work portray the experience of women. The first chapter effects a reinscription of a woman so marginalized by her community that she has no name. The fourth chapter treats the fate of a woman who cannot withstand the rifts between subject positions generated in the East and West; unable to map out her identity, she goes insane. Kingston's memoirs are also populated by the mentally deranged, retarded, and grotesque—individuals whose "difference" from the norm usually precludes their appearance in history (Blinde, 64).

Fredric Jameson, a critic who is highly skeptical of postmodern literature, might well dismally categorize *The Woman Warrior* as a typical postmodern text: a "heap of fragments" produced by a fragmented self. In many ways, it could appear as if the self, or narrator, arranging the memoirs has lost its capacity to organize its past and future into "coherent experience" (71). But what if this capacity to organize past and future—a capacity inextricably linked to the ability to generate a coherent identity (72)—were not simply "lost" but consciously problematized by the text?

In the conclusion to his attack on postmodernism, Jameson discusses the phenomenon of mapping and links the ability to create spatial maps with the ability to map out identity. He cites Kevin Lynch's description of the alienated city as a space in which "people are unable to map (in their minds) either their own positions or the urban totality in which they find themselves" (89). Disalienation, by contrast, involves the "practical reconquest of a sense of place, and the construction or reconstruction of an articulated ensemble which can be retained in memory and which the individual subject can map and remap along the moments of mobile, alternative trajectories" (89). Operating, as he does, with this binary opposition of alienation and disalienation, Jameson predictably views texts that resist the call to "practical reconquests" (in this case, not of place, but of a coherent self) as poisonous signs of cultural entropy and relativism. In doing so, he fails to recognize that a postmodern text such as *The Woman Warrior* could offer another model for the mapping of "past and future."

Kingston's text can be best understood as an "interrogative text," to use Benveniste's term. This text enlists the reader in contradiction, lacks a single discourse that contains and places all others, and refuses to offer a single point of view. Kingston's novel constitutes an alternative system for organizing experience, an activity directly related to the inscription of identity. Further, this alternative model addresses specific, feminist concerns that spring from an awareness of the contradictions inherent in the discourses that structure female identity.

According to Jacques Lacan, upon entry into language (which Lacan refers to as the symbolic order), the child becomes subject to structures of language that are marked with societal imperatives. With respect to women, Catherine Belsey points out that the two fairly standard Western discourses, liberal humanist discourse and feminist discourse, offer contradictory subject positions to women.[1] Thus, even when a person is located within a single culture, the attempt to adopt a noncontradictory position can create "intolerable pressures" (65). Understandably, then, the contradictions and resultant fragmentation of identity are multiplied when an individual must contend with discourses emanating from not one, but two cultures, each governed by a separate language or symbolic system.

This is precisely the position in which Kingston's narrator, Maxine, finds herself. Not only must she struggle to locate herself within the diverse and contradictory discourses of the Western tradition, but she must also wrestle with the positions afforded by her Chinese heritage. If, as Benveniste argues, language provides the possibility of subjectivity by allowing the speaker to say "I," then the inscription of subjectivity is doubly problematized when there are two "I's" to choose from (225). As a child, the narrator is mesmerized by the English word for "I." She asks, "[H]ow could the American "I," assuredly wearing a hat like the Chinese, have only three strokes, the middle so straight?" (193). She is startled by this articulation of selfhood, which seems so foreign: "I stared so long at that middle line and waited so long for its black center to resolve into tight strokes and dots that I forgot to pronounce it" (193). The American word for "here" presents a similar difficulty. It lacks "a strong consonant to hang onto and so flat, when 'here' [in Chinese] is two mountainous ideographs" (194). With no fixed position in either symbolic system, Kingston's identity remains divided and in flux. Her tongue, having been "cut," symbolizes this division, which enables her to speak languages that are "completely different from one another" (190). Yet the positive implications of this ability are seemingly counterbalanced by negative outcomes. Her "broken" voice, which "cracks in two," becomes a source of pain and humiliation because it prevents her from achieving a form of coherence recognizable by traditional standards (191).

Yet, as suggested earlier, Kingston refuses to ignore the multiple contradictions resulting from the demands of two symbolic systems. She does not map out a polarized position either in the form of a solid identity or in the form of a "solid" genre such as autobiography. In many respects, her decision to utilize traditional narrative forms to suit her aims corresponds to the feminist strategy outlined by Teresa de Lauretis. According to de Lauretis, feminists view narrative and narrativity as mechanisms to be employed "strategically and tactically in the effort to construct *other forms of coherence*, to shift the terms of representation, to produce the conditions of representability of another—and gendered—social subject" (109; emphasis added).

With an awareness of this feminist strategy, Kingston's rejection of traditional forms of coherence does not necessarily imply the valueless incoherence and schizophrenia posited by Jameson. In fact, *The Woman Warrior*, with its trans-generic form and fluid boundaries, where genre spills into genre, constitutes a tenuous new model for the construction of identity. In particular, the final chapter, entitled "Song for a Barbarian Reed Pipe," offers a means of reconcil-ing different discourses based on incorporation rather than denial.

The text specifically addresses the proliferation of contradictory subject positions afforded to women, and it articulates the difficulty women have in mapping out a subject position in the face of these contradictions. In Kingston's case, these contradictions relate specifically to an author whose rural Chinese culture, combined with her American experience, affords particular subject positions for women. In a discussion of Chinese culture, Margery Wolf clarifies the well-established discourse sanctioning control over the female sex. Wolf states that the Three Obediences by which women were to be governed were common knowledge: as an unmarried girl, a woman must obey her father and her brothers; as a married woman, she must obey her husband; and, as a widow, she must obey her adult sons (2).

In Kingston's book, one of the most obvious challenges to this discourse sanctioning control over women is found in the story of the Woman Warrior. Tension immediately arises as a result of the juxtaposition of the book's title, *The Woman Warrior*, and the figure presented in the first chapter, "No name woman." These two figures, the warrior and the unknown aunt, and their respective stories, generated by a single culture, reflect the antithetical subject positions available to women. On one hand, as suggested by Wolf and illustrated in the story of the no name woman, the community demands that women remain subordinate as "wives and slaves." Adherence to this discourse of submission is imperative. As the narrator explains, the rural Chinese community's notion of the real is threatened when an individual's drives, whether sexual or narra-tive, challenge this discourse of submission. When the aunt disobeys this discourse, "the frightened villagers, who depended on one another to maintain the real . . . show her a personal, physical representation of the break she had made in the roundness. . . . The villagers punished her for acting as if she could have a private life" (14).

To rebel against the discourse of submission constitutes an act of violence against the community: "one human being flaring up into violence could open up a black hole, a maelstrom that pulled in the sky" (14). The mother's first words to Kingston warn her against committing just such an act of violence: "You must not tell anyone . . . what I am about to tell you." After she tells Kingston the story of the aunt, Brave Orchid repeats this warning, "Don't tell anyone you had an aunt. Your father does not want to hear her name" (5). As a result of these admonitions, Kingston decides that "sex was unspeakable and words so strong and fathers so frail that 'aunt' would do my father mysterious harm" (18). But the very fact that the story has been published makes it clear that the mother's injunction to silence has been broken or, more accurately, evaded. Kingston does not tell *anyone* about her aunt; she tells everyone. Aware that, in retelling her aunt's story, she may be as dangerous and controlling as those who sought to punish her ancestor through silence, Kingston subverts her authority by offering several versions of the tale. Sensing the pernicious aspect to the desire to "get things straight," she must resist the urge "to name the unspeakable" (6).

But Kingston must break the silence. She must write in order to locate herself, to determine how the "invisible world the emigrants built around . . . [her] childhood fits in solid America" (6). Her parents, more thoroughly Chinese, are not faced with this problem of psychic orientation. Whenever they said home, "they suspended America" (116). Kingston must rebel if she is to make sense of her cultural heritage, the "invisible world," which informs her identity. In disobeying the community, however, she risks injuring herself because the community that she betrays is already a part of her; she has been constituted according to the community's discourse. Nowhere is this made clearer than in the section entitled "White Tigers." Here a father and mother "carve revenge" on their warrior-daughter's back. They inscribe their oaths and their names in her flesh, so that even if she were killed, the text would still be legible; people could use her dead body as a weapon (41).

Body, as text, records the iterable marks of a community—marks that can be used by others. In this portrait of body-as-text, Kingston not only self-consciously foregrounds her activity as a storyteller/writer producing a text that has an independent existence from her but also indicates that her own identity and sense of place have been inscribed by her community: "[T]hey had carved their names and address on me, and I would come back" (44). Thus, when she breaks her silence to take revenge by "reporting," she takes vengeance against herself and the people she loves. In her nightmares, she becomes a vampire: "[T]ears dripped from my eyes, but blood dripped from my fangs, blood of the people I was supposed to love" (221). The tensions generated by her self-division—her awareness of the discourse that demands submission combined with her need to retell the stories in order to understand herself—suffuse the stories she narrates. Even the idealistic portrait of the woman warrior, which challenges the traditional role of female subservience, still includes traces of the discourse that designates women as inferior.

The story of the woman warrior, in contrast to the story of the no name aunt, emphasizes that women "failed if they grew up to be but wives or slaves" because they could be "heroines, swordswomen" (23). The folktale celebrates women's power and their ability to perform heroic deeds on behalf of the community. In telling the story, Kingston inscribes herself into Fa Mu Lan's tale, just as she actively entered into the story of her aunt because, as she says, "unless I see her life branching into mine, she gives me no ancestral help" (10). As a warrior, she trains body and mind, finally learning dragon ways—how to infer the whole from the parts, how to make her mind large, "as the universe is large, so that there is room for paradoxes" (35). Her female body, rather than seen as a hindrance, becomes an advantage in battle against larger, clumsier males. Bodily functions, including menstruation, become acceptable. Even the capacity to reproduce is celebrated. Kingston recognizes that, in giving birth, women write history through their bodies. As she says, women who engaged in sex "hazarded birth and hence lifetimes" (8). Therefore, in the depiction of Fa Mu Lan as a mother, the story portrays an integral part of the historical process as experienced by women.

While the discourse that celebrates the female remains dominant, elements of the opposing discourse are evident throughout; the text does not efface contradictions. Admitting that she hid her identity from her army, the narrator explains that the "Chinese executed women who disguised themselves as soldiers or students" (46). The evil Baron voices misogynist sayings: girls are "maggots in the rice. It is more profitable to raise geese than daughters" (51). When she returns home, the warrior woman tells her husband that now that her public duties are finished, she can stay with him doing farmwork and housework and giving him "more sons" (54). Essentially, she conforms to the role of wife and slave. In general, as the story of the warrior nears its conclusion, the intrusions of the opposing discourse become more frequent, until finally, the folktale collapses under its weight.

At this point, the sayings previously cast into the mouth of the evil Baron are recontextualized. The enemy is revealed to be her father and mother and other emigrant villagers (54). No longer a heroine, the narrator sees herself at the mercy of a symbolic system that renders her subservient: "[T]here is a Chinese word for the female 'I'—which is 'slave.' Break the women with their own tongues!" (56) Despite the power of the discourse advocating subservience, the story of the woman warrior is never completely repressed. In fact, it resurfaces in the second chapter, entitled "Shaman," which describes her mother's training and experience as a doctor.

Like the mythic warrior, Kingston's mother is afforded a respite from slavery. Brave Orchid lives for two years "without servitude." After completing her training, she returns home as triumphant as any female avenger. Like the female warrior, she, too, is familiar with "dragon ways" (127). Brave Orchid is also victorious in battle. While the woman warrior of the folktale struggles against evil Barons, Kingston's mother contends against "ghosts." Ultimately, Kingston reveals that this ability to do battle with ghosts is a skill that is necessary for the development of a sense of identity.

In the novel, ghosts (as well as barbarians) occupy the shifting territory outside the borders of "reality," as designated by the Chinese. Yet the supernatural continually encroaches upon daily existence. For instance, the baby of the no name aunt is called a "little ghost." When Brave Orchid's sister, Moon Orchid, confronts her Americanized husband, they are both unreal and insubstantial to each other: "[H]er husband looked like one of the ghosts passing the car windows, and she must look like a ghost from China" (178). The land of ghosts, America is filled with specters—Taxi Ghosts, Bus Ghosts, Police Ghosts. As Kingston says, "[O]nce upon a time the world was so thick with ghosts, I could hardly breathe, I could hardly walk, limping my way around the White Ghosts and their cars" (113).

Brave Orchid's ability to overcome ghosts resides in her capacity to *incorporate* the supernatural: "[M]y mother could contend against the hairy beasts whether flesh or ghost because she could eat them" (108). This ability to incorporate what lies outside the subject—the not-I—is linked to her strong sense of identity. During an encounter with the Sitting Ghost, Brave Orchid boasts, "I do not give in. . . . You have no power over a strong woman" (84). Unlike her daughter, Brave Orchid is not caught between two symbolic systems; therefore, she identifies herself more solidly as Chinese, as one of the Han. Even when she emigrates, she is not divided. She kept her Chinese name, "adding no American nor holding one in reserve for American emergencies" (90).

Although Brave Orchid's identity appears stable, Kingston is at pains to show that identity is never a solid construct. Even Brave Orchid's spirit is divided, sometimes wandering in the past with her dead children in China and her husband in America (84), sometimes keeping her sister's plane aloft and her son's boat in Vietnam afloat (132). The fragility of identity is constantly brought to the reader's attention. Moreover, the necessity of mapping out identity is revealed to be a crucial process.

After her encounter with the Sitting Ghost, Brave Orchid's classmates must help her spirit locate the To Keung School as "home" by reciting its geographic location (89). Here the mapping of identity involves both geographic and ancestral trajectories. Brave Orchid also gives a map of China to her children—she "funneled China into our ears: Kwangtung Province, New Society Village, the river Kwoo . . . 'Go the way we came so that you will be able to find our house'" (90). The narrator recalls how her mother led her children "out of nightmares and horror movies" by singing her name along with the names of her mother, father, brothers, and sisters (89). However, as barbarians born in America, the children have difficulty understanding how to use these maps to construct personal identities.

The dangers associated with an inability to orient oneself, to map out one's identity in the presence of the not-I, are dramatically illustrated in the story of Moon Orchid. Brave Orchid paid for her sister's fare, enabling Moon Orchid to leave China and come to America. But Moon Orchid, finding herself forcefully uprooted, can make little sense of the barbarians among whom she finds herself. Her nieces and nephews appear to her as "wild animals" (156), and while she assumes that they must have "many interesting savage things to say, raised as they'd been in the wilderness," she cannot comprehend them (154). The encounter with her estranged husband reinforces the fact that she does not belong in America. He tells her, "You can't belong. You don't have the hardness for this country" (177). Hardness, or solidity, is associated with America (Kingston refers to "solid America" [6]). Solidity is a trait that Moon Orchid lacks. Shortly after the encounter with her ghost-husband, Moon Orchid gives up trying to understand the American barbarians and retreats into madness.

The story of Moon Orchid's failed attempt to leave China and live in the West illustrates Jameson's point regarding the connection between the ability to make a cognitive map of a city and the ability to map one's identity. Brave

Orchid realizes that in "whisking her sister across the ocean by jet" and making her "scurry up and down the Pacific coast," Moon Orchid had misplaced herself. Her "spirit (her 'attention' Brave Orchid called it) scattered all over the world" (181). In trying to help her sister locate herself and regain her identity, Brave Orchid chants her sister's new address to her. She tries, to no avail, to help Moon Orchid create a map that would "anchor [her] . . . to this earth" (182).

In effect, Moon Orchid's madness represents one way of dealing with multiple discourses. Rather than effect a more positive exchange with the not-I, in this case, Western culture, Moon Orchid rejects it altogether. As a result, her discourse ceases to include variety. As Brave Orchid explains, "[M]ad people have only one story that they talk over and over" (184). At the asylum, Moon Orchid is content because difference has been abolished: "no one ever leaves . . . we are all women here" (185). She delights in the narcissistic belief that the world is one and that everyone understands each other: "[W]e speak the same language, the very same. They understand me, and I understand them" (185). Her madness reflects a primary desire for nondifferentiation. This extreme form of narcissism involves the "impossible, imaginary attempt to totally integrate the self" (LaCapra, 72). Within the novel, Moon Orchid's fate functions as a warning, illustrating that attempts at denying the existence of contradictory discourses and self-division are dangerous. As Suzanne Juhasz states, the association of women with madness in Kingston's text is shown as "the alternative to their achievement of self-identity" (182).

Throughout the text, polarized and reductionist stances of any kind are revealed to be unsatisfactory methods for grappling with the presence of contradictions. The narrator takes up such a position when she tortures her weak, silent schoolmate. Determined to fit into solid America, Kingston rejects her Chinese self and projects it onto the "soft" Chinese girl who refuses to speak. Kingston divides herself, viewing with contempt the bonelessness and liquidity of her victim, who seems to be all tears and snot. But Kingston's binary stance ultimately collapses when she finds herself "crying and sniffling," behaving exactly like the girl she despises (109). A similar attempt to eradicate difference occurs when Kingston determines to confess her "secret list" to her mother. Her motive stems from a narcissistic desire similar to Moon Orchid's desire for sameness. As Kingston says, "[I]f only I could let my mother know the list, she—and the world—would become more like me, and I would never be alone again" (230). But Kingston can never regress to this state of original oneness.

In the story of the poet Ts'ai Yen, an alternative model is offered for the construction of identity. This model affords a more positive engagement with what lies beyond the world designated by a particular symbolic system—an engagement that does not eradicate discontinuity and separateness. Kingston first alludes to this model in the preamble to the story of her grandmother who loved opera. In introducing the tale, the narrator recalls that the story was told to her recently by her mother: "[T]he beginning is hers, the ending, mine" (240). This model of assimilation and incorporation has, in fact, been operative throughout the novel. The stories Kingston overheard as a child have all been translated, elaborated on, and finally passed on to the reader.

As indicated before, the most powerful articulation of this model of incorporation is conveyed through the final story of Ts'ai Yen. According to the story, the poet, who lived in the first century, is captured by barbarians. Carried far from home, she lives among the barbarians in the desert for twelve years and bears the chieftain two sons. Her sons do not speak her language, and they mock her. One night, she hears the barbarian's music. Until this time, she had thought that the death whistles that emanated from their arrows were the only music they were capable of producing. While playing their flutes, the barbarians strive to produce a high note beyond the range of possibility—an icicle in the desert. After hearing this music, Ts'ai Yen retires to her tent and begins to sing a song "so high and clear, it matched the flutes." Her words "seemed to be Chinese but the barbarians understood their sadness and anger . . . Her children did not laugh, but eventually sang along" (243). Later, when she is rescued and reunited with her people, Ts'ai Yen brings her songs back from the savage lands: "'Eighteen stanzas for a Barbarian Reed Pipe' . . . It translated well" (243).

The poet's position as exile among barbarians is analogous to Kingston's position as Chinese American. Kingston, like Ts'ai Yen, is dislocated and must struggle to make sense of contradictory discourses if she is to comprehend her identity. Ts'ai Yen's ability to incorporate the music of the barbarians corresponds to Kingston's ability as "outlaw knotmaker" (190). Her power to weave together the contradictory elements of Chinese and American discourses represents a more positive engagement with the not-I—an engagement where the not-I, far from being excluded and repressed, is able to recognize itself. The high note captured in the poet's voice can be likened to the stories Kingston narrates—stories begun by her Chinese mother and concluded by the American daughter. These hybrid narratives enable Kingston to represent her identity. Yet the structure of the narratives implies a more fragile "form of coherence," an unstable form with the tenuous existence of an icicle in the desert.

Ultimately, Kingston's text, with its depiction of the narrator's unstable subject position, offers an alternative model for portraying female identity—one that resists organizing "past, present, and future into coherent experience," to use Jameson's words. As I have illustrated, rather than dismiss the complexities generated by her dual heritage, Kingston foregrounds these difficulties and allows them to inform the design of the work as a whole. She does not take up a polarized position in an attempt to "name the unspeakable." Instead, Kingston reconceptualizes the traditional form of the novel to create a postmodern text—a transformation that lends support to Virginia Woolf's claim that women writers must abandon traditional literary forms if they hope to inscribe their own conceptions of female identity in literature.

NOTE

1. In *Critical Practice*, Belsey states that women participate both in the liberal humanist discourse of "freedom, self-determination and rationality and at the same time in the specifically feminine discourse . . . of submission, relative inadequacy and irrational intuition" (65).

REFERENCES

Belsey, Catherine. *Critical Practice*. London: Methuen, 1980.

Benveniste, Emile. *Problems in General Linguistics*. Trans. Mary Elizabeth Meek. Coral Gables, FL: University of Miami Press, 1971.

Blinde, Patricia Lin. "Icicle in the Desert: Form and Perspective in the Works of Two Chinese-American Women Writers." *MELUS* 6.3 (1979): 51-72.

de Lauretis, Teresa. *Technologies of Gender: Essays on Theory, Film, and Fiction*. Bloomington: Indiana University Press, 1987.

Hong Kingston, Maxine. *The Woman Warrior: Memoirs of a Girlhood Among Ghosts*. New York: Random House, 1977.

Hutcheon, Linda. "The Politics of Representation." *Signature* 1 (1989): 23-44.

Jameson, Fredric. "Postmodernism, or the Cultural Logic of Late Capitalism." *New Left Review* 146 (1984): 53-92.

Juhasz, Suzanne. "Maxine Hong Kingston's Narrative Technique." *Contemporary American Women Writers: Narrative Strategies*. Ed. Catherine Rainwater and William J. Scheick. Lexington: University Press of Kentucky, 1985.

LaCapra, Dominick. *History and Criticism*. Ithaca, NY: Cornell University Press, 1985.

Wolf, Margery. *Revolution Postponed: Women in Contemporary China*. Stanford, CA: Stanford University Press, 1985.

Woolf, Virginia. *A Room of One's Own*. London: Granada, 1982.

Born of a Stranger: Mother-Daughter Relationships and Storytelling in Amy Tan's *The Joy Luck Club*

Gloria Shen

Amy Tan's first work, *The Joy Luck Club* (1989),[1] is a challenge to the novel as a "narrative paradigm" (Jameson, 151) in several ways: form, narrative structure, and narrative techniques. It is not a novel in the sense that only one story, "his story" is presented; it is a work of sixteen "her stories." The stories are "presented" not by one single third-person narrator either from her particular perspective or from the various "points of view" of the characters. These are narrative techniques conventionally associated with the novel of the nineteenth and twentieth centuries. The book is divided into four main sections; the stories are told from the viewpoints of four Chinese mothers and their Chinese American daughters. The only exception is Suyuan Woo, who, having recently died, speaks not for herself but through her daughter, Jing-mei. The daughter tells her mother's stories as she takes her mother's place at the mahjong table and on the fateful trip to China. The stories, "told" by the three mothers and four daughters at different times and in different settings, resemble fragments of stories collected by a sociologist and randomly put together, rather than carefully constructed narratives set in a deliberate order by an author. In other words, *The Joy Luck Club* employs an unusual narrative strategy. In this chapter, I explore the connection between the narrative strategy employed in *The Joy Luck Club* and the relationships between the Chinese mothers and their American-born daughters.

In *The Joy Luck Club*, important themes are repeated in the stories like musical leitmotifs and presented from slightly different angles in order to give the reader a continuous sense of life as well as a full understanding of the significance of each event. The unique structure of *The Joy Luck Club* allows the unconnected fragments of life, revealed from different but somewhat overlapping perspectives by all the "reliable" narrators, to unfold into a meaningful, continuous whole so that the persistent tensions and powerful bonds between mother and daughter, between generations, may be illuminated through a montage effect on the reader.

The traditional novel as a "narrative paradigm" (Jameson, 151) entails a set of rules that bestow legitimacy upon certain narrative forms and preclude certain other forms. Jameson expounds the notion of "narrative paradigm" by claiming that the "forms" of the novel as the "inherited narrative paradigms" are: "the raw material on which the novel works, transforming their 'telling' into its 'showing,' estranging commonplaces against the freshness of some unexpected 'real,' foregrounding convention itself as that through which readers have hitherto received their notions of events, psychology, experience, space, and time" (151). The "inherited narrative paradigms" determine rules of the game and illustrate how they are to be applied. The rules define what has the right to be said and done in the culture in question. Oral narrative forms, such as popular stories, myths, legends, and tales, are thus viewed as belonging to a "savage, primitive, underdeveloped, backward, alienated" mentality, composed of opinions, prejudice, ignorance and ideology (Lyotard, 19). As Lyotard notes, oral narrative forms have been deemed fit for women and children only and have not been rightly considered as appropriate or competent forms to be subsumed under the category of the novel. As a Western-conceived notion, the "narrative paradigm" of the novel thus excludes various minority subnarrative traditions, including women's. Structurally, *The Joy Luck Club* is an interesting example because it rejects artificial unity and espouses the fragmentary, one of the main features of postmodernism.[2]

The dissolution of unity in the traditional novel, best manifested in the "fragmentation" of the work, serves to highlight different themes that evolve around the mother-daughter relationship. *The Joy Luck Club* is divided into four sections, each of which consists of four stories. Each of the four sections of the book begins with a prologue, a brief narrative illustrative of the theme of that section. The Joy Luck Club is a monthly mahjong gathering to which the generation of the Chinese mothers has belonged for decades and with which the generation of the American daughters has grown up. Like four Chinese boxes, the complexity of the narrative structure is revealed through stories told within stories by the mothers to the daughters. In this manner, Tan directly puts forward the views, feelings, emotions, and thoughts of her characters, stressing the mixture of action, consciousness, and subconsciousness. In the chapter "Without Wood," a daughter tells about a dream she once had as a child that reveals subconsciously the daughter's strong desire to resist the clutching influence of the mother on her. In this dream, the daughter finds herself in a playground filled with rows of sandboxes. In each sandbox there is a doll. Haunted by the feeling that her mother knows exactly which doll she will pick, the daughter deliberately chooses a different one. When the mother orders the guardian of the gate to the dreamworld to stop her, the little girl becomes so frightened that she remains frozen in place (186).

Tan's storytelling technique reveals the complexity of the dark, invisible mind of cultural consciousness and subconsciousness best portrayed by the stories within stories. In *The Joy Luck Club*, Tan moves with swiftness and ease from one story to another, from one symbol or image to another. In a sense, *The Joy Luck Club* can be properly called a collection of intricate and haunting memories couched in carefully wrought stories. Tan has purposely externalized the eight characters' mental world by allowing each of them to tell her own story in a deceptively simple manner, thus allowing the reader to plunge into the mind of the characters. The motives, desires, pains, pleasures, and concerns of the characters are thereby effectively dramatized. This particular writing strategy allows Tan to transcend the conventional novelistic dichotomy of preferred "showing" and undesirable "telling." The stories thus tell us a great deal about individual characters, their reaction to each other, and their activities together. Because the stories are all told in the mothers' and the daughters' own voices, we are spared the pressing question with which the reader of a conventional novel is constantly bombarded with: Am I dealing with a "reliable" or "unreliable" narrator? While immersed in particular and individual perspectives, the reader of *The Joy Luck Club* also confronts the more general and lasting concerns of many generations. Unlike Maxine Hong Kingston's *The Woman Warrior*, which relates the life experience of one woman and concentrates on one single family, the stories in *The Joy Luck Club*, with its characters and circumstances skilfully interwoven, presents a continuous whole more meaningful than the sum of its parts.

In *The Joy Luck Club*, Tan probes the problematic mother-daughter relationship in sixteen separate stories spanning two generations of eight women. Though the eight characters are divided into four families, the book itself is concerned more with an unmistakable bifurcation along generational lines: mothers, whose stories all took place in China, and daughters, whose stories deal with their lives in America. Though the mothers all have different names and individual stories, they seem interchangeable in that they all have similar personalities—strong, determined, and endowed with mysterious power—and that they all show similar concerns about their daughters' welfare. As a result, the mothers are possessively trying to hold onto their daughters, and the daughters are battling to get away from their mothers. The four mothers and four daughters are different, but their differences remain insignificant as the action of the novel is focused on the persistent tensions and powerful bonds between them.

Tan's characters are seen in both detail and outline. The first-person testimonies allow the reader to examine each of the characters closely and to develop a sense of empathy with each of them; but, at the same time, the testimonies reveal a pattern, particularly in the way the mothers and daughters relate to one another. The purpose of this treatment is obvious: to portray the mother and daughter relationship as both typical and universal.

In Tan's novel, The Joy Luck Club is a bridge uniting both space and time. The Joy Luck Club connects the sixteen intricately interlocking stories and helps to reveal and explain the infinite range and complexity of mother-daughter relationships. Within the narrative, it joins two continents and unites the experiences of the mothers and the daughters. The American daughters are alien to Chinese culture as much as they are to their mother's uncanny, Chinese ways of thinking. To the daughters, cultural and ethnic identity is possible only when they can fully identify themselves with their mothers through their maturation into womanhood. The sharing of cultural experiences between mothers and daughters through the device of storytelling transforms structurally isolated monologues into meaningful dialogues between mother and mother, daughter and daughter, and, more important, mother and daughter and coalesces the sixteen monologues into a coherent whole. While the mother and daughter relationships are unique in the ethnic context of Tan's novel, they also have a universal aspect. Indeed, all women share this experience, regardless of time and space. An-mei Hsu is puzzled by both the specific and universal qualities of the mother-daughter relationship. Raised traditionally, she was taught to swallow her desires, her bitterness, and the misery of others. Rejecting her upbringing, she tries to instill in her daughter a strong sense of self. Unfortunately, her daughter is a passive individual. An-mei Hsu is thus convinced that regardless of their respective upbringing, mothers and daughters are somehow condemned to being similar: "And even though I taught my daughter the opposite, still she came out the same way! Maybe it is because she was born to me and she was born a girl. And I was born to my mother and I was born a girl. All of us are like stairs, one step after another, going up and down, but all going the same way" (215).

Through her structural experiments with the elements of fiction and her storytelling device, and with the testimonial mode of characterization, Tan has pushed her novel beyond the merely conventional practice of the novel (to mimic the convention of the appearance of life, as done by many traditional novelists). Instead, she tries to do away with "his story" and present "her life" from the perspectives of the individual women characters in the form of loosely connected monologues. These monologues serve to translate as faithfully as possible the intricate relationship that can exist between a mother and her daughter.

Tan's extensive use of symbols and images creates a mood of expression that reveals and explains the infinite range and complexity of these mother-daughter relationships. Each of the four sections of The Joy Luck Club begins with a prologue, defining the theme of that section while disclosing certain aspects of the problem in the mother-daughter relationship. The first prologue contains a cluster of images that highlight the nature of this relationship in the book and summarize the whole novel. This prologue centers around an old woman who remembers that, while still in Shanghai, she bought a swan for a small sum. The swan, according to the vendor, was once a duck who had managed to stretch his neck in the hope of becoming a goose. On the boat sailing to America, the old woman swore to the swan that she would one day have a daughter whom no one would look down upon, for she would speak only perfect English. In order for this daughter to know her mother's meaning, she would give her the swan (17).

However, upon arriving in America, the swan is confiscated, and the old woman is left with only one of the swan's feathers. This feather is far too insignificant for her to convince anyone, least of all her daughter, how beautiful the swan was. Furthermore, the daughter she had hoped for has become an unsympathetic "stranger" who does not even speak her language. The prologue thus ends on a poignant note. Indeed, year after year, the mother waits for the moment when she would be able to tell her daughter in perfect American English that the feather is far from worthless, for it symbolizes all of her "good intentions" (17).

The prologue sets the tone and the reasons for the tensions and conflicts in the mother-daughter relationship. The "swan" and the "old woman" who sailed across the ocean together, "stretching their necks toward America" (17), are an emblem of the four mothers who came to the United States, hoping to give their daughters a better life than the one they had in China. The "good intentions" are clearly stated. But the mother, left with an almost worthless feather, is condemned to wait patiently many years until the daughter is finally mature enough to come back to her, to appreciate her, and to reconstruct the beautiful swan from the feather. The swan is therefore emblematic of both the mother's new life in America and, more important, her past one in China, an experience the mother wants to communicate to her daughter. However, only a mature daughter, who has overcome the psychological and cultural gap separating her from her mother is capable of coming to terms with this experience.

The mother-daughter relationship is the central issue and focal point in the dialogues between the mothers and daughters in Tan's book. The novel traces the psychological development of the American daughter and her final acceptance of the Chinese mother and what the Chinese mother stands for. Jing-mei Woo, who replaces her recently deceased mother at the mahjong table, is the first to tell a story on behalf of her mother; she is also the very last daughter to recount her own story. It is interesting to note that when she is asked by her three "aunts" to go to China in order to fulfill her mother's long-cherished wish to meet her lost twin babies, Jing-mei shocks and upsets them with her confused yet honest remark that she would not know what to tell her sisters because she did not really know her mother: "What will I say? What can I tell them about my mother?" (40)

The mothers are all frightened by this response. Indeed, they sense in it the confusion of their own daughters. In Jing-mei, they recognize their own daughters, all as ignorant and as unmindful of the truths and hopes their mothers brought over with them from China (40). Ironically, the accomplishment of the mother's dream for her daughter, a dream that entailed her physical removal from the motherland, results in multifarious problems in the relationship with her daughter.

In Tan's novel, the Chinese mothers are all strong-willed, persistent, hard to please, and overly critical. They often make their presence and their goodwill look like outrageous impositions rather than tacit influences. When, for example, Jing-mei Woo describes her mother's New Year crab dinner, we learn that, although she does not like this dish, she is obliged to eat it since her refusal to do so would constitute a rejection of her mother's love (202). The food and the advice offered by the mothers are hard to refuse not only because they are a symbol of love but also because they tend to carry the full weight of maternal authority. That is why Waverly Jong is convinced that telling one's mother to be quiet would be tantamount to committing suicide (173). In another example, Waverly tries to make her mother accept her American boyfriend by showing her a fur coat that he has given her as a token of his love. Totally dejected by her mother's antagonism toward her boyfriend, whom the mother does not consider good enough for her daughter, Waverly Jong feels distressed at not being able to shake off her mother's clutching influence. When she looks once again at the coat her mother has just finished criticizing, she becomes convinced that it is, indeed, shabby (169).

The mother's wish for the daughter to live a better life than the one she had back in China is revealed in the conversation between the Chinese woman and her swan on her journey to America in the novel's first prologue. Ironically, this wish becomes the very source of the conflicts and tensions in their relationship. This is made perfectly clear by Jing-mei Woo when she half-jokingly, half-remorsefully recalls her ever-agonizing childhood, a period during which her mother unsuccessfully attempts to transform her into a child prodigy. In order to prepare Jing-mei for a future that she hopes will be brilliant, Suyuan Woo nightly submits Jing-mei to a series of tests while forcing her to listen to countless stories about amazing children (133-34). Mother and daughter finally settle on Jing-mei's becoming a concert pianist, and Jing-mei begins to take piano lessons from Mr. Old Chong, a retired piano teacher who happens to be deaf. As a result, the daughter manages to get away with playing more or less competently while her teacher conducts an imaginary piece of music in his head (148).

Another daughter, Rose Hsu Jordon, is married to a "foreigner" who wishes to divorce her. Her mother, An-mei Hsu, urges her to speak up in the hope of saving her marriage. She does this by juxtaposing the Chinese way with the American way. The Chinese way consists of not expressing one's desires, not speaking up, and not making choices. The American way consists of exercising choices and speaking up for oneself. An-mei Hsu raised Rose in the American way. She hoped that this would allow her daughter to lead a better life than the one she had in China. Indeed, in China people had no choice. Since they could not speak up, they were forced to accept whatever fate befell them (241). An-mei Hsu reminds Rose that by not speaking up, she "can lose her chance forever" (215).

The frustration that Waverly's mother, Lindo Jong, feels is shared by all the mothers. This frustration is best summarized in her painful and poignant confession during the course of which she accuses herself of being responsible for the way Waverly has turned out. Her sense of responsibility stems from the fact that she is the one who wanted Waverly to have the best of both worlds, and it leads her to openly berate herself for not being able to foresee that her daughter's American circumstances would not necessarily mix well with her Chinese reality (254).

The alienation between mother and daughter often stems either from a lack of understanding or from various forms of miscommunication. While the daughters, all born in America, entirely adapt to the customs and language of the new land, the immigrant mothers still hold onto those of China. All the mothers feel their daughters' impatience when they speak Chinese and are convinced that their daughters think they are stupid when they attempt to communicate with them in broken English (40-41). If Jing-mei is initially reluctant to carry out her mother's long-cherished wish to be reunited with her two lost sisters, it is mainly because she believes that she and her mother have never understood one another. The language barrier that existed between them was such that both mother and daughter imperfectly translated each other words and meanings (37).

In a tragicomic incident that exemplifies the futile attempt to bridge the mother-daughter gap, Lindo Jong is proudly speaking to her daughter about Taiyuan, her birthplace. Waverly mistakes Taiyuan for Taiwan and is subsequently visibly irritated when her mother loudly corrects her. The daughter's unintentional mistake, combined with the mother's anger, destroys their attempt to communicate. Consequently, they are both plunged, once again, into a steely silence (183). In another example of Tan's lightness of touch straining with ambivalence, Lena St. Clair defines her mother as a "displaced person" who has difficulties expressing herself in English. Born in Wushi, near Shanghai, she speaks Mandarin and only a little English. Lena's father, who spoke only a few canned Chinese expressions, always insisted that his wife learn English. Unable to express herself clearly in English, she communicates through gestures and looks and sometimes in a broken English punctuated by hesitations and frustration. Her husband thus feels justified in putting words in her mouth (106).

The mothers' inability to speak perfect American English has multiple ramifications. For one thing, as they themselves have not lived in a foreign country, the daughters are left with the false impression that their mothers are not intelligent. As a result, the daughters often feel justified in believing that their mothers have nothing worthwhile to say. Furthermore, when mother and daughter share neither the same realm of experience and knowledge nor the same concerns, their differences are not marked by a slip of the tongue or the lack of linguistic adroitness or even by a generational gap, but rather by a deep geographical and cultural cleft. When the mother talks about American ways, the daughter is willing to listen; when the mother shows her Chinese ways, the daughter ignores her. The mother is thus unable to teach her daughter the Chinese ways of obeying parents, of listening to the mother's mind, of hiding her thoughts, of knowing her own worth without becoming vain, and, most important of understanding why "Chinese thinking is best" (254).

The gulf between the Old World and the New, between Chinese mother and American daughter, is exacerbated by the ethnic and racial biases against the Chinese that the young daughter has to deal with on a regular basis. A conversation between Waverly and her mother, Lindo Jong, shows that even as a young child, the daughter is fully aware of the hurtful effect these prejudices have had on the Chinese mother, who has not adjusted well to the life and customs of the new land. One night, while Lindo Jong is brushing her daughter's hair, Waverly, who has overheard a boy in her class discuss Chinese torture, wickedly asks her the following question: "Ma, what is Chinese torture?" Visibly disturbed by this question, Lindo Jong sharply nicks her daughter's skull with a hairpin. She then softly but proudly answers that Chinese people are proficient in many areas. They "do business, do medicine, do painting . . . do torture. Best torture" (91).

While the Chinese mother seems able readily to shrug off the detrimental influence of ethnic and racial biases, she cannot help but feel the effect of them upon her daughter. Lindo Jong is unable to overcome the painful reality that sets her apart from her daughter. She is ashamed because she knows that the daughter she is so proud of is ashamed of her and of her Chinese ways (255). The constantly growing cleavage of ethnic and national identity drives the daughter to make persistent efforts to Americanize herself in order to lessen her mother's commanding influence.

The daughters' battles for autonomy and independence from powerful imposing mothers are relentless, and the confrontations between mothers and daughters are fierce. In the chapter "Without Wood," daughter Rose Hsu Jordan describes the decision she made as a child in her dream to pick a different doll from the one her mother expected her to choose (186). Another daughter, Jing-mei, adopts a self-defensive strategy against her mother's expectation that she be a child prodigy by disappointing her whenever she can. She does this by getting average grades, by not becoming class president, by not being accepted into Stanford University, and finally by dropping out of college (142). By consistently failing her mother, Jing Mei manages to assert her own will.

The struggle between mother and daughter is equally ferocious. It often takes the form of psychological warfare between the two. Waverly Jong, a child prodigy chess player, envisages this struggle as a chess game in which her mother is transformed into a fierce opponent whose eyes are reduced to "two angry black slits" (100). The struggle is also expressed in physical and verbal fights. When, for example, the daughter Lena St. Clair overhears a mother and daughter who live next door shouting and fighting, she is not overly surprised when she learns from the daughter that both of them "do this kind of stuff all the time" (142).

This type of painful and dramatic confrontation also characterizes the relationship between Jing-mei Woo and her mother, Suyuan. Following a rather violent physical fight, Jing-mei Woo accuses her mother of wanting her to be someone she is not. Suyuan responds to this accusation by telling her that only two types of daughters exist: obedient daughters and disobedient daughters. Following this pronouncement, the daughter screams that she wishes that she was not her mother's daughter. When Suyuan reminds her that this is something that cannot be changed, Jing-mei utters the worst possible thing that a Chinese daughter could ever say to her mother: "Then I wish I'd never been born! I wish I were dead! Like them" (142). This "them" refers to the twin babies whom her mother was forced to abandon in China while attempting to escape the invading Japanese troops. Before Jing-mei realizes what a mindless thing she has just said, Suyuan, badly hurt, falls silent, backs out of the room, and like a small leaf in the wind, appears "thin, brittle, lifeless" (142).

In spite of the daughters' successful resistance and rejection of their influence, the mothers valiantly refuse to give up. After having tried many different strategies throughout their lives, the mothers finally discover that storytelling is the best way to reach the hearts and minds of their daughters. Realizing that sharing her past with her daughter might be the last and only trump card she has in order to "save" her daughter, Ying-ying St. Clair decides to give it a try. Her decision, nevertheless, reflects her awareness of the nature of the clash—the daughter's lack of ethnic and cultural identity, which Ying-ying is convinced will lead to her daughter's unhappiness. By telling her past to a daughter who has spent all of her life trying to slip away from her, Ying-ying St. Clair hopes to reclaim her, "to penetrate her skin and pull her to where she can be saved" (242). Jing-mei Woo's dying mother also realizes that her daughter's problem similarly stems from her refusal to embrace her Chinese roots. Indeed, before her trip to China, Jing-mei relentlessly denies her Chinese heritage. On the train to China from Hong Kong, Jing-mei finally comes to terms with her true identity. Reflecting on her past, she admits to feeling different. Furthermore, she is now prepared to concede: "[M]y mother was right. I am becoming Chinese" (267).

The device of storytelling by women to women is employed extensively throughout the novel as a means to achieve various ends. For instance, it is the means by which Lindo Jong is physically set free. As a young girl, Lindo managed to get out of an arranged marriage. She accomplished this feat by inventing stories about her husband's ancestor's wish for him to marry a servant girl. The mothers also resort to storytelling when trying to impart daily truths and knowledge to the daughters. Through storytelling, they hope to help their daughters rise above negative circumstances or simply avoid unknown dangers. Waverly Jong remembers her mother's telling her a story about a girl who carelessly ran into a street and was subsequently killed by a taxi (90). Lena St. Clair remembers the story her mother made up about a young woman who fell in love with an irresponsible man and had a baby out of wedlock (106). After her mother's maid tells the child An-mei Hsu about the rape that led to her mother's shameful position as the third concubine of a wealthy man, An-mei Hsu realizes that she is now better able to grasp the meaning of many of the things that previously escaped her (237). For the mother, Ying-ying St. Clair, telling her daughter about her past is a tangible proof of her love. In sharing her past with her daughter, she hopes to counter the fact that her daughter has no *chi*, no spirit. Lena's lack of *chi* is Ying-ying's greatest shame, and her stories become a means by which she hopes to help her submissive daughter regain her "tiger spirit" (252).

Telling Lena about her past is absolutely necessary because both mother and daughter are "tigers" and both are "lost . . . unseen and not seeing, unheard and not hearing" (67). By learning about her mother's past, Lena becomes better equipped to fight back and restore her happiness (marital happiness, in her case) in much the same way her mother did in the course of her own life. For Ying-ying St. Clair, who has already waited far too long to tell Lena her story, storytelling is also a positive experience since it allows her to find herself, to remember that long ago she "wished to be found" (83).

Through the sharing of personal experiences, a reconciliation between mothers and daughters is reached. The daughters realize that their mothers have always had their best interests at heart. Echoing the old woman and the swan in the first prologue at the beginning of the novel, mother Lindo Jong explains her feelings most poignantly: "I wanted everything for you to be better. I wanted you to have the best circumstances, the best character. I didn't want you to regret anything" (265). Because their own lives in China had been circumscribed by social and parental constraints that invariably led to pain, humiliation, and tragedy, the mothers all came to America to give their daughters a better life. However, daughters must first understand the real circumstances surrounding their mothers: how they arrived in their new country, how they married, how hard they tried to hold onto their Chinese roots. Once they have understood this, the daughters are better able to understand why they themselves are the way they are. Ultimately, this understanding will also lead them to finally appreciate their mothers. The mothers try very hard to leave an imprint of themselves on their daughters through various means. For the mother Lindo Jong, names carry a symbolic significance. She tells her daughter that the reason she named her Waverly is that, when she gave birth to her, they lived on a street with the same name. In naming her thus, she was convinced that her daughter would feel that she belonged on that street and that when it would come time for her to leave home, she would take with her a "piece" of her mother (265). While Waverly is left with a "piece" of her mother in her name, An-mei Hsu inherits from her mother a ring of watery blue sapphire, and Jing-mei receives a necklace with a jade pendant from hers. These pieces of jewelry are also symbolic of their mothers' continued presence in their lives. However, the daughters' acceptance of, and identification with, their mothers does not take place until all of them come into contact with their mothers' past through stories. Thus, after her mother's death, when she sets foot on Chinese land for the first time in her life, Jing-mei learns about her mother's long- cherished wish. Also during this trip, she discovers the meaning of her mother's name as well as the meaning of her own name: her mother's, Suyuan, means "Long-cherished Wish," and hers, Jing-mei, means "Younger Sister of Pure Essence." After learning the hidden meanings of these names, Jing-mei is full of remorse: "I think about this. My mother's long-cherished wish. Me, the younger sister who was supposed to be the essence of the others. I feed myself with the old grief, wondering how disappointed my mother must have been" (281).

The sharing of cultural experience between mother and daughter through the device of storytelling transforms the naive, self-protective daughters, who try hard to move away from, or surpass, their ethnic roots, into the mature daughters who are appreciative of their mother's Chinese ways. Through storytelling, the daughters come to accept their mothers' and their own race and are willing to seek their ethnic and cultural roots. Jing-mei goes to China and reunites with her twin sisters. Waverly and her American husband go to China together with her mother and spend their honeymoon there (184).

With a new consciousness, the mature daughter sees her mother in a new light. As Waverly Jong puts it: "[I]n the brief instant that I had peered over the barriers I could finally see what was really there: an old woman, a wok for her armor, a knitting needle for her sword, getting a little crabby as she waited patiently for her daughter to invite her in" (183-84). The daughter's defiance turns out to be baseless, and the "scheming ways" of the mother who seemed relentless in her pursuit of her daughter's weakest spots prove to be unfounded (180). After her mother's death, Jing-mei Woo also realizes, for the first time, that Schumann's music, which as a child she had played at a fateful recital, is in fact, composed of two parts: "Pleading Child" and "Perfectly Contented." Interestingly, it is the former piece that she played so poorly. While in mourning for her mother, Jing-mei also comes to the realization that she has always been biased by a one-sided view of life and by a poor opinion of her mother. When she plays the two pieces of music together, she suddenly understands that they are "two halves of the same song" (144). Schumann's music thus serves as a metaphor used by Tan to highlight the relationship between mother and daughter. This relationship encompasses, like Schumann's music, two phases of the human experience. At times, these phases may appear to be contradictory, but, in fact, they are really two natural and complementary stages of life. Tan thus seems to imply that a complete and holistic experience of life requires an understanding and an acceptance of both phases.

The novel ends with the arrival of Jing-mei Woo in China, the "motherland," where the three sisters are reunited and where Jing-mei finally accepts her Chinese identity. Jing-mei had to leave the West and travel all the way to China before she was able to realize that both her mother and China are in her blood. Only when she has reached maturity is she able to close the geographical gap and come to terms with her ethnic, cultural, and racial background. In doing so, she transcends the psychological gap that had alienated her from her mother and from herself. When the struggles and battles are over, when the daughter is mature enough to be able to accept the mother and identify with what she stood for, what was formerly considered a hateful bondage is revealed to be a cherished bond.

NOTES

I wish to thank Anne Brown and Marjanne Goozé for their thoughtful reading, critique, and assistance with this chapter.

1. Amy Tan was born in Oakland, California, in 1952. Her parents left China and came to the United States in 1949, leaving behind three young daughters. The communist revolution of 1949 prevented them from sending for their daughters after they had settled down in the United States. Tan was twelve years old before she learned of her sisters' existence. Recently, Tan and her mother were reunited with them in China. Tan wrote her first short story in 1985 after having joined Squaw Valley, a writers' workshop. In 1989, she published her first novel, *The Joy Luck Club*. See Amy Ling's *Between Worlds* for a brief description of Amy Tan's life.

2. The rejection of organic unity and concentration on the fragmentation of language games, of time, of the human subject, of society itself, are an attitude widely shared among postmodernists. For detailed discussions on various attempts made against totality by postmodernists, see Jean-François Lyotard's *The Postmodern Condition* and Fredric Jameson's *The Political Unconscious*.

REFERENCES

Hong Kingston, Maxine. *The Woman Warrior: Memoirs of a Girlhood Among Ghosts*.
    New York: Random House, 1977.
Jameson, Fredric. *The Political Unconscious: Narrative as a Socially Symbolic Act*.
    Ithaca, NY: Cornell University Press, 1981.
Ling, Amy. *Between Worlds: Women Writers of Chinese Ancestry*. New York: Pergamon
    Press, 1990, 137-38.
Lyotard, Jean-François. *The Postmodern Condition: A Report on Knowledge*. Manchester:
    Manchester University Press, 1984.
Ong, Walter J. *Orality and Literacy. The Technologizing of the Word*. New York:
    Methuen, 1982.
Tan, Amy. *The Joy Luck Club*. New York: Putnam, 1989.

The Ambivalence of Mirroring and Female Bonding in Paule Marshall's *Brown Girl, Brownstones*

Laura Niesen de Abruña

> If the relationship being studied is itself a mirroring, then when the scholar who "attempts to untangle" finds herself reflected in the parts which "try to separate and delineate," she is both observing a mirroring and acting it out. (Jane Gallop, "The Monster in the Mirror," 17)[1]

Like many twentieth-century women writers who draw their inspiration from the English-speaking Caribbean, Paule Marshall concentrates on the nature of bonding among women characters in her 1959 novel *Brown Girl, Brownstones*. An investigation should be made of the possibilities of mirroring (a metaphor for the emotional idea of bonding) and syncretism (a term implying a reconciliation of cultural or racial differences) among women characters in the fiction of writers, such as Paule Marshall, who examine the experiences of African-Caribbean women living in the United States or England.[2]

Mirroring was first reflected in feminist literary criticism in the 1981 publication of Ronnie Scharfman's article "Mirroring and Mothering," published in a feminist special issue of *Yale French Studies*. Since then, critics have been inspired to examine female bonding in literature written by women and to analyze the ways women's literature uses images of the mirror and reflection to signify female bonding (Scharfman, 88). As Scharfman points out, the concept of mirroring comes from psychology, particularly from D. W. Winnicott's work (91). He was one of the first object relations psychologists to use the metaphor of the mirror in a chapter entitled "Mirror-Role of Mother and Family in Child Development." This work suggests that when a baby looks into its mother's face, it ordinarily sees itself. But when the baby observes only the mother's face and mood, then the mother is not a mirror; the consequence for the baby is not the experience of love but alienation (Winnicott, 111-18).[3] The important point is not the truth value of Winnicott's analysis but the narrative value it provided to literary critics who had found a way of interpreting female bonding as positive and powerful.

Taking this optimistic approach to bonding, much contemporary feminist literary criticism argues that the women characters best able to survive form a bond, a type of strong "mirroring" relationship with other women. Yet, there is often a hidden assumption in such analyses (or wish-fulfillment fantasies) that this bonding transcends differences of race and class and is always positive and empowering. Such arguments have enlisted the aid of Nancy Chodorow and Carol Gilligan to explain the potential for closeness between women, especially mothers and daughters. However, these psychoanalytic critics have also argued that, despite the potential for tremendous closeness, the bonding between mother and daughter is fraught with ambivalence. In addition, feminists have long pointed out the sometimes emulous nature of women's interactions as the result of being disempowered in the society or simple antifeminism. Still others, such as Judith Fetterley, have investigated the process of "immasculation" by which women identify against themselves or their own interests. There are clear limitations to the nature of female bonding.

Closer investigation of bonding shows that differences in power, race, and class appear to be so important that they sometimes prove completely resistant to any type of same-gender bonding. Race, because of the history of slavery and enforced labor—as well as endemic bigotry—is often the major division in the United States, overpowering even the issues of gender and class. So, a safer statement about mirroring is that it can cut both ways, positively and negatively—and all of the shadowy stages in between. To put it another way, the mirror can be a one-way mirror reflecting opacity or a two-way mirror reflecting a positive image of the self. (Scharfman has also discussed the nature of the two-way mirror used in this sense [93].) Certainly, Jean-Paul Sartre's well-known theories of the "look" of the other implied that the "regard" of the other turned one into an object. Jacques Lacan's presentation of the mirror stage argues that the image of the self seen by an infant in the mirror is an alienated image of that self (6). In both of these discussions, the mirroring is negative. Similarly, in her article "My Monster/My Self," Barbara Johnson argues that the self is the monster and that the monster is related to the mother. Jane Gallop, commenting on this connection in an article entitled "The Monster in the Mirror: The Feminist Critic's Psychoanalysis," states that the urgent question is whether the monster in the mirror is the self or the mother. According to Gallop, it is unclear whether seeing the "self," which may be a narcissistic looking, is any better than seeing an "other" who must be viewed at a distance and somewhat objectively (16).

But Winnicott and Chodorow are not pointing to a falsely imposed choice between narcissism and objective study. This choice would follow from taking the metaphor of the mirror too literally. Their work does imply that in a mother's relationship with a child, she can express (reflect, in the metaphor) approval of the child, thereby enhancing the child's self-esteem. While this is the case for both male and female children, Chodorow points out that in the many cultures in which male and female gender roles are sharply differentiated, male children do not maintain as much contact with the mother as do female children. The very fact of sexual differentiation makes identification harder between mother and son than it can be between mother and daughter. Both factors would promote close identification of mother with daughter and daughter with mother.

While all claims concerning something as large as bonding between mothers and children must be approached very carefully, the idea of same-gender female bonding as a powerful emotional force in literature by women is certainly borne out by examination of that body of writing. Analysis shows that such bonding is there but that it is a complicated interaction demanding to be analyzed through each literary work rather than found out on the basis of theory. Purely theoretical speculations on the connection between the text as mother and the reader as daughter often blur differences between the literary situations for fictional women and the physical situations for women existing outside literary works.

Paule Marshall's novel *Brown Girl, Brownstones* is a good starting point for literary analysis because this book deals with the issue of female relationships. Not surprisingly, in Marshall's work, the mirror of female bonding reflects many faces, and the major character, Selina Boyce, sees a monster in the mirror as often as she sees the positive self. In *Brown Girl, Brownstones*, Paule Marshall examines the problems generated by a young woman's adolescence as well as the tensions she experiences between U.S. and West Indian cultures. Part of this novel is autobiographical, since Marshall's own parents emigrated to the United States during the years of World War I. Although Marshall grew up in a "Bajan" community in Brooklyn, the Caribbean culture was always present in her life, and she also returned to Barbados to understand the culture. Part of the novel is also about the difficulties that changing cultures imposes on same-gender bonding, even within the nuclear family.

Growing up in Brooklyn, Marshall's major character, Selina Boyce, at first makes a simplistic choice to reject the coldness of the other Barbadian exiles—and especially her mother—because they have embraced the worst of North American materialism. But by the novel's conclusion, Selina has developed a deeper understanding of the Barbadians' behavior as influenced by racism, and she develops an understanding of the women's strength and endurance. Throwing off one of the two bangles worn by every Barbadian girl, Selina decides to return to Barbados to seek the human values her parents lost through emigration.

Brown Girl, Brownstones attempts to chart this progress from simple rejection to identification and tolerance through Selina's efforts to bond with other women. At the beginning of the novel Selina rejects her mother, Silla, her sister Ina, and all of their friends in the Barbadian community in order to seek her identity in the outside culture. Selina attempts to identify with her new friend, Rachel Fine, with whom she dances at Hunter College. Before the year's major concert, Rachel and Selina share a moment of intimacy, exchanging confidences about their lovers. Selina tells Rachel stories of her Barbadian lover Clive, about whom her sister and mother know nothing: "Very calmly, her eyes reflecting the scant light and Rachel kneeling before her, with the darkness like a high tent around them, Selina told of her plan and of Clive" (279).

Here, the mirroring between the two women is positive, although qualified by a sense of evanescence that even they feel. They are loath to go on stage, where they must assume their public masks of white woman and black woman. They both linger, hesitant to leave their place of intimacy because they know that the outside world will soon separate them and drive them apart (280). This feeling is prescient because immediately after the dance, Selina meets an older white woman who shows her how fragile her moment with Rachel really was. There is other evidence that Rachel and Selina are too remote in culture to understand one another. The daughter of wealthy white parents, Rachel thinks of the Caribbean as a place for lusty romances on cruise ships. As she explains to Selina, she met her boyfriend Bobby on a week's cruise to Jamaica and Haiti. She regards the islands as a place for a vacation and the trip as adjunct to their "honeymoon" on a type of private yacht (280). As well intentioned as she is, Rachel is something of a snob and would be incapable of understanding the experience of Selina's mother in the sugarcane fields of Barbados or the ambivalence of Selina's father toward the Caribbean.

Selina's experience with Rachel is a gentler version of interracial misunderstanding that Clive recalls earlier in the novel. He once tried to maintain a friendship with a white man, but he habitually asked Clive what it felt like to be black and tried to compare a nightmare in which he felt "some irrecoverable loss" (254) to the way Clive must feel all the time. Clive then realized that the "friend" had never seen him as anything other than the racial "Other" whose identity must be explained as a "loss." His perspective on the failed relationship is a distanced tolerance. He asks himself what purpose it would serve to lash out at the other man. At least he was trying to communicate: "And why hurt people when they're so damn fragile inside . . . ?" (254). Gazing into the white world, then, is looking into a one-way mirror. Neither Selina nor Clive has been able to achieve identification with white friends.

The extreme and climactic example of this one-way mirroring comes, ironically, in an intense scene between two women. After Selina has danced with her friends, she accompanies one of them back to her apartment, where she is confronted for the first time by the girl's mother. Selina's own mother warned her to expect not friendship but hostility from her white acquaintances and their families, but Selina did not believe them dangerous until this point. The older woman suddenly leans forward and places her hand on Selina's knee to ask if her parents were from the South. Although the question is not in itself offensive, the woman's attitude seems to be exasperated, and the hand on the knee seems, to Selina, to be condescending and even "indecent" (287). Eventually, the woman succeeds in finding an avenue through which to feel superior when Selina says that her parents come from the West Indies: "The woman sat back, triumphant. 'Ah, I thought so. We once had a girl who did our cleaning who was from there . . .' She caught herself and smiled apologetically. 'Oh, she wasn't a girl, of course. We just call them that. It's a terrible habit'" (287). Although Selina might expect the image of her hope and youth to be reflected in the woman's regard, the white woman's pale eyes reflect only one thing—that Selina is black and must be made to feel inferior to her own family: "Those eyes were a well-lighted mirror in which, for the first time, Selina truly saw—with a sharp and shattering clarity—the full meaning of her black skin" (289). "And," the narrator says, "knowing was like dying" (289). She is thus reduced to the object of the older woman's gaze.

Robbed of her "self" as subject, Selina experiences a ritual death of that self, accompanied by an emotion so powerful that it not only robs her of her "self" but also convinces her that the others—even Rachel—have sought to steal her sense of self-worth: "The thrust of hate at that moment was strong enough to sweep the world and consume them" (289). The older woman inflicts additional damage in the form of an internalization of self-doubt, for Selina is reminded of her insecurity, "the part of her which had long hated her for her blackness and thus begrudged her each small success like the one tonight" (289). This death ends Selina's hopes of merging with the white society but gives birth to a desire to bond with Barbadian women. The glass (mirror) that Selina has been holding while talking to the woman slips and splinters on the floor, releasing Selina from the hold of the woman's voice. The pain, which might announce a death or a birth, seems necessary for her reentry into the Barbadian community. The dance she has performed at the recital was an enactment of the birth-to-death cycle (275), which Selina had to mime on stage before she enacts this experience in her own spiritual life after the dance is over.

Before rebirth, she must confront at least two monsters in the mirror. In the store window where she hides from her humiliation, Selina gazes at her reflection, "the way a child looks at himself in the mirror" (290). The first confrontation is with the nature of racism as a scapegoating of the oppressed. She remembers what Clive said about the dynamics between himself and white people. Her dark face must represent to them what they fear most—their own potential for doing ill (291): "The woman, confronted by her brash face, has sensed the arid place within herself and had sought absolution in cruelty" (291). Selina now sees the true reflection of racism as the whites' projection of their own fears and insecurities onto the physically different. Even more important, Selina understands that, in looking at her image, she causes her own fears and insecurities to arise: "Her sins rose like a miasma from its fetid bottom. . . . They were unbearable suddenly, monstrous" (291). The image of herself engendered by others and even reflected in her own self-image would be reflected in every eye she met and in every corner of her life. Like the other Barbadians whom she simply rejected, she would have to kill the monster in the mirror to keep it from destroying her, inside and outside. Until then her "real face" would not emerge.

When Selina's dream of acceptance by the majority culture dies, she can reexamine her ties to the Barbadian women. While Selina feels conflict about her identification with her mother, Vergie, Florrie, and even Beryl, there remain psychological and cultural ties with her community and her family that prevent their image in the mirror from becoming a completely opaque hatred. The white woman can reflect only complete negativity because she refuses to accept Selina's humanity or her womanhood, which are readily and even lovingly conceded by Silla and the other black women in the novel. Because of that love, Selina can now become one with Miss Thompson, the woman who was mutilated by a white man attempting to rape her; one with the mother, who endured rather than commit suicide; one with Virgie and Florrie, who persisted in finding worth within their culture. She could not see her "real face" reflected in their eyes until she had experiences the suffering that hurt them. Whereas she earlier rejected her sister Ina as a member of the women's "cult of blood and breasts" (62), Selina now accepts the pull of both as something linking her with her sister.

Early in the novel Selina rejects the Barbadian women and their values. When Florrie Trotman attempts to establish a sense of kinship with her by touching her breast, Selina becomes enraged. Yet, she also becomes aware of the ways that this connection bonds her to the other women: "It was the rite which made her one with Florrie's weighty bosom and Virgie Farnum's perennially burgeoning stomach" (78). Even though her ties with her mother have been stretched to their limits, Selina can finally reinscribe herself into the community of Barbadian women of whom her mother is the center. Through their strength Selina can find the courage to face the majority world in which she is defined as the Other.

Selina's relationship with her mother seems at first a mirroring that cuts two ways. On one hand, the independence makes them very similar; on the other hand, the mother's bitterness has caused her to lose touch with the spiritual and creative sides of herself. At the beginning of the novel, the strong mother is represented as a potential death threat to those who confront her. Silla, called "the mother" rather than "Selina's mother" or simply "mother," is the sole source of income for her family. Silla and other characters such as Miss Thompson indicate that the women are the major source of strength in this community. Their fight for basic survival is strengthened by their continual interaction. Most of the conversation in the novel takes place in Silla's kitchen, a place of respite for the women of the community who find their interaction, regardless of the topic of conversation, empowering. In her essay on her own career, "The Making of a Writer: From the Poets in the Kitchen," Marshall claims that such women in her real past also held talks in the kitchens of her neighborhood and used language to gain some control over their lives (7).[4]

After the confrontation with the white woman, Selina can make peace with her mother since the tie that binds them is too strong—and now too valuable—to break completely. Whatever their personal tensions, the mother is the positive mirror that will allow Selina to internalize the mirror within herself so that she views her own image positively. As she wins the Barbadian Association's scholarship, Selina gazes at her people's eyes and finds herself reflected there. As she moves down the aisle, Selina sees her own experience reflected in the many faces around her. In them she senses a source of endurance and mystery that she had not noticed before and was moved with admiration: "A thought glanced her mind as Cecil Osborne held her face between his ruined hands and kissed her: love was the greater burden than hate" (302). Acknowledging the bond with her mother but deciding to leave for Barbados, Selina tells her mother that she really is her child, psychologically (307). She reminds her mother that she herself left home when she was eighteen in order to gain her independence: "I used to love hearing that. And that's what I want" (307). The bonding between Silla and Selina is not a confused merging but an acknowledgment of the worth of each self, each self needing and demanding to assert its separate existence from the other woman.

As many cultural critics have pointed out, bonding between women of different races is very difficult, especially if one is in the majority and the other is marginalized through class and historical situations. In the case of the African-Caribbean woman living in the United States, the comprehension of the "Otherness" found in African-Caribbean women is made even more difficult by the history of slavery and the presence of racism. If one believes that one's being is precisely the result of one's culture and society, then there could be no possibility of bonding because, as JanMohamed claims, "one's culture is what formed that being" (65). In Marshall's novel, the mirroring between Selina and the older white woman is negative because the woman is the product of white, upper-class privilege; she can reflect only what excludes Selina and thereby makes her feel worthless. Although the woman is a stereotype, she signals the near impossibility of syncretism between an African-Caribbean woman from a poor family, exiled in the United States, and a white woman of European descent living in a wealthy Manhattan neighborhood. Such a compounding of differences in race, culture, class, and ethnic background negates any bonding that could take place through similarity in gender.

After such a monster has been unleashed, how can the literary critic agree with the novel's statement that love is a greater responsibility than hate? Perhaps by paying careful attention to the nature of female bonding as ambivalent rather than transcendent. The novel argues that bonding among women who share ties of family, race, culture—and gender—can be tremendously powerful, just as feminist literary critics have argued. There is the possibility that some type of bonding can take place between white women such as Rachel Fine and black women such as Selina Boyce. The treatment of Rachel is generally positive and admits some space for interracial relationships within the argument of the novel. To survive, however, their friendship would need to resist tremendous pressures from the outside and the large difference between them. It is significant that Marshall does not choose to follow this bonding; Selina would not have found her deepest satisfaction in her relationship with Rachel. The way the novel is written implies that white and middle-class American literary critics, even when female, must be careful in speaking of positive female bonding, especially in literature written by recent arrivals in the United States whose cultures are different from the majority culture. Such critics should be aware and beware of using the literary text as a mirror in which they see projected their own wishes, no matter how well intentioned they are. Critics should not claim to find instances of interracial mirroring if they are the products of their own fantasies. Where interracial mirroring does exist, one must be careful about explaining its nature and limits. If Jane Gallop's caveat is correct, feminist literary critics must realize the seduction of the mirror lest they themselves—we ourselves—become monstrous.

NOTES

1. I am much indebted to Jane Gallop for her helpful criticism of my ideas about female bonding during a 1988 National Endowment for the Humanities Summer Seminar on "Issues in Feminist Theory."

2. For an investigation of female bonding in West Indian women writers, particularly Phyllis Shand Allfrey, Zee Edgell, Paule Marshall, Jamaica Kincaid, Merle Hodge, and Jean Rhys, see my article, "Twentieth-Century Women Writers from the English-Speaking Caribbean."

3. The signal importance of this passage is recognized not only by Scharfman but also by Gallop, who analyzes Scharfman's reading of Winnicott (Gallop, 18).

4. I am indebted to several conversations with critic Lucy Wilson for my observations on the importance of the kitchen as a location for women's empowerment through language. Wilson has explained the importance of language in Paule Marshall's work in a conference paper, "The Fiction of Exile: Paule Marshall's 'Contrapuntal Vision,'" given in 1989 at the annual meeting of the Association of Caribbean Studies.

REFERENCES

Chodorow, Nancy. *The Reproduction of Mothering: Psychoanalysis and the Sociology of Gender*. Berkeley: University of California Press, 1978.

Fetterley, Judith. *The Resisting Reader: A Feminist Approach to American Fiction*. Bloomington: Indiana University Press, 1978.

Gallop, Jane. "The Monster in the Mirror: The Feminist Critic's Psychoanalysis." *Feminism and Psychoanalysis*. Ed. Richard Feldstein and Judith Roof. Ithaca, NY: Cornell University Press, 1989, 13-24.

Gilligan, Carol. *In a Different Voice: Psychological Theory and Women's Development*. Cambridge: Harvard University Press, 1982.

JanMohamed, Abdul R. "The Economy of Manichean Allegory: The Function of Racial Difference in Colonialist Literature." *Critical Inquiry* 12 (1985): 59-87.

Johnson, Barbara. "My Monster/My Self." *Diacritics* 12.2 (1982): 2-10.

Lacan, Jacques. "The Mirror Stage." *Écrits: A Selection*. Trans. Alan Sheridan. New York: Norton, 1966, 1-7.

Marshall, Paule. *Brown Girl, Brownstones*. New York: Feminist Press, 1959.

———. "The Making of a Writer: From the Poets in the Kitchen." *Merle and Other Stories*. London: Virago, 1985.

Niesen de Abruña, Laura. "Twentieth-Century Women Writers from the English-Speaking Caribbean." *Modern Fiction Studies* 34.1 (1988): 85-96.

Scharfman, Ronnie. "Mirroring and Mothering in Simone Schwarz-Bart's *Pluie et Vent sur Télumée Miracle* and Jean Rhys' *Wide Sargasso Sea*." *Yale French Studies* 62 (1981): 88-106.

Winnicott, D. W. "Mirror-Role of Mother and Family in Child Development." *Playing and Reality*. New York: Basic Books, 1971.

No Place for Identity: Jeannette Lander's Migrating Women's Aesthetic

Tobe Levin

"I'm a foreigner, and I mean to keep it that way." (Huston, 1113)[1]

In any attempt at placing identity in international women's writing, Jeannette Lander, winner of the 1976 Villa Massimo Prize, stands out as a stimulating subject. Born in 1931 in New York City, she accompanied her Polish-Jewish immigrant parents to Atlanta, where her father opened a grocery store in the black quarter of the city and made a home for his family above it. After publishing some poetry in Yiddish and English while still in the United States, Lander, who emigrated at age twenty-eight to Germany, earned her doctorate in 1966 from the Free University of Berlin, prelude to the monographs she was to write (in German) on Pound and Yeats, journal articles, and television scripts. Her works of fiction include *One Summer in the Week of Itke K.* [*Ein Sommer in der Woche der Itke K.*] (1971), which I discuss here, *On Foreign Soil* [*Auf dem Boden der Fremde*] (1972), and a collection of short stories, *A Bird in the Hand . . .* [*Ein Spatz in der Hand . . .*] (1972). Two additional novels follow: *Daughters* [*Die Töchter*] (1976) and *Myself Alone* [*Ich, allein*] (1980), reprinted 1988). In 1985, she moved for twelve months to Sri Lanka but returned to West Berlin the following year.[2]

The author's own migrations testify to a lifestyle that meets her aesthetic under the postmodern arch, particularly in her first macaronic work of fiction, *One Summer in the Week of Itke K.*, a text addressed to German-speaking readers but dependent on multilinguality, code switching, and heteroglossia for its effect. It illustrates a point I hope to make in this chapter: just as languages interact and change one another over time, so is identity formation, as a function of our "native" tongue, constantly in flux. If, as Lacanians assert, subjectivity depends on escaping the semiotic, nonsemantic code to enter the symbolic father tongue, Lander's text raises interesting questions by dramatizing a linguistic community in which not a single one of a multitude of codes remains as it was before the mix. English words enter Yiddish sentences; Yiddish terms enter black English; black English becomes double-negated German; and the High

German used breaks native speaker rules. German compounds words, but not with Lander's liberty, as in "Tessie . . . fearslookslistens for George" [Tessie . . . angstschauthorcht nach George (*Ein Sommer*, 30)]. The question for feminist readers becomes, What happens to the Law of the Father, the experience of a single tongue that opposes the masculine One to the "female" Other when language itself is no longer One but also many, illusive and changing within the fluidity of time and space?

Lander's fiction, idiosyncratic as it is, enters a corpus of multilingual texts. Her literary kin include writers I would envision from roughly three perspectives. First, there are those whose oeuvre greets the world in a tongue other than their author's native one and who may or may not be the bilingual writers whose polyglot production Elizabeth Klosky Beaujour analyzes so well in *Alien Tongues*. The obvious examples of Vladimir Nabokov, Joseph Conrad, Samuel Beckett, Elsa Triolet, Anzia Yeyierska, and I. B. Singer come to mind, as well as contemporaries Nancy Huston, Monique Wittig, Susanne de Lotbinière-Harwood, and increasing numbers of immigrants using their host nation's language in their texts—for instance, Turks in German. The second focus illuminates Lander's Judaism. In "Jeannette Lander and Ronnith Neumann's Utopian Quest for Jewish Identity in the Contemporary West German Context," Leslie A. Adelson discusses Lander's second novel and concludes that *On Foreign Soil* "conveys both the notion of being a stranger in a foreign territory *and* the curious (but for Jews traditional) paradox of finding one's grounding in precisely that foreignness" (117). I would go even further to argue, like Huston claiming the benefits of "reassuring strangeness," that identity itself is illusive and illusionary: the multilingual, like the multicultural, displaces the self-identical, making it unknowable because it remains in flux. Illustrating this is Henry Roth's *Call It Sleep*, presenting a third perspective from which to view the work of Lander. In "Between Mother Tongue and Native Language: Multilingualism in Henry Roth's *Call It Sleep*," Hana Wirth-Nesher points out two techniques also shared by Itke's author. These are strategies to "simulate the experience of the immigrant child protagonist [or] to translate these experiences for [the] general . . . reader" (297). Like *One Summer in the Week of Itke K.*, "*Call It Sleep* is a classic example of a work in which several cultures interact linguistically, thematically, and symbolically" (Wirth-Nesher, 297). Focusing on the ideal audience for specifically Jewish texts, Wirth-Nesher concludes: "Both bilingualism and diglossia are central concepts in any discussion of Jewish literature, for they presuppose that a truly competent reader must be in command of more than one language, and consequently more than one culture" (298).

The resistance to multiculturalism cannot be underestimated. I would like to think of this chapter as a contribution to the urgent struggle feminists are waging outside the academy, especially around issues of national identity and exclusion. Take, for instance, the tail end of the BMW I'm chasing down the Autobahn: "Everyone's a foreigner, almost everywhere." This timely bumper sticker began appearing in 1988, weakly reminding German motorists of a smoldering xenophobia soon to erupt, mainly in the East after reunification, and sow increasing alarm in my dark-skinned and Jewish fellow residents of Germany. In her tales, Lander speaks to our fears.

One Summer in the Week of Itke K. offers insights into issues of identity and expression in an era of increasing intolerance by replacing the fixed essences of racial stereotyping with dramas of subject and subjectivity formation. Lander's Jewish female protagonist, growing up in the black ghetto of Atlanta, glides toward, around, through, and along ever-shifting frontiers of ethnic and linguistic specificity. Language mélange plays a dominant thematic role in the text. "Place presents itself to us as a condition of human experience," notes geographer J. Nicholas Entrikin (1), and for Itke, Atlanta is primarily Jewish and black, apprehended through the adolescent's layered subjectivity. The young girl's city consists of an apartment above the grocery; of Simpson Street in front and the streetcar tracks; of the lovers' field behind the shades Mamma pulls, where a victory garden is planted. Characteristic, too, are Biggsmamma's veranda and other neighboring shanties; a competent white and a markedly inferior black school, a synagogue, and a sanctified house of worship "that was really a warehouse, not a church" [daß . . . ein Lagerhaus war und keine Kirche (180)]. The evening sun shines on "dirt [Dreck], garbage [Abfall], asphalt [Asphalt]," and transforms the "mud" [Schlamm] into "dust" [Staub] (189). The rich air carries the aroma of magnolias.

The year is 1942. Itke, the second of three daughters, celebrates her fifteenth birthday as the globe reels, anti-Semites in the Old World, and racists in the New World fracturing her growing sense of self. Because she lives in the black community, she perceives her locale not as polarized but as indefinite if measured by the impossibility of communicating in a single tongue. Site gives way to sound in the portrait of this city, whose "normal" life expresses itself in transmutations of language. From Tatte Kovsky's, Mammanui's, and their children's mouths come Yiddish threaded with Polish and English, Hebrew proverbs, songs, and shreds of prayer; the clientele speaks black English disguised as double-negatived German and sequined with Jewish idiom. The narrator, Itke, at times in the first, at other times in the third person, uses High German and, once in a while, standard English. If not "untranslatable" (Mueller, n.p.), the text is certainly inimitable. In critic Salcia Landmann's words:

The novel is written in a language tailored to this very unique world: sentences are pre- and antilogical, set off by rhythmical interludes, fantastic neologisms, whose elements recombine or are broken up, then swirled together to surface again and again. In the midst of all this, the Yiddish-English salad bar, from which the good-hearted father chooses when chatting with his black women customers; they in turn take up the shreds of his Yiddish jargon and idioms, enriching their own speech fragments. The whole thing is jazz, is pop, is an ideal instrument with which to reflect this extraordinary world. (n.p.)

Thus, counter to the actual southern city supposedly segregated into distinct cultural and linguistic entities, textual Atlanta appears to be ceaselessly changing, and the groups to which stereotypes most easily apply—the blacks, the Jews—influence one another, changing each other in a process without end.

Setting out with humanistic notions of identity, particularly, the Jewish cult/culti-
vation of the chosen—Itke calls it "tending our Otherness" [Das Anderssein
pflegen (19)] while simultaneously insisting on the dignity of a "Mensch"—the
narrative spirals toward a state of radical decenteredness, transgressing codes of
which critic Sybille Wirsing writes: "[T]he rules of this linguistic household
seduce the author again and again into setting off fresh little revolutionary
wordbombs" (n.p.), but not in the service of *l'art pour l'art*. Rather, Lander's
"lexicon and circumstances don't give you a moment's peace. The news is that
you ought to prefer standing out, not holding on to the habitual. Security is mere
illusion" (n.p.).

This insecurity simply echoes the facts of history. In the 1920s, Itke's father,
Tatte Kovsky, had been forced to flee conscription in Poland. Once he has taken
over the Jägel's grocery in Atlanta's ghetto, the store stages lively "down home"
scenes reminiscent of Maya Angelou or Zora Neale Hurston and, with its
upstairs apartment, forms the heart of young Itke's town. Boundaries exist but,
like the endlessly pregnant Russian dolls, are embedded in one another. The
following passage, opening the novel, suggests this imbrication:

Itke.
Nappy-haired, dark-eyed Itke lives in a ring in a ring. The innermost is Yiddish. The
middle, black American. The outermost is whiteprotestantamerican in the Deep South.
Itke-I. In her fourteenth summer. Deep Southern summers start in May.
Lives in her apartment, the Yiddish apartment, above the grocery and general store,
the "Krom" store for a black clientele in the black quarter in the ever larger, faster better
growing city of Atlanta where an exception is made for the white grocer so that he can
live in the apartment adjoining his store in the black quarter.
Doesn't live among her own. Itke, with long dark locks combed and arranged
morning after morning by European motherhands (Oi ayoi, a yiddische Mammenui), goes
to school with natives, 150% blond from the inside out for generations in the Deep
South. Itke with Rebecca-eyes, Rebecca and Ruth, morning after morning, by black
hands the cornbread muffins baked, in mama Kovsky's kosher kitchen chewed, in the
sheetwhite school digested, in the outermost ring. Not among her own.

[Itke.
Itke mit krausem Haar, mit dunklen Augen, lebt in einem Kreis in einem Kreis in
einem Kreis. Der innerste ist jiddisch. Der mittlere ist schwarzamerikanisch. Der äußere
ist weißprotestantischamerikanisch tief im Süden.
Itke-ich. Im vierzehnten Sommer. Tiefsüdensommer beginnen im Mai.
Lebt in ihrer Wohnung, der jiddischen Wohnung, über dem Lebensmittel- und
Kolonialwarenladen, dem "Kromladen" für Negerkundschaft im Negerviertel in der
immer größer, schneller, besser werdenden Stadt Atlanta, wo ein weißer Lebensmittel-
händler ausnahmsweise in der Wohnung wohnen darf, die an seinen Laden anschließt,
auch im Negerviertel.
Lebt nicht unter ihresgleichen. Erste Generation Itke, mit langen dunklen Locken
Morgen für Morgen von europäischen Mammahänden gekämmt und gelegt (Oi ayoi, a
jiddische Mammaniu), geht in die Schule unter Einheimischen, hundertundfünfzigprozent
blond von innen her seit Generationen im tiefen Süden. Itke mit Rebekkaaugen, Rebekka
und Ruth, Morgen für Morgen Maismehlbrötchen, die Negerhände backen, in Mamma

Kovskys koschere Küche kauend, in der blaßweißen Schule verdauend, im Außenkreis. Nicht unter ihresgleichen. (13)]

The key term here is *not*: not ever among her own. For to reside with Old World parents in the black quarter of Atlanta is to live a contradiction disruptive to the formation of any essentially fixed identity. Of course, to know you are not among your own presupposes knowledge of your own, your contours and culture. But as Shaul Stampfer reminds us, "[M]igration is one of the central themes in the history of the Jewish people" (220). With migration come the stresses of exile: Itke has no choice but to negotiate a self. At times, she finds black and Jew joined in negativity, playing together the Other to the Protestants' majority. But at other moments Jews pale, as Tatte Kovsky whitens in the eyes of the blacks even though treated like a Jew—humiliated and abused—by the Christian police. Itke, however, still a Jewish child, longs for the culture most appealing to her, on the street:

Saturday evenings Luther put up his stand on the corner and began to grill spare ribs on the hot coals, spare ribs basted with a real spicy tomato sauce whose aroma brought out all the neighbors. . . . He poked his extra long fork into the coals, turned the sizzling ribs over on the grill, casually splattering sauce here and there, crying out in a strange loud singsong: "Barbecued spare-ribs! Hot off the coals!"

[Sonnabend abends schlug Luther seinen Stand an der Ecke auf und begann auf Holz-kohlen Schweinerippchen zu braten, Schweinerippchen mit einer besonders pikanten Tomatensauce bestrichen, deren Aroma die ganze Gegend anlockte. . . . Er stocherte mit der überlangen Gabel in den Kohlen, drehte die zischenden Rippen auf dem Rost, spritzpadderte Sauce unbekümmert hin und her, schrie mit einem merkwürdig singenden Schreiton: "Barbecued spare-ribs! Hot off the coals!" (13-14)][3]

The senses of smell and hearing celebrate a culture making virtue of neces-sity, the cheapest, fattiest, least meaty parts of the pig having become delicacies that tempt the narrator looking out from behind the screen, ironically both enabled and disabled, "ItkewhiteJewish, with an apron pocket full of money and a heart full of the commandment never to eat pork" [Itkeweißjüdisch, mit Kitteltaschen voller Geld und dem Herzen voll mit dem Verbot, Schweinefleisch zu essen (147)]. Itke, however, is not left desirous for long. "Kimm arein, es is busy, Itke," the girl hears, pulled away from the street and back into the store to the chords of her mother's code-mixing refrain, "Oi, Itkele, at home every-thing, but everything was different" [Oi! Itkele, inder alten Heem is alles, alles, anderesch gewe'en (14)].

Atlanta, then, for the narrator, though American born and raised, cannot be home but acts as a site of difference demanding narrative creation of a fluctuat-ing self. Lander dramatizes this community-in-difference through both character-ization and the use of allegory: each chapter sections itself into scenes corre-sponding to stage directions for what the author holds to be analogous folk art forms, the minstrel show and the Dybbuk. To illustrate, Chapter 1 is headed:

Minstrel Show, in which Itke describes the rings of her environment in order to discern their boundaries.

Scene 1: Itke sings the song of the Rebecca-eyed woman among the clarinette voices of the Blacks.

Scene 2: Papa and Momma play the melody of Otherness with keys and window-shades.

[*Minstrel-Schau*, in der Itke die Kreise ihrer Umwelt beschreibt, um festzustellen, welche Grenzen sie haben.

1. Auftritt: Itke singt das Lied einer Rebekka-äugigen unter den Klarinettenstimmen der Neger.

2. Auftritt: Tatte und Mamma spielen die Melodie vom Anderssein auf Schlüsseln und Rollo. (11)]

Here the form of minstrelsy fleshes out with unaccustomed content, the reference to Rebecca binding black and Jew in their Old Testament allegiances, while at the same time Rebecca, chosen wife of a polygamous patriarch, suggests the gendered exile of exogamy. The double message, fracturing and joining, repeats itself in the ring, boundary and continuity, and in the key, opening and locking away. Finally, both the minstrel and the Dybbuk masquerade as multiples of selves. In the latter, for example, a young man dies of thwarted love, enters his beloved as a spirit on her wedding day, driving her to perform the dance of madness that frees her, ironically liberating by doubling her.[4] Lander claims that in "*One Summer in the Week of Itke K.* a curious marriage of these two art forms takes place" (n.p.). Although the white in blackface might seem a co-optation of minority culture, it refers back to an art form that arose in response to slavery but that preserves elements of African rhythms, hence illustrating once again a point the narrative conspires to convey: there is no origin, no authentic self-identical culture to return to or create oneself out of, but only a dialectical interweaving of elements influenced by a concrete history, one of whose dominant traits is the displacement of entire peoples.

This refusal of fixity, however, does not lead to a desert of abstraction. Lander's narrative is sensually satiating, awash in discrete detail. Betty Bergland offers a thought-provoking theory of reading immigrant and displaced women writers that focuses us even more sharply on the complicity between narrative plenitude and the subtext of absence. In a talk on "Postmodernism and the Subject of Autobiography: Reconstructing the 'Other,'" Bergland takes three Jewish immigrants—Mary Antin, Anzia Yezierska, and Emma Goldman—publishing in English, not their native tongue, to illustrate her application of Bakhtin's chronotope as a lens through which "the subjectivities of those constructed as Other in the culture" can be appreciated (4). Bergland mediates Bakhtin's view for us as follows: because human beings are always imagined in detail, inserted in time and space, the mathematical coinage chronotope constitutes a "category" emphasizing the inseparability of these dimensions, and, Bakhtin claims, when applied to literature, the term "makes narrative events concrete" (250). Consequently, the abstract elements in fiction, "the philosophical and social generalizations, ideas, analyses of cause and effect—gravitate toward the chronotope and through it take on flesh and blood, permitting the imaging power of art to do its work. Such is the presentational significance of the chronotope" (84-85). Defined by Bakhtin as a "*time-space*" (42), the chronotope in Lander's writing highlights those precise features, era and place, that show Itke's Atlanta at its most revealing and, at the same time, mediate against any monodimensional posture of identity.

Here is one example. Joe Louis has just won the world heavyweight crown for the fifth time, but jubilation is no less raucous and pungent than in 1937. Mammenui at the window watches her black neighbors dancing in the streets when Tatte calls her, "Listen, Hannahle, are you listening?" [Heerst, Hannele, heerst?] The radio announcer has just said:

And now for the news. Reliable sources report that Hitler and his followers are solving the "Jewish question" through persecution! through annihilation! Only the most rapid intervention by American bombers.

[nunmehr zuverlässige Berichte. Hitler und seine feilen Anhänger lösen das "Juden-problem" durch Verfolgung! durch Vernichtung! Nur das schnellste Eingreifen ameri-kanischer Bomber. (65)]

We know that the bombers did not intervene; they refused to destroy the tracks leading to Auschwitz. The allusion evokes the world's hostility to Jews, a clue Mammenui follows in turning away from the window, away from the present as Blacks rejoice in symbolic empowerment, the chronotope of ghetto street/Joe Louis victory. Instead of taking pleasure in her neighbors' strength, the Jewish mother returns to Poland and the history of Jewish impotence. She remembers the long walk to the often-frozen river with the heavy water bucket because Jews were forbidden to use the village spring. The school on the other side of town also closed its doors to her. Observing Mammenui take her place beside Tatte to read the Yiddish paper, Itke thinks of herself as another genera-tion but reflects on marginality again within the chronotope:

Mommapapa let me sit at the window, at the window in the space between their ring of worry and the surrounding ring of the carefree, putting on the victory parade outside, living, enjoying what I, sitting at the window, let pass me by; Itke beyond the ring, inside the ring-around; Itke in the space built by a window from which everything is visible of which you can't take part.

[Mammatatte ließen mich am Fenster sitzen, am Fenster in der Zone zwischen ihrem Kreis der Sorge und dem umkreisenden Kreis der Sorg losen, der draußen . . . den Triumphzug . . . veranstalteten, erlebten, genossen, den ich am Fenster sitzend an mir vorbeirollen ließ; Itke jenseits des Kreises, diesseits des Umkreises; Itke in der Zone, die ein Fenster bildet, von dem aus man alles sieht, woran man nicht teilhat. (67)]

Distanced from herself by the third person, Itke moves farther and farther from the already decentered center. The pane of glass repeats the opening image of the door, serving as a filter that allows to pass through it the spectral, auditory, and olfactory environment but excludes the gustatory and the tactile, that is to say, the intimate.

Intimacy is achieved in one of the final vignettes. If one of the strongest Jewish customs is "to marry exclusively among one's religioracialtribal comrades" [ausschließlich unter ihren Glaubensrassenvolksgenossen zu heiraten (44)], Itke symbolically but incompletely breaches that border when, at the end of the novel, she slips through the fence into a field with her cousin Sonny to undergo her (hetero)sexual initiation. Her partner is a Jew, but Itke remains during the act less attentive to him than to the sounds wafting from the open window above their heads where Jimmielee vociferously fuses with the black man called Brother, the men's nicknames resonating with the rules of kinship while inviting their transgression. Tribe and family continue to serve as anchors of identity, but links in their chains are coming loose.

Lander's Atlanta thus invites the adolescent to enter a number of cultures, but only conditionally. She can stroll, for example, on Peachtree Street (43): with her twelve B'nai B'rith sisters, Itke promenades unmolested along the thoroughfare of the outer ring, stops at a drugstore for a 485-calorie sundae before going to the movies to see *Tarantala*, sitting downstairs—both activities "chronotopic," their meaning derived from the concrete history of blacks and whites in the Deep South. After all, Itke's friend Jimmielee would have been barred from both sundae eating and movie viewing so that the activity reverberates with Itke's ironic white privilege, double-edged because passing might be possible but only momentarily, as a masquerade in contexts devoid of intimacy.

Yet anti-Semitism, as a counter to white privilege, remains invisible to the middle ring. Take, for instance, the neighbor Mrs. Stevens's tale of her son's death:

The first ones was already coming on with they burning crosses, three in a row, all in white like ghosts and only two holes to look through. Riding high and the cross in they hands, I'm tellin' ya, Miss Itke, three in a row. They come up Simpson Street along here in fron of this store where we sitting right now, and behind them three more and behind them three more and slow as death, so he'p me God.

[Da kamen die ersten schon angeritten mit ihren Kreuzen brennend, drei nebeneinander in einer Reihe, ganz weiß wie die Geister und nor zwei Löcher zum Durchgucken. Hoch geritten und die Kreuze in Händen, brennende Kreuze sag'ich Dir, Miss Itke, drei nebeneinander. So kamen sie die Simpson Street lang hier vor diesem Laden, wo wir hier sitzen, und hinter ihnen noch drei und hinter ihnen noch drei, und langsam wie der Tod, so rette mich Gott. (57)]

Yes, the Ku Klux Klan marched through the ghetto to intimidate blacks, and although the parade past the grocery threatens the Jews as well, Itke's neighbors do not see her endangerment. Quite the contrary: the community targets Tatte's Krom in the final scenes, raising some difficult issues. Even if the Jews are scapegoated as whites, is the failure to see them as Jews, the erasure of their Jewishness, a sign of anti-Semitism on the part of blacks?

The narrative answers simply by highlighting Tatte's difference from the pale majority, dramatically evident in his handling of the following incident. When a hit-and-run white cop mangles five-year-old Blue, Tatte rushes to the hospital with her, disregarding the "whites only" signs to actually find a doctor whose spontaneous humanity induces him to treat the bleeding child, but she dies nonetheless. Her murder leads to the looting of Tatte's store. Labeled by critic Georg Zivier "a miniature in Black of the Night of Crystal" (n.p.), the event shows how fragile Itke's security is. An illusory harmony returns with Tatte's mitzvah, as Jews would label his response: ordered not to sell his food on the pretext that it might be damaged, he gives it away. In the final tableau, the short, stocky immigrant bicycles through the ghetto, his list of customers in hand. He knows whose next paycheck comes in two weeks, who would otherwise go without were it not for the groceries he distributes. But generosity, reminder of a structural inequality of power, does not dissolve the differential separating customer and merchant. Despite his humane motive, the benefactor is the historically, if only relatively, privileged. Yet I, for one, resist the erasure of this relativity.

Lander's tale of Itke thus tries to underwrite the resemblances in the innermost rings, representing two diaspora peoples of Zion who are metaphorical kin. The black minister preaches: "I tell you tonight, he ain't chosen no other for his work but the children of Israel" [Ich sag'euch heutabend: er hat nicht auserkoren kein'/ andren für sein Werk, nur die Kinder von Israel (185)]. Old Testament stories, the deliverance from slavery, the importance of Moses—these bind the blacks and the Jews. More important, however, is the plastic image with which I conclude. Itke has returned from the Sanctified Church to find her parents kneeling in the backyard, momma crying, Tatte with his arm around her, burying a frying pan: the new cook has violated Kashrut, the prescribed division of cooking utensils according to whether meat or milk dishes are served. Itke's commentary:

Oh—the frying pan, traif, unkosher eggs cooked in it. It's got to be buried in God's earth, to stay there week after week. God's clean earth recleans the unclean. Newly born, the pan will be dug up. In wonder after wonder the pious God reveals himself. Oh—Biggsmamma paints in the holy circle of the blue stones. My momma buries the impure.

[Oh—die treefene Pfanne, darin gebraten worden ist das nicht koschere Fleisch. Begraben wird sie in Gottes Erde, dort zubleiben Woche um Woche. Gottes reine Erde reinigt wieder das Unreine. Neu geboren wird die Pfanne ausgegraben. In Wunder um Wunder offenbart sich dem Frommen sein Gott. Oh—Biggsmamma mahlt im heiligen Kreis der blauen Steine. Meine Mamma gräbt Verunreinigtes ein. (190)]

The sarcastic tone marks a break: Itke's ancestral spirituality leaves her as empty as Biggsmamma's voodoo while at the same time seeming restively alive. The older women live anchored in an understanding counter to the "increasingly larger, faster, better growing city of Atlanta [immer größer, schneller, besser werdenden Stadt Atlanta (13)], but the younger suffers her contingent, partial access to at least three worlds, the white, modern Western one and those of her traditional elders, Jews and blacks.

In Lander's sequel, Yvonne, autobiographical heroine of *On Foreign Soil* (1972), leaves her Atlanta grocery as a pregnant, Jewish eighteen-year-old married to a West Berliner and settles in "German-speaking Germany" [Deutschsprachland]. When, after fifteen years of wedded life, Yvonne's husband lets loose with "You, you filthy Jew" [Du dreckiger Jude, du], Yvonne has enough composure to ask herself whether rage speaks the truth or anger is clichéd. But the vilification pushes her to leave (though temporarily) what has been a progressively deteriorating marriage: she takes her teenage son back to visit her parents in Atlanta, only to discover that they, having left the tenements, now replicate the bigotry of whites. When her father asks the classic question, "Yvonne, how can a Jew live in Germany?" [Yvonnele: Wie kann ein Jude in Deutschland leben? (189)]. The answer is: as a foreigner and, in contrast to suburbanites, with greater self-awareness. In Yvonne's view, her parents' prosperous Jewish community has lost its integrity by denying its history. As Daghild Bartels notes: "From fear of annihilation they counterfeit themselves. To preserve themselves" (n.p.). Yvonne is afloat in her postmodern sadness. Displacement alone—in linguistic, geographic, and psychoanalytic guises—processes identity. Who you are remains a function of where you—momentarily—are. As critic Sybille Crack notes, "Foreign soil is everywhere" (n.p.). There is no place for identity.

NOTES

This chapter is based on two talks, the first at the session "Displaced Women," Modern Language Association Convention, Washington, D.C., December 30, 1989, and the second at the German Society for American Studies Annual Convention [Deutsche Gesellschaft für Amerikastudien Jahrestagung], Bonn, June 12, 1990. I would like to thank Heidrun Suhr, Angelika Bammer, and Sabine Bröck-Sallah for inviting me to speak in their sessions. For an excellent discussion of Lander's work, unavailable at the time this article was written, see Leslie A. Adelson, *Making Bodies, Making History: Feminism and German Identity* (Lincoln, NE: University of Nebraska Press, 1993).

1. All translations are my own.

2. I was privileged to meet her in December 1990, in Essen, where we both participated in the symposium "Jewish Culture and Femininity in Modernism" ["Jüdische Kultur und Weiblichkeit in der Moderne"]. The symposium, organized by Sigrid Weigel and Inge Stefan, took place December 13-16, 1990, at the Wissenschaftszentrum Nordrhein-Westfalen, Kulturwissenschaftliches Institut.

3. Text within quotes in English in the original.

4. For more information on S. Ansky's *The Dybbuk*, readers are referred to David S. Roskies, "Yiddish Literature" in *The Schocken Guide to Jewish Books*, edited by Barry W. Holtz (New York: Schocken, 1992, 266).

REFERENCES

Adelson, Leslie A. "Jeannette Lander and Ronnith Neumann's Utopian Quest for Jewish Identity in the Contemporary West German Context." *New German Critique* 50 (Spring/Summer 1990): 113-34.

Bakhtin, M. "The Bildungsroman and Its Significance in the History of Realism (Toward a Historical Typology of the Novel)." *Speech Genres and Other Late Essays*. Ed.

Caryl Emerson and Michael Holquist. Trans. Vern W. McGee. Austin: University of Texas Press, 1986, 10-59.

Bartels, Daghild. "Paradoxien." Review of *Auf dem Boden der Fremde* by Jeannette Lander. *Frankfurter Rundschau*, 14 February 1974.

Beaujour, Elizabeth Klosky. *Alien Tongues: Bilingual Russian Writers of the 'First' Emigration*. Ithaca, NY: Cornell University Press, 1989.

Bergland, Betty. "Postmodernism and the Subject of Autobiography: Reconstructing the 'Other.'" Maine Conference on Autobiography, University of Southern Maine, September 29-October 1, 1989.

Bondy, Francois. Review of *Auf dem Boden der Fremde* by Jeannette Lander. *Die Zeit*, February 9, 1973.

Crack, Sybille. "Zu Hause in der Fremde." Review of *Auf dem Boden der Fremde* by Jeannette Lander. *Stuttgarter Zeitung*, July 21, 1973.

Entrikin, J. Nicholas. *The Betweenness of Place: Towards a Geography of Modernity*. Baltimore: Johns Hopkins University Press, 1991.

Huston, Nancy. "La Rassurante étrangeté." *Les Temps Modernes* 425 (December 1981): 1111-17.

Lander, Jeannette. *Auf dem Boden der Fremde*. Frankfurt am Main: Insel, 1972.

———. *Ich, allein*. Frankfurt am Main: Autoren Edition; 1980. Frankfurt am Main: Fischer, 1988.

———. *Ein Sommer in der Woche der Itke K*. Frankfurt am Main: Insel, 1971.

———. *Ein Spatz in der Hand. . . .* Frankfurt am Main: Insel, 1972.

———. *Die Töchter*. Frankfurt am Main: Insel, 1976.

Landmann, Salcia. "Juden vom Negergetto." Review of *Ein Sommer in der Woche der Itke K*. by Jeannette Lander. *St. Galler Tageblatt*, January 1, 1973.

Mueller, Dennis. Review of *Ein Sommer in der Woche der Itke K*. by Jeannette Lander. *Books Abroad. An International Literary Quarterly*, January 1973.

Stampfer, Shaul. "The Geographic Background of East European Jewish Migration to the United States Before World War I." *Migration Across Time and Nations*. Ed. Ira Glazer and Luigi de Rosa. New York: Holmes and Meier, 1986, 220-30.

Wirsing, Sybille. "Nackte Halbwahrheiten. Jeannette Landers 'Sachgeschichten.'" Review of *Ein Spatz in der Hand . . .* by Jeannette Lander. *Die Zeit*, January 10, 1973.

Wirth-Nesher, Hana. "Between Mother Tongue and Native Language: Multilingualism in Henry Roth's *Call It Sleep*," *Prooftexts* 10 (1990): 297-312.

Zivier, Georg. "Liebenswerte Leute in Kovskys Kramladen. Jeannette Landers Roman 'Ein Sommer in der Woche der Itke K.'" *Der Tagespiegel*, November 28, 1971.

Expatriate Afro-American Women as Exotics

Marilyn Elkins

For many an Afro-American, perhaps the biggest impact of his move to a new land is the discovery that, to many foreigners, his black skin is desirable. What had been stigma in America becomes stylish in Europe. (Dunbar, 197)

For Afro-American male artists, Europe has offered the intellectual and artistic acceptance often denied them in their native America. Richard Wright, James Baldwin, and Chester Himes have written about this affirmation in positive terms. But novels about black female expatriates provide more limited endorsements of the experience. Instead, such works portray black women's expatriatism as narcissism—a hybrid form that conflates exoticism and exploitation—rather than as affirmation. The use female characters make of this experience depends ultimately upon their ability to find self-knowledge that allows them to transcend their societies. The major works written by black women novelists about such experience—Nella Larsen's *Quicksand*, published in 1928, Toni Morrison's *Tar Baby*, published in 1981, and Andrea Lee's *Sarah Phillips*, published in 1984—have heroines who accomplish this task with varying degrees of success. Using Larsen's novel as an intertextual reference, the later novels depend on many of her ideological premises. However, they explore fuller and richer self awareness for their heroines.

Each of the novels has a heroine who initially chooses to become an expatriate, indicating her sense of exile from America. Helga, the major character of Larsen's *Quicksand*, leaves Harlem, searching for a place to belong among her white relatives who live in Denmark. Eventually, she finds that she often feels alienated by her treatment as exotic. But when she returns to America, she is trapped in the quicksand of the novel's title: a marriage and kids with a southern minister. Jadine, the focus of Morrison's novel, is doubly exiled. She makes her first appearance in the novel when she is living with her aunt and uncle, housekeepers for a white, American family on an island in the Carribean. After working in Paris as a top model, she has returned to her family, attempting to discover her authenticity. After a difficult relationship with Son—whose sexuality and southern upbringing are reminiscent of that presented in Larsen's Southern minister—Jadine avoids the quicksand of Larsen's character. In the novel's closing scene, she flies to Paris with no clear purpose other than escape. She no longer views her American roots as essential. Sarah, the main character in Lee's novel, is living in Paris, ruminating about where she will go when she returns to America. Her first-person narrative traces the events that have brought her to Paris as a prologue to effecting her complicated return to the United States.

The novels' heroines share characteristics that appear to make them versions of the classic "tragic mulatto." Yet each of the novels subverts the normal expectations of that genre.[1] These shared characteristics include education, light skin, and other physical characteristics that make them fit white society's pre-scriptions for beauty. Like the protagonists in the convention, each woman vacillates because she is unsure whether to choose the black or white world. While Lee's protagonist shares many of the physical traits and the educational background of the others, her motivation for going to Paris and her ultimate return stem from a source that is less connected to racial concerns. She eschews the material accoutrements of the successful white world, and her sense of self-worth depends less on her physical beauty.

The authors' descriptions of these women underscore their "white" character-istics. Helga Crane, Larsen's main character, is the child of a Danish mother and a black American father. Her skin is like "yellow satin"; she has "sensitive" lips, a "good" nose, "delicately chiseled" ears, and "curly blue-black hair" that "tumbled, falling unrestrained about her face and on to her shoulders" (3). Morrison endows Jadine with a face that has graced "every magazine in Paris" (40), including the cover of *Elle* (44). She is referred to by Gideon as "the yalla," and he warns Son that such women have to choose being black, and "most don't choose it" (155). Sarah Phillips describes herself as "tall and lanky and light-skinned, quite pretty in a nervous sort of way" (4); she is described by her three French male friends as "notre Négresse pasteurisée" (11).

Striving to convert themselves into art objects, each of these women enhances her physical characteristics for her preferred societal role.[2] Helga's initial decision to leave Naxos, the boarding school where she teaches, stems partly from her hatred of the drab colors she is forced to wear (38-39). Once she arrives in Harlem, she deliberately combines her beauty and clothing to get the effect she wants; when she attends a party shortly before her departure for Denmark, she decides to wear her black net dress that is touched with orange when she remembers the more conservative Anne's words: "There's not enough of it, and what there is gives you the air of something about to fly" (124). She chooses the dress as a symbol of her pending departure and her difference from her more conservative Harlem friends. Her need to create herself as object extends to her surroundings as well; she spends much of her Naxos salary on furnishings for her room and spends much of her time arranging her surround-ings into an artful backdrop for her beauty.

Like this earlier counterpart, Jadine and Sarah also use clothes for special effects. As Mary Jane Lupton points out, Jadine deliberately chooses her clothing for the impression it creates; for her first outing with Son, she selects a peasant dress to tempt him, and many of her efforts at transforming Son center on changing his dress (417).[3] Her Christmas gifts to Ondine and Sydney consist of clothes that they will never wear but that fit Jadine's conception of how she thinks they should dress. The gifts are Jadine's attempt to create an artistically esthetic family background for herself (90).

Sarah chooses her clothes to make her look like a "wood nymph," to "convey a sexy jeune fille air worthy of Claudine at school" (96). Her literary impulses dictate her artistic embellishment of self: she selects her clothes to help her look like an aspiring writer, reciting Donne on her way to meet her professor, having made herself "look as beautiful and mysterious as" she can, slicking back her hair, rimming her eyes with dark color, and donning high heels (98). At her father's funeral, when she wears the black clothing provided by the members of his church, she considers "how expensive and beautiful" she looks and is filled with "self-congratulatory excitement," assuming "an affected manner, hoping that passers-by in the March night would see and admire [her] as a tragic heroine" (112).

A desire to create a more beautiful self, displayed in appropriate surroundings and clothes, underpins the decisions of Helga and Jadine to go to Europe; Sarah's decision comes from an impulse to escape her conservative upbringing. While all three women leave America partly because of racism, they also seek escape from aspects of self that they do not like or accept. Perhaps because of its being set in the 1920s, Larsen's articulation of racial tension as a deciding factor for Helga's departure is the most direct and straightforward. The overt racism that Helga experiences from both races was more socially acceptable; therefore, it is more readily apparent. She flees Naxos because she sees the hypocritical attitudes of the staff who try to whiten their students as much as possible, teaching black students that their blackness is inferior and must be hidden, sublimated, or removed. Helga realizes that "she hadn't really wanted to be made over" (16), yet she also feels a sense of shame that "evidently there were parts of her she couldn't be proud of" (17). When she decides to leave Harlem, she flees being "yoked to these despised black folk" (121). Contemplating her race in the interior of a Harlem nightclub, she is "blind to its charm, purposely aloof and a little contemptuous" (131). She also resents her friends' rejection of people who go "about with white folk" (133) and admires Audrey Denney's "assurance, the courage, so placidly to ignore racial barriers and give her attention to people" (136). Yet Helga refrains from making this step herself because "it would be foolish, and *so ugly*" (134; emphasis added).

Denmark offers Helga the opportunity to have the clothes and surroundings that she seeks as setting for her beauty; she can more easily enhance herself as object. Earlier she has assessed what she wants as "material security, gracious ways of living, a profusion of lovely clothes, and a goodly share of envious admiration" and "happiness," although "her conception of it had no tangibility" (23-24). Her fantasies of Denmark are a "blissful sensation of visualizing herself in different, strange places, among approving and admiring people, where she would be appreciated, and understood" (126). When she arrives in Denmark, "she took to luxury as the proverbial duck to water. And she took to admiration and attention even more eagerly" (147). She now has what she wants: "leisure, attention, beautiful surroundings. Things. Things. Things" (147). As a result Helga has an "augmented sense of self-importance" and appreciates fully her ability to "enhance what was already in one's possession" (163). Eventually she gives "herself up wholly to the fascinating business of being seen, gaped at, desired" (163).

Yet she does not receive the understanding that she also craves. The adoration also isolates: "[T]rue, she was attractive, unusual, in an exotic, almost savage way, but she wasn't one of them. She didn't at all count" (155). She begins to miss black people, and although she is shamed initially by the performance of the blacks in the circus, she returns to it because of her homesickness (182-85). When she hears Dvorak, she thinks of spirituals, realizes how much she misses Negroes, and for the first time can identify with her father's "facile surrender to the irresistible ties of race" (207). Returning to Harlem, she has a difficult time admitting that her return is permanent, but she likes "the sharp contrast to her pretentious stately life in Copenhagen" (214). Helga also refuses to acknowledge the inherent superficiality within her creation of self as object. While the novel criticizes the emotional emptiness in Helga's European stay, Larsen also portrays Helga as unable to learn from the experience.

Like Larsen, Morrison uses her novel to attack such reification. Morrison suggests that Jadine makes wrong choices because of her inability to read character. Jadine's artistic ability has been limited by "too many art history courses" so that she sees "planes and angles and miss[es] character" (158). Morrison carefully delineates Jadine's limited abilites as a pictorial artist, juxtaposing them with Jadine's superior ability to enhance her physical self. When she is initially insulted by Son, she begins an artistic re-creation of their confrontation as she will tell it to her friends, removing and changing the parts that reflect negatively upon her. Encountering him after he has bathed and shed his beard, she still focuses on her misguided, artistic perceptions. She converts him to object, preferring to sketch him. She brings along her crayons and sketch pad on their picnic. Her attempts at drawing, however, leave her "wishing once more that she had had genuine talent in her fingers" (181). During her struggle with the swamp women whose femaleness she resists, she looks down at "the pad with Son's face badly sketched" (182): a wry comment on her insistence on her limited artistry when faced with real things—Son's genuinely handsome face, the exceptional femaleness of these women and the African woman in yellow who spat at her in Paris. As she leaves L'Arbe de la Croix to return to Paris, she makes the same mistake that she makes with her photographs in Eloe. She looks at Alma as an art object, wishing once more that she had real talent to draw the girl's eyes.

However, her ability to enhance her own beauty and create an artistic backdrop for its display is superior. Recognizing it as a commodity, she went to Europe, she tells Son, because she "thought there might be a fourth choice" from "marrying a dope king or doctor," modeling, or teaching art (225). Yet in Paris she becomes a successful model who adorns her natural beauty with jewels and raw silk. Moving mainly in a white world, she "needed only to be stunning, and to convince them she was not as smart as they were" (126). Ignoring her superior intellect, she adopts this role, which called for "only charm—occasionally panache" (127). Paris affords her the opportunity to be the object of adulation, to date a variety of white men, and to create a fantasy world for herself that is carefully arranged. Even the meals that she prepares to celebrate have been "printed in *Vogue* and *Elle* in a manner impressive to a twenty-five-year-old" (45). Yet this world loses meaning for Jadine when she encounters the authenticity of a "woman much too tall," with "too much hip, too much bust" (45).[4] This authenticity, which eludes Jadine in her role as artist, inspires her with a combination of love and hate, making her feel "lonely and inauthentic" and sending her back to her Aunt Ondine in a search for self (48). But this reaction is mixed. She also belittles this authenticity, as she does Son's, by measuring it by white standards. Thus, she reminds and consoles herself that the woman in yellow would be laughed out of the lobby of the modeling agency.

When Jadine returns to Paris, she is still fleeing. Her return seems a negation, a return to the world of vanity that offers her no opportunity to be more than art object. Her fear that Ryk, her French lover, may only want "any black girl who looks like me, talks and acts like me" suggests that she distrusts a white European male's ability to see her individuality. The text hints that Ryk may indeed be preoccupied with women who are racially different from him: he is unfaithful to Jadine with a woman named Nina Fong.[5]

Although Sarah does not go to Paris in search of beautiful things and refuses to allow Henri to buy her clothes, she savors the admiration that she inspires. Henri refers to her as "'Reine d'Afrique, petite Indienne" (5); places her, naked, on a wooden box to praise and criticize her body; tells her she is beautiful; and shows her off to his friends in cafés, discos, and the famous Paris drugstores (7). Sarah has come to Europe with "an unfocused snobbery, vague literary aspirations, and a lively appetite for white boys" (4). While "white boys [were] the forbidden fruit" of her mother's generation, in the circles that Sarah frequented at Harvard, "such pairings were just about required, if one was to cut any dash at all" (97). Sarah is interested in cutting a dash. She is pleased with the attention that she receives from all three boys. Having sexual relations in her own variation of a ménage à trois serves as rebellion against her black bourgeois background. To one of the Philadelphia Negroes that Morrison's Sydney refers to, Sarah struggles to deny her background. Europe offers her the opportunity to enter "a world where life was aimless and sometimes bizarre—a mixture that suited [her] desire for amnesia" (5).

Along with her bourgeois background, she wants to forget the racism that she has suffered in America. When Sarah enters the previously all-white Quaker elementary school that she attends, she feels as embarrassed by the black cook's greeting as she feels by the stares that she receives from the white students who watch her constantly. Uncomfortable thinking about the black people "who worked at the school," she wants desperately to "really fit in, and if . . . the rulers of the Olympian band of suntanned, gold-bangled popular girls, shimmering in their Fair Isle sweaters, had so much as crooked a finger," she would have deserted her only friend, Gretchen (56). When she is offered the part of the colored maid in the school play, she realizes that "it was simply . . . a matter of knowing where you stood" (58). Although the students in her school did not jeer at her, they shut her off socially "with a set of almost imperceptible closures and polite rejections" (54).

Yet Sarah's stay in Paris does not fulfill her longing to be included and understood. She knows that the boys with whom she shares the apartment are far closer to each other than she will ever "be to either of them" (9). When Henri describes her as being the child of a part redskin and Jewish Irlandaise who was raped "by a jazz musician as big and black as King Kong, with sexual equipment to match," she is not offended by the racism since this hip brand of humor has punctuated the circles that she hung out with at Harvard. Yet the tale shows her that she will be unable to escape her "portion of America" (12). She realizes that she cannot be ruthless enough to "cut off ties with the griefs, embarrassments, and constraints of a country, a family" and cannot join "the ranks of dreaming expatriates for whom Paris can become a self-sufficient universe" (15). Her decision to return to America is an acceptance of her family, racial, and national identity. Like young people of many races, including most of the other international sojourners who pass through the Neuilly apartment, Sarah rebels to forge her own identity.

Having integrated the various aspects of her consciousness, she can return to America, embrace the mother and brother whom she loves, and accept her father's death. She is ready to seize the gauntlet passed on to her at his funeral to "do something out of the ordinary" with her life (113). She no longer needs the thrill of motion that "moved in a direction away from anything" she has known to obliterate her loss (117). Sarah recognizes that her expatriate experience has been filled "with the experimental naughtiness of children reacting against their training" (15). This self-knowledge enables her to convert self into subject. Her story serves as explanation not only of how she came to be in Paris but of how she came to be in the world as well. Her self-knowledge indicates her growth and transcendence, a change that surpasses any development experienced by Helga or Jadine.

But Sarah's love for, and closeness with, her family make her different. She is the only protagonist of these novels who has the inner strength to incorporate her individual self—her active sexuality, her need for adventure, and her literary talent—with her strong sense of family ties. She is capable of making what she acknowledges will be a "complicated return" (15). Her story details a strong, loving relationship with her father that permits her to acknowledge her own sexuality in a nonthreatening way.

For Helga and Jadine, however, lack of self-knowledge and racial identity links inextricably with their sensuality. They cannot incorporate sexuality without loss of self-respect. Since attitudes toward sex were more repressed during the 1920s, Helga's refusal seems most apparent and, perhaps, justified. Her denial guides much of her movement throughout the novel. It dictates her sudden departure for Denmark and undergirds her decision to return.[6] Hortense Thornton suggests that Helga's rejection of Olsen masks her sexual repression

(299), but Larsen's portrayal of the repression begins early in the novel. Sexually unawakened until her meeting with Anderson, Helga has experienced her sexual attractiveness only as power to be used over her fiancé: "[H]is mute helplessness against that ancient appeal by which she held him pleased her and fed her vanity—gave her a feeling of power" (18). Only with Anderson does she start to feel "that urge for service, not now for her people, but for this man who was talking so earnestly of his work, his plans, his hopes" (45). She feels "shame" but "is stirred" by "actual desire to stay" (45). But Anderson misreads her reaction, calling her a lady of "dignity and breeding," and she experiences "turmoil" (46). Anderson's description of her as a "lady" implies that she must deny the sexual impulse he has aroused. If she responds—as she does to his passionate kiss later in the novel—she risks losing his respect. To remain the carefully crafted object, she must not feel. Since part of the appeal of such a creation is its inaccessibility, she is imprisoned by her own artistry.

This scene with Anderson precedes her flight from Naxos; a scene observing Anderson with Audrey Denney precedes her sailing to Denmark; her rejection of Olsen is followed by thoughts of Anderson, and she thinks that she is "glad that I refused him [Olsen]" (198); and Anderson's refusal of her sends her into the arms of Reverend Green. She dances between the horns of the dilemma shaped by her inner needs for authentic sexuality and her ego needs for adulation. She is unable to wed the parts of her dissociated self, an inability that is exacerbated by the artistic Olsen. Anderson's rejection of her pushes her to the church, and, as McDowell points out, the description of this scene "unambiguously simulates sexual excitement and orgasmic release" (xx). The shouting and musical release of the church parallel the sexual release that Helga sought dancing in Harlem's nightclubs. Unable to act upon her sexuality as Sarah Phillips does, it becomes a trap for Helga that forms the true quicksand of the novel's title. Larsen's novel delineates the dangers of sublimating sexuality into vanity. Damned to failure whether she marries Olsen or Green, Helga's refusal of self-knowledge reduces her to fragmentation.

Morrison uses Jadine to add an interesting twist to Larsen's idea; in Morrison's version of the story Jadine's quicksand is her inability to trust the character and intensity of her womanhood.[7] Like Helga, Jadine is also orphaned; her father's absence from the novel goes unexplained. Both women's careers as art objects are financed by white males. Valerian, the white employer of Jadine's uncle, plays the role given to Helga's Danish uncle. Jadine's sexuality is also consciously repressed. Until she meets Son, she makes an effort to keep "the small dark dogs galloping on silver feet" under control because their release frightens her (94). She is not innocent; she is afraid to relinquish control, to unleash her sexuality because she misinterprets its power as an opportunity for others to dominate—rather than admire—her. Even her private sexual fantasies have a narcissistic quality. The autoeroticism of the scenes with the fur coat have a magazine-slick, *Playboy* quality to them. Her reaction confuses Jadine, who finds "there was something a little fearful about the coat. No, not fearful, seductive" (112). Morrison's language underscores the connection between admiration, sex, and fear for Jadine, and she continues the connection with

Jadine's reaction to Son's improved appearance: "[S]he was holding tight to the reins of dark dogs with silver feet. For she was more frightened of his good looks than she had been by his ugliness" (158).

The narrator's approval of Jadine's sexual awakening by Son is apparent in Morrison's language: "She was completely happy. After all those sexually efficient men, all those foreplay experts and acrobats, and the nonverbal equipment men, his wildness and fumbling, his corny unselfconscious joy was like blue-sky water" (225). The words mingle sex with fantasy and myth and link Son to nature: "He was still life, babies, cut glass, indigo, hand spears, dew, cadmium yellow, Hansa red, moss green and the recollection of a tree that wanted to dance with her" (230). Yet his genuine love cannot replace Jadine's need for adulation. For Ondine and Sydney have not taught her the value of either her heritage or her sexuality. Childless themselves, they have glorified in Jadine's accomplishments without teaching her to love and respect her heritage or even the other blacks with whom she has contact.[8] So she returns to Paris with the appropriate backdrop of her sealskin coat, after "doing her eyes" (288), contrasting her art with Alma's natural "eyes of a curious deer" that Jadine has no real talent to draw (289). Unwilling to accept her sexuality, she prefers adulation that will ensure her alienation. She finds this imprisoning objectification preferable to being "barely noticeable in (and never selected from) that stampede" that she is a part of in America (126).

Larsen's and Morrison's protagonists choose opposite answers to the question of their permanent domicile, but their European experience fails as affirmation of self. Offering no art except the text of their artistically enhanced bodies and faces, Helga and Jadine present a cogent argument against reification of self. A European experience for artists of such limited scope only re-inforces their weakness. Lee's character, however, has talent that extends beyond the body as text. Her voice tells her story, suggesting that she has converted her experience, not her physical self, into art. Admitting that her return will be complicated, she avoids the simplistic and ultimately unfulfilling decisions of Helga and Jadine. Sarah emerges as much more like those male narrators who survive the "fire" and live to tell the story.

Using the expatriate experience to criticize female objectification, all three novels reach a similar conclusion: the individual, female self emerges no more nourished by unqualified acceptance than by unqualified rejection. Certainly, acceptance as an exiled, exotic Other does not guarantee self-acceptance. As evidenced by its effect upon Helga and Jadine, such objectification carries its own psychological damage. Since Sarah makes this discovery, Lee's novel suggests that if the expatriate experience enhances feelings of self-worth, they must already be established, perhaps as a result of strong familial ties. As a result, *Sarah Phillips* constitutes an important revision of the earlier novels. Its Afro-American heroine converts the expatriate experience into a recognition and affirmation of her female individuality.

NOTES

1. This convention is discussed fully by Barbara Christian (35-61). Generally, these stories depict a martyred figure whose suffering is sued to symbolize the absurdity of racism.

2. For the underlying ideas in my analysis of this aspect of these protagonists, I am indebted to Susan Gubar for her discussion of woman as art object and her analysis of women who create art using "the only materials at hand—their bodies, their selves" (249).

3. For an excellent discussion of additional uses that Morrison makes of clothing in the novel, see Lupton's article, especially 416-19.

4. Peter Erickson analyzes the maternal symbolism in Morrison's portrayal of the African woman in "Images of Nurturance."

5. For another look at Morrison's treatment of the dehumanizing aspect of being loved only for one's race, see her portrayal in *Song of Soloman* of Empire State, who suffers when he learns that "his white wife loved not only him, not only this other black man, but the whole race" (128).

6. Much of my understanding of the importance of Helga's denial of her sexuality comes from the essays of Cheryl Wall and Deborah E. McDowell.

7. Although Lauren Lepow argues convincingly that what Jadine is all about are "self-creation and self-perpetuation against the odds of the dualistic world" (376), her interpretation of the novel's attitude toward Jadine seems to conflict directly with Morrison's own statement that the African woman is the transcendent character with "the real chic . . . the one that is very clear in some deep way about what her womanhood is" (Naylor and Morrison, 572).

8. James Coleman's essay points out that Ondine and Sydney are partly responsible for Jadine's lack of wholeness and offers an excellent interpretation of important political questions that are raised in the novel.

REFERENCES

Christian, Barbara. *Black Women Novelists: The Development of a Tradition, 1892-1976.* Westport, CT: Greenwood Press, 1980.

Coleman, James. "The Quest for Wholeness in Toni Morrison's *Tar Baby.*" *Black American Literature Forum* 20.1-2 (1986): 63-73.

Dunbar, Ernest. *Black Expatriates: A Study of American Negroes in Exile.* New York: Dutton, 1968.

Erickson, Peter B. "Images of Nurturance in Toni Morrison's *Tar Baby. College Language Association Journal* 28.1 (1984): 11-32.

Gubar, Susan. "'The Blank Page' and the Issues of Female Creativity." *The Madwoman in the Attic: The Woman Writer and the Nineteenth-Century Literary Imagination.* Ed. Sandra M. Gilbert and Susan Gubar. New Haven, CT: Yale University Press, 1979, 243-61.

Larsen, Nella. *Quicksand.* 1928. New York: Greenwood Press, 1969.

Lee, Andrea. *Sarah Phillips.* New York: Penguin, 1984.

Lepow, Lauren. "Paradise Lost and Found: Dualism and Edenic Myth in Toni Morrison's *Tar Baby.*" *Contemporary Literature* 28.3 (1987): 363-77.

Lupton, Mary Jane. "Clothes and Closure in Three Novels by Black Women." *Black American Literature Forum* 20.4 (1986): 409-21.

McDowell, Deborah E. Introduction. *Quicksand and Passing*. New Brunswick, NJ: Rutgers University Press, 1986, ix-xxxv.

Morrison, Toni. *Song of Soloman*. New York: Knopf, 1977.

————. *Tar Baby*. 1981. New York: New American, 1982.

Naylor, Gloria, and Toni Morrison. "A Conversation." *Southern Review* 21.3 (1985): 567-93.

Thornton, Hortense. "Sexism as Quagmire: Nella Larsen's Quicksand." *College Language Association Journal* 16 (March 1973): 285-91.

Wall, Cheryl. "Passing for What? Aspects of Identity in Nella Larsen's Novels." *Black Literature Forum* 20.1-1 (1986): 97-111.

Index

About the Editors and Contributors

FIONA R. BARNES teaches English literature and composition at Santa Fe College in Gainesville, Florida. She has published articles on Michelle Cliff and Nadine Gordimer, and is currently revising her dissertation, "Geography, Gender and Genre: Women's Postcolonial Novels of Development." She is also co-editing two collections of essays, one on Michelle Cliff and the other entitled *Making Home: Contemporary Women Writers and the Politics of Home.*

NANCY TOPPING BAZIN is Professor of English at Old Dominion University, Norfolk, Virginia, where she has served as Director of Women's Studies and Chair of the English Department. She is the author of *Virginia Woolf and the Androgynous Vision* (1973) and co-editor of *Conversations with Nadine Gordimer* (1990). In addition to several essays on Woolf and Gordimer, she has published articles on women's studies, curriculum transformation, and such writers as Doris Lessing, Marge Piercy, Edith Wharton, Margaret Atwood, Buchi Emecheta, Bessie Head, Mariama Bâ, Anita Desai, and Athol Fugard. She has participated in faculty development projects in Postcolonial literature, Third World studies (with trips to the Ivory Coast, Tanzania, and Morocco), and East Asian studies (with a trip in 1989 to Japan and China). She teaches courses entitled Contemporary World Literature and Literature of the Developing World. She is writing a book on Nadine Gordimer.

ANNE E. BROWN is Associate Professor of French at the University of New Brunswick, Canada, where she teaches Québécois women writers and African literature. She has published articles and delivered conference papers on Québécois and African women writers and on Acadian literature. She is the author of an essay titled "Unhiding the Hidden: Writing During the Quiet Revolution" in *The Anatomy of Gender. Women's Struggle for the Body* (1992). Dr. Brown also serves on the editorial board of *Studies in Canadian Literature/Études en littérature canadienne*, and on the advisory board of *Revue de l'Association de linguistique appliquée.*

ANNICK CHAPDELAINE is Associate Professor of French and Translation at McGill University in Montréal, Canada. She has published articles and presented papers on translation studies, language and culture, women's studies, and Québec sci-ence fiction writers. Her main research interests are discourse analysis and feminist literary theory. She is presently directing a research group (funded by the Social Sciences and Humanities Research Council of Canada), whose project is to retranslate William Faulkner's *The Hamlet* into French using both a practical and a theoretical perspective.

MARILYN ELKINS teaches ethnic and women's literature at California State University-Los Angeles. She edited and wrote the introduction and epilogue for *The Heart of a Man* (1992). Dr. Elkins also edited the critical collection, *August Wilson: A Casebook*, which contains her essay and introduction. She has published articles on Frances E. W. Harper and Kay Boyle.

MARLENE GOLDMAN is a graduate of the Department of English at the University of Toronto, where she teaches Canadian literature. Her thesis, "No Man's Land: Re-Charting the Territory of Female Identity in Selected Fictions by Contempo-rary Canadian Women Writers," focuses on the images of maps and map-making within a variety of postmodern texts. She has published an article on Alice Munro in *Studies in Canadian Literature/Études en littérature canadienne* and an essay on Aritha von Herk's works in *Canadian Literature*. Other research interests include the portrayal of women in film. She has worked as an associate editor at the *Malahat Review* and has taught Women's Studies at the University of Victoria, British Columbia.

VERA F. GOLINI is Associate Professor of Italian and Chair of Italian and French Studies at St. Jerome's College (federated with the University of Waterloo in Ontario, Canada). Dr. Golini's research centers on issues in contemporary Italian literature. She has lectured extensively in both Canada and the United States and has published articles on Italian futurism, and Italian women writers in the Renaissance and at the turn of the century. She is cur-rently completing a translation of a collection of short stories by Dacia Maraini.

MARJANNE E. GOOZÉ is Associate Professor at the University of Georgia, where she teaches German and Women's Studies. She has contributed widely to the scholarship on Bettina von Arnim, including a long review essay in *Bettina Brentano-von Arnim: Gender and Politics*. She has published on the nineteenth-century German women authors Rahel Varnhagen and Karoline von Günderrode, as well as on Goethe, Hölderlin, and Kafka. Her research focuses on women's personal narratives and she has published an article, "The Definitions of Self and Form in Feminist Autobiography Theory," in *Women's Studies: An Interdisci-plinary Journal*.

ANNE-MARIE GRONHOVD is Assistant Professor of French at Gustavus Adolphus College, where she teaches French literature, Québécois women writers, and Women's Studies. She has published articles and delivered conference papers on Marcel Proust, Marguerite Duras, and Québécois women writers. She writes reviews for *French Review* and is on the editorial board of *Journal of Durassian Studies*. Presently her research focuses on Marcel Proust and the writings of Québécois Women Writers and J. M. G. Le Clézio.

SUZANNE KEHDE, who teaches at California Polytechnic State University, San Luis Obispo, is working on a book on the imbrications of nationalism, imperialism, colonialism, identity, subjectivity, and engenderment in twentieth-century British and postcolonial fiction. She has published articles on the intersections of engenderment and imperialism in the work of such diverse writers as Walter Van Tilburg Clark, David Henry Hwang, Graham Greene, and Henry James. Her article, "Voices From the Margin," appeared in *Feminism and Dialogics*, in addition to another article on Spivak, Bakhtin, and Vygotsky. Her play, *Everything You Always Wanted*, was produced by the Wichita State University Theater.

MARKETTA LAURILA is Assistant Professor of Spanish at Louisiana State University, where she teaches contemporary Latin American literature and Hispanic women writers in the Department of Foreign Languages and Literatures. She is also a member of the Women and Gender Studies Faculty. She has written articles and presented papers on Elena Garro, Isabel Allende, and Marta Traba and is currently writing a book on representations of violence in narratives by Latin American women writers.

TOBE LEVIN teaches with the University of Maryland, European Division and the American Studies Department, J. W. Goethe Universität, Frankfurt am Main. Her research interests include literature by Jewish and African American women. A cofounder of Women's International Studies Europe (W.I.S.E.) and a steering group member representing Germany, she has also co-edited (with Angelika Köster-Lossack) a special issue of *Women's Studies Quarterly* (1992) on Women's Studies in Europe.

DEANNA MADDEN has taught at the University of Hawaii at Manoa, State University of New York at Plattsburgh, and the University of Miami. Her publications include an essay on women in dystopian novels in *Misogyny in Literature: An Essay Collection* (1992) and articles on gender roles and women writers. Her short stories have appeared in literary journals.

LAURA NIESEN DE ABRUÑA is Associate Professor of English at Ithaca College in Ithaca, New York, where she teaches contemporary American fiction, American literature, and Caribbean literature. She is the author of *The Refining Fire: Herakles and Other Heroes in T. S. Eliot's Works* and has published extensively on T. S. Eliot, Mark Twain, Jean Rhys, Joan Riley, and West Indian literature.

SHEILA J. PETTY is Assistant Professor of Film and Video at the University of Regina, Canada. She has published essays on African film in *Parachute*, *Canadian Journal of Communication*, *Cineaction*, *Society for Visual Anthropology Review*, *Afterimage*, and *Films d'Afrique*. She is working on a book on African cinema and female spectators.

SUSAN PORTER is a lecturer in English literature at the University of Saskatchewan in Saskatoon, Canada. Her areas of concentration are British Renaissance and nineteenth-century American literature and literary theory. Her dissertation was titled: "Domination and Dissent: Gender Duality and Patriarchal Authority." An earlier version of the chapter in this book was published in *The Canadian Journal of Irish Studies* for December 1989. She has also delivered papers on Daniel Defoe's *Roxana* and is currently working on the relationship between domestic and political power structures in the late Shakespearean romances.

SUSAN CANTY QUINLAN is Associate Professor of Romance Languages at the University of Georgia, where she teaches Portuguese, Luso-Brazilian literature and Women's Studies. She is the author of *The Female Voice in Contemporary Brazilian Narrative* (1991), is coauthor of *Connecting Threads: Brazilian Feminist Discourse*, and has written articles on contemporary Brazilian narratives. Currently, she is working on *Connecting Threads*.

EVA RUESCHMANN, who was born in Berlin, received her doctorate in Comparative Literature at the University of Massachusetts at Amherst and is currently a Visiting Assistant Professor at Hampshire College. She has published and presented conference papers on a variety of topics, including the intersections of sister relations and race in Jessie Fauset's and Dorothy West's novels, the cinema of Alan Rudolph, psychoanalytic theory and criticism, films of Max Orphuls and Margarethe von Trotta, and madness and female identity in the writings of Janet Frame and others. Future projects include a psychoanalytic reading of sister relationships in twentieth-century literature and film and research in new approaches to European and American modernism.

PEGGY SHARPE is Associate Professor and teaches Portuguese and Luso-Brazilian literature at the University of Illinois. Aside from numerous articles on nineteenth- and twentieth-century Brazilian women writers, she has published a critical edition of Nísia Floresta's nineteenth-century work on the need for social and educational reform for women, *Opúsculo humanitário* (1989) and a monograph study of the Portuguese novelist, Eça de Queirós: *Espelho na rua: A cida-de na ficça de Eça de Queirós* (1991). She is presently completing a coauthored book of essays on the intellectual history of Brazilian feminist discourse, *Connecting Threads: Brazilian Feminist Discourse*.

GLORIA SHEN is Assistant Professor in the Department of Comparative Literature at the University of Georgia. Her research interests include literary theories, poetics, philosophy of language, the relationship of language, thought and culture, and cross-cultural issues in race and gender. She has published articles on comparative poetics, narrative techniques, society and literature, and problems of women's literature.

KAYANN SHORT is an instructor at the University of Colorado at Boulder. Her essay on *This Bridge Called My Back* appeared in *Genders* and she is co-editor of *Sexual Artifice* (1994). She is currently completing a book that examines the oppositional strategies of the feminist press movement in the United States from 1969 to the present.

ARLETTE M. SMITH is a member of the College Language Association Research Committee. She retired as Associate Professor of French at Temple University in Philadelphia, where she taught since 1970. A specialist in twentieth-century French literature, she has also lectured on Francophone-African and Caribbean literatures at various universities and cultural institutes. Her articles and reviews have appeared in *French Review*, *The Dictionary of Literary Biography*, *Revue CELFAN*, *CELACEF Bulletin*, *Africana Journal*, *Le Petit Courier*, and *Journal of Modern Literature*.

MARGARETA THOMPSON teaches Russian language and literature and Swedish. Her publications include several translations of Russian prose and poetry and articles on Soviet literature. Thompson has recently completed an edition of Mikhail Kuraev's *Night Patrol and Other Stories* (1994). She is currently completing an edition of the literary criticism of Vladimir Lakshin and is writing a biography of the poet and editor Aleksandr Tvardovskii.